Fifth Edition

GARDEN STATE

GOLF GUIDE

*Complete Coverage of
All New Jersey's
Public and Private
Golf Courses*

Esther Kaplan & Debra Wolf

Weathervane Press

GARDEN STATE GOLF GUIDE
Esther Kaplan & Debra Wolf

Published by Weathervane Press

ISBN 0-9645830-6-2

Printed in the United States of America

Library of Congress Cataloging in Publication Data

1. GARDEN STATE GOLF GUIDE - Title

2. Golf Guide

3. New Jersey

4. Kaplan, Esther

5. Wolf, Debra

Cover Design by Susan Steeg

CONTENTS

PREFACE   5

HOW TO USE THIS BOOK   7

North East Region   13
Bergen and Passaic Counties

North West Region   43
Sussex, Warren and Morris Counties

East Central Region   95
Essex, Union and Hudson Counties

West Central Region   127
Somerset, Middlesex, Mercer and Hunterdon Counties

Upper Shore Region   187
Monmouth and Ocean Counties

South West Region   245
Burlington, Camden, Gloucester and Salem Counties

Lower Shore Region   293
Atlantic, Cape May and Cumberland Counties

MAPS

North East   11
North West   41
East Central   93
West Central   125
Upper Shore   185
South West   243
Lower Shore   291

INDEX   327

ACKNOWLEDGMENTS

We would like to acknowledge and thank the people who helped us put together this golf guide. Susan Steeg's graphic design talent is always appreciated. We could never have had so many details without the staff, pros and managers at the golf courses listed herein. The opportunity to golf at these varied courses contributed to our ability to provide information and to give accurate descriptions. Many thanks to everyone who assisted us in creating the fifth edition of **The Garden State Golf Guide**.

Please note: The information in this book was provided by the personnel at the courses and country clubs. Every effort was made to provide accurate data. However, errors may have occurred, and the authors do not claim that every word is accurate and complete. In some cases, the yardages for the individual holes may not agree with the totals shown; nevertheless the total yardages are correct. Information regarding fees, reservation policies and access, is always subject to change without notice and should be verified before planning to play at any of these courses. There may have been changes since the time of the interviews.

PREFACE

Golf is a sport that is appealing to both men and women, from the young to the advanced in years. Why is golf such a universal attraction? Most sports require power, speed and stamina. Golf, on the other hand, utilizes more subtle skills such as finesse, judgment and coordination, so that strength and physical endurance are not necessarily the dominant factors. This makes it the perfect sport for everyone and explains its soaring popularity. We wrote those words 10 years ago for the first edition of the **Garden State Golf Guide.** Looking back over the many years we have been researching and writing this book, we can count over 58 new golf courses built in New Jersey! Interest in golf has become more intense and consequently, not only are there a number of new courses in various stages of planning and construction, but the existing ones are upgrading, refurbishing and expanding. With all these changes and additions, we realized that this fifth edition of the book would be most timely. Now, more than ever, women, youngsters and teenagers have discovered what tried and true golfers have known for years; time spent playing golf can fascinate you, challenge you, introduce you to new friends and places, keep you in touch with nature and help you to stay physically fit.

It's interesting that the small state of New Jersey has some of the world's finest golf facilities. Highly rated **Baltusrol** is just one of the many outstanding courses located in the state. Besides well known private golf clubs such as **Somerset Hills, Plainfield, Ridgewood** and **Alpine,** there are many less well known but worthy of high regard. **Metedeconk National, Panther Valley, TPC at Jasna Polana** and the recently completed **Shadow Isle** are of comparable status. In addition, New Jersey has some fine publicly owned courses; namely **Sunset Valley, Hominy Hill** and **Charleston Springs.** Privately owned, but open to the public, are **Shore Gate** and **Sand Barrens** near Atlantic City, **Pine Barrens,** upscale and outstanding **Sea Oaks, Pine Hill** and **Twisted Dune.** Sussex County is humming with golf activity. When we first started researching New Jersey courses in the mid-nineties, one of the owners of what is presently Crystal Golf Resorts told us with great enthusiasm that this northwestern part of the state would become a golf mecca. Now that group consists of **Crystal Springs, Black Bear, Ballyowen, Wild Turkey, Minerals** (formerly the **Spa**) and **Great Gorge.** A most spectacular country clubhouse, luxurious hotel facilities as well as many outdoor and indoor sports venues are part of the attraction there. In the southern part of the State, golf development has not been neglected. More than 10 new courses in the greater Atlantic City area have appeared on the scene. The latest creation, **Vineyard Golf,** is the only course in the state built at a winery with abundant grape vines on the property. Farther to the southwest is the highly acclaimed **River Winds** in the Region where **Scotland Run** was completed a few years ago. Another area of explosive growth of golf courses has been seen in adult communities and developments. We now identify over 30 of them and still counting!

With a state the size of New Jersey, it is possible to travel from one end to the other and still enjoy a leisurely round of golf. Why not take the time to learn about the great golfing opportunities within your reach? New Jersey offers play in the mountains, at the seashore, in the Pinelands and varied terrain in between. The diversity of golf courses can satisfy the budget minded as well as those willing to pay more for beautiful views, excellent facilities and challenging experiences.

In addition to its magnificent array of golf facilities, the bountiful natural beauty of New Jersey makes its residents justifiably proud. With extensive white sand beaches at the Jersey shore, rolling hills of the Watchung and Ramapo Mountains, lush wooded valleys, rich farmlands and well preserved Pinelands, it is fittingly referred to as the "Garden State". Some areas are well known to tourists and draw many visitors from near and far. However, New Jersey offers attractions that are often undiscovered while its more densely populated and developed sectors are familiar and overwhelm the image of the state. There are many New Jersey residents who are not aware of the picturesque horse farms, miles of undeveloped rural areas, many parks, forests and even wildlife sanctuaries. From High Point State Park in the northernmost part of Sussex County to Cape May Migratory Bird Refuge in the southernmost section of Cape May, New Jersey will amaze you with its beauty and natural wonders.

HOW TO USE THIS BOOK

Introduction

We have divided the 21 counties of the State of New Jersey into seven geographical regions. A scrupulous effort has been made to include all the Garden State's golf courses and we have personally visited every one.

Private and Public Golf Courses

Private means the course is open only to members and their guests. Initiation fees and yearly membership dues vary greatly. To obtain specific information, call the individual club. If you belong to a private club, it is possible for your pro to make arrangements with another club for you to play there.

Various private courses are located within adult communities. These are open only to residents of the community and their guests. If you are considering a move to an adult community, it might be a good idea to inquire about playing a round of golf at that facility.

Public is defined as courses that are open to the public and include the following categories:
1. County or municipally owned and operated courses with special rates and reservation policies
2. Daily fee courses open to the public at daily fee rates
3. Resort courses open to the public with reduced rates for hotel guests

Semi-Private Courses with memberships available at widely varying costs offering reduced or pre-paid daily fees and tee time priorities. These clubs also encourage daily fee players.

Name, Address and Telephone Number

On each page, we listed the full name of the club and its address. In a few cases, we have abbreviated Country Club as CC and Golf Club or Golf Course as GC. For some, a special number for tee time reservations is given.

Within each region, the courses are arranged alphabetically and therefore listed that way at the beginning of each region. An easy way to find an individual course by name is to refer to the **index** for its page number. The numerical dots on the regional maps give the **approximate** location of the courses with respect to major highways and towns.

Course Information

The first paragraph on each course page includes the number of holes on the course, days and months open, types of memberships and reservation policies. Most New Jersey courses that are open all year or most of the year are dependent on "weather permitting." It is therefore advisable to call in advance for the latest tee time information, as well as for seasonal rate policies. Most private clubs are open six days a week and usually close on Mondays.

Amenities

This box contains a generally self-explanatory check list of the amenities at each course. However, when there are exceptions or clarifications, they are so noted in the text, i.e. Driving Range is checked but practice is limited to irons, or Pull Carts are checked but allowed only during certain hours or days.

Power Carts: Most courses encourage the use of power carts; a few do not offer them at all.

Pull Carts: Those courses that permit the use of pull carts may or may not provide them for rent as well. Power caddies are sometimes available for rent.

Food: When this item is checked, the facility offers anything from a limited snack bar or vending machines to a full-service restaurant and bar.

Outings: Many clubs make their facilities available to groups of more than 12 golfers for outings usually sponsored by corporations, charities, townships or club members. Most private clubs encourage outings on the days they are closed to their members (usually Mondays). Some clubs limit their outings to member sponsored only.

Caddies: Generally not offered at public courses. Check with individual clubs for their caddie policy.

Soft Spikes: Where required, so noted. Some clubs are now strongly recommending them. Call in advance for policy.

Fees

The fee schedule indicates the prevailing rates, however, it is recommended that you contact the course to make sure it has not been revised. Rates given are for peak times and vary seasonally. Published rates are subject to change but generally do not vary greatly from one year to the next.

Weekday: Monday to Friday*
Weekend: Saturday, Sunday and holidays: *some courses include Friday as part of the weekend.

Daily: Greens fee for daily play

Res/ID: County or township resident with current yearly permit.

Twilight: Twilight starting time differs from club to club in and off-season: check in advance with club.

Cart fees: Generally given for two people in a power cart. Sometimes listed per person (pp).

Course Description

The course description helps you discover what course would be most appropriate and appealing for you. We have discussed degree of difficulty, variety, length and special features. The scorecard shown below each course description gives additional details on course rating, slope and yardages. Whenever possible, information describing what is unique or unusual about these courses has been included; such as historical, anecdotal or interesting features. These descriptions might offer golfers some clue for course strategy.
Many nine hole courses have an additional tee box for the second nine to give the golfer playing 18 holes some added variety. Moreover, courses that have more than two nine hole sets allow combinations of play, i.e. Blue-Red, Blue-White and Red-White.

Course Directions
The first line of directions gives you the course number as indicated on the regional map. Directions progress from major highways to secondary highways to local roads and finally to the club. Care has been taken to alert the driver to landmarks or other helpful navigational features. It is recommended that you bring along a good New Jersey map to track your route in more detail as the maps provided herein show only **approximate** locations.

Professional Staff

Manager, Director of Golf: May manage more than just the golf operation.
Supt: Superintendent of greens.
Pro: Head professional is listed; some courses have assistant pros as well. If the pro is PGA affiliated, it is shown following the name.
Architect: The name of the architect(s), year built or redesigned.
Estab: Indicates when the club originated.

Scorecard

Course Rating is an indication of how difficult the course is to a scratch golfer (one who shoots par or better). The higher the rating, the greater the difficulty.

Slope is useful as a comparison of relative difficulty between courses with the higher slope number indicating the more difficult course. It is determined by accredited members of a local golf association.
The usual categories rated on the scorecard on each page of this book are: **Blue, White** and **Red** tees. Many courses are offering additional tee boxes which are indicated on the actual scorecard. Some tee positions are designated by other colors or names. In some cases, we have put yardages on the scorecard under Blue but there are also Black tees for Professional yardages and we have mentioned in the description the total yardages from the back or the tips to indicate the true length of the course.

New

Golf courses that were in construction at the time of our last **Garden State Golf Guide** edition and have opened recently, or are scheduled to open in 2005 or later or are in construction as we go to press are designated with a "NEW" on their page.

Internet

We have included information about web sites and email addresses when available, such as:
Web sites: www.anygolfclub.com
email: info@anyclub.com

NORTH EAST REGION

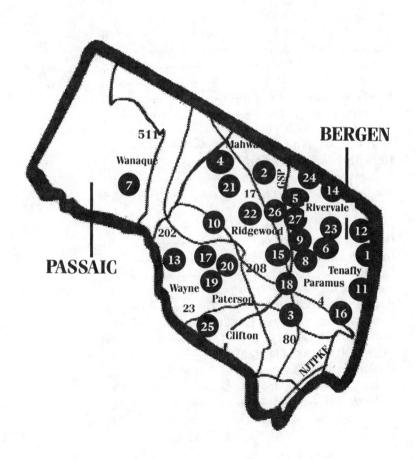

NORTH EAST REGION

Public Courses appear in **bold italics**

	Map #	Page #
Alpine Country Club (1)		13
Apple Ridge Country Club (2)		14
Arcola Country Club (3)		15
Bergen Hills CC (23)		16
***Darlington Golf Course* (4)**		17
Edgewood Country Club (5)		18
***Emerson Country Club* (6)**		19
***Glenwild Greens* (7)**		20
Hackensack Golf Club (8)		21
Haworth Country Club (9)		22
***High Mountain Golf Club* (10)**		23
Knickerbocker Country Club (11)		24
Montammy Golf Club (12)		25
North Jersey Country Club (13)		26
Old Tappan Golf Course (14)		27
***Orchard Hills Golf Course* (15)**		28
***Overpeck County Golf Course* (16)**		29
Packanack Golf Club (17)		30
***Paramus Golf & Country Club* (18)**		31
***Passaic County Golf Course* (19)**		32
Preakness Hills Country Club (20)		33
Ramsey Golf & Country Club (21)		34
Ridgewood Country Club (22)		35
***Rockleigh Golf Course* (24)**		36
Upper Montclair Country Club (25)		37
***Valley Brook GC* (26)**		38
White Beeches Golf & CC (27)		39

ALPINE COUNTRY CLUB

80 Anderson Ave., Demarest, NJ 07627   **(201) 768-2121**
www.alpinecc.org

Alpine is an 18 hole course open 6 days a week from March through December. Guests may play accompanied by a member. Tee times are not required.

- •Driving Range
- •Practice Green
- •Power Carts
- Pull Carts
- •Club Rental
- •Caddies
- •Lockers
- •Showers
- •Food
- •Clubhouse
- •Outings
- •Soft Spikes

Course Description: Alpine, one of the most difficult courses in Bergen County, is known for its lush old trees and steep hills. A.W. Tillinghast, the designer of Alpine and Baltusrol as well, followed the contours of the rolling terrain to create a beautiful challenging course. The golfer must be prepared for sidehill, uphill and downhill lies in order to score well here. The greens are fast; many are two tiered. For example, the tenth, a straight uphill par 4, has a blind tee shot and an approach to a small green; a memorable hole! The 18th is a long par 5 that finishes a round of golf that can be frustrating but very enjoyable. There will be some more water in play when the course is redesigned in 2005.

Directions: Bergen County, #1 on Northeast Map
Pal. Interstate Pkwy. to Exit 2, Alpine. At STOP, go left onto Rte. 9W South. Go right at first light onto Closter Dock Rd., then at Anderson Ave., make a left to club on left.

Hole	1	2	3	4	5	6	7	8	9	Out	BLUE	Rating 73.1
BLUE	418	372	331	381	136	436	598	191	510	3373		Slope 139
WHITE	407	350	315	369	127	412	545	166	500	3191		
Par	4	4	4	4	3	4	5	3	5	36	WHITE	Rating 71.6
Handicap	3	9	11	7	17	1	5	15	13			Slope 135
RED	393	272	290	312	110	299	472	153	443	2744		
Par	5	4	4	4	3	4	5	3	5	37	RED	Rating 73.8
Handicap	7	9	11	13	17	3	1	15	5			Slope 130
Hole	10	11	12	13	14	15	16	17	18	In		Totals
BLUE	339	394	316	478	300	404	191	317	570	3309	BLUE	6711
WHITE	317	362	301	452	291	385	184	304	561	3157	WHITE	6348
Par	4	4	4	4	4	4	3	4	5	36	Par	72
Handicap	4	8	16	2	14	6	18	10	12			
RED	216	354	283	443	280	310	164	246	455	2751	RED	5471
Par	4	4	4	5	4	4	3	4	5	36	Par	74
Handicap	14	2	10	6	12	4	18	16	8			

Manager: Larry Savvides   **Pro:** Kevin Syring, PGA   **Supt:** Steven Finamore
Architect: A.W. Tillinghast 1928

APPLE RIDGE COUNTRY CLUB PRIVATE

269 East Crescent Ave., Mahwah, NJ 07430   (201) 327-8000

Apple Ridge is an 18 hole course that is open 6 days a week, from Mar. 1 to Dec.31. Guests may play accompanied by a member. Tee time reservations are necessary for weekends.

- •Driving Range
- •Practice Green
- •Power Carts
- Pull Carts
- •Club Rental
- •Caddies

- •Lockers
- •Showers
- •Food
- •Clubhouse
- •Outings
- •Soft Spikes

Course Description: The Hal Purdy designed Apple Ridge is considered a very sporty course with undulating fairways, small well-bunkered greens and several challenging water holes. It is known for its well maintained tree lined fairways. From the ninth hole, there is a spectacular view of the New York City skyline. The 13th hole is a true test of golf; 447 yards from the blues with a lake guarding the green, the golfer has to make the right club decision or wind up in the water.

Directions: Bergen County, #2 on Northeast Map
Take Rte. 17 North to Lake St., Ramsey Exit. At first light, make a left onto East Crescent Ave; club is on the right.

Hole	1	2	3	4	5	6	7	8	9	Out	BLUE	Rating 70.5
BLUE	411	381	161	501	415	174	397	363	446	3249		Slope 130
WHITE	386	354	133	476	402	160	382	339	420	3052		
Par	4	4	3	5	4	3	4	4	4	35	WHITE	Rating 69.3
Handicap	5	9	17	13	1	11	7	15	3			Slope 127
RED	362	330	109	453	352	146	367	316	394	2829		
Par	4	4	3	5	4	3	4	4	5	36	RED	Rating 73.8
Handicap	3	7	17	1	11	15	5	13	9			Slope 128
Hole	10	11	12	13	14	15	16	17	18	In		Totals
BLUE	203	368	322	447	563	358	411	188	515	3375	BLUE	6624
WHITE	184	345	307	423	540	341	388	171	493	3192	WHITE	6244
Par	3	4	4	4	5	4	4	3	5	36	Par	71
Handicap	10	8	12	2	4	16	6	18	14			
RED	165	322	290	397	450	324	330	155	472	2905	RED	5734
Par	3	4	4	5	5	4	4	3	5	37	Par	73
Handicap	16	8	10	6	2	12	14	18	4			

Manager: Tom Savvides   **Pro:** John Curry, PGA   **Supt:** Wayne Remo
Architect: Hal Purdy 1966

ARCOLA COUNTRY CLUB

P.O.Box 158, Paramus Rd., Paramus, NJ 07652   (201) 843-9800

Arcola is an 18 hole private course that is open 7 days a week all year (Mondays after 11AM). Guests may play accompanied by a member. Tee time reservations are not required.

- **Driving Range**
- **Practice Green**
- **Power Carts**
- Pull Carts
- **Club Rental**
- **Caddies**

- **Lockers**
- **Showers**
- **Food**
- **Clubhouse**
- **Outings**
- **Soft Spikes**

Course Description: Arcola is a gently rolling parkland type course nestled in the hills of Paramus with impressive views, particularly from the first hole. Three ponds come into play on this tightly bunkered challenging golf course. With the surrounding commercial development, it is surprising to find such a well-maintained layout in this location. Rees Jones and Roger Rulewich are two of several architects who have taken part in the improvements here. Arcola will have improvements on the bunkers and work done on the tee boxes in 2005 and is expected to be re-rated.

Directions: Bergen County, #3 on Northeast Map
From the GWBridge, take Rte. 4 West to the Paramus Road exit. Bear right off exit to course which is immediately on the right.

Hole	1	2	3	4	5	6	7	8	9	Out	BLUE	Rating 73.7
BLUE	436	209	348	389	431	406	204	503	521	3447		Slope 131
WHITE	418	186	317	371	412	380	186	476	494	3240		
Par	4	3	4	4	4	4	3	5	5	36	WHITE	Rating 72.0
Handicap	6	16	18	2	8	4	14	12	10			Slope 128
RED	402	141	283	314	329	341	111	414	413	2748		
Par	5	3	4	4	4	4	3	5	5	37	RED	Rating 72.7
Handicap	13	15	7	1	11	9	17	3	5			Slope 123
Hole	10	11	12	13	14	15	16	17	18	In		Totals
BLUE	432	164	587	346	162	531	352	440	409	3423	BLUE	6870
WHITE	406	154	566	326	150	514	336	419	396	3267	WHITE	6503
Par	4	3	5	4	3	5	4	4	4	36	Par	72
Handicap	5	15	1	13	17	9	11	3	7			
RED	339	96	508	294	132	474	305	395	281	2824	RED	5572
Par	4	3	5	4	3	5	4	5	4	37	Par	74
Handicap	8	16	2	12	18	4	10	6	14			

Manager: Bill Hoferer   **Pro:** Bill Burgess, PGA   **Supt:** Barney Misiura
Architects: Herbert Barker 1909, **Renov:** Rees Jones, Roger Rulewich

BERGEN HILLS COUNTRY CLUB `PUBLIC`

660 River Vale Rd., River Vale, NJ 07675
www.bergenhillscc.com

(201) 391-2300

Bergen Hills is an 18 hole course open all year 7 days a week. Tee time reservations may be made up to 2 weeks in advance. Outings are welcomed here requiring 2 weeks notice for 12 or more players. Multiple membership categories.

- •Driving Range
- •Practice Green
- •Power Carts
- •Pull Carts
- •Club Rental
- •Soft Spikes
- •Lockers
- •Showers
- •Food
- •Clubhouse
- •Outings

Fees	Weekday	Weekend
Mon-Thur	$69	$99
Fri	$79	
Twilight	$49M-Fri	$59
Power carts included		

Course Description: The immaculately maintained Bergen Hills (formerly RiverVale CC) is a narrow course with gently rolling land and tough, targeted well bunkered greens, many of which are elevated. A round here commences with a par 4 384 yd hole that requires a blind uphill approach shot. The difficult 4th hole is a dogleg left; the 18th, features a picturesque pond that fronts the slope to the green. The long par 3 5th is 233 yards from the back tees offering trees in play, deep rough on the left and a bunkered putting surface. Several holes have great views of the Tappan Reservoir.

Directions: Bergen County, #23 on Northeast Map
Pal.Int.Pkwy. to Exit #6W. At 4th light, go left on Blue Hill Rd.(water on left). Go 1.4 miles. Blue Hill Rd. becomes Orangeburg Rd. in River Vale. Go left on River Vale Rd. Club is 1/4 mile on left.

Hole	1	2	3	4	5	6	7	8	9	Out	BLUE	Rating 70.7
BLUE	384	325	482	351	233	475	364	133	540	3287		Slope 130
WHITE	365	308	471	321	215	454	334	123	522	3113		
Par	4	4	5	4	3	4	4	3	5	36	WHITE	Rating 69.5
Handicap	3	15	7	11	5	1	13	17	9			Slope 126
RED	326	302	410	267	156	408	309	98	479	2755		
Par	4	4	5	4	3	5	4	3	5	37	RED	Rating 74.9
Handicap	7	11	1	13	15	3	9	17	5			Slope 128

Hole	10	11	12	13	14	15	16	17	18	In		Totals
BLUE	394	345	336	167	508	468	380	164	375	3137	BLUE	6470
WHITE	372	337	325	161	488	450	365	155	364	3017	WHITE	6123
Par	4	4	4	3	5	5	4	3	4	36	Par	72
Handicap	4	14	10	16	6	12	8	18	2			
RED	338	271	268	156	417	442	307	148	302	2649	RED	5353
Par	4	4	4	3	5	5	4	3	5	37	Par	74
Handicap	8	16	12	14	4	2	10	18	6			

Gen. Mgr: John Napier **Dir. of Golf:** Tom McGuinness, PGA **Supt:** Oscar Bucaro
Architects: Orrin Smith & Donald Ross 1930

DARLINGTON GOLF COURSE

PUBLIC

277 Campgaw Rd., Mahwah, NJ 07430   **(201) 327-8770**

Darlington is an 18 hole Bergen County Course open 7 days a week from mid-March to mid-Dec. County residents can obtain IDs for $25. (Srs. $18). There is a computerized reservation system for tee times up to 7 days in advance; call 343-4441. Direct # for conditions call 327-8778.

- •Driving Range
- •Practice Green
- •Power Carts
- •Pull Carts
- •Club Rental
- •Soft Spikes

- •Lockers
- •Showers
- •Food
- •Clubhouse
- •Outings

Fees	Weekday	Weekend
ReswID	$18	$23
Non-reg	$40	$48
NonNJ	$55	$55
Sr/Jr	$9	$20
Power carts	$24	$24

Course Description: Set in a heavily wooded county park, Darlington, with its rolling hills and lush greens, is an appealing example of a popular public course. Although not extremely long, the par fours are a sure test of the golfer's skill. The pleasant scenery can lull the unwary player into thinking this is just a walk in the woods; however, an errant shot can find the golfer in those woods with an unplayable lie. Some consider the long par 4 ninth the most picturesque hole. This championship style course offers an enjoyable golf experience to players of all levels. A full service driving range is adjacent to the course.

Directions: Bergen County, #4 on Northeast Map
Take Rte. 17 North to Rte. 202 South. Pass Ramapo College to Darlington Ave. & turn left. Follow to Campgaw Rd. & turn right. Go 1&1/4 miles & turn left into course before the Police Academy.

Hole	1	2	3	4	5	6	7	8	9	Out	BLUE	Rating 70.6
BLUE	480	175	365	362	189	379	372	390	470	3182		Slope 122
WHITE	452	155	355	352	170	355	357	375	448	3019		
Par	5	3	4	4	3	4	4	4	4	35	WHITE	Rating 68.8
Handicap	9	17	11	13	15	3	7	5	1			Slope 118
RED	380	119	290	313	155	320	320	288	420	2605		
Par	5	3	4	4	3	4	4	4	4	35	RED	Rating 69.9
Handicap	9	17	11	13	15	3	7	5	1			Slope 117
Hole	10	11	12	13	14	15	16	17	18	In		Totals
BLUE	452	500	175	369	489	344	176	382	415	3302	BLUE	6484
WHITE	402	483	150	340	463	325	154	363	350	3030	WHITE	6049
Par	4	5	3	4	5	4	3	4	4	36	Par	71
Handicap	2	8	18	12	10	14	16	4	6			
RED	361	423	131	298	432	295	122	321	312	2695	RED	5300
Par	4	5	3	4	5	4	3	4	4	36	Par	71
Handicap	2	8	18	12	10	14	16	4	6			

Manager: Walter Wargaski   **Supt:** Dave Warner
Architect: Nicholas Psiahas 1975

EDGEWOOD COUNTRY CLUB PRIVATE

449 River Vale Rd., River Vale, NJ 07675   **(201) 666-1200**
www.edgewoodnj.com

Edgewood is a 27 hole course with 3 separate nines; Red, White & Blue. It is open 6 days a week and closes in January. Guests play accompanied by a member. Tee time reservations are necessary on weekends.

•Driving Range	•Lockers
•Practice Green	•Showers
•Power Carts	•Food
Pull Carts	•Clubhouse
•Club Rental	•Outings
•Caddies	•Soft Spikes

Course Description: Formerly a dairy farm in Bergen County, Edgewood's three nines were built as a public facility then later became a private club. The predominantly flat tree lined terrain has wide fairways and deep bunkers. Many holes present trouble; out-of-bounds, ponds and creeks demand careful placement of the tee shot or the approach to the well bunkered greens. The Blue offers the most dramatic layout with sharp doglegs and water holes. The meandering 5th hole on the Red is known as the "Willow Hole" because of the many willow trees. The course is constantly being updated. The scorecard below shows the Red Course above & the Blue below and their combined ratings and slopes.

Directions: Bergen County, #5 on Northeast Map
Pal.Pkwy. North to Exit 6W. At 4th STOP, go left onto Blue Hill Rd.(water on left); for 1.4 miles. Road becomes Orangeburg Rd. in RiverVale. Go left onto RiverVale Rd. Club is on right.

Hole	1	2	3	4	5	6	7	8	9	Out	BLUE	Rating 71.9
BLUE	325	516	365	201	442	510	352	158	449	3318		Slope 134
WHITE	311	474	340	174	413	496	334	144	434	3120		
Par	4	5	4	3	4	5	4	3	4	36	WHITE	Rating 69.9
Handicap	6	5	4	8	1	2	7	9	3			Slope 129
RED	297	461	327	168	337	421	305	135	412	2863		
Par	4	5	4	3	4	5	4	3	5	37	RED	Rating 71.3
Handicap	4	2	6	8	3	1	5	9	7			Slope 120
Hole	10	11	12	13	14	15	16	17	18	In		Totals
BLUE	370	366	380	194	497	519	193	374	191	3084	BLUE	6402
WHITE	349	345	334	180	447	506	148	354	181	2874	WHITE	5994
Par	4	4	4	3	5	5	3	4	3	35	Par	71
Handicap	3	5	1	7	6	2	8	4	9			
RED	320	331	279	152	420	405	106	336	162	2511	RED	5374
Par	4	4	4	3	5	5	3	4	3	35	Par	72
Handicap	3	6	4	7	1	5	9	2	8			

Manager: Danny Palazzola   **Pro:** Keith Larsen, PGA   **Supt:** Paul Dotti
Architect: Orrin Smith 1946

EMERSON GOLF CLUB

99 Palisade Ave., Emerson, NJ 07630   **(201) 261-1100**
www.emersongolfclub.com

Emerson is an 18 hole course open 7 days a week all year. Weekday memberships are available with unlimited golf and cart fees & weekend starting times. Tee times may be made up to 5 days in advance, members up to 8 days. Carts required on weekends.

<table>
<tr><td>

• **Driving Range**   • **Lockers**
• **Practice Green**   • **Showers**
• **Power Carts**   • **Food**
• **Pull Carts**   • **Clubhouse**
• **Club Rental**   • **Outings**
• **Soft Spikes**

</td></tr>
</table>

Fees	Weekday	Weekend
M-Th $58	(Fri$79)	$85
Twi	$48(1:30)	$58(3PM)
Jr	$25	
Price includes cart		

Course Description: The front nine of the Emerson golf course plays longer and straighter than the tighter and shorter back. The course is maintained very well. The signature third hole, a 468 yard par 4, tees off into the wind and finishes hitting to a small green. Six par 4s are over 400 yards; the par 3 16th is over 200 yards. By stressing ready golf, fast play is encouraged and golfers enjoy the well paced rounds. On a crowded weekend, players can reasonably expect no more than 4 & 1/2 hours to complete a round of 18 holes.

Directions: Bergen County, #6 on Northeast Map
GWBr. to Rte. 4 West to Kinderkamack Rd./RiverEdge exit. Make a left at light onto Kinderkamack Rd. Go 4-5 mi. to town of Emerson, cross RR tracks, make immediate right onto Emerson Plaza E. for 300 yds. Go left onto Palisade Ave.to club on right.

Hole	1	2	3	4	5	6	7	8	9	Out	BLUE	Rating 71.5
BLUE	519	176	474	390	422	460	349	192	567	3549		Slope 121
WHITE	495	162	437	340	413	436	341	162	545	3331		
Par	5	3	4	4	4	4	4	3	5	36	WHITE	Rating 70.1
Handicap	9	17	1	15	5	3	13	11	7			Slope 119
RED	474	157	366	284	351	372	263	134	431	2832		
Par	5	3	4	4	4	4	4	3	5	36	RED	Rating 70.8
Handicap	3	17	9	13	5	1	15	11	7			Slope 117
Hole	10	11	12	13	14	15	16	17	18	In		Totals
BLUE	418	167	518	431	406	395	204	418	443	3400	BLUE	6949
WHITE	390	140	499	380	377	376	176	403	415	3156	WHITE	6487
Par	4	3	5/4	4	4	4	3	4	4/5	35	Par	71
Handicap	4	18	10	12	16	6	14	8	2			
RED	374	131	351	265	346	370	145	309	408	2699	RED	5531
Par	4	3	5/4	4	4	4	3	4	4/5	35	Par	71
Handicap	4	18	6	14	8	2	10	16	12			

Manager: Gautam Patankar   **Supt:** Paul Sutter
Architect: Alec Ternyei 1968

GLENWILD GREENS

102 Glenwild Ave., Bloomingdale, NJ 07403   **(973) 283-0888**
wwwglenwildgreens.com

Glenwild Greens is a 9 hole par 3 course. Memberships are available. Tee time reservations are not necessary.

Driving Range	Lockers
•**Practice Green**	Showers
Power Carts	
•**Pull Carts**	•**Food**
•**Club Rental**	Clubhouse
•**Soft Spikes**	•**Outings**

Fees	Weekday	Weekend
Daily	$10	$13
Sr	$8	$13
Jr	$8	$10
2nd nine	$5	$6

Course Description: Carved out of the woods with considerable grade changes and elevated tees, Glenwild Greens has lush fairways and a variety of challenging holes. Two ponds affect play on two holes. One might get the impression that this is an easy par 3 layout but there is much more of interest to the course. Plenty of room between holes is provided to avoid collisions with other players. Glenwild is a great place to practice one's short game. An excellent learning center has been established here for Jrs.

Directions: Passaic County, #7 on Northeast Map
Rte. 80 to Exit 53, then Rte. 23 North to Rte. 287 North to Exit #53. Go left on Hamburg Tpke. at light. After 1 & 1/2 miles, bear right up hill on Glenwild Ave. Club is 1/2 mile on right.

Hole	1	2	3	4	5	6	7	8	9	Out	BLUE	Rating
BLUE												Slope
WHITE	65	85	75	125	135	100	110	100	170	965		
Par	3	3	3	3	3	3	3	3	3	27	WHITE	Rating
Handicap												Slope
RED												
Par											RED	Rating
Handicap												Slope

Hole	10	11	12	13	14	15	16	17	18	In		Totals
BLUE											BLUE	
WHITE											WHITE	965
Par											Par	27
Handicap												
RED											RED	
Par											Par	
Handicap												

Owner: Alex MacKenn   **Manager/Pro:** Bruce Chamberlain   **Supt:** Ron Silvius
Built: 1994

HACKENSACK GOLF CLUB

Soldier Hill Rd., Oradell, NJ 07649   **(201) 261-5505**

Hackensack is a private 18 hole course open 6 days a week and closes in Jan. Tee time reservations are not required. Guests may play accompanied by a member.

```
• Driving Range    • Lockers
• Practice Green   • Showers
• Power Carts      • Food
  Pull Carts       • Clubhouse
• Club Rental      • Outings
• Caddies          • Soft Spikes
```

Course Description: Designed in 1928 by architect Charles Banks, Hackensack offers diversity and challenge for any level player. The large bunkers and tree lined fairways make strategic shot placement a must. This is one of the longer courses in Bergen County with 5 difficult par 4s over 400 yards each from the blue tees. The club's Rees Jones renovation in 1996 was to reposition the bunkers. The signature 18th hole always seems to stimulate discussion by touring pros who visit here; it is a dogleg left with a bunker and mound on the right and an uphill shot to a hidden green. Hackensack is the home club of Jim McGovern, winner of the 1993 Houston Open.

Directions: Bergen County, #8 on Northeast Map
GSP to Exit #165. Go East on Oradell Ave. to Forest. Turn left, then right on Soldier Hill Rd. Club is on left. From Rte. 4 East or West; take Kinderkamack Rd. North in River Edge to Oradell. Go left on Soldier Hill to club on right.

Hole	1	2	3	4	5	6	7	8	9	Out	BLUE	Rating 72.2
BLUE	470	429	224	392	377	142	378	524	421	3357		Slope 134
WHITE	440	421	197	383	357	132	355	500	401	3186		
Par	5	4	3	4	4	3	4	5	4	36	WHITE	Rating 70.9
Handicap	15	1	13	5	11	17	9	7	3			Slope 131
RED	416	406	150	373	296	122	267	474	346	2850		
Par	5	5	3	4	4	3	4	5	4	37	RED	Rating 73.2
Handicap	7	5	15	1	9	17	13	3	11			Slope 131

Hole	10	11	12	13	14	15	16	17	18	In		Totals
BLUE	510	425	184	337	336	522	405	160	402	3281	BLUE	6638
WHITE	503	404	177	312	324	502	392	148	387	3149	WHITE	6335
Par	5	4	3	4	4	5	5	3	4	36	Par	72
Handicap	8	2	16	12	14	10	4	18	6			
RED	468	329	139	278	325	439	384	133	325	2820	RED	5670
Par	5	4	3	4	4	5	5	3	4	37	Par	74
Handicap	6	14	18	2	8	4	12	16	10			

Manager: Norman Forsyth   **Pro:** Michael Dezic, PGA   **Supt:** Richard Lane
Estab: 1899   **Architects:** Charles Banks 1928   Rees Jones 1996

HAWORTH COUNTRY CLUB

PRIVATE

5 Lake Shore Dr., Haworth, NJ 07641   **(201) 384-7300**

Haworth is an 18 private course open all year 6 days a week. Tee time reservations may be made in advance. Full and weekday memberships are available. Guests may play accompanied by a member.

- •Driving Range
- •Practice Green
- •Power Carts
- •Pull Carts
- •Club Rental
- Caddies
- •Lockers
- •Showers
- •Food
- •Clubhouse
- •Outings
- •Soft Spikes

Course Description: The Robert Trent Jones renovation at Haworth is spectacular indeed; water in play and deceptively contoured fairways make it more challenging and interesting than ever. Beautiful wild flowers have been planted all over giving a natural colorful ambience. The first hole, a long par five 561 yds. from the back, requires a shot over a pond for the approach to the green. The par 3 eleventh has overhanging trees, water to carry and a green surrounded by bunkers; a daunting hole. The 12th is hilly with ponds on 2 sides and a sloped right to left fairway hitting out of a narrow chute. The course at Haworth is a fair and true test of golf.

Directions: Bergen County, #9 on Northeast Map
Rte.4 West to River Rd. Exit. (After Fairleigh Dick. Univ.) At light, which is River Rd. turn left. Take River Rd. (approx. 4 mi.) to Hasbrouck Blvd. and turn right. Make a left at Grant Av. and left at Sunset Ave. to Lake Shore Drive and follow straight to club.

Hole	1	2	3	4	5	6	7	8	9	Out	BLUE	Rating 71.1
BLUE	540	377	198	343	355	530	360	200	397	3300		Slope 132
WHITE	519	345	181	304	326	499	327	166	351	3108		
Par	5	4	3	4	4	5	4	3	4	36	WHITE	Rating 68.2
Handicap	1	13	7	15	17	3	11	9	5			Slope 124
RED	489	329	150	276	298	473	278	136	303	2732		
Par	5	4	3	4	4	5	4	3	4	36	RED	Rating 70.8
Handicap	1	5	15	13	11	3	9	17	7			Slope 125

Hole	10	11	12	13	14	15	16	17	18	In		Totals
BLUE	421	185	378	453	150	364	436	206	539	3132	BLUE	6432
WHITE	385	159	343	420	119	342	400	177	513	2858	WHITE	5876
Par	4	3	4	5	3	4	5	3	5	36	Par	72
Handicap	2	8	12	14	18	10	16	6	4			
RED	359	138	314	392	103	334	370	150	480	2640	RED	5372
Par	5	3	4	5	3	4	4	4	4	36	Par	72
Handicap	4	16	8	10	18	12	6	14	2			

Manager: Akio Nakahara   **Pro:** Charles Podmayersky, PGA   **Supt.** John Emmolo
Architects: Albert Zakorus 1966   Robert Trent Jones 1999

HIGH MOUNTAIN GOLF CLUB

845 Ewing Ave., Franklin Lakes, NJ 07417 **(201) 891-4653**
www.highmountaingolf.com

High Mountain is an 18 hole course open to the public 7 days a week from mid-March to mid-Dec. Memberships are available. Starting times required for Wed, Thurs, & Fr. 8AM-3PM. Course is open to the public weekends after 2 PM (no advance tee time.)

- •Driving Range
- •Practice Green
- •Power Carts
- •Pull Carts
- •Club Rental
- •Soft Spikes
- •Lockers
- •Showers
- •Food
- •Clubhouse
- •Outings

Fees	Weekday	Weekend
Daily(M-Th)	*$66	*$77
Twi(4PM)	$27	$30
Mbrs(+cart)	$12	$16
*Power carts (req.) included		

Course Description: The popular semi-private High Mountain is a well maintained playable course with bent-poana grass fairways and bent grass greens. Contoured tree lined fairways, natural ponds and creeks add to its interest. The 4th hole is long (522 from the back) with a second shot over a pond to a tricky uphill green. The par 5 16th, 579 yards from the whites, requires an accurate approach shot over water which is in play on a total of five holes. The back nine is tighter and longer than the front.

Directions: Bergen County, #10 on Northeast Map
Rte. 4 West to Rte. 208 North. Take Ewing Ave. exit and turn left. Club is about 1 mile from exit on left.

Hole	1	2	3	4	5	6	7	8	9	Out	BLUE	Rating 70.8
BLUE	369	385	195	522	150	415	345	365	140	2886		Slope 123
WHITE	350	373	183	511	135	405	331	353	136	2777		
Par	4	4	3	5	3	4	4	4	3	34	WHITE	Rating 69.3
Handicap	10	6	12	4	18	2	14	8	16			Slope 119
RED	305	356	167	443	115	389	314	313	127	2529		
Par	4	4	3	5	3	4	4	4	3	34	RED	Rating 70.9
Handicap	4	4	15	4	13	4	5	5	14			Slope 123
Hole	10	11	12	13	14	15	16	17	18	In		Totals
BLUE	404	480	183	412	403	327	587	200	465	3461	BLUE	63516
WHITE	392	445	162	403	392	307	579	189	455	3324	WHITE	6185
Par	4	5	3	4	4	4	5	3	5	37	Par	71
Handicap	5	13	15	7	3	17	1	9	11			
RED	311	425	132	390	298	276	461	166	438	2897	RED	5426
Par	4	5	3	4	4	4	5	3	5	37	Par	71
Handicap	11	9	15	3	5	17	1	13	7			

Manager: Turgy Irtz   **Pros:** Joe & Pat Lawlor, PGA   **Supt:** Eliot Lewis
Architect: Alec Ternyei 1967

KNICKERBOCKER C.C.

188 Knickerbocker Rd., Tenafly, NJ 07670   (201) 568-4034

Knickerbocker is a private 18 hole course open 6 days a week and closed in Jan. & Feb. Guests play accompanied by a member. Tee time reservations are not necessary.

•**Driving Range**	•**Lockers**
•**Practice Green**	•**Showers**
•**Power Carts**	•**Food**
Pull Carts	•**Clubhouse**
•**Club Rental**	•**Outings**
•**Caddies**	•**Soft Spikes**

Course Description: Nestled in the middle of abundantly treed Tenafly is Knickerbocker Country Club. This very well maintained course has narrow fairways, a flat front nine and a hilly back. It is deceptively challenging. The approach shots are difficult to the true and very fast, undulating greens. On the long, demanding par 4 twelfth, the golfer drives from an elevated tee to a wide fairway; water is in play both off the tee and on the second shot. The signature par 3 sixth is quite picturesque.

Directions: Bergen County, #11 on Northeast Map
Take Rte. 9W to Clinton Ave., Tenafly. Go left all the way down Clinton Ave. over the RR tracks to Knickerbocker Rd. and make a left. Club is on left; pro shop is on right.

Hole	1	2	3	4	5	6	7	8	9	Out	BLUE	Rating 71.9
BLUE	390	533	422	172	357	182	428	391	349	3224		Slope 131
WHITE	380	518	414	145	343	168	420	383	339	3110		
Par	4	5	4	3	4	3	4	4	4	35	WHITE	Rating 70.9
Handicap	9	5	3	15	11	17	1	7	13			Slope 129
RED	366	469	365	109	306	148	341	370	315	2789		
Par	4	5	4	3	4	3	4	4	4	35	RED	Rating 74.6
Handicap	9	1	5	17	11	15	7	3	13			Slope 133
Hole	10	11	12	13	14	15	16	17	18	In		Totals
BLUE	497	164	430	540	387	357	312	223	494	3404	BLUE	6628
WHITE	486	156	421	525	379	341	302	207	483	3300	WHITE	6410
Par	5	3	4	5	4	4	4	3	5	37	Par	72
Handicap	10	18	2	4	6	8	16	14	12			
RED	458	124	404	445	373	325	294	192	447		RED	5851
Par	5	3	5	5	4	4	4	4	5	39	Par	74
Handicap	4	16	6	2	8	10	14	18	12			

Manager: Keith Tierney   **Pro:** Ed Whitman, PGA   **Supt:** Sam Juliano
Architect: Donald Ross 1914

MONTAMMY GOLF CLUB

Route 9W, Alpine, NJ 07620 **(201) 768-9000**

Montammy is an 18 hole course open 6 days a week, eleven months a year (closed January). Guests play accompanied by a member. Tee times may be reserved 1 week in advance for weekends. Call extension #169 for the pro shop.

- •**Driving Range**   •**Lockers**
- •**Practice Green** •**Showers**
- •**Power Carts**   •**Food**
-   Pull Carts   •**Clubhouse**
- •**Club Rental**   •**Outings**
- •**Caddies**   •**Soft Spikes**

Course Description: Montammy is a hilly course built on the New Jersey Palisades. It is fairly narrow and tree-lined. The par 3 fourth has a blind uphill tee shot to the undulating green. Landing there does not guarantee a two putt as the breaks are tricky and the surface is fast and interesting. The par 4 seventh, considered the signature hole, is a severe dogleg right with a second shot over a pond. A pond on the right on the par 5 fifth makes the hole more challenging. This same pond can lure a slice on the 3rd hole which now plays longer as the tee box has been moved back. The course is constantly being upgraded and is maintained extremely well. Caddies are required before 2 PM.

Directions: Bergen County, #12 on Northeast Map
G.W.Br. to Pal.Int.Pkwy. to Exit #1. Go right at exit to light. Turn right at light onto 9W and proceed north. After light at Tenafly, watch for club entrance on left.

Hole	1	2	3	4	5	6	7	8	9	Out	BLUE	Rating 73.2
BLUE	405	502	383	196	542	416	343	211	429	3427		Slope 135
WHITE	383	482	354	180	514	390	323	175	393	3194		
Par	4	5	4	3	5	4	4	3	4	36	WHITE	Rating 71.0
Handicap	5	7	13	15	1	3	11	17	9			Slope 130
RED	338	440	310	148	454	351	277	158	303	2779		
Par	4	5	4	3	5	4	4	3	4	36	RED	Rating 71.5
Handicap	5	7	9	15	3	1	11	17	13			Slope 126
Hole	10	11	12	13	14	15	16	17	18	In		Totals
BLUE	385	558	404	528	146	455	354	221	380	3431	BLUE	6858
WHITE	358	534	361	501	120	422	329	186	359	3170	WHITE	6364
Par	4	5	4	5	3	4	4	3	4	36	Par	72
Handicap	8	4	12	10	18	2	16	14	6			
RED	301	430	295	439	89	370	306	168	257	2655	RED	5434
Par	4	5	4	5	3	5	4	3	4	37	Par	73
Handicap	10	2	12	6	18	4	16	14	8			

Director of Golf: Mike Burke, Jr., PGA   **Supt:** Jim Swiatlowski
Architect: Frank Duane 1966

25

NORTH JERSEY COUNTRY CLUB PRIVATE

Hamburg Turnpike, Wayne, NJ 07470   **(973) 595-5150**
www.northjerseycc.com

North Jersey is a private 18 hole course open 6 days a week and closed in January. Guests may play accompanied by a member. Tee time reservations are necessary for weekends only.

•Driving Range	•Lockers
•Practice Green	•Showers
•Power Carts	•Food
Pull Carts	•Clubhouse
•Club Rental	•Outings
•Caddies	•Soft Spikes

Course Description: The beautiful, hilly and well maintained North Jersey CC is one of the more difficult courses in this part of the state. With small, undulating greens and tree lined fairways, there is little room for errant shots. The golfer is forced to negotiate many uneven lies. The rugged terrain as well as the blind shots on many holes add to the challenge. Several renovations have taken place in the bunkering of the course and in the clubhouse. Recently, the rotation of the holes has been switched to facilitate an easier start of the round. The club hosted the NJ State Open in 1995.

Directions: Passaic County, #13 on Northeast Map
Rte. 80 West to Rte. 23 North to Alps Rd. and make a right. Make a right on Ratzer Rd. and at 1st traffic light, make a left onto Valley Rd. At 1st light, make a right onto Hamburg Tpke. Club is 3/4 mile on left.

Hole	1	2	3	4	5	6	7	8	9	Out	BLUE	Rating 72.5
BLUE	495	429	335	159	425	439	524	136	397	3339		Slope 136
WHITE	482	414	315	138	413	423	503	131	385	3204		
Par	5	4	4	3	4	4	5	3	4	36	WHITE	Rating 70.4
Handicap	11	1	13	15	3	5	9	17	7			Slope 133
RED	423	368	290	125	343	414	488	127	374	2952		
Par	5	4	4	3	4	5	5	3	4	37	RED	Rating 74,5
Handicap	9	3	13	15	7	11	1	17	5			Slope 134
Hole	10	11	12	13	14	15	16	17	18	In		Totals
BLUE	380	371	372	160	371	164	467	534	398	3217	BLUE	6556
WHITE	353	355	361	153	358	152	400	509	379	3020	WHITE	6224
Par	4	4	4	3	4	3	4	5	4	35	Par	71
Handicap	10	12	4	16	14	18	2	8	6			
RED	312	315	348	118	351	132	350	459	351	2736	RED	5688
Par	4	4	4	3	4	3	4	5	4	35	Par	72
Handicap	14	10	2	16	12	18	4	6	8			

Manager: Ed LaPadula   **Pro:** Chris Dachisen, PGA   **Supt:** Gary Arlio
Architect: Walter Travis 1923 **Estab.** 1894

OLD TAPPAN GOLF COURSE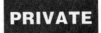

83 De Wolf Rd., Old Tappan, NJ 07675   **(201) 767-1199**

Old Tappan is a 9 hole municipally owned course with a membership only policy. It is open 6 days a week from 3/15--12/30. All Old Tappan residents are eligible to join. There is a waiting list for non-residents. Tee time reservations are not necessary.

Driving Range	•Lockers
•Practice Green	•Showers
•Power Carts	•Food
•Pull Carts	•Clubhouse
•Club Rental	•Outings
Caddies	•Soft Spikes

Course Description: The well maintained Old Tappan has very good drainage and is therefore playable soon after rain. The course features large undulating greens and its many trees help to define the fairways. The par 3 third presents a beautiful view of the lake and requires a well struck tee shot; one must make sure to stay clear of the pond. On the par 3 sixth hole the golfer must hit onto a green elevated 50 feet above the fairway. Old Tappan residents are lucky to have this little gem virtually in their backyards.

Directions: Bergen County, #14 on Northeast Map
Pal.Int.Pkwy. to Exit #6W, Orangeburg. Proceed West on Veterans Memorial Rd. for 1 mile to Blaisdell Rd. which becomes DeWolf. Turn left on DeWolf to course ahead on left. **OR** Piermont Rd. to Broadway in Norwood. Left on Broadway; bear left to Central Ave. At Old Tappan Rd. go right then left onto DeWolf to club.

Hole	1	2	3	4	5	6	7	8	9	Out	BLUE	Rating 68.2
BLUE												Slope 123
WHITE	362	290	202	414	352	112	412	415	517	3076		
Par	4	4	3	4	4	3	4	4	5	35	WHITE	Rating 69.0
Handicap	7	17	11	1	9	15	5	3	13			Slope 115
RED	352	277	186	397	338	95	407	405	504	2961		
Par	4	4	3	5	4	3	4	5	5	37	RED	Rating 71.3
Handicap	2	11	13	9	4	14	1	5	3			Slope 118

Hole	10	11	12	13	14	15	16	17	18	In		Totals
BLUE											BLUE	
WHITE	352	277	186	397	338	95	407	405	504	2961	WHITE	6037
Par	4	4	3	4	4	3	4	4	5	35	Par	70
Handicap	8	18	12	4	10	16	6	2	14			
RED	275	228	150	384	263	81	334	398	434	2547	RED	5508
Par	4	4	3	5	4	3	4	5	5	37	Par	74
Handicap	12	18	16	10	15	17	8	6	7			

Manager/Pro: Doug Meeks, PGA   **Supt:** Paul Pariscondola
Architect: Hal Purdy 1969

ORCHARD HILLS GOLF COURSE PUBLIC

404 Paramus Rd., Paramus, NJ 07652   **(201) 447-3778**

Orchard Hills is a 9 hole county course open 6 days a week and closed Dec. 15 to Mar. 15. For tee times: call county reservation system at 343-4441. Prices below are for 9 hole/18 hole rounds for county residents with ID, other rates for 18 holes.

Driving Range	Lockers
•**Practice Green**	Showers
•**Power Carts**	Food
•**Pull Carts**	•**Clubhouse**
•**Club Rental**	•**Outings**

Fees	Weekday	Weekend
ReswID	$18	$23
Non-reg	$40	$48
NonNJ	$55	$55
Sr/Jr	$9	$20
Power carts	$24	$24

Course Description: Orchard Hills is on the grounds of Bergen Community College and is quite well maintained. Somewhat hilly with plenty of interesting holes, it is a welcome place to play in Bergen County. The par 3 fourth requires an accurate shot over water to a small green. The first hole has a tree in the fairway that makes shots to the green difficult. The 9th hole requires a long drive, otherwise, the prudent golfer needs to lay up or risk landing in the pond that lurks about a 100 yards from the green.

Directions: Bergen County, #15 on Northeast Map
Rte. 4 East or West to Paramus Rd. Make a right on Paramus Rd. and go for approximately 1 & 1/2 miles. On right is entrance to Bergen Community College. Enter & follow signs to course on left.

Hole	1	2	3	4	5	6	7	8	9	Out	BLUE	Rating
BLUE												Slope
WHITE	280	325	465	180	268	325	347	199	387	2776		
Par	4	4	5	3	4	4	4	3	4	35	WHITE	Rating 67.7
Handicap	9	5	7	4	8	1	6	3	2			Slope 109
RED	269	310	461	164	254	313	330	187	376	2664		
Par	4	4	5	3	4	4	4	3	4	35	RED	Rating 70.0
Handicap	9	5	7	4	8	1	6	3	2			Slope 113
Hole	10	11	12	13	14	15	16	17	18	In		Totals
BLUE											BLUE	
WHITE											WHITE	
Par											Par	70
Handicap												
RED											RED	
Par											Par	70
Handicap												

Manager: Bob Pallotta   **Supt:** Peter Evans
Built: 1920s

OVERPECK GOLF COURSE

East Cedar Lane, Teaneck, NJ 07666   **(201) 837-3020**

Overpeck is one of four Bergen County 18 hole public courses. It is open 7 days a week from mid March to mid Dec. For computerized tee time reservations: call 343-4441 7 days in advance for county residents, 1 day for non res. @$1.50pp.

•**Driving Range**	•**Lockers**
•**Practice Green**	•**Showers**
•**Power Carts**	•**Food**
•**Pull Carts**	•**Clubhouse**
•**Club Rental**	•**Outings**

Fees	Weekday	Weekend
ReswID	$18	$23
Non-reg	$40	$48
NonNJ	$55	$55
Sr/Jr	$9	$20
Power carts	$24	$24

Course Description: Wide open and relatively flat, Overpeck gets quite busy in season. The many water hazards provide interest and some challenge, and many golfers make their way using pull carts. There are brooks, streams, ditches and lakes to carry. Overpeck's greens are moderate in size with some break. The back nine is considered more difficult than the front.

Directions: Bergen County, #16 on Northeast Map
Take Rte. 4 to Teaneck Rd. South to Cedar Lane. Go left on Cedar Lane; club is at end of road.

Hole	1	2	3	4	5	6	7	8	9	Out	BLUE	Rating 72.2
BLUE	528	362	188	330	430	441	479	130	342	3230		Slope 125
WHITE	486	350	155	318	418	415	454	122	325	3043		
Par	5	4	3	4	4	4	5	3	4	36	WHITE	Rating 70.7
Handicap	7	13	15	11	3	1	5	17	9			Slope 121
RED	400	291	111	296	320	398	413	93	281	2603		
Par	5	4	3	4	4	4	5	3	4	36	RED	Rating 70.8
Handicap	7	13	15	11	3	1	5	17	9			Slope 118

Hole	10	11	12	13	14	15	16	17	18	In		Totals
BLUE	410	392	489	371	217	434	379	506	156	3354	BLUE	6584
WHITE	368	381	458	354	192	413	366	489	131	3152	WHITE	6195
Par	4	4	5	4	3	4	4	5	3	36	Par	72
Handicap	4	10	8	12	6	2	·16	14	18			
RED	238	316	400	298	131	340	312	438	117	590	RED	5193
Par	4	4	5	4	3	4	4	5	3	36	Par	72
Handicap	4	10	8	12	6	2	16	14	18			

Manager: Tina Tedesco   **Supt:** Doug Richardson
Architect: Michael Burris 1960

PACKANACK GOLF CLUB

7 Osborne Terrace, Wayne, NJ 07470   **(973) 694-9754**

Packanack is a 9 hole private course open 6 days a week and closed between Dec. and March. Guests play accompanied by a member. Tee time reservations are necessary on weekends.

•**Driving Range**	•**Lockers**
•**Practice Green**	•**Showers**
•**Power Carts**	•**Food**
•**Pull Carts**	•**Clubhouse**
•**Club Rental**	•**Outings**
Caddies	•**Soft Spikes**

Course Description: Scenic Packanack is flat and tight with water in play on every hole. The medium sized greens are maintained in excellent condition. The signature hole is the par 3 sixth, 180 yards over a lake; more water lurks along the left side. Recent improvements have been made on the drainage ditches. The members here live around Packanack Lake, a community that has tennis courts and beach property for swimming. The scorecard below provides the total yardages from the 2nd set of tees that give variety for those who go around twice.

Directions: Passaic County, #17 on Northeast Map
Rte. 80 West to Rte. 23 North to Packanack Lake Rd. and go right. Watch for Osborne Terrace and turn right. Clubhouse is on the right.

Hole	1	2	3	4	5	6	7	8	9	Out	BLUE	
BLUE												
WHITE	470	474	211	325	321	180	413	290	327	3064		
Par	5	5	3	4	4	3	4	4	4	36	WHITE	Rating 69.5
Handicap	9	7	3	5	13	15	1	17	11			Slope 124
RED	445	438	158	263	265	136	384	269	237	2616		
Par	5	5	3	4	4	3	5	4	4	37	RED	Rating 69.8
Handicap	7	1	9	6	2	5	8	4	3			Slope 125
Hole	10	11	12	13	14	15	16	17	18	In		Totals
BLUE											BLUE	
WHITE										3056	WHITE	6120
Par											Par	72
Handicap												
RED										2629	RED	5245
Par											Par	74
Handicap												

Manager: Bill Caldwell   **Pro:** Ben Karalis, PGA   **Supt:** Doug Vogel
Architect: Geoffrey Cornish 1965

PARAMUS GOLF & CC

314 Paramus Rd., Paramus, NJ 07652   **(201) 447-6079**

Paramus is an 18 hole course open 7 days a week all year. Memberships are available. Registered players make tee times the day before in person. Non-reg. may call 10-10:30 AM for play after 1PM that day. Fees paid in cash only. 2nd # is 447-6067.

Driving Range	
• Practice Green	• Lockers
• Power Carts	• Showers
• Pull Carts	• Food
• Club Rental	• Clubhouse
• Soft Spikes	• Outings

Fees	Weekday	Weekend
ParRes.Reg.	$12	$17
Par res	$17	$22
NJ Res(reg)	$24	$34
NJ Res	$34	$44
Sr Discounts	$2 off	
Power carts	$24	$12/ (9)

Course Description: Stephen Kay's five year improvement plan to refurbish Paramus has resulted in a well maintained course enjoyable for all players. The course has been tightened and is extremely popular. The 218 yard par 3 17th has a well bunkered, postage stamp sized elevated green. The signature par 3 12th is made interesting by the stone mausoleum to the right of the green. On the 8th, a dogleg par 4, the golfer encounters water if the tee shot is too long and straight, making it especially hazardous from the forward tees. The difficult 9th hole, 589 yards from the back, is rarely reached in two. The reconstructed 11th, 12th and 13th holes are longer and trickier than ever before. There is a modified driving range.

Directions: Bergen County, #18 on Northeast Map
Take Rte. 4 West to Paramus Rd; travel north & follow signs toward Bergen Community College. Course is on right just after Century Rd.

Hole	1	2	3	4	5	6	7	8	9	Out	BLUE	Rating 69.6
BLUE	343	372	371	314	145	271	371	409	589	3185		Slope 118
WHITE	322	347	338	295	114	247	351	376	544	2934		
Par	4	4	4	4	3	4	4	4	5	36	WHITE	Rating 67.1
Handicap	11	5	7	13	15	17	9	1	3			Slope 113
RED	259	233	293	275	89	226	239	300	481	2395		
Par	4	4	4	4	3	4	4	4	5	36	RED	Rating 66.4
Handicap	11	5	9	13	17	15	7	3	1			Slope 109

Hole	10	11	12	13	14	15	16	17	18	In		Totals
BLUE	332	508	171	489	332	172	360	218	406	2988	BLUE	6173
WHITE	316	475	158	478	302	156	336	191	378	2790	WHITE	5724
Par	4	5	3	5	4	3	4	3	4	35	Par	71
Handicap	8	14	8	16	10	12	6	2	4			
RED	263	380	123	410	282	108	277	121	344	2308	RED	4703
Par	4	5	3	5	4	3	4	4	4	36	Par	72
Handicap	10	2	18	4	12	16	8	14	6			

Manager/Pro: Madeline Cassano, LPGA   **Supt:** Ken Krausz
Built: 1975   **Architect:** Stephen Kay (redesign 1998)

PASSAIC COUNTY GOLF COURSE PUBLIC

207 Totowa Rd., Wayne, NJ 07470   (973) 881-4921

Passaic County Golf Course has 36 holes and is the only public course in Passaic County. It is open 7 days a week all year. Private memberships are available. Golfers get tee times based on when they arrive at the course.

- •Practice Range   •Lockers
- •Practice Green   •Showers
- •Power Carts   •Food
- •Pull Carts   •Clubhouse
- •Club Rental   •Outings

Fees	Weekday	Weekend
Resident	$16	$19
Non-res	$45	$50
Sr/Jr	$11	$14
Power carts	$22	$12/9

Course Description: Passaic County Golf Course offers many water hazards, long fairways and large greens creating a challenge for all levels of play. The Red course is flat and wooded, the Blue is hilly, tree lined and open. The first hole on the Red is 453 yards from the whites and designed long to avoid congestion at the beginning of the round. It is relatively flat with a dogleg surrounded by many beautiful trees. Water makes the hole more interesting. When this course opened in 1931, there was a $1.00 greens fee on weekends! The scorecard below is for the Red course.

Directions: Passaic County, #19 on Northeast Map
Rte. 80 West to Exit #55, Union Blvd., Totowa. Go left on Totowa Rd. and follow curved road for approx. 2 miles. Course is on right.

Hole	1	2	3	4	5	6	7	8	9	Out	BLUE	Rating
BLUE	471	348	449	400	386	187	540	199	370	3350		Slope
WHITE	453	340	436	390	378	176	532	188	360	3253		
Par	4	4	4	4	4	3	5	3	4	35	WHITE	Rating 71.2
Handicap	3	13	5	7	9	15	1	17	11			Slope 122
RED	420	325	426	378	365	140	506	130	340	3030		
Par	5	4	5	4	4	3	5	3	4	37	RED	Rating 74.8
Handicap	3	13	5	7	9	15	1	17	11			Slope 128
Hole	10	11	12	13	14	15	16	17	18	In		Totals
BLUE	395	454	375	218	280	448	435	228	419	3252	BLUE	6602
WHITE	385	446	370	198	275	438	425	220	408	3165	WHITE	6418
Par	4	4	4	3	4	4	4	3	4	34	Par	69
Handicap	10	2	12	18	14	4	6	16	8			
RED	326	432	352	170	261	399	404	208	394	2946	RED	5976
Par	4	5	4	3	4	5	5	3	5	38	Par	75
Handicap	10	2	12	18	14	4	6	16	8			

Manager/Supt: Nick Roca
Architect: Martin O'Laughlin 1931

PREAKNESS HILLS CC

1050 Ratzer Rd., Wayne, NJ 07470   **(973) 694-2910**

Preakness Hills is an 18 hole course open 6 days a week and closed in January and February. Guests play accompanied by a member. Tee time reservations are necessary on weekends.

•**Driving Range**	•**Lockers**
•**Practice Green**	•**Showers**
•**Power Carts**	•**Food**
Pull Carts	•**Clubhouse**
Club Rental	•**Outings**
•**Caddies**	•**Soft Spikes**

Course Description: For players and naturalists, Preakness Hills is a challenging course in a majestic setting. A large pond stocked with bass and carp may be found on the property. Cranes and other colorful birds are ever-present. Golfers must be accurate to avoid trouble especially with the tee shot over a pond to the 18th green which is just in front of the magnificent clubhouse. The par 4 15th hole, a dogleg right, has water to be wary of as well. The 13th green is double-tiered. The sixth hole is densely treed and well-bunkered with a "bowling alley" fairway; careful placement is well rewarded. The 17th hole, 498 yards from the back tees, has 5 bunkers on the left and 2 on the right of the green. Caddies are required until 3 P.M.

Directions: Passaic County, #20 on Northeast Map
Rte. 80 West to Rte. 23 North. Exit on Alps Rd. & take it to Ratzer Rd. Turn right and club is ahead on right.

Hole	1	2	3	4	5	6	7	8	9	Out	BLUE	Rating 72.4
BLUE	480	356	381	441	508	224	428	162	420	3400		Slope 130
WHITE	438	345	377	400	499	210	424	151	411	3255		
Par	5	4	4	4	5	3	4	3	4	36	WHITE	Rating 71.2
Handicap	15	13	3	7	5	11	9	17	1			Slope 128
RED	353	283	334	327	465	188	379	141	398	2868		
Par	4	4	4	4	5	3	4	3	5	36	RED	Rating 73.3
Handicap	5	15	3	13	1	11	7	17	9			Slope 135

Hole	10	11	12	13	14	15	16	17	18	In		Totals
BLUE	497	310	403	359	370	407	187	498	146	3177	BLUE	6577
WHITE	475	300	389	344	365	390	168	489	129	3049	WHITE	6304
Par	5	4	4	4	4	4	3	5	3	36	Par	72
Handicap	10	12	6	2	14	4	16	8	18			
RED	426	219	346	283	336	335	152	408	109	2614	RED	5482
Par	5	4	4	4	4	4	3	5	3	36	Par	72
Handicap	6	12	10	2	14	4	16	8	18			

Manager: Richard MacBain   **Pro:** Robert Foster, PGA   **Supt:** Jon O'Keefe
Architect: Willie Tucker 1926

RAMSEY GOLF & COUNTRY CLUB PRIVATE

105 Lakeside Dr., Ramsey, NJ 07446   **(201) 327-3877**
www.ramseygcc.com

Ramsey is a private 18 hole course open 6 days a week and closed Jan. & Feb. Guests may play accompanied by a member. Tee time reservations are necessary summer weekend mornings.

•Driving Range	•Lockers
•Practice Green	•Showers
•Power Carts	•Food
•Pull Carts	•Clubhouse
•Club Rental	•Outings
Caddies	•Soft Spikes

Course Description: Ramsey's golf course circles a peaceful residential development and surrounds 3 spring fed lakes. The course was built after the houses were in place, a difficult task indeed. It was originally the 220 acre Ramsey Estates; the pro shop was converted from a stable, then to a bowling alley and later to its present state. The "Abbey Restaurant", of Norman architecture, is constructed of all natural stones. The original 6 hole course was begun in 1940; Hal Purdy added the 2nd 6 holes about 30 years ago. In 1995, he finished the challenging job of fitting in the final 6 to make this a regulation 18 hole facility. Ramsey is tight, scenic and well maintained; a lovely amenity for NJ golfers and especially the homeowners who are entitled to automatic membership. A major renovation was completed in 2004.

Directions: Bergen County, #21 on Northeast Map
GSP to Rte. 17 North to Allendale exit; at first light, make a right onto Franklin Tpke, (Rte. 507). Pass 1 light, club is ahead on left.

Hole	1	2	3	4	5	6	7	8	9	Out	BLUE	Rating 67.2
BLUE	525	165	290	168	329	372	274	161	423	2707		Slope 117
WHITE	515	160	280	160	316	357	264	156	413	2621		
Par	5	3	4	3	4	4	4	3	4	34	WHITE	Rating 66.3
Handicap	3	15	13	9	17	5	7	11	1			Slope 115
RED	485	135	270	112	310	309	254	131	403	2409		
Par	5	3	4	3	4	4	4	3	5	35	RED	Rating 68.4
Handicap	1	17	9	15	11	7	5	13	3			Slope 115
Hole	10	11	12	13	14	15	16	17	18	In		Totals
BLUE	505	155	376	136	306	383	178	500	294	2833	BLUE	5540
WHITE	475	150	371	124	296	378	163	475	282	2714	WHITE	5335
Par	5	3	4	3	4	4	3	5	4	35	Par	69
Handicap	2	14	4	18	12	8	16	6	10			
RED	441	122	370	114	221	333	151	430	275	2457	RED	4866
Par	5	3	4	3	4	4	3	5	4	35	Par	70
Handicap	2	16	6	18	14	8	12	4	10			

Manager: Cheryl Veltman   **Pro:** Mark Mitchell, PGA   **Supt:** Chad Mathieu
Architect: Hal Purdy 1965

RIDGEWOOD COUNTRY CLUB PRIVATE

96 West Midland Ave., Paramus, NJ 07450   **(201) 225-6521**

Ridgewood is a 27 hole course open 6 days a week and closed in Feb. Guests play accompanied by a member. Tee time reservations are not necessary.

•Driving Range	•Lockers
•Practice Green	•Showers
•Power Carts	•Food
Pull Carts	•Clubhouse
•Club Rental	•Outings
•Caddies	•Soft Spikes

Course Description: This tree-lined championship course was designed in 1928 by A.W. Tillinghast. It is rated as one of the top hundred courses in the country in no small part due to the challenge presented by the tee shots. On the West Course, the par 4 ninth hole is 427 yards, a dogleg right with a cavernous bunker guarding the left front of the green. The sixth on the Center Course is called the "nickel & dime" hole. You either end up with a five or a ten depending on the accuracy of your approach shot. In 2001, Ridgewood hosted the Senior PGA Championship. The scorecard below is for the West & East courses.

Directions: Bergen County, #22 on Northeast Map
Take Rte. 4 East or West to Rte. 17 North. Take the 2nd Midland Ave. exit. Travel approximately 1/2 mile to club on right.

Hole	1	2	3	4	5	6	7	8	9	Out	BLUE	Rating 71.5
BLUE	371	384	202	597	413	151	420	569	427	3534		Slope 136
WHITE	358	363	181	531	403	137	380	559	419	3331		
Par	4	5	3	4	5	4	3	4	4	36	WHITE	Rating 69.3
Handicap	7	4	9	6	1	2	8	5	3			Slope 124
RED	340	347	136	456	394	124	305	515	334	2951		
Par	4	4	3	5	5	3	4	5	4	37	RED	Rating 73.4
Handicap	5	3	9	2	6	8	7	1	4			Slope 133
Hole	10	11	12	13	14	15	16	17	18	In		Totals
BLUE	375	177	567	414	407	229	460	403	379	3411	BLUE	6945
WHITE	350	155	544	390	374	205	428	393	369	3208	WHITE	6539
Par	4	3	5	4	4	3	4	4	4	35	Par	71
Handicap	6	9	2	4	3	8	1	7	5			
RED	325	136	507	405	358	187	413	382	328	3041	RED	5997
Par	4	3	5	5	4	3	5	4	4	37	Par	74
Handicap	7	9	1	5	3	8	2	4	6			

Manager: Larry Kelly   **Pro:** David Reasoner, PGA   **Supt:** Todd Raisch
Estab: 1890 **Architect:** A.W. Tillinghast 1928

ROCKLEIGH GOLF COURSE

PUBLIC

15 Paris Ave., Rockleigh, NJ 07647 **(201) 768-6353**

Rockleigh is a public county course with three nines & is open from mid-March to mid-Dec. 7 days a week. Call 343-4441 for automated tee times up to 7 days in advance (until midnight of the night before.) There is a reservation fee. Scorecard below is Red/White. Resident ID cards are available.

Driving Range
- **Practice Green**
- **Power Carts**
- **Pull Carts**
- **Club Rental**
- **Soft Spikes**
- **Lockers**
- **Showers**
- **Food**
- **Clubhouse**
- Outings

Fees	Weekday	Weekend
ReswID	$18	$23
Non-reg	$40	$48
NonNJ	$55	$55
Sr/Jr	$9	$20
Power carts	$24	$24

Course Description: The traditional design of Rockleigh, the only Bergen County course that has 27 holes, offers something for every level of player. It is wide-open with gently rolling hills and mid-sized greens. The Red course is considered the most challenging, highlighted by the 4th hole which is hilly and has water in play. The White is flatter and the Blue has as the longest hole, the par 5 #8 with a length of 536 yards. Beautiful views of the Palisades can be enjoyed here. The course gets quite busy; as many as 600 people per day play on a weekend. Scorecard below is Red/White; rating & slope are an average of all 3 courses.

Directions: Bergen County, #24 on Northeast Map
Palisades Pkwy. to Exit #5S. Take Rte. 303 South which becomes Livingston Ave. Turn left at the 4th light, Paris Ave., and proceed to course on right. OR Rte. 9W North to Closter Dock Rd. and turn left. Go right on Piermont, then left on Paris to club on left.

Hole	1	2	3	4	5	6	7	8	9	Out	BLACK	Rating
BLACK	374	342	422	179	540	525	479	232	436	3529		Slope
WHITE	358	328	395	161	459	485	453	202	403	3244		
Par	4	4	4	3	5	5	4	3	4	36	WHITE	Rating 68.2
Handicap	6	9	2	8	5	4	1	7	3			Slope 115
RED	320	276	360	95	430	416	352	145	275	2669		
Par	4	4	4	3	5	5	4	3	4	36	RED	Rating 68.2
Handicap	6	9	2	8	5	4	1	7	3			Slope 115

Hole	10	11	12	13	14	15	16	17	18	In		Totals
BLACK	301	453	411	216	377	534	181	466	344	3283	BLACK	6812
WHITE	289	403	365	188	346	483	165	493	322	3054	WHITE	6298
Par	4	4	4	3	4	5	3	4/5	4	35/36	Par	71/72
Handicap	7	1	4	8	5	2	9	3	6			
RED	255	344	310	122	316	398	130	416	294	2585	RED	5254
Par	4	4	4	3	4	5	3	5	4	36	Par	72
Handicap	7	1	4	8	5	2	9	3	6			

Manager: Leo Odabashian   **Supt:** Rebecca Hawkins
Architects: Robert Trent Jones 1964 (*Blue*)   Alfred Tull 1958 (*Red & White*)

UPPER MONTCLAIR CC

PRIVATE

177 Hepburn Rd., Clifton, NJ 07012   **(973) 779-7505**
umccgolf@aol.com

Upper Montclair is a private 27 hole course open 6 days a week all year. Guests play accompanied by a member. Tee time reservations are not necessary. The scorecard below is for the East & South courses.

> •**Driving Range**   •**Lockers**
> •**Practice Green**   •**Showers**
> •**Power Carts**   •**Food**
> •**Pull Carts**   •**Clubhouse**
> •**Club Rental**   •**Outings**
> •**Caddies**   •**Soft Spikes**

Course Description: This championship course was originally designed as 36 holes by A.W. Tillinghast for Upper Montclair but the GSPkway took 9 away, Robert Trent Jones then redesigned the course for 27 holes. The fairways are tree lined and well maintained. Many of the immaculately groomed greens are elevated and all are fast with subtle breaks. Water on the par 4 third hole requires a well placed tee shot followed by a demanding second shot. Characteristic of Robert Trent Jones are the long tee boxes and narrow fairways. Members can never tire of the variety of play on this course.

Directions: Passaic County, #25 on Northeast Map
Garden State Pkwy. to Exit # 153. Take Rte. 3 East. Almost immediately, make a right to the club entrance on Rte. 3.

Hole	1	2	3	4	5	6	7	8	9	Out	BLUE	Rating 73.6
BLUE	440	182	550	300	185	520	400	370	430	3467		Slope 136
WHITE	427	170	535	370	165	500	365	350	401	3283		
Par	4	3	5	4	3	5	4	4	4	36	WHITE	Rating 71.4
Handicap	1	8	3	6	9	4	5	7	2			Slope 136
RED	410	160	415	335	140	410	350	330	355	2905		
Par	5	3	5	4	3	5	4	4	4	37	RED	Rating 73.4
Handicap	2	8	3	6	9	1	7	5	4			Slope 127
Hole	10	11	12	13	14	15	16	17	18	In		Totals
BLUE	420	495	425	355	375	180	390	215	590	3445	BLUE	6912
WHITE	410	478	408	340	357	168	360	195	550	3266	WHITE	6549
Par	4	5	4	4	4	3	4	3	5	36	Par	72
Handicap	4	3	1	7	6	9	5	8	2			
RED	356	385	355	320	325	135	350	170	469	2826	RED	5731
Par	4	5	5	4	4	3	4	3	5	37	Par	74
Handicap	4	2	3	7	6	9	5	8	1			

Manager: Robert Paskill   **Pro:** Matt Malario, PGA   **Supt:** Bob Dickison
Architect: A.W. Tillinghast 1901   **Redesign:** Robert Trent Jones 1929

VALLEY BROOK GOLF CLUB

SEMI-PRIVATE

15 RiverVale Rd., RiverVale, NJ 07675   (201) 664-5886
www.valleybrookgolfclub.com

Valley Brook is a public 18 hole course open 7 days a week, all year. Memberships are available as well as reserved weekend starting times. Tee times: up to 5 days in advance. Carts are required on weekends.

•Driving Range	•Lockers
•Practice Green	•Showers
•Power Carts	•Food
•Pull Carts	•Clubhouse
•Club Rental	•Outings
•Soft Spikes	

Fees	M-Th	Weekend
	$70	$95
Fri	$75	
Twi	$40	$65
Power carts	included	

Course Description: Valley Brook, located on the grounds of the former Pascack Brook golf course, is a totally redesigned championship facility. Bent grass greens fairways and tees make this course a delight to play. There is challenging bunkering around every hole. The par 3 9th has a carry over water into the prevailing wind. The 13th, a go-for-broke par 5, makes the golfer work the ball in both directions. Eight of the holes have additional tee markers. The driving range is well situated and offers a good practice area. This meticulously-groomed layout is a major attraction for area golfers.

Directions: Bergen County, #19 on Northeast Map
Rte. 4 W to Kinderkamack Rd. Exit. & go left (north) on Kind. Rd. for 5.5 miles & turn right onto Old Hook Rd & pass Pascack Valley Hospital. Before next light, go left onto Emerson Rd. Go to end & go right onto RiverVale Rd. Course is 1/2 mile on right.

Hole	1	2	3	4	5	6	7	8	9	Out	BLUE	Rating 69.8
BLUE	330	495	183	395	580	384	233	422	166	3188		Slope 126
WHITE	310	480	153	370	552	361	188	396	140	2950	.	
Par	4	5	3	4	5	4	3	4	3	35	WHITE	Rating 68.1
Handicap	13	3	17	7	1	11	9	5	15			Slope 123
RED	240	420	116	280	440	281	146	325	110	2358		
Par	4	5	3	4	5	4	3	4	3	35	RED	Rating 66.8
Handicap	13	3	17	7	1	11	9	5	15			Slope 112
Hole	10	11	12	13	14	15	16	17	18	In		Totals
BLUE	314	315	198	488	337	396	437	178	360	3023	BLUE	6211
WHITE	300	294	161	464	319	357	402	167	337	2801	WHITE	5751
Par	4	4	3	5	4	4	4	3	4	35	Par	70
Handicap	12	14	18	2	10	6	4	16	8			
RED	246	260	123	421	293	307	349	143	300	2432	RED	4790
Par	4	4	3	5	4	4	4	3	4	35	Par	70
Handicap	12	14	18	2	10	6	4	16	8			

Manager: Gautam Patkner   **Pro:** Kent Smith,PGA   **Supt:** Mike Sunshine
Architects: *Pascack Brook* John Handwerg Jr. 1962 *Valley Brook* Bill Boswell 2001

WHITE BEECHES GOLF & CC

70 Haworth Dr., Haworth, NJ 07641   **(201) 385-8531**

White Beeches is a private 18 hole course open 6 days a week and closed for the month of Feb. Guests play accompanied by a member. Reserved tee times are suggested for weekends.

•**Driving Range**	•**Lockers**
•**Practice Green**	•**Showers**
•**Power Carts**	•**Food**
Pull Carts	•**Clubhouse**
•**Club Rental**	•**Outings**
•**Caddies**	•**Soft Spikes**

Course Description: White Beeches is a relatively flat, parkland style course with an abundance of trees and many doglegs. The greens are postage stamp in size and extremely hard to hold. Excellent chipping and putting skills are necessary to get up and down. The player faces a difficult decision on the par 5 eleventh hole where a brook crosses the fairway; to lay up on the second shot or to try to carry the green. The 18th is a daunting finishing hole, a par 3 over water. The tee boxes have recently been redone.

Directions: Bergen County, #27 on Northeast Map
From Rte. 4, take Kinderkamack Road North to Oradell. Go right on Oradell Ave. to blinking light and make a left on Grant Ave. and right on Sunset. Turn left on Haworth Dr. to club on left..

Hole	1	2	3	4	5	6	7	8	9	Out	BLUE	Rating 72.1
BLUE	392	326	527	349	374	148	299	570	368	3353		Slope 128
WHITE	371	289	514	331	365	134	285	557	354	3200		
Par	4	4	5	4	4	3	4	5	4	37	WHITE	Rating 70.9
Handicap	3	13	5	11	7	17	15	1	9			Slope 135
RED	351	255	405	322	353	420	262	500	340	2949		
Par	4	4	5	4	4	4	3	5	4	37	RED	Rating 72.2
Handicap	3	15	7	11	9	17	13	1	5			Slope 132
Hole	10	11	12	13	14	15	16	17	18	In		Totals
BLUE	396	509	366	185	429	366	336	428	215	3230	BLUE	6519
WHITE	376	481	346	174	413	347	315	411	202	3065	WHITE	6254
Par	4	5	4	3	4	4	4	4	3	35	Par	72
Handicap	6	8	10	18	2	14	12	4	16			
RED	355	421	310	162	401	329	284	400	145	2807	RED	5439
Par	4	5	4	3	5	4	4	5	3	37	Par	74
Handicap	8	2	12	16	4	14	10	6	18			

Manager: George Arnold   **Pro:** Brian Gaffney, PGA   **Supt:** Eugene Huelster
Architects: Val Flood 1902   Walter Travis 1919   Alfred Tull 1950

COMING ATTRACTIONS

As a service to our readers, we must include information about the exciting new Meadowlands project set to open in 2006. Phase 1, also referred to as the *Meadowlands Golf Resort Village*, will be developed on approximately 785 acres in Lyndhurst, Rutherford and North Arlington in Bergen County and Kearny in Hudson County. Along with the preservation of hundreds of acres of open areas from current landfills, there are plans for four 18 hole links style golf courses, two private and two public, hotels, retail space, condominums, biking and walking trails, a rail line and much more. For additional information, go to the www.meadowlansmiracle.com website.

NORTHWEST REGION

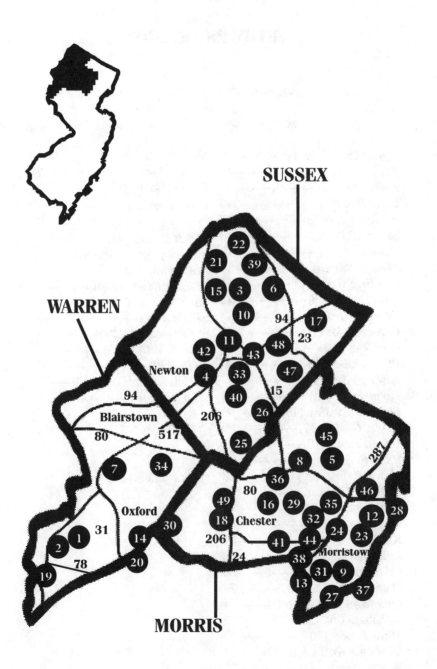

SUSSEX

WARREN

MORRIS

NORTHWEST REGION

Public Courses appear in *bold italics*

Map (#)	Page #	Map (#)	Page #
Apple Mountain (1)	43	Mt. Tabor (32)	76
Architect's Golf Club (2)	44	Newton (33)	77
Ballyowen (3)	45	Panther Valley (34)	78
Bear Brook (4)	46	Peace Pipe (35)	79
Berkshire Valley (5)	47	Picatinny Golf Club*(36)	80
Black Bear (6)	48	*Pinch Brook* (37)	81
Black Oak (49)	49	Rockaway River (38)	82
Blair Academy (7)	50	*Rock View* (39)	83
Bowling Green (8)	51	*Rolling Greens* (40)	84
Brooklake CC (9)	52	Roxiticus Golf Club (41)	85
Crystal Springs (10)	53	*Skyview* (42)	86
Culver Lake (11)	54	Spring Brook (44)	87
Deer Run (12)	55	*Sunset Valley* (45)	88
Fairmount CC (13)	56	*Twin Willows* (46)	89
Fairway Valley (14)	57	Wallkill Country Club (47)	90
Farmstead (15)	58	*Wild Turkey* (48)	91
Flanders Valley (16)	59		
Great Gorge (17)	60		
Green Pond (18)	61		
Harkers Hollow (19)	62		
Hawk Pointe (20)	63	*Military Course	
Hidden Acres (21)	64		
High Point (22)	65		
Knoll East (23)	66		
Knoll West (24)	67		
Lake Lackawanna (25)	68		
Lake Mohawk (26)	69		
Madison Golf Club (27)	70		
Meadows Golf Club (28)	71		
Mendham Golf Club (29)	72		
Mine Brook (30)	73		
Minerals Golf Club (43)	74		
Morris County (31)	75		

APPLE MOUNTAIN GOLF & CC   PUBLIC

369 Hazen Oxford Rd., Belvidere, NJ 07823   **(908) 453-3023**
www.applemountaingolf.com

Apple Mountain is an 18 hole public course open 7 days a week all year. Memberships are available. Tee times: up to 2 weeks in advance.

Driving Range	• **Lockers**
• **Practice Green**	• **Showers**
• **Power Carts**	• **Food**
• **Pull Carts**	• **Clubhouse**
• **Club Rental**	• **Outings**
• **Soft Spikes**	

Fees	Weekday	Weekend
Daily	$23	$37
After 12PM	$21	$31
Power carts 12pp, after12 $8pp		

Course Description: Apple Mountain is a hilly scenic well-maintained golf course. Although there are many beautiful mature trees lining the fairways, additional ones are planted periodically and tees are upgraded on a regular basis. Water comes into play on eleven holes. The severe dogleg left and water to carry on the signature par 5 third hole makes it a formidable challenge. The unique par 6 17th is a 650 yard downhill dogleg. The greens have variety; some are elevated, some are two-tiered. The 13th and 15th holes are at high elevations and the Delaware Water Gap can be seen in the distance. The Top of the Green Restaurant is an added attraction.

Directions: Warren County, #1 on Northwest Map
Rte. 80W to Exit #12 (Hope). Left @ Stop sign onto Rte.521S (becomes Rte.519S). Go straight thru light @Rte.46 to 4-way flashing light. Left onto Rte.623 for 4/10 mile; take 2nd left onto Rte. 624. Go 1 mile up hill to club on right.

Hole	1	2	3	4	5	6	7	8	9	Out	YELLOW	Rating 71.1
YELLOW	284	381	560	170	394	379	401	397	229	3160		Slope 122
WHITE	262	365	501	120	364	362	372	379	135	2860		
Par	4	4	5	3	4	4	4	4	3	35	WHITE	Rating 67.5
Handicap	16	4	2	18	6	14	12	8	10			Slope 114
RED	232	321	453	109	262	273	265	371	122	2408		
Par	4	4	5	3	4	4	4	4	3	35	RED	Rating 69.7
Handicap	16	4	2	18	6	14	12	8	10			Slope 120
Hole	10	11	12	13	14	15	16	17	18	In		Totals
YELLOW	201	376	373	568	339	261	419	656	280	3200	YELLOW	6360
WHITE	130	356	351	541	327	182	372	632	260	3151	WHITE	6011
Par	3	4	4	5	4	3	4	5	3	35	Par	70
Handicap	15	17	7	5	9	13	3	1	11			
RED	111	332	312	457	294	159	331	559	250	2805	RED	5213
Par	3	4	4	5	4	3	4	6	4	37	Par	72
Handicap	15	17	7	5	9	13	3	1	11			

Manager: Drew J. Kiszonak   **Pro**: Rob Hirt, PGA   **Supt:** Mike Tate
Built: 1973

ARCHITECTS GOLF CLUB

PUBLIC

700 Strykers Rd., Phillipsburg, NJ 08865   **(908) 213-3080**
www.thearchitectsclub.com

The Architects Golf Club is an 18 hole course open to the public 7 days a week all year. Memberships are available. Tee times: 14 days for public. A full service clubhouse is planned for 2005.

<table>
<tr><td>

• **Driving Range**
• **Practice Green**
• **Power Carts**
  Pull Carts
• **Club Rental**
• **Soft Spikes**

• **Lockers**
  Showers
• **Food**
• **Clubhouse**
• **Outings**

</td><td>

Fees	M-Thurs	Weekend
Daily	$75	$100
Fri	$85	

Power carts included

</td></tr>
</table>

Course Description: Each hole is built in the style of the classic architects of the past such as Old Tom Morris, C. B. MacDonald, Donald Ross, Tillinghast, Seth Raynor. Alister Mackenzie, George Crump, Charles Banks, Walter Travis and Dick Wilson. Inspired by these legendary designers, Stephen Kay consulted with historian Ron Whitten. The beautifully manicured property consists of rolling open farm fields with spectacular views of the surrounding mountains. Water affects play on the 9th and again on the par 5 13th. The course, 6863 yds from the back tees, varies in elevation by a full 95 feet. To simulate playing conditions, the driving range contains carved mounds and undulations.

Directions: Warren County, #2 on Northwest Map
Rte.78W to Exit 3. Go to traffic light at St. James and turn right. Make 1st left onto Strykers Rd. Course is 2 miles on the right.

Hole	1	2	3	4	5	6	7	8	9	Out	GOLD	Rating .71.6
GOLD	500	185	510	422	345	135	400	174	410	3081		Slope 127
BLUE	485	165	497	405	335	116	375	163	395	2936		
Par	5	3	5	4	4	3	4	3	4	35	BLUE	Rating 70.4
Handicap	15	9	5	7	13	17	3	11	1			Slope 125
RED	404	122	414	350	283	100	331	110	337	2451		
Par	5	3	5	4	4	3	4	3	4	35	RED	Rating 71.0
Handicap	15	9	5	7	13	17	3	11	1			Slope 123

Hole	10	11	12	13	14	15	16	17	18	In		Totals
GOLD	358	523	182	494	454	432	443	180	385	3451	GOLD	6532
BLUE	348	500	159	475	400	405	423	171	355	3236	BLUE	6172
Par	4	5	3	5	4	4	4	3	4	36	Par	71
Handicap	14	10	16	6	4	2	8	18	12			
RED	291	437	138	407	354	352	350	142	311	2782	RED	5233
Par	4	5	3	5	4	4	4	3	4	36	Par	71
Handicap	14	10	16	6	4	2	8	18	12			

Pro/Manager: Keith Hicklin, PGA   **Supt**: Dave Eichner
Architect: Stephen Kay 2001

BALLYOWEN GOLF CLUB

105-137 Wheatsworth Rd., Hamburg, NJ 07419   **(973) 827-5996**
www.crystalgolfresort.com

Ballyowen is an 18 hole course open 7 days a week Mar.-Dec. Reserve card members have privileges and discounts at Black Bear, Crystal Springs, Wild Turkey, Great Gorge and Minerals. Tee times: 7 day advance, 12 day for mbrs.

•**Driving Range**	•**Lockers**
•**Practice Green**	•**Showers**
•**Power Carts**	•**Food**
Pull Carts	•**Clubhouse**
•**Club Rental**	•**Outings**
•**Soft Spikes**	•**Caddies**

Fees	Weekday	Weekend
Daily	$100	$125
After 3PM	$60	$80
Power carts	included	

Course Description: With panoramic views of the Kittatinny Mountains in the distance, Ballyowen takes advantage of the unique natural landscape. The property was reclaimed from a former quarry and is virtually treeless. Over 7000 yards from the tips, multiple tee locations give golfers of all skill levels a chance to enjoy this links style layout. The architect specializes in environmentally sensitive design. The broad verdant rolling contoured fairways, the bent grass greens, the wind shifts and the wheat-like native grasses in the rough, make this an unusual and challenging course with a true Irish flavor. The kilted staff and beautiful clubhouse enhance the old world impression here. Named by *New Jersey Golfer* in 1998 #1 public course in NJ.

Directions: Sussex County, #3 on Northwest Map
Rte. 80 West to Exit 53. Take Rte. 23 North approx. 30 miles to Hamburg. Go left on Rte.94S for 2 miles to Wheatsworth Rd. Turn left & go 1 mi. to course on right.

Hole	1	2	3	4	5	6	7	8	9	Out	BLUE	Rating 71.2
BLUE	351	312	546	180	530	174	384	395	393	3265		Slope 125
WHITE	328	282	505	159	509	159	347	374	364	3027		
Par	4	4	5	3	5	3	4	4	4	36	WHITE	Rating 70.0
Handicap	13	11	3	17	5	15	1	7	9			Slope 122
RED	286	212	423	95	422	107	285	283	282	2395		
Par	4	4	5	3	5	3	4	4	4	36	RED	Rating 66.9
Handicap	11	13	1	17	3	15	5	7	9			Slope 106

Hole	10	11	12	13	14	15	16	17	18	In		Totals
BLUE	482	161	328	360	448	167	420	490	387	3243	BLUE	6508
WHITE	460	140	315	338	409	143	394	475	365	3039	WHITE	6066
Par	5	3	4	4	4	3	4	5	4	36	Par	72
Handicap	12	18	14	8	4	16	2	10	6			
RED	396	87	247	303	354	99	355	357	310	2508	RED	4903
Par	5	3	4	4	4	3	4	5	4	36	Par	72
Handicap	12	18	14	6	4	16	2	10	8			

Manager: Adam Donlin   **Pro:** Dave Glenz, PGA   **Supt:** Brad Sparta
Architect: Roger Rulewich 1998

BEAR BROOK GOLF CLUB

527 Route 94, Fredon Township, NJ 07860

www.bearbrookgolf.com

(973) 383-2327

Bear Brook is a semi-private 18 hole course open 7 days a week from Apr. 1 to Nov. 28th. Tee times: 7 days public, 10 days mbrs. Rates include carts. A full service clubhouse is planned for 2005.

Driving Range	**•Lockers**
•Practice Green	**• Showers**
•Power Carts	**•Food**
Pull Carts	**•Clubhouse**
•Club Rental	**•Outings**
•Soft Spikes	

Fees	**Weekday**	**Weekend**
Daily	$50	$67
Twi 2PM	$35	$50
Carts included		
Senior rates M-Thurs		

Course Description: Bear Brook is built within a gated community of estate homes and golf villas. On the first hole, the golfer is confronted with a daunting tee shot over protected wetlands and a 2nd to a severely elevated contoured green. The layout is hilly former farmland. On #14, the long hitters will face a challenge; it is a 700 yard par 5 and very narrow. The par 3 15th is like #12 at Augusta, a stream and a moat surround the peninsula green. A brook crosses the 18th fairway. Golfers new to this course should be happy with a 2 putt due to fast and undulating greens. Water is in play on 6 holes.

Directions: Sussex County, #4 on Northwest Map
Rte.80W to Exit 25/Rte. 206North; follow for 10 miles; left onto County Rd.618 West: follow to end (approx.2.3 mi.) Go left on Rte. 94 South, club is 2 miles on left.

Hole	1	2	3	4	5	6	7	8	9	Out	BLACK	Rating 73.0
BLACK	400	376	212	362	314	600	358	381	160	3163		Slope 141
WHITE	386	366	192	354	296	556	312	350	155	2967		
Par	4	4	3	4	4	5	4	4	3	35	WHITE	Rating 70.0
Handicap	5	9	7	15	13	1	11	3	17			Slope 134
RED	350	287	132	284	218	493	251	105	111	2231		
Par	4	4	3	4	4	5	4	4	3	35	RED	Rating 67.9
Handicap	5	9	7	15	13	1	11	3	17			Slope 113

Hole	10	11	12	13	14	15	16	17	18	In		Totals
BLACK	355	200	420	360	706	158	415	382	356	3352	BLACK	6515
WHITE	349	181	395	332	585	145	360	356	351	3045	WHITE	6021
Par	4	3	4	4	5	3	4	4	4	35	Par	70
Handicap	14	16	8	10	2	18	4	6	12			
RED	273	101	252	294	418	97	315	326	258	2421	RED	4652
Par	4	3	4	4	6	3	4	4	4	35	Par	70
Handicap	14	16	8	10	2	18	4	6	12			

Director of Golf/Mgr: Elliott Chick   **Sup't:** Jim Rusnic
Architect: Roger Rulewich redesign 2001

BERKSHIRE VALLEY GOLF COURSE

PUBLIC

28 Cozy Lake Rd., Jefferson Twp, NJ 07438   **(973) 208-0018**
www.morrisparks.net

Berkshire Valley is the newest 18 hole course of the Morris County Parks. It is open. 4/1 to 11/30 & closed Tuesdays. ID is valid at Flanders Valley, Pinch Brook & Sunset Valley. Automated tee times: residents 7 days. Clubhouse to open Spring 2005.

- **Driving Range**
- **Practice Green**
- **Power Carts**
- Pull Carts
- **Club Rental**
- **Soft Spikes**

- **Lockers**
- **Showers**
- **Food**
- **Clubhouse**
- **Outings**

NEW

Fees	Weekday	Weekend
Res/ID	$50	$60
Sr.	$40	
Non res	$65	$75
Twilight rates available		
Power carts $14pp/(2) $17(1)		

Course Description: It took imagination to create Berkshire Valley out of a former quarry. The first 5 holes are along a mountain ridge, the remaining in a valley filled with natural wetlands and ponds that are in play. The Rockaway River can be found along holes 6, 7, 8 and 15. Environmental restrictions were overcome with great ingenuity. The course can be characterized by spectacular views, a variety of holes, forced carries and abounding wildlife. The signature par 3 12th contains the old stone elephant house foundation from the days when Barnum & Bailey used this property. 6810 yards from the back tees, golfers will find this scenic course both challenging and interesting.

Directions: Sussex County, #5 on Northwest Map
Rte. 80 to Exit 34B. Take Rte. 15 North and go right Berkshire Valley Road. Proceed 7 miles and make right on Cozy Lake Road to course.

Hole	1	2	3	4	5	6	7	8	9	Out	BLUE	Rating 71.1
BLUE	378	240	509	365	328	187	535	383	373	3298		Slope 120
WHITE	363	210	487	354	308	157	495	365	367	3106		
Par	4	3	5	4	4	3	5	4	4	36	WHITE	Rating 68.0
Handicap	3	9	11	13	15	17	7	1	5			Slope 115
RED	284	126	395	273	275	92	418	305	367	3106		
Par	4	3	5	4	4	3	5	4	4	36	RED	Rating 66,9
Handicap	5	15	1	9	3	17	7	11	13			Slope 113

Hole	10	11	12	13	14	15	16	17	18	In		Totals
BLUE	382	335	162	408	275	528	183	373	410	3056	BLUE	6354
WHITE	367	286	142	417	230	513	151	316	367	2789	WHITE	5895
Par	4	4	3	4	4	5	3	4	4	35	Par	71
Handicap	2	14	18	4	16	10	8	6	12			
RED	297	213	83	317	203	390	131	262	313	2209	RED	4647
Par	4	4	3	4	4	5	3	4	4	35	Par	71
Handicap	4	10	16	2	18	6	14	8	12			

Manager/Pro: Tim Markt   **Supt:** Mark Jaretsky
Architect: Roger Rulewich 2004

BLACK BEAR GOLF CLUB

PUBLIC

138 Route 23 North, Franklin, NJ 07416   **(973) 827-5996**
www.crystalgolfresort.com

Black Bear is an 18 hole course open 7 days a week from Mar. to Dec. Rewards Card mbs. have discounts and pref. tee times for Crystal Springs, Minerals, Ballyowen, Wild Turkey & Great Gorge. Tee times: Mbrs 12 days in advance, non-mbrs. up to 10 days.

- •Driving Range
- •Practice Green
- •Power Carts
- Pull Carts
- •Club Rental
- •Soft Spikes

- •Lockers
- •Showers
- •Food
- •Clubhouse
- •Outings

Fees	Weekday	Weekend
Daily	$59	$79
Twi	$39	$49
Power carts included		

Course Description: The 6,673 yard layout of Black Bear combines the spectacular beauty of the Kittatinny mountain area with an array of amenities that rivals any golf facility in the Metropolitan area. There is a diversity of topography, an abundance of wildlife and remarkable scenery. This course is the headquarters for the well known David Glenz Golf Academy. There are two distinct nines on 280 acres of a former farm; the front weaves in and out of forests and sloping terrain, while the back offers interesting mounding. The long par 5 13th hole is situated at the base of a mountain and plays up to a large elevated green which is 40 feet above the tee off point.

Directions: Sussex County, #6 on Northwest Map
Rte. 80 West or East to Exit 53. Take Rte. 23 North for approximately 26 miles to Franklin. Course is 1/2 mile north of Rte. 517 intersection; (entrance is shared with Weis Supermarket.)

Hole	1	2	3	4	5	6	7	8	9	Out	BLACK	Rating 72.2
BLACK	384	506	445	406	195	566	204	343	420	3490		Slope 130
WHITE	349	451	394	386	158	500	142	295	400	3075		
Par	4	5	4	4	3	5	3	4	4	36	WHITE	Rating 67.8
Handicap	9	11	1	5	17	13	7	15	3			Slope 124
RED	240	382	329	310	120	437	122	251	305	2496		
Par	4	5	4	4	3	5	3	4	4	36	RED	Rating 67.7
Handicap	11	3	5	9	17	1	15	13	7			Slope 116

Hole	10	11	12	13	14	15	16	17	18	In		Totals
BLACK	382	148	385	555	164	275	496	389	389	3183	BLACK	6673
WHITE	335	123	350	496	137	230	455	340	342	2808	WHITE	5873
Par	4	3	4	5	3	4	5	4	4	36	Par	72
Handicap	8	18	4	2	16	14	12	6	10			
RED	266	103	335	366	111	164	380	267	297	2260	RED	4756
Par	4	3	4	5	3	4	5	4	4	36	Par	72
Handicap	8	16	10	4	18	14	2	6	12			

Manager: Art Walton   **Pro:** Dave Glenz, PGA   **Supt:** Eric Tomzick
Architects: Jack Kurlander, David Glenz 1996

BLACK OAK GOLF CLUB

PRIVATE

Bartley Rd., Long Valley, NJ 07853   **(908) 876-9887**
www.blackoakgolfclub.com

Black Oak is a private 18 hole golf club that is scheduled to open some time in 2006. It will be open 6 days a week and closed from about Nov. 15-March 15th. A full service stone and wood clubhouse will be built after the club opens.

- Driving Range
- Practice Green
- Power Carts
- Pull Carts
- Club Rental
- Caddies
- Lockers
- Showers
- Food
- Clubhouse
- Outings
- Soft Spikes

Course Description: Longtime & well known NJ golf professional, David Glenz is the architect for Black Oak. Built on 300 acres of mostly heavily wooded property, it will be a traditional 7000 acre layout. The design follows the contours of the land with broad fairways and some elevation changes. 12 holes will be quite hilly with water in play on 3 holes. This new par 72 course is expected to be the 1st in NJ certified at the Silver Level by the Audobon Sanctuary Program, an honor due to the careful environmental sensitivity utilized in the development. Complete practice facilities will include a par 3 hole. Future personnel details were unavailable at press time.

Directions: Morris County, #49 on Northwest Map
Rte. 80W to Exit 27. Take Rte 206S and make right onto Bartley Rd. Follow Bartley approx. 3 miles to course on left.

Hole	1	2	3	4	5	6	7	8	9	Out	BLACK	Rating
BLACK	370	430	425	180	420	175	520	430	545	3495		Slope
BLUE												
Par	4	4	4	3	4	3	5	4	5	36	BLUE	Rating
Handicap												Slope
RED												
Par											RED	Rating
Handicap												Slope
Hole	10	11	12	13	14	15	16	17	18	In		Totals
BLACK	205	315	425	190	560	410	445	555	445	3550	BLACK	7045
BLUE											BLUE	
Par	3	4	4	3	5	4	4	5	4	36	Par	72
Handicap												
RED											RED	
Par											Par	
Handicap												

Architect: David Glenz 2005

BLAIR ACADEMY GOLF COURSE `PUBLIC`

600 Park St., Blairstown, NJ 07825 **(908) 362-2021**

Blair Academy is a 9 hole course open 7 days a week from mid March to end of Nov., weather permitting. Memberships are available. Reserved tee times generally not necessary.

Driving Range
•**Practice Green**
Power Carts
•**Pull Carts**
•**Club Rental**
Soft Spikes
Lockers
Showers
Food
Clubhouse
Outings

Fees Weekday Weekend
$13/9 $18/18 $15/9 $20/18
Twilight reduced rates
Discounts for Srs. & Jrs.

Course Description: The layout at Blair Academy is beautifully maintained and very hilly. Power carts are not allowed at all, consequently walkers get a good workout. Deep bunkers surround the greens and on a number of holes the green can't be seen from the tee. The scenery is beautiful especially in Autumn. The 9th hole was moved recently. The course is usually uncrowded except when the school golf team practices. Different tees may be used for the second nine. The par 3 second has both the tee and the green elevated.

Directions: Warren County, #7 on Northwest Map
Rte. 80 West to Exit #12. Go right toward Blairstown onto Rte. 521 for 5 miles. At end, make left and after Coastal Sta., make right onto Park St. Pass 2 STOP signs to Blair Academy gate. Follow signs to golf course.

Hole	1	2	3	4	5	6	7	8	9	Out	BLUE	Rating
BLUE												Slope
WHITE	372	188	375	267	503	186	491	138	350	2870		
Par	4	3	4	4	5	3	5	3	4	35	WHITE	Rating
Handicap	5	13	7	1	9	15	11	17	3			Slope
RED	360	132	241	257	405	149	423	118	300	2385		
Par	4	3	4	4	5	3	5	3	4	35	RED	Rating
Handicap	4	8	3	2	6	7	5	9	1			Slope

Hole	10	11	12	13	14	15	16	17	18	In		Totals
BLUE											BLUE	
BLUE	372	182	375	267	503	207	491	157	356	2910	WHITE	5780
Par	4	3	4	4	5	3	5	3	4	35	Par	70
Handicap	6	14	8	2	10	16	12	8	4			
GOLD	362	180	358	257	462	172	463	124	327	2705	RED	5090
Par	4	3	4	4	5	3	5	3	4	35	Par	70
Handicap	3	7	1	4	5	8	6	9	2			

Manager/Pro: Hal Eaton   **Supt:** Joe Antonioli   **Built:** 1920's

BOWLING GREEN GOLF CLUB SEMI-PRIVATE

53 Schoolhouse Rd., Milton, NJ 07438   **(973) 697-8688**
www.bowlinggreengolf.com

Bowling Green is a semi-private 18 hole course open to the public 7 days a week from mid March until mid-Dec. Memberships are available. Call 14 days in advance for tee times, members 19 days.

•**Driving Range**	•**Lockers**
•**Practice Green**	•**Showers**
•**Power Carts**	•**Food**
•**Pull Carts**	•**Clubhouse**
•**Club Rental**	•**Outings**
•**Soft Spikes**	

Fees	M-Thurs	Fri-Sun
Daily	$53	$82
Twi 9 holes	$33 (2PM)	
Power carts	$10pp	
After 12:	$20 pp	

Course Description: With Bowling Green Mountain as a backdrop, this picturesque course is appealing to nature lovers as well as all levels of golfers. The tee shot over water on the #1 handicap fourth hole requires accuracy and water is still in play on the approach to the green. The 601 yard long 18th is made more difficult by the uphill terrain leading to the putting surface. The drives out of a chute of pines on the 5th and 10th holes make them both challenging and memorable. Attentive rangers assist the players in maintaining the pace of play. Carts are not mandatory.

Directions: Morris County, #8 on Northwest Map
Rte.80 West to Exit 34B. Take Rte.15N for 4 & 1/2 miles; turn right on Weldon Rd. for 6 miles to intersection at Red Barn. Bear right, make first left on Schoolhouse Rd. Club on left.

Hole	1	2	3	4	5	6	7	8	9	Out	BLUE	Rating 72.4
BLUE	358	375	220	482	351	417	431	210	492	3336		Slope 131
WHITE	330	359	198	456	331	397	405	184	474	3134		
Par	4	4	3	5	4	4	4	3	5	36	WHITE	Rating 70.3
Handicap	13	7	15	1	11	3	5	17	9			Slope 126
RED	298	285	178	420	262	266	314	110	382	2515		
Par	4	4	3	5	4	4	4	3	5	36	RED	Rating 68.3
Handicap	13	7	15	1	11	3	5	17	9			Slope 121
Hole	10	11	12	13	14	15	16	17	18	In		Totals
BLUE	389	167	403	351	493	350	199	400	601	3353	BLUE	6689
WHITE	363	144	381	291	474	313	176	376	572	3090	WHITE	6224
Par	4	3	4	4	5	4	3	4	5	36	Par	72
Handicap	10	16	4	12	8	14	18	6	2			
RED	265	120	282	265	357	239	145	312	466	2451	RED	4966
Par	4	3	4	4	5	4	3	4	5	36	Par	72
Handicap	10	16	4	12	8	14	18	6	2			

Manager: Bruce Salmon   **Pro:** John Klocksin, PGA   **Supt:** Dave Mayer
Architect: Geoffrey Cornish 1965

BROOKLAKE COUNTRY CLUB

139 Brooklake Rd., Florham Park, NJ 07932   **(973) 377-6751**

Brooklake is an 18 hole course open 6 days a week from Apr.1 to Dec 10th. Guests play accompanied by a member. Tee time reservations are not necessary.

•**Driving Range**	•**Lockers**
•**Practice Green**	•**Showers**
•**Power Carts**	•**Food**
Pull Carts	•**Clubhouse**
•**Club Rental**	•**Outings**
Caddies	•**Soft Spikes**

Course Description: Brooklake is relatively flat and well treed with tricky, carefully manicured greens and water in play on seven holes. The layout begins with a long, well bunkered, picturesque and treacherous par 3. The fifth is a lengthy par 4 that has a stream running through the fairway. The tenth hole has an island green, one of many obstacles to posting a low score. The tee shot over water on the par 3 17th is to a narrow target surrounded by bunkers. The signature par 5 18th hole is 630 yards with a creek and sparkling pond confronting the golfer.

Directions: Morris County, #9 on Northwest Map
Rte. 80W or E to Rte. 287S. Exit at Rte. 24E. Take the Florham Park exit to Columbia Tpke. (Rte. 510). Make right onto Ridgedale Ave. Turn left onto Brooklake Rd. to club on right.

Hole	1	2	3	4	5	6	7	8	9	Out	BLUE	Rating 73.8
BLUE	190	517	380	185	466	360	342	419	574	3433		Slope 132
WHITE	183	500	372	175	436	329	330	411	566	3302		
Par	3	5	4	3	4	4	4	4	5	36	WHITE	Rating 72.2
Handicap	11	13	5	17	1	15	9	3	7			Slope 130
RED	164	480	320	126	385	278	315	400	465	2933		
Par	3	5	4	3	4/5	4	4	4/5	5	36/38	RED	Rating 71.8
Handicap	11	13	5	17	1	15	9	3	7			Slope 128
Hole	10	11	12	13	14	15	16	17	18	In		Totals
BLUE	402	427	390	420	517	452	167	168	630	3502	BLUE	7006
WHITE	371	387	382	387	502	412	157	157	585	3340	WHITE	6642
Par	4	4	4	4	5	4	3	3	5	36	Par	72
Handicap	2	12	6	10	16	8	18	14	4			
RED	300	325	345	325	480	305	133	100	500	2813	RED	5383
Par	4	4	4	4	5	4	3	3	5	36	Par	73
Handicap	6	10	8	12	4	14	16	18	2			

Manager: Mario Fastiggi   **Pro:** Frank Esposito, Jr., PGA   **Supt:** Scott Carpenter
Architect: Herb Strong 1921

CRYSTAL SPRINGS GOLF CLUB · PUBLIC

123 Crystal Springs Rd., Hamburg, NJ 07419 **(973) 827-5996**
www.crystalgolfresort.com

Crystal Springs is an 18 hole course open to the public Mar. to Dec. 7 days a week. Memberships are available. Rewards card gives discounts & pref. tee times (12days) for Balllyowen, Black Bear, Wild Turkey, Minerals and Great Gorge.

- •Driving Range •Lockers
- •Practice Green •Showers
- •Power Carts •Food
- Pull Carts •Clubhouse
- •Club Rental •Outings
- •Soft Spikes

Fees	Weekday	Weekend
Daily	$65	$90
Twi 3PM	$45	$55
Power carts included		

Course Description: Crystal Springs is a course of breathtaking views and dramatic golf holes, a truly unique experience. A links layout, it has moguls and hills on every hole and large contoured greens, some multi-tiered. Water is in play on 6 holes. The signature par 3 11th has a tee shot from an 80 foot elevation down a limestone cliff to a large butterfly shaped green. The sparkling azure blue, spring fed quarry on the left is the repository of many balls. The par 3 9th requires accuracy over a pond to a green surrounded by bunkers. From the tee on the 10th, a par 4, it is a carry over water to a severe dogleg left and an uphill shot to a two-tiered green with a beautiful view. Crystal Springs is considered one of the most challenging courses in NJ.

Directions: Sussex County, #10 on Northwest Map
Rte. 80 West to Exit 53. Take Rte. 23 North (approx. 28 mi.) through Franklin and just before Hamburg, make a right onto Rte. 517 North. Course is 3 miles ahead on left.

Hole	1	2	3	4	5	6	7	8	9	Out	BLUE	Rating 72.1
BLUE	536	393	405	455	103	376	399	526	140	3364		Slope 132
WHITE	403	356	383	403	113	343	366	493	130	3090		
Par	5	4	4	5	3	4	4	5	3	37	WHITE	Rating 69.7
Handicap	7	3	1	11	17	9	13	5	15			Slope 126
RED	453	313	323	375	100	303	332	443	106	2748		
Par	5	4	4	5	3	4	4	5	3	37	RED	Rating 70.5
Handicap	7	9	5	1	17	11	13	3	15			Slope 123

Hole	10	11	12	13	14	15	16	17	18	In		Totals
BLUE	380	186	508	145	518	125	389	383	363	2997	BLUE	6361
WHITE	347	186	475	125	510	105	356	350	330	2784	WHITE	5874
Par	4	3	5	3	5	3	4	4	4	35	Par	72
Handicap	10	14	6	16	2	18	4	8	12			
RED	297	105	425	100	465	85	305	300	280	2363	RED	5111
Par	4	3	5	3	5	3	4	4	4	35	Par	72
Handicap	6	18	4	14	2	16	10	8	12			

Manager: Art Walton   **Pro:** Dave Glenz, PGA   **Supt:** Craig Worts
Architect: Robert Von Hagge 1990

CULVER LAKE GOLF CLUB

PUBLIC

E. Shore of Culver Lake Rd., Branchville, NJ 07826   (973) 948-5610

Culver Lake is a 9 hole course open 7 days a week between March and December. Tee time reservations are not necessary. Memberships are available. Tuesday is Ladies Day and discounts prevail. Improvements are being made to the clubhouse.

Driving Range
- Practice Green
- Power Carts
- Pull Carts
- Club Rental
Soft Spikes

- Lockers
- Showers
- Food
- Clubhouse
- Outings

Fees	Weekday	Weekend
9 holes	$11	$15
18 holes	$15	$21
Power carts	$6/9	$11/18
Sr discounts on weekends		

Course Description: In 1962, Culver Lake reopened as a golf course. For a while the property had been used as a game preserve; much of the wildlife from that period remain and still roam here. The greens are tight, wooded, small and well-maintained; some are contoured. When playing the second nine, the 14th becomes a 504 yard par 5 with OB on the right and a postage stamp green. The pond off the 1st tee has been enlarged and a new drainage system has been installed recently.

Directions: Sussex County, #11 on Northwest Map
Rte. 80 West to Exit 34B (Sparta). Take Rte. 15N to Rte. 206N and go 4 & 1/2 miles to the East Shore of Culver Lake Rd. Make a right and go 1 mile to course.

Hole	1	2	3	4	5	6	7	8	9	Out	BLUE	Rating
BLUE												Slope
WHITE	129	339	142	302	408	391	163	336	297	2507		
Par	3	4	3	4	4	4	3	4	4	33	WHITE	Rating 65.0
Handicap	18	7	17	11	2	3	15	5	9			Slope 109
RED	124	300	140	270	402	360	135	220	224	2175		
Par	3	4	3	4	5	4	3	4	4	34	RED	Rating 68.6
Handicap												Slope 118
Hole	10	11	12	13	14	15	16	17	18	In		Totals
BLUE											BLUE	
WHITE	171	361	168	331	504	397	174	349	324	2779	WHITE	5286
Par	3	4	3	4	5	4	3	4	4	34	Par	67
Handicap	13	4	16	12	1	6	14	10	8			
RED											RED	4350
Par											Par	68
Handicap												

Manager/Supt: Robert Lupine   **Built:** 1962

DEER RUN GOLF & TENNIS CLUB

1 Gettysburg Way, Lincoln Park, NJ 07035   **(973) 694-0758**

Deer Run is a 9 hole course found within a private condo development. It is open all year 7 days a week. Guests play accompanied by a member. Tee time reservations are not necessary.

•**Driving Range**	Lockers
•**Practice Green**	Showers
•**Power Carts**	Food
•**Pull Carts**	•**Clubhouse**
•**Club Rental**	•**Outings**
Caddies	•**Soft Spikes**

Course Description: Deer Run is a very walkable links type golf course surrounded by lovely town homes. It is wide open, generally flat with some contour. Water in the form of ponds is in play on four holes. The greens are large and well maintained. An improved sprinkler system has been installed. The layout is in excellent shape with a new driving range and full practice facility. Two sets of tees are offered to give variety and make the course play like 18 holes.

Directions: Morris County, #12 on Northwest Map
Take Rte.80 to Exit 52. At exit make right & then turn left onto Two Bridges Rd. Go over a bridge and turn left at STOP sign (still Two Bridges). Continue to another STOP and turn left. Go up hill & make left onto Pinebrook Rd. Go 1 mi. & turn left into Deer Run development and to golf course.

Hole	1	2	3	4	5	6	7	8	9	Out	BLUE	Rating 69.2
BLUE	436	485	344	401	222	427	390	380	150	3122		Slope 122
WHITE	408	475	329	359	165	414	338	372	142	3022		
Par	4	5	4	4	3	4	4	4	3	35	WHITE	Rating 70.5
Handicap	2	10	16	8	15	5	13	12	18			Slope 124
RED	397	393	225	291	125	313	321	327	134	2526		
Par	5	5	4	4	3	4	4	4	3	36	RED	Rating 69.6
Handicap	1	5	15	7	13	3	11	9	17			Slope 112
Hole	10	11	12	13	14	15	16	17	18	In		Totals
BLUE											BLUE	6470
WHITE											WHITE	6044
Par											Par	70
Handicap												
RED											RED	5052
Par											Par	72
Handicap												

Pro: Marty Vybihal, PGA   **Supt:** Jason Morgan
Built: 1980s   **Architect:**(remodel) Robert McNeil 1999

FAIRMOUNT COUNTRY CLUB

400 Southern Blvd., Chatham, NJ 07928 **(973) 377-8901**

Fairmount is an 18 hole private golf club open 6 days a week and closed in February. Guests may play accompanied by a member. Tee time reservations are necessary for weekends.

•**Driving Range**	•**Lockers**
•**Practice Green**	•**Showers**
•**Power Carts**	•**Food**
Pull Carts	•**Clubhouse**
•**Club Rental**	•**Outings**
•**Caddies**	•**Soft Spikes**

Course Description: Fairmount is a typical Hal Purdy design featuring crown style greens that fall off on all sides. It is relatively tight, flat, long and difficult, with creeks and ponds affecting play on 8 holes. It borders the Great Swamp, a National Refuge, so the course stays soft all year. The signature par 4 fourteenth is one of several great doglegs; its green has a severe break. The tee boxes have been rebuilt recently and the 10th hole has been extended. The 2005 NJ State Open will be held here.

Directions: Morris County, #13 on Northwest Map
GSP or NJ Tpke to Rte. 78West. Exit at Rte. 24West, then take the Summit-River Rd. exit. Go straight to 4th light and make a left on Noe Ave. Proceed to the end and turn right onto Southern Blvd. and to the club on the right.

Hole	1	2	3	4	5	6	7	8	9	Out	BLUE	Rating 73.0
BLUE	553	400	415	156	338	429	172	527	346	3336		Slope 138
WHITE	536	387	410	150	332	419	152	514	342	3242		
Par	5	4	4	3	4	4	3	5	4	36	WHITE	Rating 72.2
Handicap	3	9	1	15	11	5	17	7	13			Slope 134
RED	502	357	395	132	252	401	131	429	429	2930		
Par	5	4	5	3	4	5	3	5	4	38	RED	Rating 75.6
Handicap	3	9	1	15	11	7	17	5	13			Slope 138
Hole	10	11	12	13	14	15	16	17	18	In		Totals
BLUE	553	478	359	217	408	524	405	198	430	3396	BLUE	6757
WHITE	367	470	350	203	399	512	396	193	421	3311	WHITE	6553
Par	4	5	4	3	4	5	4	3	4	36	Par	72
Handicap	12	4	14	15	10	2	8	18	6			
RED	351	433	335	177	377	449	337	173	403	3035	RED	5933
Par	4	5	4	3	4	5	4	3	5	36	Par	74
Handicap	12	4	14	16	2	6	8	18	10			

Manager: Jim Hoppenstadt   **Pro:** Mark Giuliano, PGA   **Supt:** Vince Bracken
Architect: Hal Purdy 1958

FAIRWAY VALLEY GOLF CLUB PUBLIC

76 Mine Hill Rd., Washington, NJ 07882   (908) 689-1530

Fairway Valley is a 9 hole course open to the public 7 days a week all year weather permitting. Memberships are available. Tee times may be made up to 2 weeks in advance.

Driving Range
- Practice Green
- Power Carts
- Pull Carts ·
- Club Rental
- Soft Spikes

Lockers
Showers
- Food
- Clubhouse
- Outings

Fees	Weekday	Weekend
9 holes	$15	$18
18 holes	$21	$27
Srs	$14/9	$19/18
Power carts	$10/9	$12/18

Course Description: Fairway Valley is a flat, wide open, scenic and easy to walk facility. Originally built as a 6 hole layout, played 3 times for 18, it was converted later into the present nine. It provides wonderful practice for beginners. Ponds are encountered on the 4th, 7th and 8th holes. The par 4 fifth could be considered the signature hole, the #1 handicap from the back tees requiring a shot to a narrow fairway and an approach to a target green. A Gold set of tees has been added. On weekends and holidays this course becomes quite busy.

Directions: Warren County, #14 on Northwest Map
Rte.80 West to Exit 26(Budd Lake). Take Rte.46W to Hackettstown. Make right onto Rte.57W for approx. 10 miles, crossing over Rte.31. Road is now Main St., Washington. At 1st light, make right onto Belvedere Ave. Go straight, at 4 way STOP sign, road becomes Mine Hill. Course is 1 mile up on right.

Hole	1	2	3	4	5	6	7	8	9	Out	BLUE	Rating 68.0
BLUE	490	312	300	140	410	138	480	185	480	2935		Slope 120
WHITE	475	297	280	130	346	135	386	149	471	2669		
Par	5	4	4	3	4	3	4	3	5	35	WHITE	Rating 65.4
Handicap	4	2	9	8	1	7	3	5	6			Slope 117
RED	450	282	220	118	326	130	336	129	414	2405		
Par	5	4	4	3	4	3	5	3	5	36	RED	Rating 67.4
Handicap	2	6	7	9	4	8	3	5	1			Slope 120

Hole	10	11	12	13	14	15	16	17	18	In		Totals
BLUE											BLUE	5870
WHITE											WHITE	5338
Par											Par	70
Handicap												
RED											RED	4810
Par											Par	72
Handicap												

Manager/Supt: Jim Stern   **Built:** 1960s

57

FARMSTEAD GOLF & CC

PUBLIC

88 Lawrence Rd., Lafayette, NJ 07848

www.farmsteadgolf.com

(973) 383-1666

Farmstead is a 27 hole course open to the public 7 days a week from Mar. to Dec. Tee times; 2 weeks in advance. Limited memberships are available. Carts req'd before 2PM weekends and holidays. 10% off on green fees if booked online.

Driving Range	•Lockers
•Practice Green	•Showers
•Power Carts	•Food
•Pull Carts	•Clubhouse
•Club Rental	•Outings
•Soft Spikes	

Fees	M-Thurs	Fri-Sun
Daily	$30	$61*
After 2	$20	$26
Sr M-Fri $39/cart		
Power carts $14pp *cart incl		

Course Description: Farmstead is more challenging than the golfer realizes at first glance. The Valley nine, although short, is very tight having 7 holes with out of bounds on the right. A good short game is essential to conquer the undulating greens throughout the course. On the longer Lakeview & Clubview nines, the trees and doglegs can block shots that miss the fairway. All the layouts are well contoured and heavily treed. The signature par 3 9th on Lake is an all water carry to a virtual island green; the 4th has a new putting area. On Club, the green is now a peninsula. The scorecard below is for Lakeview and Clubview.

Directions: Sussex County, #15 on Northwest Map
Rte. 80 West to Exit 34B. Go north on Rte. 15 for 15 miles. At intersection for Rte. 94, turn left onto Rte. 623S. Go 3.5 miles to course on left.

Hole	1	2	3	4	5	6	7	8	9	Out	BLUE	Rating 71.9
BLUE	357	433	219	550	561	238	384	367	201	3310		Slope 129
WHITE	285	380	182	508	503	219	369	304	124	2874		
Par	4	4	3	5	5	3	4	4	3	35	WHITE	Rating 68.7
Handicap	8	1	6	3	4	2	5	7	9			Slope 123
RED	226	370	126	474	444	166	306	234	93	2439		
Par	4	4	3	5	5	3	4	4	3	35	RED	Rating 68.3
Handicap	6	4	8	2	1	7	3	5	9			Slope 116
Hole	10	11	12	13	14	15	16	17	18	In		Totals
BLUE	368	410	189	586	497	353	350	437	180	3370	BLUE	6680
WHITE	356	384	188	497	458	329	343	432	172	3159	WHITE	6033
Par	4	4	3	5	5	4	4	4	3	36	Par	71
Handicap	4	2	6	3	7	8	9	1	5			
RED	329	282	154	432	343	225	270	408	105	2548	RED	4987
Par	4	4	3	5	4	4	4	5	3	36	Par	71
Handicap	4	5	7	1	3	8	6	2	9			

Manager: Sandy Howarth   **Pro:** Scott Pruden, PGA   **Supt:** Bob Phoebus
Built: Phoebus Family 1960s

FLANDERS VALLEY GOLF COURSE   PUBLIC

81 Pleasant Hill Rd., Flanders, NJ 07836   **(973) 584-5382**
www.morrisparks.net

Flanders Valley has two 18 hole layouts, Blue-White and Red-Gold. It is run by the Morris County Park Commission & open 7 days a week from Apr. 1 to Nov. 30. Res ID$35. Automated phone system reservations 7 days in advance for res. Others call in day of play for tee time. Reservation fees $2.50pp res., $5pp for non-res.

Driving Range	
•**Practice Green**	•**Lockers**
•**Power Carts**	•**Showers**
•**Pull Carts**	•**Food**
•**Club Rental**	•**Clubhouse**
•**Soft Spikes**	Outings

Fees	Weekday	Weekend
Res/ID	$22	$27.50
Sr.	$17	
Non-res	$38	$45
Power carts	$14pp	
9 hole fees available		

Course Description: Rated by Golf Digest as one of the top 100 public courses, in the US, Flanders Valley has a well deserved reputation. Extremely busy in season, the course has tree lined narrow fairways and very large undulating greens, some tiered. There is water in play on several holes. The 7th, on the Red course is a long par 4 with a creek running across it. Recently some bunkers have been renovated and the drainage system improved. The scorecard below is for the Red-Gold layout. Most tournaments are played on White-Blue. Although somewhat difficult to get a choice tee time in advance, single walk-ons often get to play.

Directions: Morris County, #16 on Northwest Map
Take Rte. 80 to Exit 27A. Take Rte. 206S approximately 3 mi to 3rd light and make left onto Main St., Flanders. Follow road to course on left.

Hole	1	2	3	4	5	6	7	8	9	Out	BLUE	Rating 71.6
BLUE	380	510	413	371	149	541	478	166	396	3404		Slope 126
WHITE	361	487	398	351	135	526	455	151	379	3243		
Par	4	5	4	4	3	5	4	3	4	36	WHITE	Rating 70.5
Handicap	4	5	2	6	9	3	15	8	7			Slope 123
RED	304	409	355	286	111	466	412	120	346	2809		
Par	4	5	4	4	3	5	5	3	4	37	RED	Rating 71.8
Handicap	5	4	2	7	9	1	5	8	6			Slope 123
Hole	10	11	12	13	14	15	16	17	18	In		Totals
BLUE	476	192	403	550	362	213	426	394	350	3366	BLUE	6770
WHITE	476	162	380	528	332	189	410	369	340	3186	WHITE	6429
Par	5	3	4	5	4	3	4	4	4	36	Par	72
Handicap	2	8	3	1	6	7	4	5	9			
RED	422	141	338	451	298	150	332	314	285	2731	RED	5540
Par	5	3	4	5	4	3	4	4	4	36	Par	73
Handicap	1	7	2	3	4	8	5	6	9			

Manager: Bob Stegner   **Pro:** Renee Klose, LPGA   **Supt:** Mark Johnson
Architects: original 27 Hal Purdy 1963   Rees Jones last nine 1982

GREAT GORGE COUNTRY CLUB PUBLIC

Route 517, McAfee, NJ 07428   (973) 827-7603
www.play27.com

Great Gorge CC is a privately owned 27 hole course open to the public 7 days a week
from mid March to the end of Nov. Reservations may be made up to 30 days in
advance for tee times. Part of Crystal Golf Resorts, the Rewards card is honored here.

•Driving Range	•Lockers
•Practice Green	•Showers
•Power Carts	•Food
Pull Carts	•Clubhouse
•Club Rental	•Outings
•Soft Spikes	

Fees	Weekday	Weekend
Daily(M-Thurs) $59		$89
Fri.	$69	
After 3 PM	$35	$49
Sussex res. discounted		
Power carts included		

Course Description: A tight, picturesque shot maker's course, Great Gorge has three
holes rated among the best public golf holes in the Garden State. The layout which is
surrounded by the Kittatinny Mts. is hilly with quarry rocks lining some of the fairways.
The Quarry and Lake nines are considered by many the most difficult combination with
a rating from the Blues of 73.4 and slope of 132. The signature #1 on the Lake nine
features an elevated tee and a very small green with water on the right. Five sets of
tees give golfers of all levels appropriate yardages. Pace of play is carefully monitored.
The scorecard below is for the Quarry and Rail nines.

Directions: Sussex County, #17 on Northwest Map
Rte. 80 West to Exit 53. Take Rte. 23N to Hamburg. Go right to Rte. 94N. At light, go
straight up hill (road becomes Rte. 517N.) Go approx. 1/10th mi. to the Legends Hotel
and golf course. Driveway is 1/4 mi. on the right.

Hole	1	2	3	4	5	6	7	8	9	Out	BLUE	Rating 72.9
BLUE	175	592	230	364	443	180	449	502	427	3308		Slope 129
WHITE	167	538	191	352	434	170	403	490	422	3077		
Par	3	5	3	4	4	3	4	5	4	35	WHITE	Rating 70.8
Handicap	8	3	6	7	2	9	1	5	4			Slope 129
RED	134	488	152	318	395	114	367	436	283	2907		
Par	3	5	3	4	4	3	4	5	4	35	RED	Rating 68.6
Handicap	8	3	6	7	2	9	1	5	4			Slope 124
Hole	10	11	12	13	14	15	16	17	18	In		Totals
BLUE	456	429	182	341	156	586	519	412	383	3450	BLUE	6758
WHITE	440	360	166	328	151	566	498	370	373	3292	WHITE	6369
Par	4	4	3	4	3	5	5	4	4	36	Par	71
Handicap	3	1	8	7	9	2	5	6	4			
RED	321	335	136	293	128	518	455	319	347	3019	RED	5926
Par	4	4	3	4	3	5	5	4	4	36	Par	71
Handicap	3	1	8	7	9	2	5	6	4			

Manager: Joe Galan   **Pro:** Terry Manziano, PGA   **Supt:** David Brubaker
Architect: George Fazio 1970

GREEN POND GOLF CLUB

PUBLIC

765 Green Pond Rd., Marcella, NJ 07866   **(973) 983-9494**

Green Pond is a privately owned 9 hole course open to the public 7 days a week from April through November. Reserved tee times are not necessary.

Driving Range	Lockers
Practice Green	Showers
•**Power Carts**	•**Food**
•**Pull Carts**	•**Clubhouse**
•**Club Rental**	Outings
Soft Spikes	

Fees	Weekday	Fri-Sun
Daily	$21	$27
Power carts	$17/9	$32/18

Course Description: Short, hilly and narrow, Green Pond gives the golfer a chance to develop skill with irons. A dogleg has been created on the signature par 4 7th and the hole has been lengthened to 450 yards. The par 3 finishing hole requires an accurate tee shot to carry over a pond that makes this ninth and eighteenth, if you play the lay-out twice, a demanding and interesting experience. A new scorecard is now available but not reflected below.

Directions: Morris County, #18 on Northwest Map
Rte. 80 West to Exit 37. Take Green Pond Road north for 6 miles. Course is on the left.

Hole	1	2	3	4	5	6	7	8	9	Out	BLUE	Rating
BLUE												Slope
WHITE	485	320	332	129	474	178	355	314	128	2715		
Par	5	4	4	3	5	3	4	4	3	35	WHITE	Rating
Handicap	3	9	7	17	1	13	5	11	15			Slope
RED	470	250	300	120	434	132	260	228	112	2306		
Par	5	4	4	3	5	3	4	4	3	35	RED	Rating
Handicap	3	9	7	17	1	13	5	11	15			Slope
Hole	10	11	12	13	14	15	16	17	18	In		Totals
BLUE											BLUE	
WHITE											WHITE	2715
Par											Par	35
Handicap												
RED											RED	2306
Par											Par	35
Handicap												

Owner/Manager: Bob Enholm

HARKERS HOLLOW GOLF CLUB PRIVATE

950 Uniontown Rd., Phillipsburg, NJ 08865 (908) 859-0448

Harkers Hollow is a private 18 hole course located in Harmony Township. It is open all year 7 days a week, weather permitting. Pro shop is closed Dec. 24-Mar.14. Guests play accompanied by a member. Members may call in advance for tee times.

- •Driving Range
- •Practice Green
- •Power Carts
- •Pull Carts
- •Club Rental
- Caddies
- •Lockers
- •Showers
- •Food
- •Clubhouse
- •Outings
- •Soft Spikes

Course Description: Harkers Hollow is a hilly course with numerous uneven lies that are more up and downhill on the front nine and sidehill on the back. The small greens are fast with considerable break; a creek runs through eight of the fairways. The par 5 4th is the signature hole with a stadium sized, contoured multi-tiered green that slopes back to front and is difficult to hold. Great care is taken to keep the greens consistent.

Directions: Warren County, #19 on Northwest Map
Rte. 80W to Exit 12, Blairstown-Hope. Take Rte. 521S for 1 mile. At blinker, road becomes Rte. 519S. Continue about 18 mi. to course on left. OR take Rte.78W to Exit #3, Phillipsburg. Go to the 2nd traffic light and go right onto Rte. 519N. Proceed about 4 miles to club on right.

Hole	1	2	3	4	5	6	7	8	9	Out	BLUE	Rating 72.0
BLUE	420	375	376	524	157	422	423	429	154	3280		Slope 128
WHITE	408	365	365	510	148	413	411	419	148	3187		
Par	4	4	4	5	3	4	4	4	3	35	WHITE	Rating 71.1
Handicap	7	5	11	1	15	13	9	3	17			Slope 126
RED	359	303	356	439	107	402	358	355	99	2778		
Par	4	4	4	5	3	5	4	4	3	36	RED	Rating 71.6
Handicap	11	9	13	1	15	5	7	3	17			Slope 127

Hole	10	11	12	13	14	15	16	17	18	In		Totals
BLUE	501	189	391	392	390	371	202	403	432	3271	BLUE	6551
WHITE	492	179	379	378	376	362	194	395	417	3174	WHITE	6361
Par	5	3	4	4	4	4	3	4	4	35	Par	70
Handicap	2	16	8	4	14	12	18	10	6			
RED	442	169	327	309	299	285	178	331	355	2695	RED	5473
Par	5	3	4	4	4	4	3	4	4	35	Par	72
Handicap	2	16	8	10	6	14	18	12	4			

Manager: Bob Bolig **Pro:** Peter Dachisen, PGA **Supt:** Donald Zeffer
Architect: Robert White 1929

HAWK POINTE GOLF CLUB

294 Rte. 31 South, Washington, NJ 07882   **(908) 689-1870**
www.hawkpointegolf.com

Hawk Pointe is a semi-private 18 hole course open to the public 7 days a week. It closes Dec. thru Feb. Memberships are available. Tee times: 14 day advance for mbrs; 7 day non-mbrs.

•**Driving Range**	**Lockers**
•**Practice Green**	•Showers
•**Power Carts**	•**Food**
•Pull Carts	•**Clubhouse**
Club Rental	•**Outings**

Fees	Weekday	Weekend
Daily	$80	$95
Power carts included		

Course Description: Set in the rolling hills of the New Jersey countryside, this fairly new championship 18hole layout offers golfers scenic vistas, rugged terrain and a wonderful playing experience. Bent grass is used throughout the beautifully conditioned wide fairways & large greens. A charming stone kiln at the back of the first green adds to the ambience here. The 7th green has a tricky approach shot with a steep drop to the back. The par 3 13th has a very wide three tiered green and the 15th features a split fairway with trouble in-between. Some consider the 10th the signature hole offering a scenic view of a granite outcropping from a nearby mountain. Every effort was made to preserve the natural surroundings.

Directions: Warren County, #20 on Northwest Map
Rte. 80W to Rte. 78W to Exit #17/Clinton. Take Rte. #31 North for approx. 9 miles to club on right. OR Rte.80 to Rte.46W to Hackettstown, to 57W for 8 mi. to 31S for 1 mi.

Hole	1	2	3	4	5	6	7	8	9	Out	BLUE	Rating 70.9
BLUE	485	427	401	168	397	318	510	348	136	3152		Slope 131
WHITE	433	394	370	122	341	295	456	336	128	2853		
Par	5	4	4	3	4	4	5	4	3	36	WHITE	Rating 67.4
Handicap	5	3	11	15	7	13	1	9	17			Slope 120
RED	386	284	239	93	324	225	401	303	103	2405		
Par	5	4	4	3	4	4	5	4	3	36	RED	Rating 68.0
Handicap	3	9	11	15	5	13	1	7	17			Slope 119
Hole	10	11	12	13	14	15	16	17	18	In		Totals
BLUE	495	357	352	168	361	547	174	360	431	3222	BLUE	6374
WHITE	397	290	268	122	326	500	160	340	395	2782	WHITE	5635
Par	5	4	4	3	4	5	3	4	4	36	Par	72
Handicap	6	8	10	18	12	2	16	14	4			
RED	397	290	268	122	326	500	160	340	395	2384	RED	4789
Par	4	4	4	3	4	5	3	4	4	36	Par	72
Handicap	4	10	12	18	14	2	16	6	18			

Dir. of Golf: Bob Ross   **Pro:** John Suter, PGA   **Supt:** Dave Reece
Architect: Kelly Blake Moran, 2000

HIDDEN ACRES GOLF COURSE · PUBLIC

Ayers Rd., Hainesville, NJ 07851   **(973) 948-9804**

Hidden Acres is a 9 hole privately owned course open to the public 7 days a week from April through November. Tee time reservations are not necessary.

Driving Range	
• **Practice Green**	Lockers
• **Power Carts**	Showers
• **Pull Carts**	Food
• **Club Rental**	Clubhouse
• **Soft Spikes**	Outings

Fees	Weekday	Weekend
Daily	$14	$14
Power carts	$12/9	$24/18

Course Description: At Hidden Acres, the first 3 holes are wide open; the last six are more tree lined. The greens are small and of average speed. The par 3 ninth requires a tee shot over a pond. The course is a very friendly family operation that is constantly being upgraded and is playable for all skill levels.

Directions: Sussex County, #21 on Northwest Map
Rte. 80 West to Exit 34B. Take Rte. 15N and continue as it becomes Rte. 206N. In Hainesville, at De Angeli's Restaurant, turn left. At "T", turn right and then first left onto Rte. 646. Proceed for 1mile and turn right onto Ayers Rd and golf course.

Hole	1	2	3	4	5	6	7	8	9	Out	BLUE	Rating
BLUE												Slope
WHITE	290	410	500	140	340	280	175	425	165	2725		
Par	4	4	5	3	4	4	3	5	3	35	WHITE	Rating
Handicap	9	1	2	6	5	8	4	7	3			Slope
RED	250	340	380	140	290	270	125	410	145	2350		
Par											RED	Rating
Handicap												Slope

Hole	10	11	12	13	14	15	16	17	18	In		Totals
BLUE											BLUE	
WHITE											WHITE	5450
Par											Par	70
Handicap												
RED											RED	4700
Par											Par	70
Handicap												

Manager: Pam Green   **Supt:** Harry Green
Architect: Harold Green 1977

HIGHPOINT COUNTRY CLUB   **PUBLIC**

Clove Rd., Montague, NJ 07827   **(973) 293-3282**

Highpoint ia an 18 hole course open 7 days a week and closed in Jan. & Feb. Various memberships are available. Tee times may be made 2 weeks in advance. Tues: Senior Day, Thurs: Ladies Day.

•**Driving Range**	•**Lockers**
•**Practice Green**	•**Showers**
•**Power Carts** ·	•**Food**
Pull Carts	•**Clubhouse**
•**Club Rental**	•**Outings**
Soft Spikes	

Fees	Weekday	Weekend
Daily	$45	$60
After 3PM	$37	
Fees include cart		

Course Description: Highpoint is a traditional links course, narrow with no parallel fairways. Overlooking beautiful Holiday Lake and with several creeks in evidence throughout the course, water comes into play on 14 holes. The first hole is a daunting par 5 dogleg requiring substantial carry over water on the approach shot. The greens are fast some sharply two tiered. Try not to land above the hole. People travel to Highpoint from PA, NY and other parts of NJ.

Directions: Sussex County, #22 on Northwest Map
Rte. 80 West to Exit 34B. Take Rte. 15N which becomes Rte. 206N. Continue approx. 15 mi. to Clove Rd. (Rte. 653) and turn right. Club is 3 miles up on the right.

Hole	1	2	3	4	5	6	7	8	9	Out	BLUE	Rating 73.3
BLUE	500	330	428	532	213	448	215	442	411	3519		Slope 128
WHITE	481	312	392	513	197	416	196	420	394	3321		
Par	5	4	4	5	3	5	3	4	4	37	WHITE	Rating 71.6
Handicap	9	17	3	11	7	13	15	1	5			Slope 126
RED	465	265	367	408	208	351	155	415	315	2949		
Par	5	4	4	5	4	5	3	4	4	38	RED	Rating 70.0
Handicap	1	13	5	11	17	7	15	3	9			Slope 120
Hole	10	11	12	13	14	15	16	17	18	In		Totals
BLUE	522	408	378	348	190	551	302	433	132	3264	BLUE	6783
WHITE	518	377	362	305	140	506	278	404	115	3005	WHITE	6326
Par	5	4	4	4	3	5	4	4	3	36	Par	73
Handicap	6	8	12	14	16	4	10	2	18			
RED	429	349	298	285	68	425	137	295	120	2406	RED	5355
Par	5	4	4	4	3	5	3	4	3	35	Par	73
Handicap	4	4	15	4	13	4	5	5	14			

Manager/Supt: Bret Roby
Built: Gerald Roby 1960s

KNOLL EAST GOLF CLUB

PUBLIC

Knoll & Greenbank Rd., Parsippany, NJ 07054   **(973) 263-7115**

Knoll East is owned by the township of Parsippany and is open to the public from March to December, 7 days a week. Tee time reservations are not necessary during the week. On weekends: book in person for that day or call after 6AM for tee times 11AM or later that same day.

Driving Range	
•**Practice Green**	Lockers
•**Power Carts**	Showers
•**Pull Carts**	•**Food**
•**Club Rental**	•**Clubhouse**
•**Soft Spikes**	•**Outings**

Fees	Weekday	Weekend
Res/ID	$11	$15.50
Non-res	$22	$31
Mbrs 6-8AM		$8.50
Power Carts	$28.50	$17/9

Course Description: Knoll East is a wide open golf course with scenic views especially spectacular during the fall foliage season. The course is not very long but care must be taken on several of the fairways which are tight. The well bunkered greens are small and in good condition, the 18th severely sloped. The signature par 5 5th challenges the golfer to shape the drive hugging the right but avoiding the creek to be in a good position for a shot to the green. A creek runs across the 7th fairway. The long par 3 third requires accuracy; an errant shot does not yield an easy recovery.

Directions: Morris County, #23 on Northwest Map
Rte. 80 West to Exit 47, Parsippany. Take Rte. 46W to 2nd light and make a right onto Beverwick Rd. Go about 2 mi. and turn left at end of road. At 2nd driveway, turn right and follow signs to club entrance. From Rte. 287, see directions for Knoll West.

Hole	1	2	3	4	5	6	7	8	9	Out	BLUE	Rating
BLUE												Slope
WHITE	390	431	230	348	476	307	313	182	337	3014		
Par	4	4	3	4	5	4	4	3	4	35	WHITE	Rating 67.9
Handicap	5	1	9	11	3	17	13	15	17			Slope 112
RED	365	415	197	315	443	247	260	152	313	2707		
Par	4	5	3	4	5	4	4	3	4	36	RED	Rating 67.9
Handicap	5	3	7	11	1	17	13	15	9			Slope 112
Hole	10	11	12	13	14	15	16	17	18	In		Totals
BLUE											BLUE	
WHITE	503	325	154	376	127	347	543	165	330	2870	WHITE	5884
Par	5	4	3	4	3	4	5	3	4	35	Par	70
Handicap	6	10	16	4	18	12	2	14	8			
RED	472	300	135	348	117	315	525	135	255	2602	RED	5309
Par	5	4	3	4	3	4	5	3	4	35	Par	71
Handicap	4	12	14	6	18	10	2	16	8			

Manager/Pro: Victor Conticchio, PGA   **Supt:** John Grady
Architect: Hal Purdy 1960s

KNOLL WEST COUNTRY CLUB

Knoll & Greenbank Rd., Parsippany, NJ 07054   **(973) 263-7110**

Knoll West is an 18 hole course owned by the township of Parsippany open 7 days a week from Mar. to Dec. There is a waiting list for memberships. Tee times; members may reserve up to 1 week in advance. Public may play when time is available.

Driving Range	•**Lockers**
•**Practice Green**	•**Showers**
•**Power Carts**	•**Food**
•**Pull Carts**	•**Clubhouse**
•**Club Rental**	•**Outings**
•**Soft Spikes**	

Fees	Weekday	Weekend
Res/mbr	$12.50	$17
Mbrs	$25	$34
Non/mbr	$37.50	$51
Power Carts $29.50		

Course Description: The original clubhouse, destroyed by fire, was rebuilt on a high knoll, thus the name Knoll. The course was the brainchild of a few extremely wealthy men who wanted a superb private layout for their golfing pleasure. The 339 acre design is one of the finest for a semi-private club in New Jersey. It is long with many bunkers along the fairways protecting the difficult greens, characteristic of Charles Banks. The 439 yard par 4 18th is a favorite due to its long, narrow well-bunkered green. The course is steadily being improved. Power carts are required until 3:30PM.

Directions: Morris County, #24 on Northwest Map
Rte. 80 to Rte. 287N to Exit #45 at Wootton St. At 2nd STOP, make right onto Vreeland Ave. Go 1/2 mile down hill and follow signs on right to Knoll East & West. For access via Rte.80 and Rte. 46, see directions to Knoll East.

Hole	1	2	3	4	5	6	7	8	9	Out	BLUE	Rating 72.4
BLUE	416	445	194	394	550	154	367	416	388	3324		Slope 127
WHITE	409	426	188	383	525	142	355	406	380	3214		
Par	4	4	3	4	5	3	4	4	4	35	WHITE	Rating 71.3
Handicap	5	1	15	9	3	17	13	7	11			Slope 125
RED	374	361	148	303	430	130	330	384	355	2815		
Par	5	4	3	4	5	3	4	4	4	36	RED	Rating 74.1
Handicap	3	7	15	13	1	17	11	5	9			Slope 127
Hole	10	11	12	13	14	15	16	17	18	In		Totals
BLUE	391	418	383	248	430	530	383	170	439	3392	BLUE	6716
WHITE	385	407	370	217	410	520	371	158	427	3265	WHITE	6479
Par	4	4	4	3	4	5	3	4	4	35	Par	70
Handicap	10	6	14	12	2	8	16	18	4			
RED	359	386	356	189	365	493	345	145	400	3038	RED	5853
Par	4	5	4	4	4	5	4	3	5	38	Par	74
Handicap	10	6	12	16	8	2	14	18	4			

Manager: Pat De Falco   **Pro:** Steele King, PGA   **Supt**: John Grady
Architect: Charles Banks 1929

LAKE LACKAWANNA G C

155 Lake Drive, Stanhope, NJ 07874   **(973) 448-1313**

Lake Lackawanna is a 9 hole course open to the public 7 days a week all year weather permitting. Tee time reservations are not necessary.

<table>
<tr><td>Driving Range
•**Practice Green**
•**Power Carts**
•**Pull Carts**
•**Club Rental**
Soft Spikes</td><td>Lockers
Showers
•**Food**
Clubhouse
Outings</td></tr>
</table>

Fees	**Weekday**	**Weekend**
Daily/9	$12	$16
18 holes	$15	$20
Sr./Jr.	$14/9	$19/18
Power carts $5pp/9		

Course Description: Lake Lackawanna is a pleasant, mostly flat nine hole wide open course, good for practicing your game. Its hill reaches an elevated green on the 8th; the 9th has an elevated tee to a long downhill par 3. The new owner is doing a major upgrade by lengthening holes, redoing fairways and rebuilding the tee boxes. For 2005, the course will be longer than shown below with a lower par making the layout more challenging. Two holes have water in play. The course will be rated in the Spring.

Directions: Sussex County, #25 on Northwest Map
Take Rte.80West to Exit 25. Take Rte.206North for 3 traffic lights. Go right at Barones Restaurant for 1 and 1/4 mile. At the sign for Lake Lackawanna Golf Course, make a right on Hemiover Ave. Proceed 2 blocks to course on left.

Hole	1	2	3	4	5	6	7	8	9	Out	BLUE	Rating
BLUE												Slope
WHITE	315	165	150	215	135	400	440	200	220	2240		
Par	4	3	3	3	3	4	5	4	3	32	WHITE	Rating
Handicap	3	7	6	4	8	1	2	9	5			Slope
RED												
Par											RED	Rating
Handicap												Slope
Hole	10	11	12	13	14	15	16	17	18	In		Totals
BLUE											BLUE	
WHITE											WHITE	4480
Par											Par	64
Handicap												
RED											RED	
Par											Par	
Handicap												

Manager: Mike Byrne   **Supt:** Fred Jackson

LAKE MOHAWK GOLF CLUB

471 West Shore Trail, Sparta, NJ 07871   **(973) 729-9200**
www.lakemohawkgolfclub.com

Lake Mohawk is an 18 hole private course open 6 days a week from March through December. Guests play accompanied by a member. Tee time reservations are necessary for weekends. Caddies are available only on weekends.

•**Driving Range**	•**Lockers**
•**Practice Green**	•**Showers**
•**Power Carts**	•**Food**
•**Pull Carts**	•**Clubhouse**
•**Club Rental**	•**Outings**
•**Caddies**	•**Soft Spikes**

Course Description: This challenging hilly golf course situated above Lake Mohawk is surrounded by many lovely homes. It is short with elevated greens and tees: deer abound. A stream meanders through the back nine providing interest to this picturesque course. The first hole, a 452 yard par 4, is made more difficult by dense woods on the left, out of bounds on the right and an uphill second shot to a well bunkered green. On weekends, use of electric carts is required.

Directions: Sussex County, #26 on Northwest Map
Rte.80W to Exit 34B and take Rte. 15N for approx. 8.5 mi. to Sparta/Mohawk Bus. District exit. Continue straight onto Rte. 181N approx. 2.5 mi.to 2nd light. Go left down hill to STOP sign. Continue across the Plaza onto West Shore Trail. Keep left at fork, proceed 2 mi. Club on right.

Hole	1	2	3	4	5	6	7	8	9	Out	BLUE	Rating 70.9
BLUE	452	368	471	193	334	312	444	408	174	3156		Slope 130
WHITE	442	363	451	170	330	302	404	380	160	3002		
Par	4	4	5	3	4	4	4	4	3	35	WHITE	Rating 70.1
Handicap	1	5	7	15	9	17	3	11	13			Slope 128
RED	432	326	405	151	328	250	394	309	135	2730		
Par	5	4	5	3	4	4	5	4	3	37	RED	Rating 73.1
Handicap	1	9	7	15	3	17	5	11	13			Slope 126
Hole	10	11	12	13	14	15	16	17	18	In		Totals
BLUE	495	528	194	428	148	314	383	439	195	3124	BLUE	6280
WHITE	490	518	187	415	133	305	370	425	175	3018	WHITE	6020
Par	5	5	3	4	3	4	4	4	3	35	Par	70
Handicap	12	4	14	6	18	16	8	2	10			
RED	406	457	169	408	120	300	334	411	132	2737	RED	5467
Par	5	5	3	5	3	4	4	5	3	37	Par	74
Handicap	6	2	16	12	18	10	8	4	14			

Manager: Eugene Savron   **Pro:** Davis De Rosa, PGA   **Supt:** Eric Carlson
Architect: David Sewell 1927

MADISON GOLF CLUB

Green Avenue, Madison, NJ 07940   **(973) 377-5264**

Madison is a 9 hole private golf course open 6 days a week, from March 15 through December 15. Guests play accompanied by a member. Tee time reservations are required on weekends.

•**Driving Range***	•**Lockers**
•**Practice Green**	•**Showers**
•**Power Carts**	•**Food**
•**Pull Carts**	•**Clubhouse**
Club Rental	•**Outings**
Caddies	•**Soft Spikes**

Course Description: An extremely well-maintained hilly course, Madison is characterized by small well bunkered greens and narrow tree lined fairways. On two of the holes it is necessary to hit over a road. The dogleg right par 4 sixth requires careful club selection; its green is two-tiered. On the signature 9th, also a par 4, a tree is in the middle of the fairway affecting the second shot. A renovation in 2003 enlarged the tee boxes. Members have differing yardages as an option for the 2nd nine. The NJ Assistant Pro Match Play Tournament is held here annually.

Directions: Morris County, #27 on Northwest Map
Rte. 80 to Rte. 287S to Exit 35. Take Rte. 124 East into downtown Madison. Turn right at Waverly which becomes Green Ave; club is on the right. From GSP, exit at #142. Take Rte. 78 West to Rte.24 West to Chatham. Then take Rte. 124 West to Madison and turn left into Waverly and follow as above.

	1	2	3	4	5	6	7	8	9	Out	BLUE	Rating
BLUE												Slope
WHITE	154	254	202	217	391	334	138	155	374	2153		
Par	3	4	3	3	4	4	3	3	4	31	WHITE	Rating 63.1
Handicap	15	11	9	7	1	5	13	17	3			Slope 123
RED	150	250	200	210	328	281	137	150	370	1859		
Par	3	4	3	4	4	5	3	3	5	34	RED	Rating 64.5
Handicap	15	7	9	11	1	5	13	17	3			Slope 112
Hole	**10**	**11**	**12**	**13**	**14**	**15**	**16**	**17**	**18**	**In**		Totals
BLUE											BLUE	
WHITE	158	263	210	226	400	341	158	160	381	2240	WHITE	4393
Par	3	4	3	3	4	4	3	3	4	31	Par	62
Handicap	16	12	10	8	2	6	14	18	4			
RED	154	254	202	217	328	281	140	155	374	2052	RED	3911
Par	3	4	3	4	4	5	3	3	5	34	Par	68
Handicap	16	8	10	12	2	6	14	18	4			

Pro: Craig Lindsey, PGA   **Supt:** Keith Rose
Built: 1896

MEADOWS GOLF CLUB

79 Two Bridges Rd., Lincoln Park, NJ 07035   **(973) 696-7212**
www.meadowsgolfclub.com

Meadows is an 18 hole course open to the public 7 days a week all year. Tee times are first come, first served weekdays and 7 days in advance on weekends.

Driving Range	
•Practice Green	•Lockers
•Power Carts	•Showers
•Pull Carts	•Food
•Club Rental	•Clubhouse
•Soft Spikes	•Outings

Fees	M-Fri	Weekend
Daily	$36	$59
After 12PM		$48
Srs	$19	
Power Carts $15pp		
Twillight rates available		

Course Description: The Meadows underwent a major renovation a few years ago. The course now measures more than 6300 yards and 2 new par 4s have been created which results in no back to back par 3s. Also, new bunkers as well as cart paths throughout the property were added. The layout is predominantly flat and open, with water in play on 15 of the holes. The par 3 9th has a substantial carry over water and is 249 yards from the back tees. A computerized sprinkler system has been installed.

Directions: Morris County, #28 on Northwest Map
Rte. 80 to Exit 52. Make a left onto Two Bridges Rd. Go to the end and turn left. Course is on the right about 1/2 mile ahead.

Hole	1	2	3	4	5	6	7	8	9	Out	BLUE	Rating 70.9
BLUE	394	375	495	109	402	386	433	343	249	3186		Slope 127
WHITE	375	360	482	114	397	376	408	343	219	3074		
Par	4	4	5	3	4	4	4	4	3	35	WHITE	Rating 69.2
Handicap	11	7	9	17	1	13	5	15	3			Slope 124
RED	321	301	395	80	329	256	308	288	146	2424		
Par	4	4	5	3	4	4	4	4	3	35	RED	Rating 67.9
Handicap	15	9	3	17	1	13	7	11	5			Slope 117

Hole	10	11	12	13	14	15	16	17	18	In		Totals
BLUE	310	140	508	430	129	383	379	402	356	3037	BLUE	6345
WHITE	308	116	482	430	129	373	361	377	356	2932	WHITE	6006
Par	4	3	5	4	3	4	4	4	4	35	Par	70
Handicap	14	16	8	4	18	6	10	2	12			
RED	278	90	392	340	96	277	333	299	300	2405	RED	4829
Par	4	3	5	4	3	4	4	4	4	35	Par	70
Handicap	14	16	6	10	18	8	4	2	12			

Manager: Dennis Rogers   **Supt:** Andy Shuckers
Architects: Frank Duane 1963   Hank Finelli 1999

MENDHAM GOLF CLUB

PRIVATE

Golf Lane, Mendham, NJ 07945   **(973) 543-7297**

Mendham Golf Club, known as Mendham Golf & Tennis Club, is an 18 hole private course open 6 days a week from April through November. Guests play accompanied by a member. Tee times are arranged when members arrive.

- **Driving Range**
- **Practice Green**
- **Power Carts**
- **Pull Carts**
- **Club Rental**
- Caddies
- **Lockers**
- **Showers**
- **Food**
- **Clubhouse**
- Outings
- **Soft Spikes**

Course Description: Mendham is a relatively short and narrow layout with rolling hills demanding all varieties of shots. The back is longer and more wide open than the short tight front nine. The signature par 4 6th, with a large oak tree in the middle of the fairway, has one of the six ponds that come into play, and exemplifies the difficulties of the layout. The 18th, considered one of the premiere holes in Morris County, has a narrow driving area, out of bounds on the left, woods on the right and a brook in front of the two-tiered small green. Total yardages and ratings below are from Black, Blue and Red tees.

Directions: Morris County, #29 on Northwest Map
Rte.80 to Rte.287S towards Morristown. Take exit #33 (Harter Rd.) and turn left. Make left onto Rte. 202S & go 2 miles to Tempe Wicke Rd. At light (Jockey Hollow Park), go right. Go 3.4 mi & turn right at Kenneday Rd. Club is 500 yds. ahead on right.

Hole	1	2	3	4	5	6	7	8	9	Out	BLACK	Rating 71.9
BLACK	347	386	492	391	155	371	203	520	366	3231		Slope 130
BLUE	340	360	465	340	140	352	135	480	330	2942		
Par	4	4	5	4	3	4	3	5	4	36	BLUE	Rating 70.9
Handicap	14	8	12	2	18	6	16	4	10			Slope 127
RED	321	268	463	308	127	298	121	425	262	2593		
Par	4	4	5	4	3	4	3	5	4	36	RED	Rating 71.7
Handicap	12	10	4	2	18	14	16	6	8			Slope 128
Hole	10	11	12	13	14	15	16	17	18	In		Totals
BLACK	564	432	183	352	221	423	343	555	376	3449	BLACK	6682
BLUE	540	366	170	330	150	360	330	525	360	3131	BLUE	6411
Par	5	4	3	4	3	4	4	5	4	36	Par	72
Handicap	1	9	17	13	11	5	15	3	7			
RED	443	366	98	325	147	55	300	479	355	2868	RED	5187
Par	4	4	5	4	3	5	4	3	4	36	Par	72
Handicap	5	9	17	11	15	7	13	1	3			

Pro: Tom Staples, PGA   **Supt:** Chris Boyle
Architect: Alfred Tull 1961

MINE BROOK GOLF CLUB

500 Schooleys Mtn. Rd., Hackettstown, NJ 07840 **(908) 979-0366**
www.minebrookgolfclub.com

Mine Brook is a privately owned 18 hole course open to the public 7 days a week all year. Tee times; up to 1 week in advance, two weeks for season pass holders. Carts are required before 2PM on weekends. Call for add'l rates and discounts.

Driving Range
• Practice Green
• Power Carts
• Pull Carts
• Club Rental
• Soft Spikes

• Lockers
• Showers
• Food
• Clubhouse
• Outings

Fees	Weekday	Weekend
Daily	$34.50	$60w/cart
Srs	$26.50	
Power carts $16pp		
Twilight rates available.		

Course Description: Golfers from NJ, PA & NY flock to play this par 70, traditional links style course, formerly called Hidden Hills. The challenging sporty and scenic layout has something for every level of player. There are 6 holes with ponds and lakes affecting play; the fairways are lined with mature trees. The signature par 5 15th is difficult due to its length and dogleg left. The long 18th, a 575 par 5, is bordered by the Musconetcong River. The bunkers and greens have been redone recently and the drainage improved. The course is now owned and operated by Arnold Palmer Golf Management.

Directions: Morris County, #30 on Northwest Map
Rte. 80 West to Exit 26. Take Rte. 46W to Hackettstown and go left at East Ave. At next light, make left onto Schooley's Mountain Rd. Course is 2 lights on left.

Hole	1	2	3	4	5	6	7	8	9	Out	BLUE	Rating 70.8
BLUE	465	180	395	384	320	380	147	383	445	3089		Slope 131
WHITE	450	160	351	368	310	375	112	364	430	2920		
Par	5	3	4	4	4	4	3	4	4	35	WHITE	Rating 68.9
Handicap	14	16	10	6	12	8	18	4	2			Slope 130
RED	425	115	300	350	275	333	87	320	415	2620		
Par	5	3	4	4	4	4	3	4	5	36	RED	Rating 66.5
Handicap	14	16	10	6	12	8	18	4	2			Slope 118

Hole	10	11	12	13	14	15	16	17	18	In		Totals
BLUE	385	430	135	380	202	475	335	200	575	3117	BLUE	6349
WHITE	367	338	115	356	160	457	326	196	552	2867	WHITE	5987
Par	4	4	3	4	3	5	4	3	5	35	Par	70
Handicap	9	1	17	11	5	7	13	15	3		·	
RED	300	296	100	285	117	432	321	174	460	2486	RED	5505
Par	4	4	3	4	3	5	4	3	6	36	Par	72
Handicap	9	1	17	11	5	7	13	15	3			

Manager/Pro: Don Zauner, PGA   **Supt:** Kevin Taggert
Built: 1919, 2nd nine James M. Rocco 1965

MINERALS GOLF CLUB

Route 94, McAfee, NJ 07428

(973) 827-5996

www.crystalgolfresort.com

Minerals is a 9 hole course open 7 days a week and closed between November and March. Rewards card give discounts at Crystal Springs, Ballyowen, Great Gorge, Wild Turkey and Black Bear. Tee times: mbs 12 days in advance, public, 7 days.

Driving Range	
•Practice Green	Lockers
•Power Carts	Showers
•Pull Carts	•Food
•Club Rental	•Clubhouse
•Soft Spikes	•Outings

Fees	Weekday	Weekend
Daily	$20	$39
Twi	$18	$22
Early bird	$18	$25
Power carts included		

Course Description: Minerals is a picturesque executive course offering five par 3s and four par 4s. The signature par 3 4th requires a shot of 180 yards over a pond in front of a rock wall. This hilly and challenging layout is a demanding test of golf. It is embraced by a development of condo units. Stay and play packages are available through the recently renovated luxury hotel, part of the Crystal Springs Golf and Spa Resort, which includes a Day Spa, Conference Center and a complete Sports Facility.

Directions: Sussex County, #43 on Northwest Map
Rte. 80 West to Exit 53. Take Rte. 23N for about 30 miles to Rte.94N (Hamburg) & turn right.. Bear right and at next light, cross RR tracks and go 1 mile to entrance. Sign reads "The Spa & Hotel at Crystal Springs."

Hole	1	2	3	4	5	6	7	8	9	Out	BLUE	Rating 62.8
BLUE	346	178	363	181	323	231	407	176	100	2305		Slope 104
WHITE	316	136	337	150	292	186	374	153	100	2044		
Par	4	3	4	3	4	3	4	3	3	31	WHITE	Rating 60.2
Handicap	9	11	7	3	13	5	1	17	15			Slope 99
RED	281	103	294	88	265	152	312	131	100	1726		
Par											RED	Rating 62.1
Handicap												Slope 97

Hole	10	11	12	13	14	15	16	17	18	In		Totals
BLUE											BLUE	4610
WHITE											WHITE	4088
Par											Par	62
Handicap												
RED											RED	3452
Par											Par	62
Handicap												

Manager: Helene Reinsma **Pro:** David Glenz, PGA **Supt:** Glen Wright
Architect: Robert Trent Jones 1988

MORRIS COUNTY GOLF CLUB

36 Punch Bowl Rd., Convent Station, NJ 07961   **(973) 539-1188**

Morris County is an 18 hole private course open six days a week. It operaties all year weather permitting. Guests play accompanied by a member. On weekends, tee time reservations are an option.

•**Driving Range**	•**Lockers**
•**Practice Green**	•**Showers**
•**Power Carts**	•**Food**
Pull Carts	•**Clubhouse**
•**Club Rental**	•**Outings**
•**Caddies**	•**Soft Spikes**

Course Description: Nestled in the contours of the rolling terrain, Morris County is a beautiful old hilly course. The greens are small and undulating; the fairways tree-lined. A blind tee shot on the difficult and long par 4 7th forces long drivers to be careful otherwise the golfer is left with a downhill second shot to a semi punch bowl green located even further below. The signature par 3 13th, "Redan", has an elevated green with a difficult slope. Many holes have been named for world famous ones. The 18th, "Home," features another highlight, a double dogleg.

Directions: Morris County, #31 on Northwest Map
From Rte. 80, take Rte. 287S toward Morristown. Proceed to 2nd Morristown exit (Rte. 24, Madison Ave). Go left at top of ramp and continue 1.3 miles after 3 traffic lights, to Punch Bowl Rd. Turn left and go 1 mile past RR tracks. Club is on the left.

Hole	1	2	3	4	5	6	7	8	9	Out	BLUE	Rating
BLUE												Slope
WHITE	315	492	116	363	308	319	448	422	403	3186		
Par	4	5	3	4	4	4	4	4	4	36	WHITE	Rating 69.8
Handicap	16	12	18	10	14	8	2	6	4			Slope 124
RED	275	475	103	312	297	288	448	312	397	2908		
Par	4	5	3	4	4	4	5	4	5	38	RED	Rating 73.0
Handicap	15	1	18	5	13	7	3	9	11			Slope 123
Hole	10	11	12	13	14	15	16	17	18	In		Totals
BLUE											BLUE	
WHITE	443	509	311	177	410	220	402	186	405	3053	WHITE	6249
Par	4	5	4	3	4	3	4	3	4	34	Par	70
Handicap	1	11	17	9	3	15	5	13	7			
RED	433	379	308	171	384	172	359	164	320	2690	RED	5598
Par	5	4	4	3	5	3	4	3	4	35	Par	73
Handicap	6	2	12	10	14	16	4	17	8			

Manager: David Harnois   **Pro:** Ted O'Rourke, PGA   **Supt:** William Carrick
Architect: Seth Raynor 1894

MT. TABOR COUNTRY CLUB

PRIVATE

Country Club Road, Mt. Tabor, NJ 07878   **(973) 627-5995**

Mt. Tabor is a private 9 hole course open from April 1 to November 1, 6 days a week. Guests play accompanied by a member. Tee time reservations are advised on weekends.

- •Driving Range
- •Practice Green
- •Power Carts
- •Pull Carts
- •Club Rental
- Caddies

- •Lockers
- •Showers
- •Food
- •Clubhouse
- •Outings
- •Soft Spikes

Course Description: A challenging, tight course, Mt. Tabor has small undulating greens and many uneven lies. Accuracy is the key to scoring well on this nine hole layout. Throughout the scenic hilly terrain, there are creeks across and along the fairways. The signature par 4 13th has an old tree in the middle of the fairway that affects both the tee and second shots; the green slopes away front to back. The club changes the tee position for the second nine with differing yardages as shown on the scorecard below. Mt. Tabor celebrated its centennial in 2000.

Directions: Morris County, #32 on Northwest Map
Rte. 80 To Exit #39. Take Rte. 53 South for about 2 miles. Make a left on Country Club Road to club.

Hole	1	2	3	4	5	6	7	8	9	Out	BLUE	Rating
BLUE												Slope
WHITE	255	283	430	400	140	171	311	465	344	2799		
Par	4	4	4	4	3	3	4	5	4	35	WHITE	Rating 67.9
Handicap	13	15	5	1	17	11	7	3	9			Slope 122
RED	250	265	430	392	138	147	303	417	328	2670		
Par	4	4	5	5	3	3	4	5	4	37	RED	Rating 71.7
Handicap	13	15	5	1	17	11	7	3	9			Slope 127
Hole	10	11	12	13	14	15	16	17	18	In		Totals
BLUE											BLUE	
WHITE	240	274	365	462	198	151	307	433	355	2785	WHITE	5584
Par	4	4	4	5	3	3	4	4	4	35	Par	70
Handicap	14	12	6	2	18	16	10	4	8			
RED	236	258	360	457	185	136	296	417	338	2683	RED	5353
Par	4	4	4	5	4	3	4	5	4	37	Par	74
Handicap	14	12	6	2	18	16	10	4	8			

Pro: Glenn Hollterman, PGA   **Supt:** Curt Gandolfo   **Built: 1900**

NEWTON COUNTRY CLUB

25 Club Rd., Newton, NJ 07860   **(973) 383-9394**

Newton is a private 18 hole course open 6 days a week from April through December, weather permitting.. Guests play accompanied by a member. Tee time reservations are not necessary.

•**Driving Range**	•**Lockers**
•**Practice Green**	•**Showers**
•**Power Carts**	•**Food**
•**Pull Carts**	•**Clubhouse**
Club Rental	•**Outings**
Caddies	•**Soft Spikes**

Course Description: Newton is a difficult, hilly course with uneven lies and small greens. The atmosphere is quiet and peaceful. Water can be found mainly on the par 4 18th, a beautiful signature hole. The golfer tees off from a hill to a dogleg left; the second shot is over a pond to an elevated green guarded by a stone wall. From the blues and whites, the 8th is the #1 handicap hole, a long par 4. Originally, this course was the nine hole Sussex Country Club.

Directions: Sussex County, #33 on Northwest Map
Rte. 80 to Exit 34B. Take Rte.15 North for about 6 miles. Take the Newton exit to Rte. 517. Stay on the Newton-Sparta Road to club on the right.

Hole	1	2	3	4	5	6	7	8	9	Out	BLUE	Rating 70.9
BLUE	350	385	360	162	368	181	355	429	525	3115		Slope 133
WHITE	340	375	353	147	353	174	350	417	502	3011		
Par	4	4	4	3	4	3	4	4	5	35	WHITE	Rating 69.8
Handicap	9	11	7	17	13	15	5	1	3			Slope 130
RED	305	365	274	137	343	123	345	409	453	2754		
Par	4	4	4	3	4	3	4	5	5	36	RED	Rating 71.8
Handicap	11	7	13	15	9	17	5	3	1			Slope 127
Hole	10	11	12	13	14	15	16	17	18	In		Totals
BLUE	369	532	393	178	356	419	355	174	404	3180	BLUE	6295
WHITE	354	518	378	164	336	404	342	147	389	3032	WHITE	6043
Par	4	5	4	3	4	4	4	3	4	35	Par	70
Handicap	12	2	6	16	14	4	10	18	8			
RED	266	436	305	107	268	350	285	107	303	2427	RED	5181
Par	4	5	4	3	4	4	4	3	4	35	Par	71
Handicap	12	2	6	16	14	4	10	18	8			

Manager: Steve Kerrins   **Pro:** Robin Kohberger, PG   **Supt:** Les Carpenter
Architects: Front nine: Gordon & Gordon 1904   Back: 1969

PANTHER VALLEY GOLF & CC

PRIVATE

Route 517, Hackettstown, NJ 07840
www.panthervalleygolf&cc.com

(908) 852-6120

Panther Valley is a private 18 hole course open 6 days a week. It closes the beginning of Dec. and reopens Apr. 1. Guests play accompanied by a member. Reserved tee times are suggested for weekends.

- •**Driving Range**
- •**Practice Green**
- •**Power Carts**
- Pull Carts
- •**Club Rental**
- •**Caddies**

- •**Lockers**
- •**Showers**
- •**Food**
- •**Clubhouse**
- •**Outings**
- •**Soft Spikes**

Course Description: Located on a former estate in the woods of western New Jersey, and measuring 6827 yards from the championship tees, Panther Valley is a beautiful and hilly course. The rural setting is abundant with wildlife; deer, muskrat, beaver and even an occasional black bear have been spotted. The golfers stop at a halfway house for food after the front nine. The course has Penn Cross bent grass fairways and greens. The latter are fast and undulating, a true test of skill. From the signature 9th hole, players can see water on one side and mountains in the distance. The handsome clubhouse and separate golf shop were rebuilt after a fire in 1989. Panther Valley has one of the most picturesque driving ranges in the Northeast.

Directions: Warren County, #34 on Northwest Map
Rte.80W to Exit 19 Hackettstown-Andover. At exit, turn left onto Rte. 517. The club is one mile ahead on the right.

Hole	1	2	3	4	5	6	7	8	9	Out	BLUE	Rating 71.1
BLUE	510	169	388	360	431	162	523	411	418	3372		Slope 133
WHITE	488	153	378	345	398	151	502	391	389	3195		
Par	5	3	4	4	4	3	5	4	4	36	WHITE	Rating 69.4
Handicap	9	15	7	13	3	17	11	1	5			Slope 126
RED	452	121	349	303	381	127	471	365	370	2939		
Par	5	3	4	4	5	3	5	4	4	37	RED	Rating 72.6
Handicap	9	17	7	11	13	15	5	1	3			Slope 125
Hole	10	11	12	13	14	15	16	17	18	In		Totals
BLUE	174	501	337	184	348	361	353	355	380	2993	BLUE	6365
WHITE	161	482	314	160	330	344	337	341	360	2829	WHITE	6024
Par	3	5	4	3	4	4	4	4	4	35	Par	71
Handicap	14	2	10	18	6	8	16	12	4			
RED	118	450	283	133	283	327	310	297	329	2530	RED	5469
Par	3	5	4	3	4	4	4	4	4	35	Par	72
Handicap	18	2	4	16	6	8	14	12	10			

Manager: Jeffrey Williams   **Pro:** Daniel J. Pasternak, PGA   **Supt:** Pat Campbell
Architects: Robert Trent Jones, Sr. & Rees Jones 1969

PEACE PIPE COUNTRY CLUB   PRIVATE

2 Lee Rd., Denville, NJ 07834   **(973) 625-5041**
www.peacepipecountryclub.com

Peace Pipe is a 9 hole private golf course open all year 7 days a week. Reservations for tee times are not necessary.

•**Driving Range**	Lockers
•**Practice Green**	Showers
•**Power Carts**	•**Food**
•**Pull Carts**	•**Clubhouse**
•**Club Rental**	•**Outings**
Caddies	•**Soft Spikes**

Course Description: Peace Pipe started as a 6 hole facility and later graduated to the present layout. A new irrigation system has recently been installed. This 9 hole course is tight, short and moderately contoured with small greens. The Rockaway River is encountered on the 4th and 5th holes. The par 3 8th has a rocky area both behind the green and on the left with woods on the right, making a scenic signature hole. The 9th is a par 4 with an island green. It is advisable to check playability after a heavy rain.

Directions: Morris County, #35 on Northwest Map
Rte. 80 To Exit 39. Take Rte.46E. Go to 2nd light and turn left. Make an immediate right and at 1st light, turn left onto Diamond Springs Rd. Go 2 miles and turn right onto River Rd. Make a left onto Lee Rd. to club.

Hole	1	2	3	4	5	6	7	8	9	Out	BLUE	Rating 67.0
BLUE	286	270	398	445	201	285	263	155	323	2626		Slope 130
WHITE	271	255	372	405	184	270	248	133	313	2451		
Par	4	4	4	5	3	4	4	3	4	35	WHITE	Rating 66.0
Handicap	9	15	1	2	11	13	7	17	5			Slope 124
RED	252	225	340	345	167	245	175	120	270	2139		
Par											RED	Rating 66.3
Handicap												Slope 118
Hole	10	11	12	13	14	15	16	17	18	In		Totals
BLUE											BLUE	5252
WHITE											WHITE	4902
Par											Par	70
Handicap												
RED											RED	4278
Par											Par	70
Handicap												

Manager/Supt: David Lee
Built: Sid Lee 1960

PICATINNY GOLF CLUB

Building 121A, Picatinny, NJ 07806   (973) 989-2466

Picatinny is an 18 hole private course open 6 days a week between Apr.1 & Nov. 30. It is available to military civilian employees of the Arsenal and retired and active duty military personnel and veterans from Morris County. Tee time reservations are required.

Driving Range	•Lockers
•Practice Green	•Showers
•Power Carts	•Food
•Pull Carts	•Clubhouse
•Club Rental	•Outings
Caddies	•Soft Spikes

Course Description: Picatinny is relatively flat with small greens and heavily tree-lined fairways. On the tight front nine, there are approximately 50 bunkers. Water is in play on seven of the 18 holes. On the 17th, a short par 4, the golfer must hit over a road on the approach shot. New cart paths and bridges have recently been put in place as well as a new green on the 15th. That hole is played as a par 4 during the week and a par 5 on weekends. Golfers often find this course more difficult than it appears at first.

Directions: Morris County, #36 on Northwest Map
Rte. 80 To Exit 34B. Take Rte. 15N. After 1/4 mile, take entrance to Picatinny Arsenal. At first light, bear right, then make 1st left and turn left to Clubhouse.

Hole	1	2	3	4	5	6	7	8	9	Out	BLUE	Rating 72.7
BLUE	438	160	502	390	400	213	391	417	533	3444		Slope 129
WHITE	425	145	485	380	385	200	385	400	525	3330		
Par	4	3	5	4	4	3	4	4	5	36	WHITE	Rating 71.5
Handicap	11	17	13	9	7	15	5	3	1			Slope 127
RED	365	110	420	300	310	155	300	325	415	2700		
Par	4	3	5	4	4	3	4	4	5	36	RED	Rating 71.1
Handicap	5	15	7	9	11	3	17	1	13			Slope 122
Hole	10	11	12	13	14	15	16	17	18	In		Totals
BLUE	170	350	524	422	446	545	230	312	373	3372	BLUE	6749
WHITE	160	330	512	410	430	538	225	300	365	3270	WHITE	6519
Par	3	4	5	4	4	5	3	4	4	36	Par	72
Handicap	18	4	8	10	14	2	16	6	12			
RED	140	300	450	315	310	430	160	300	325	2730	RED	5409
Par	3	4	5	4	4	5	3	4	4	36	Par	72
Handicap	14	2	6	8	16	10	12	18	4			

Manager/Pro: Matt Mugavero, PGA   **Supt:** Chris Kunkel
Built: 1st nine 1928   2nd nine 1940

PINCH BROOK GOLF COURSE

PUBLIC

234 Ridgedale Ave., Florham Park, NJ 07932   **(973) 377-2039**
www.morrisparks.net

Pinch Brook is a Morris County course open 7 days a week from Apr. 1 to Nov. 30. Residents, who register for IDs, may make tee times 1 week in advance, $2.50pp fee. Non-residents, $5pp fee, 5 days in advance under automated program.

Driving Range
•Practice Green
•Power Carts
•Pull Carts
•Club Rental
•Soft Spikes
•Lockers
•Showers
•Food
•Clubhouse
Outings

Fees	Weekday	Weekend
Res/ID	$20.50	$26
Res/Sr	$15.50	
Non-res	$36.50	$47.50
Power cart $29/18		

Course Description: Pinch Brook, a par 65, is a flat, short and easy course to walk. The greens are large and fast. Woods may be found on either side of many holes; ponds affect play on four of them. A creek runs all the way along the left side on the ninth. For the tee shot, a big ravine confronts the golfer on the par 3 18th. Pinch Brook was originally called Canary Cottage and then Florham Park CC. Later, Morris County bought it and established it as a county course.

Directions: Morris County, #37 on Northwest Map
Rte. 80West to Rte. 287S towards Morristown. Exit at Rte. 10East (not Pleasant Ave.) Turn right onto Ridgedale Ave. Course is 3 miles ahead on the left.

Hole	1	2	3	4	5	6	7	8	9	Out	BLUE	Rating 64.2
BLUE	177	178	466	369	351	364	158	153	187	2403		Slope 105
WHITE	159	163	445	349	340	341	144	127	163	2231		-
Par	3	3	5	4	4	4	3	3	3	32	WHITE	Rating 62.5
Handicap	15	13	1	9	7	5	3	17	11			Slope 102
RED	136	143	407	333	325	325	103	109	131	2012		
Par	3	3	5	4	4	4	3	3	3	32	RED	Rating 63.4
Handicap	15	13	1	7	5	3	11	17	9			Slope 102

Hole	10	11	12	13	14	15	16	17	18	In		Totals
BLUE	174	476	385	337	343	190	177	358	164	2604	BLUE	4996
WHITE	157	453	368	327	336	169	144	337	142	2433	WHITE	4653
Par	3	5	4	4	4	3	3	4	3	33	Par	65
Handicap	18	6	8	14	2	4	16	10	12			
RED	139	408	286	301	316	124	117	314	100	2105	RED	4106
Par	3	5	4	4	4	3	3	4	3	33	Par	65
Handicap	18	4	6	14	2	10	16	8	12			

Manager: Tony Palmieri   **Pro:** Ed Koch, PGA   **Supt:** Bill Engler
Architect: Rees Jones 1983

ROCKAWAY RIVER CC

PRIVATE

39 Pocono Rd., Denville, NJ 07834   **(973) 627-4461**
email:rrccproshop@optonline.net

Rockaway River is a private 18 hole course open 6 days a week March 15 to December 31. Guests play accompanied by a member. Tee time reservations are not necessary.

•Driving Range	•Lockers
•Practice Green	•Showers
•Power Carts	•Food
Pull Carts	•Clubhouse
•Club Rental	•Outings
•Caddies	•Soft Spikes

Course Description: Rockaway River is a short, gently rolling and fairly tight course with small well-bunkered greens, some elevated. It is noted for its long par 5s. The tenth, a dogleg left par 4, can prove to be very difficult especially on the approach shot to the severely elevated landing area. On the signature par 5 18th, the Rockaway River is in play on both the tee and second shots. The river or marshland helps keep the course lush and in wonderful condition. The club hosted the Dodge Open Charity Classic from 1964-1994 and now hosts it as the NJPGA Clambake.

Directions: Morris County, #38 on Northwest Map
Rte. 80W to Exit 42B. Bear right and then make left at 2nd light onto Rte.46W. Turn right at 2nd light onto the Boulevard. At 1st light, go left onto Pocono Rd. Club is 1 mile ahead on the right.

Hole	1	2	3	4	5	6	7	8	9	Out	BLUE	Rating 72.7
BLUE	578	404	426	552	307	198	416	354	144	3379		Slope 133
WHITE	565	394	404	546	296	175	402	344	135	3261		
Par	5	4	4	5	4	3	4	4	3	36	WHITE	Rating 71.7
Handicap	3	9	7	1	11	15	5	13	17			Slope 129
RED	437	307	360	414	285	152	341	300	95	2691		
Par	5	4	4	5	4	3	4	4	3	36	RED	Rating 72.6
Handicap	7	11	1	5	9	15	3	13	17			Slope 129
Hole	10	11	12	13	14	15	16	17	18	In		Totals
BLUE	415	217	259	325	173	572	350	333	538	3182	BLUE	6581
WHITE	413	212	254	312	167	530	343	327	528	3086	WHITE	6347
Par	4	3	4	4	3	5	4	4	5	36	Par	72
Handicap	2	8	16	12	18	6	10	14	4			
RED	375	176	249	293	146	448	326	278	475	2766	RED	5457
Par	5	3	4	4	3	5	4	4	5	36	Par	73
Handicap	8	16	12	10	18	6	2	14	4			

Manager: Pat Hnatiw   **Pro:** Gregory J. Baker, PGA   **Supt:** Dave Pughe
Architect: Devereaux Emmet 1915

ROCK VIEW GOLF CLUB

PUBLIC

60 River Rd., Montague, NJ 07826   **(973) 293-9891**

Rock View is a 9 hole course open to the public 7 days a week from Apr.1 to Oct. 31. Memberships are available. Tee time reservations are not necessary.

Driving Range
- **Practice Green**
- **Power Carts**
- **Pull Carts**
- **Club Rental**
- **Soft Spikes**

Lockers
Showers
- **Food**
- **Clubhouse**
Outings

Fees	Weekday	Weekend
9 holes	$11	$11
18 holes	$17	$17
Power carts	$17/9	$29/18

Course Description: A predominantly flat layout with small greens, Rock View is located in a valley. However, the 8th and 9th are hilly; the green on the 8th is elevated. The course is good for the average golfer and considered a challenge to beat par. From the 1st hole, New York and Pennsylvania may be seen in the distance. The scenery is picturesque and the air is cool and clear. People come to play here from NY and PA as well as New Jersey.

Directions: Sussex County, #39 on Northwest Map
Rte. 80 to Exit 34B. Go north on Rte.15 to Rte. 206. Continue north up to Montague for about 5 miles and bear left onto River Rd. (Rte. 521). Club is on the right about 1 and 1/2 miles south of Port Jervis.

Hole	1	2	3	4	5	6	7	8	9	Out	BLUE	Rating
BLUE												Slope
WHITE	283	273	331	144	251	283	382	152	410	2464		
Par	4	4	4	3	4	4	4	3	5	35	WHITE	Rating
Handicap	7	5	3	9	6	4	2	8	1			Slope
RED												
Par											RED	Rating
Handicap												Slope

Hole	10	11	12	13	14	15	16	17	18	In		Totals
BLUE											BLUE	
WHITE											WHITE	4928
Par											Par	70
Handicap												
RED											RED	
Par											Par	
Handicap												

Manager/Supt: James Seeger
Built: 1935

ROLLING GREENS GOLF CLUB `PUBLIC`

214 Newton Sparta Rd., Newton, NJ 07860
www.rollinggreensgolf.com

(973) 383-3082

Rolling Greens is an 18 hole course open to the public 7 days a week all year. Annual memberships are available. Tee time reservations may be made up to 7 days in advance. Specials: Ladies/Wed $15, Seniors/ M & Thurs. $15.

Driving Range
- **Practice Green**
- **Power Carts**
- **Pull Carts**
- **Club Rental**
- **Soft Spikes**

Lockers
Showers
- **Food**
Clubhouse
- **Outings**

Fees	Weekday	Weekend
Daily	$20	$28
After 3	$14	$19
Power carts	$13pp	

Course Description: Although Rolling Greens is a relatively short course, it is rather tricky and narrow with small well bunkered greens. Flat and easy to walk, golfers encounter ponds on the par 3 9th and 18th holes. A creek runs across or alongside five other holes. Two extremely sharp L shaped doglegs can be found on the back. The fairways, tees and greens have been upgraded and are well conditioned. Rolling Greens Golf Academy with Driving Range may be found on nearby Route 206 South in Newton.

Directions: Sussex County, #40 on Northwest Map
Rte.80 West to Exit 34B. Take Rte.15 North for 11 miles, then take the 2nd Sparta exit to Rte.517S. Turn left at light; at end of exit go straight for 4 lights. Club is 1/4 mile past 4th light on the left.

Hole	1	2	3	4	5	6	7	8	9	Out	BLUE	Rating 64.5
BLUE	355	310	350	237	269	510	347	210	185	2773		Slope 116
WHITE	333	270	307	210	260	483	315	187	167	2532		
Par	4	4	4	3	4	5	4	3	3	34	WHITE	Rating 62.4
Handicap	4	9	6	11	13	2	8	16	14			Slope 103
RED	300	247	289	150	215	463	297	120	100	2181		
Par	4	4	4	3	4	5	4	3	3	34	RED	Rating 62.2
Handicap	4	9	6	11	13	2	8	16	14			Slope 104

Hole	10	11	12	13	14	15	16	17	18	In		Totals
BLUE	367	200	197	460	235	383	157	197	220	2416	BLUE	5189
WHITE	333	167	167	450	235	327	133	152	183	2147	WHITE	4679
Par	4	3	3	5	3	4	3	3	3	31	Par	65
Handicap	5	18	15	1	12	3	17	7	10			
RED	316	157	161	411	211	317	119	116	165	1973	RED	4191
Par	4	3	3	5	4	5	3	3	3	33	Par	67
Handicap	5	18	15	1	12	3	17	7	10			

Pro: Oscar Coetzee, PGA   **Supt:** Ian Kunesch
Architect: Nicholas Psiahas 1954

ROXITICUS GOLF CLUB

Bliss Rd., Mendham, NJ 07945   **(973) 543-4017**

Roxiticus is a private member owned 18 hole course open 6 days a week and closed from Christmas until Apr. 1. Guests play accompanied by a member. Tee time reservations are required on Sundays.

•**Driving Range**	•**Lockers**
•**Practice Green**	•**Showers**
•**Power Carts**	•**Food**
Pull Carts	•**Clubhouse**
•**Club Rental**	•**Outings**
Caddies	•**Soft Spikes**

Course Description: One of the finest of the Morris County courses, Roxiticus Golf Club is extremely picturesque and hilly. The thick natural woods provide a substantial buffer between the holes. This layout features narrow fairways, many uneven lies, target landing areas and truly magnificent scenery. Considered a shotmaker's course, water is in play on 8 holes. The par 3 signature 12th has an elevated tee, woods on the left, a brook and woods on the right and a pond in front. The pro shop is located in a former carriage house and is well stocked and beautifully designed.

Directions: Morris County, #41 on Northwest Map
Take Rte. 80 to Rte. 287S to Exit 30 for Bernardsville. Take Rte. 202S to center of Bernardsville and bear right onto Anderson Rd. Go about 3 miles to Bliss Rd. and turn left. Proceed 1 mile to club on the right.

Hole	1	2	3	4	5	6	7	8	9	Out	BLUE	Rating 72.5
BLUE	368	526	233	442	560	201	344	317	139	3130		Slope 135
WHITE	357	508	218	410	541	186	325	305	130	2980		
Par	4	5	3	4	5	3	4	4	3	35	WHITE	Rating 70.0
Handicap	13	5	9	1	3	11	7	15	17			Slope 132
RED	341	469	169	334	488	160	301	284	117	2663		
Par	4	5	3	4	5	3	4	4	3	35	RED	Rating 72.4
Handicap	11	3	13	5	1	9	7	15	17			Slope 134
Hole	10	11	12	13	14	15	16	17	18	In		Totals
BLUE	425	375	194	389	529	423	135	410	428	3308	BLUE	6521
WHITE	405	357	178	369	495	395	115	392	396	3102	WHITE	6118
Par	4	4	3	4	5	4	3	4	4	35	Par	70
Handicap	8	14	16	6	2	12	18	10	4			
RED	342	280	152	348	453	358	114	321	363	2731	RED	5485
Par	4	4	3	4	5	4	3	4	4	35	Par	72
Handicap	10	18	14	4	2	12	16	8	6			

Manager: Ann Chrapowicki   **Pro:** Todd Hojnacki, PGA   **Supt:** Justin Dorman
Architect: Hal Purdy 1967

SKY VIEW GOLF CLUB

226 Lafayette Rd., Sparta, NJ 07871
www.skyviewgolf.com

(973) 726-4653

Sky View is an 18 hole par 71 semi-private course. Memberships are available. Tee times: up to 7 days in advance. Super twilight and early bird specials are available as well as reduced rates for county residents.

- •**Driving Range**
- •**Practice Green**
- •**Power Carts**
- •**Pull Carts**
- •**Club Rental**
- •**Soft Spikes**
- •**Lockers**
- Showers
- •**Food**
- •**Clubhouse**
- •**Outings**

Fees	Weekday	Weekend
Daily	$59	$85
Twi 2PM $39		3PM $49
Carts are included		

Course Description: Beautiful large single family homes are built around Sky View, an extremely hilly course that overlooks Fox Hollow Lake in Sparta. The elevation changes are impressive as well as the grand sheer rock cliffs and outcroppings of stone. Trees abound and surround the difficult varieties of rough. Environmental sensitivity is displayed as the holes weave through striking natural terrain. Golfers are challenged by OB and hazards on several holes. The par 5 downhill 18th offers a lake on the left and OB driving range on the right. The uphill fairways make the course play longer. The names of the holes are descriptive giving an indication of what lies ahead. From the championship tees the course totals 6425 yards.

Directions: Sussex County, #42 on Northwest Map
Rte.80 to Exit 34B. Take Rte.15N for 12 miles to End of Freeway Sign. At jughandle, make left onto Rte 181S (Lafayette Road). Course is 1/4 mile on the right.

Hole	1	2	3	4	5	6	7	8	9	Out	BLUE	Rating 70.0
BLUE	325	530	169	540	365	175	326	435	382	3230		Slope 129
WHITE	303	506	134	471	318	145	295	396	372	2940		
Par	4	5	3	5	4	3	4	4	4	36	WHITE	Rating 67.6
Handicap	17	3	14	2	7	6	10	1	13			Slope 122
RED	283	420	105	420	291	125	270	363	352	2629		
Par	4	5	3	5	4	3	4	5	4	37	RED	Rating 69.4
Handicap	15	3	17	5	7	11	9	1	13			Slope 124

Hole	10	11	12	13	14	15	16	17	18	In		Totals
BLUE	375	126	340	382	156	490	305	175	465	2839	BLUE	6069
WHITE	344	103	292	357	152	463	275	151	465	2602	WHITE	5542
Par	4	3	4	4	3	5	4	3	5	35	Par	71
Handicap	8	12	11	5	9	15	4	16	18			
RED	313	96	252	292	140	408	250	120	455	2326	RED	4955
Par	4	3	4	4	3	5	4	3	5	35	Par	72
Handicap	6	18	14	10	8	4	2	16	12			

Manager/Pro:: Joe Kelly, PGA   **Supt**: Mike Candeloro
Architect: Robert McNeil 2000

SPRING BROOK COUNTRY CLUB

9 Spring Brook Rd., Morristown, NJ 07960   **(973) 538-7959**

Spring Brook is an 18 hole private course open 6 days a week and closed in February. Guests play accompanied by a member. Tee time reservations are necessary on weekends after 11:30AM.

> • **Driving Range**   • **Lockers**
> • **Practice Green**   • **Showers**
> • **Power Carts**   • **Food**
>   Pull Carts   • **Clubhouse**
> • **Club Rental**   • **Outings**
> • **Caddies**   • **Soft Spikes**

Course Description: A par 70 from the back tees, Spring Brook is a very picturesque, fair and enjoyable course. On 14 of the holes, the golfer encounters out of bounds and on five, water from natural springs. The tee on the outstanding 10th hole is along the water's edge. The carry is over the pond on this par 3 to a bowl-shaped green with bunkers guarding the front and both sides; too much club and the shot could land in one of two bunkers at the back. Spring Brook may be the only regulation 18 hole course in the country where there are 3 par 3s in a row. A redesign by Ken Dye, Jr. has just been completed resulting in yardage changes.

Directions: Morris County, #44 on Northwest Map
Rte. 80W to Rte. 287S to Exit 33, Harter Rd.. Go left off ramp for 3/4 mile and then a sharp right onto **Old** Harter Rd. Proceed 50 yards and make a sharp right onto Alvord Rd. to club. Entrance is straight ahead.

Hole	1	2	3	4	5	6	7	8	9	Out	BLUE	Rating 71.7
BLUE	417	223	532	386	374	495	395	428	192	3442		Slope 130
WHITE	402	195	502	362	360	487	376	413	173	3270		
Par	4	3	5	4	4	5	4	4	3	36	WHITE	Rating 70.5
Handicap	3	17	5	9	13	11	7	1	15			Slope 124
RED	323	155	395	309	347	402	361	400	122	2814		
Par	4	3	5	4	4	5	4	5	3	37	RED	Rating 72.5
Handicap	7	17	5	15	11	9	1	3	13			Slope 131

Hole	10	11	12	13	14	15	16	17	18	In		Totals
BLUE	164	210	349	448	204	427	446	417	397	3062	BLUE	6504
WHITE	162	197	335	430	193	414	441	417	393	2982	WHITE	6292
Par	3	3	4	4	3	4	5	4	4	34	Par	70
Handicap	14	16	10	2	18	6	12	4	8			
RED	95	175	322	375	168	319	404	404	322	2718	RED	5434
Par	3	3	4	4	3	4	5	5	4	35	Par	72
Handicap	18	14	8	2	16	12	4	6	10			

Manager: Michael Rudon   **Pro:** George Deitz, PGA   **Supt:** Robert Carey
Architect: Robert Hucknell 1922

SUNSET VALLEY GOLF COURSE   PUBLIC

West Sunset Rd., Pompton Plains, NJ 07444   **(973) 835-1515**
www.morrisparks.net

Sunset Valley, part of the Morris County Park System is an 18 hole course open 7 days a week from Apr.1st to Dec. 7th. ID obtained is valid at Flanders Valley, Pinch Brook & Berkshire Valley. Automated tee times: residents 7 days, registered non-res 5 days.

<table>
<tr><td>

Driving Range
- **Practice Green**
- **Power Carts**
- **Pull Carts**
- **Club Rental**
- **Soft Spikes**

- **Lockers**
- **Showers**
- **Food**
- **Clubhouse**
  Outings

</td><td>

Fees	Weekday	Weekend
Res./ID	$22	$27.50
Senior	$17	
Non.cty NJ	$38	$49
Power Cart	$17/single	$28/2

</td></tr>
</table>

Course Description: Sunset Valley is a demanding and hilly course with contoured and sloping greens. The difficult par 5 7th requires the golfer to decide whether to go for the green in two or play conservatively. The tight fairways lead up to 3 of the toughest finishing holes in the state of NJ. From the tee on the 555 yard par 5 16th, the drive should be right to left to keep the ball in the narrow fairway; the hole ends with a severe uphill leading to the green. Sunset Valley is well managed and worthwhile to play and meanwhile enjoy the spectacular views of the mountains in the distance.

Directions: Morris County, #45 on Northwest Map
Rte.80 West to Exit 53. Take Rte.23N to Newark-Pompton Tpke. Take the jughandle and cross over Rte. 23 to Jacksonville Rd. and turn left. Look for Sunset Rd. on right. Make a right and follow Sunset to club on the right.

Hole	1	2	3	4	5	6	7	8	9	Out	BLUE	Rating 71.4
BLUE	360	409	224	406	396	173	508	375	378	3229		Slope 129
WHITE	335	375	183	383	360	147	495	332	356	2966		
Par	4	4	3	4	4	3	5	4	4	35	WHITE	Rating 69.1
Handicap	13	7	15	3	5	17	1	11	9			Slope 125
RED	285	302	163	323	338	111	437	293	317	2569		
Par	4	4	3	4	4	3	5	4	4	35	RED	Rating 70.0
Handicap	13	7	15	3	5	17	1	11	9			Slope 122
Hole	10	11	12	13	14	15	16	17	18	In		Totals
BLUE	421	329	203	353	398	147	555	430	418	3254	BLUE	6483
WHITE	406	299	194	330	367	134	523	418	402	3073	WHITE	6039
Par	4	4	3	4	4	3	5	4	4	35	Par	70
Handicap	10	14	16	12	8	18	2	4	6			
RED	367	267	170	207	336	119	448	405	386	2705	RED	5274
Par	4	4	3	4	4	3	5	4	4	35	Par	70
Handicap	10	14	16	12	8	18	2	4	6			

Manager: Lou Rauch   **Dir. of Golf:** Renee Klose, LPGA   **Supt:** Joanne Eberle
Architect: Hal Purdy 1974

TWIN WILLOWS GOLF COURSE · PUBLIC

167 Ryerson Rd., Lincoln Park, NJ 07035   **(973) 692-0179**

Twin Willows is a 9 hole par 3 course located at the Lincoln Park Swim Club. It is open to the public 7 days a week from April through November. Reserved tee times are not necessary. *Management prefers golfers to wear sneakers or flat-soled shoes.

Driving Range	Lockers
•**Practice Green**	Showers
Power Carts	•**Food**
•**Pull Carts**	Clubhouse
•**Club Rental**	Outings
•**Soft Spikes***	

Fees	Weekday	Weekend
Daily	$13	$15
Sr/Jr 8AM-1PM $10		
Fees are for 9 holes		

Course Description: This course consists entirely of par 3s between 80 and 180 yards in length. It affords the player an opportunity to practice the short game. Local rule states that there is a 5 stroke limit on any hole. There is a picnic area on the premises.

Directions: Morris County, #46 on Northwest Map
Rte. 80West to Exit 53. Take Rte. 23N to 1st exit (Lincoln Park-Rte. 202). Take Rte. 202 to Ryerson Rd and turn right. Club is 1 mile ahead on right.

Hole	1	2	3	4	5	6	7	8	9	Out	BLUE	Rating
BLUE												Slope
WHITE	80	100	105	110	105	125	140	140	150	1055		
Par	3	3	3	3	3	3	3	3	3	27	WHITE	Rating
Handicap												Slope
RED												
Par											RED	Rating
Handicap												Slope
Hole	10	11	12	13	14	15	16	17	18	In		Totals
BLUE											BLUE	
WHITE											WHITE	
Par											Par	
Handicap												
RED											RED	
Par											Par	
Handicap												

Manager/Supt: Richard Ward   **Pro:** Jeffrey Ward, PGA

WALLKILL GOLF CLUB

Maple Rd., Franklin, NJ 07416   **(973) 827-9620**

Wallkill is a 9 hole private course open 7 days a week. The club closes from December to mid April. Guests play accompanied by a member. Reserved tee times are not required. Members may use a practice net in lieu of a driving range.

> Driving Range   •**Lockers**
> •**Practice Green** •**Showers**
> •**Power Carts** •**Food**
> •**Pull Carts** •**Clubhouse**
> •**Club Rental** •**Outings**
> Caddies •**Soft Spikes**

Course Description: Deceptively difficult, Wallkill is a short course with small greens. The Walkill River meanders through this very hilly course. On the 4th hole, the golfer finds both the river and a creek. The 7th is called the "teacup hole" due to the high rim around the 2 tiered green. The club, still boasting a waiting list, has added fairway bunkers and a 2nd set of tees from the Reds. Wallkill was originally designed with 6 holes for the NJ Zinc Co. officials and their guests. It was incorporated as Wallkill Golf Club in 1915 and sometime in the 1920s, it was expanded to the present 9 holes. The members are proud to show off their little "gem" in Franklin, NJ.

Directions: Sussex County, #47 on Northwest Map
Rte. 80 to Exit 53. Take Rte. 23North. When entering Franklin, make a left on Franklin Ave. (Rte. 631) past a pond and waterfall and onto Cork Hill Rd. Immediately after the municipal building, go right onto Maple Rd. Club is ahead on right.

Hole	1	2	3	4	5	6	7	8	9	Out	BLUE	Rating
BLUE												Slope
WHITE	315	169	485	225	285	398	147	512	333	2869		
Par	4	3	5	3	4	4	3	5	4	35	WHITE	Rating 67.8
Handicap	14	17	4	11	10	1	16	5	8			Slope 117
RED	268	137	350	163	234	235	116	374	246	2123		
Par	4	3	5	3	4	4	3	5	4	35	RED	Rating 67.3
Handicap	13	17	3	11	9	1	15	5	7			Slope 119

Hole	10	11	12	13	14	15	16	17	18	In		Totals
BLUE											BLUE	
WHITE	326	152	520	205	310	380	158	480	350	2881	WHITE	5806
Par	4	3	5	3	4	4	3	5	4	35	Par	70
Handicap	13	18	3	12	9	2	15	6	7			
RED											RED	4661
Par											Par	70
Handicap												

Manager/Pro: Frank Vnuk, PGA   **Supt:** Richard Fodor
Built: 1910

WILD TURKEY GOLF CLUB

PUBLIC

123 Crystal Springs Rd., Hamburg, NJ 07419
www.crystalgolfresort.com

(973) 827-5996

Wild Turkey is an 18 hole course open 7 days a week from Mar. to Dec. Rewards card for Crystal Springs, Ballyowen, Black Bear, Great Gorge and Minerals. Tee times: 15 day mbrs, 10 day public. A fabulous new clubhouse is shared with Crystal Springs.

•**Driving Range**	•**Lockers**
•**Practice Green**	•**Showers**
•**Power Carts**	•**Food**
Pull Carts	•**Clubhouse**
•**Club Rental**	•**Outings**
•**Soft Spikes**	

Fees	Weekday	Weekend
Daily	$80	$110
Twi	$60	$75
Power carts included		

Course Description: Wild Turkey is the newest addition to Sussex County's growing array of fine courses. Essentially horseshoeing around Crystal Springs and not quite as rugged, it is characterized by large landing areas, wide fairways, small greens having substantial break, trademark bunkers and some steep elevations. The course is fairly forgiving but shot-making is essential. The front is bordered by woods and OB guarding the many new homes being built in this fast growing golf community. With dramatic par 3s, the course measures 7,202 yards from the back tees. The finishing holes are very challenging, the 17th a 600+ yd. par 5, the 18th a long uphill par 4.

Directions: Sussex County, #48 on Northwest Map
Rte. 80 to Exit 53B. Take Rte. 23 North (approx. 28 miles) through Franklin and just before Hamburg make a right onto Rte. 517 North. Course is 2 miles ahead on left.

Hole	1	2	3	4	5	6	7	8	9	Out	BLUE	Rating 71.4
BLUE	387	163	519	431	450	329	181	528	371	3359		Slope 131
WHITE	369	133	485	398	408	293	164	472	351	3073		
Par	4	3	5	4	4	4	3	5	4	36	WHITE	Rating 68.7
Handicap	11	17	5	1	3	13	7	15	9			Slope 124
RED	286	103	445	322	378	253	119	324	301	2531		
Par	4	3	5	4	4	4	3	4	4	35	RED	Rating 69.0
Handicap	15	17	5	3	1	13	11	7	9			Slope 118

Hole	10	11	12	13	14	15	16	17	18	In		Totals
BLUE	218	544	380	367	187	392	170	577	361	3196	BLUE	6555
WHITE	193	497	340	343	147	342	155	535	317	2869	WHITE	5942
Par	3	5	4	4	3	4	3	5	4	35	Par	71
Handicap	10	2	14	16	12	4	18	8	6			
RED	165	435	299	300	100	318	128	462	286	2493	RED	5024
Par	3	5	4	4	3	4	3	5	4	35	Par	70
Handicap	10	6	14	16	18	4	12	2	8			

Manager: Art Walton   **Pro:** David Glenz, PGA   **Supt:** Mike Poluzzi
Architect: Roger Rulewich 2001

Golf is a game in which you put a ball 1 and 1/2 inches in diameter on a ball 8,000 miles in diameter and you try to hit the little ball without hitting the big ball.

A golfer may be careful with his money in other matters but never minds spending a small fortune on clubs, balls, lessons, fees and therapy (when his game drives him to the brink of a nervous breakdown).

(Country Club of Salem)

EAST CENTRAL REGION

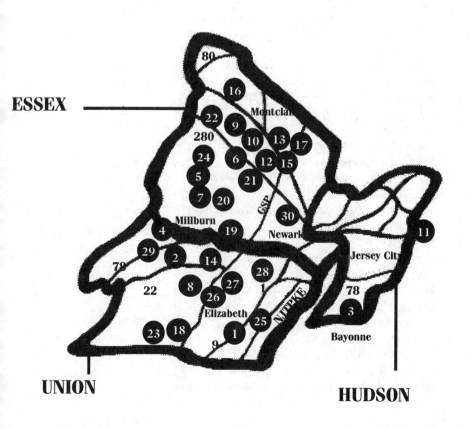

ESSEX

UNION

HUDSON

EAST CENTRAL

Public Courses appear in **bold italics**

Map (#)   Page #

Ashbrook Golf Course (1)------------------- 95
Baltusrol Golf Club (2)-------------------------- 96
Bayonne Golf Course (3)----------------------- 97
Canoe Brook Country Club (4)---------------- 98
Cedar Hill Country Club (5)-------------------- 99
Crestmont Country Club (6)------------------- 100
East Orange Golf Club (7)------------------ 101
Echo Lake Country Club (8)------------------- 102
Essex County Country Club (9)--------------- 103
Essex Fells Country Club (10)---------------- 104
Forest Hill Field Club (12)---------------------- 105
Francis Byrne Golf Course (13)----------- 106
Galloping Hill Golf Course (14)----------- 107
Glen Ridge Country Club (15)----------------- 108
Green Brook Country Club (16)--------------- 109
Hendricks Field Golf Club (17)------------ 110
Hyatt Hills Golf Course (18)---------------- 111
Liberty National Golf Club (11)--------------- 112
Maplewood Country Club (19)---------------- 113
Millburn Golf Course (20)------------------- 114
Montclair Golf Club (21)------------------------ 115
Mountain Ridge Country Club (22)----------- 116
Oak Ridge Golf Course (23)---------------- 117
Rock Spring Club (24)-------------------------- 118
Roselle Golf Club (25)-------------------------- 119
Scotch Hills Country Club (26)------------- 120
Shackamaxon Golf & CC (27)------------------ 121
Suburban Golf Club (28)----------------------- 122
Summit Municipal Golf Course (29)---------- 123
Weequahic Park Golf Course (30)--------- 124

ASH BROOK GOLF COURSE

PUBLIC

1210 Raritan Rd., Scotch Plains, NJ 07076   **(908) 756-0414**

Ash Brook, part of the Union County Parks System, is an 18 hole course open 7 days a week all year. Residents purchase ID and may reserve up to 1 week in advance, non res. with ID up to 3 days. Reciprocity for Bergen & Middlesex Srs W/ID on weekdays.

Driving Range
- **Practice Green**
- **Power Carts**
- **Pull Carts**
- **Club Rental**
- **Soft Spikes**

- **Lockers**
- **Showers**
- **Food**
- **Clubhouse**

Outings

Fees	Weekday	Weekend
Res/ID	$22	$24
Srs/ID	$14	$22
Non.res	$44	$48
Power Carts	$26(18)	$16 (9)
(Out of County Sr $28)		

Course Description: The rolling terrain at Ash Brook is relatively wooded. The course was renovated by architect, Stephen Kay with new bunkers and undulating greens, many of which are triple tiered and quite challenging. It has been rated as one of the most difficult public courses in NJ. The par 5 16th is an uphill dogleg right with a lake at the corner. Water comes into play on several other holes. Ash Brook is very busy on weekends. This facility has a 9 hole pitch and putt course on the premises.

Directions: Union County, #1 on East Central Map
GSP to Exit 135 (Central Ave). Make the 1st left at light onto Raritan Rd. At 4th light, turn right onto Lake Ave. Go 3 lights and turn left onto Old Raritan Rd. Watch for signs for golf course.

Hole	1	2	3	4	5	6	7	8	9	Out	BLUE	Rating 73.3
BLUE	417	380	420	185	511	155	435	548	426	3477		Slope 125
WHITE	377	351	389	176	471	135	400	484	392	3175		
Par	4	4	4	3	5	3	4	5	4	36	WHITE	Rating 70.1
Handicap	12	14	6	16	8	18	2	10	4			Slope 116
RED	324	332	351	136	410	115	341	426	356	2791		
Par	4	4	4	3	5	3	4	5	4	36	RED	Rating 71.8
Handicap	12	14	10	16	8	18	6	2	4			Slope 118

Hole	10	11	12	13	14	15	16	17	18	In		Totals
BLUE	428	353	539	222	466	303	525	423	180	3439	BLUE	7040
WHITE	401	342	517	193	432	287	483	386	157	3198	WHITE	6397
Par	4	4	5	3	4	4	5	4	3	36	Par	72
Handicap	11	9	5	15	1	13	3	7	17			
RED	378	303	490	170	402	278	430	338	125	2914	RED	5570
Par	4	4	5	3	5	4	5	4	3	37	Par	73
Handicap	9	11	3	15	5	13	1	7	17			

Manager: Ron Gooodwin   **Pro:** Ron Regner, PGA   **Supt:** Peter McCoy
Architect: Alfred Tull 1953 **Renovation**: Stephen Kay 1999

BALTUSROL GOLF CLUB

PRIVATE

Shunpike Rd., Springfield, NJ 07081
www.baltusrol.com

(973) 376-5160

Baltusrol has two 18 hole courses, the Upper and the Lower, open all year 7 days a week. Guests play accompanied by a member. Reservations for tee times are not necessary. The scorecard below is for the Lower course.

- •Driving Range
- •Practice Green
- •Power Carts
- Pull Carts
- •Club Rental
- •Caddies
- •Lockers
- •Showers
- •Food
- •Clubhouse
- •Outings
- •Soft Spikes

Course Description: This traditional setting is suffused with pure golf atmosphere. Jack Nicklaus won two US Opens here; numerous other championships took place at this world famous club. The finely maintained courses feature rolling fairways, a multitude of bunkers and subtle greens. The Lower is dauntingly long, particularly from the Blues. The par 5 17th is 630 yards!! John Daly was the first to reach the green in two. The signature and memorable par 3 fourth requires an accurate shot over a formidable pond to a well bunkered green. The courses have been redesigned by Robert Trent Jones and Rees Jones.

Directions: Union County, #2 on East Central Map
GSP or NJTpke to Rte. 78West. Take Rte. 24West to sign marked "Springfield, Summit, Millburn." Follow sign to Summit. You are now on Broad St. Turn left onto Orchard St. which changes to Shunpike at Morris Ave. Turn right at caution blinker into club.

Hole	1	2	3	4	5	6	7	8	9	Out	BLUE	Rating 74.5
BLUE	478	381	443	194	393	470	505	374	205	3443		Slope 140
WHITE	470	362	405	143	375	411	494	360	189	3209		
Par	5	4	4	3	4	4	5	4	3	36	WHITE	Rating 72.7
Handicap	11	7	1	17	3	5	13	9	15			Slope 139
RED	453	300	402	101	342	406	461	342	171	2978		
Par	5	4	5	3	4	5	5	4	3	38	RED	Rating 76.1
Handicap	4	14	6	18	8	12	2	10	16			Slope 135
Hole	10	11	12	13	14	15	16	17	18	In		Totals
BLUE	454	428	193	393	409	430	216	630	542	3695	BLUE	7195
WHITE	444	388	188	374	379	383	180	543	511	3390	WHITE	6637
Par	4	4	3	4	4	4	3	5	5	36	Par	72
Handicap	2	8	16	12	14	4	18	6	10			
RED	416	377	151	359	329	368	114	448	423	2985	RED	5963
Par	5	4	3	4	4	4	3	5	5	37	Par	75
Handicap	11	3	15	9	13	5	17	1	7			

Manager: Kevin Vitale **Pro:** Doug Steffan, PGA **Supt:** Mark Kuhns
Architect: A. W. Tillinghast 1922

BAYONNE GOLF CLUB

New York Harbor, Bayonne, NJ   **(845) 362-9146**
www.bayonnegolfclub.com

Bayonne Golf Club is a private 18 hole course open 6 days a week all year. Memberships are by invitation only. Guests play accompanied by a member. Tee time reservations are not necessary.

- •Driving Range
- •Practice Green
- •Power Carts
- Pull Carts
- •Club Rental
- •Caddies
- •Lockers
- •Showers
- •Food
- •Clubhouse
- •Outings
- •Soft Spikes

Course Description: With land facing NYBay and views of the Statue of Liberty and Manhattan, Bayonne Golf Club is the latest and most ambitious project for Empire Golf and Eric Bergstol. Seven years in the planning, Hudson County will have the first golf course within its borders when this 403 acre beautifully landscaped property at Constable Hook is completed in 2005. The fescue covered dunes and firm fairways & greens demand the skilled touch of an experienced golfer. The layout is a purely links style with elevation changes of over 100 feet and 13 holes on the water. Accessible by helicopter, private yacht, harbor shuttle or auto Bayonne's opening is anxiously being awaited. As we go to press, only the preliminary scorecard is available.

Directions: Hudson County, #3 on East Central Map
NJTPK to Exit #14A. Take Rte. 440 South; stay in right lane. Make a right turn at jughandle of New Hook Rd. Follow curved rd. (New Hook) to club on left.

Hole	1	2	3	4	5	6	7	8	9	Out	BLUE	Rating
BLUE	390	405	185	560	160	320	440	575	430	3452		Slope
WHITE												
Par	4	4	3	5	3	4	4	5	4	36	WHITE	Rating
Handicap												Slope
RED												
Par											RED	Rating
Handicap												Slope
Hole	10	11	12	13	14	15	16	17	18	In		Totals
BLUE	470	230	450	570	210	305	470	530	440	3675	BLUE	7160
WHITE											WHITE	
Par	4	3	4	5	3	4	4	5	4	36	Par	72
Handicap												
RED											RED	
Par											Par	72
Handicap												

Architect: Eric Bergstol 2005

CANOE BROOK COUNTRY CLUB PRIVATE

1108 Morris Turnpike, Summit, NJ 07901   (908) 277-2683

Canoe Brook is a private club with 36 holes. It is open 6 days a week, all year, weather permitting. Guests play accompanied by a member. Tee time reservations are not necessary.

•**Driving Range**	•**Lockers**
•**Practice Green**	•**Showers**
•**Power Carts**	•**Food**
Pull Carts	•**Clubhouse**
•**Club Rental**	•**Outings**
•**Caddies**	•**Soft Spikes**

Course Description: An original C.H. Alison design, Canoe Brook's South course is considered one of the most difficult in NJ due to its length, small greens, penalizing rough, numerous bunkers and its tree-lined fairways. Water comes into play, most daunting on the par 3 10th where bunkers surround the green. Featured on the North is the par 3 14th where a lake extends up to the green making this hole a beautiful and difficult signature. Both layouts have had extensive redesign by Robert Trent Jones and Rees Jones. The club hosts qualifying rounds for the US Open and hosted the Women's National Amateur of 1938, '83 and '90. The scorecard below is for the North course.

Directions: Union County, #4 on East Central Map
GSP or NJTpke to Rte. 78W to Exit 48. Take Rte. 24West to Summit Ave. exit. Go through light on north service road. Club is ahead on the right.

Hole	1	2	3	4	5	6	7	8	9	Out	BLUE	Rating 74.1
BLUE	399	572	390	362	173	442	212	528	417	3495		Slope 135
WHITE	380	534	358	346	148	402	184	501	401	3254		
Par	4	5	4	4	3	4	3	5	4	36	WHITE	Rating 71.9
Handicap	7	1	13	11	17	5	15	9	3			Slope 131
RED	358	460	323	282	110	352	153	435	355	2828		
Par	4	5	3	4	5	4	3	4	4	36	RED	Rating 74.0
Handicap	7	1	9	6	2	5	8	4	3			Slope 134
Hole	10	11	12	13	14	15	16	17	18	In		Totals
BLUE	374	173	538	391	226	382	431	455	601	3571	BLUE	7066
WHITE	360	148	512	370	201	360	395	424	567	3337	WHITE	6591
Par	4	3	5	4	3	4	4	4	5	36	Par	72
Handicap	12	18	4	14	10	16	8	6	2			
RED	333	125	434	326	166	331	334	330	496	2875	RED	5703
Par	4	3	5	4	3	4	4	4	5	36	Par	72
Handicap	12	18	2	8	14	16	6	10	4			

Manager: Rudolf Fisher   **Pro:** Greg Lecker, PGA   **Supt:** Tom Ashfield
Architects: South: Charles Alison 1924 **North:** Alfred Tull, Walter Travis 1902

CEDAR HILL COUNTRY CLUB

100 Walnut St., Livingston, NJ 07039   **(973) 992-6455**

Cedar Hill is a private 18 hole course open 6 days a week from Mar. 1 to Nov. 30. Guests play accompanied by a member. Tee times may be made 2 or 3 days in advance for weekends.

•Driving Range	•Lockers
•Practice Green	•Showers
•Power Carts	•Food
Pull Carts	•Clubhouse
•Club Rental	•Outings
•Caddies	•Soft Spikes

Course Description: Cedar Hill is known for its fast, undulating, small greens. Some consider the par four 4th hole the most difficult due to the out of bounds along the right side of the fairway. Its severely sloped green is well protected by bunkers. The back nine includes a memorable par 3 that goes downhill to an elevated green surrounded by bunkers. The par 5 18th is a good uphill finishing hole. Accuracy is a necessity in order to score well at Cedar Hill. Every bunker and tee is presently being upgraded to make the course more interesting and challenging.

Directions: Essex County, #5 on East Central Map
GSP or NJTpke to Rte.280 West. Exit at 4A (Eisenhower Parkway). Follow parkway for 6 traffic lights (approx. 3 miles) to Walnut Street and turn right. Club is ahead on left.

Hole	1	2	3	4	5	6	7	8	9	Out	BLUE	Rating 70.9
BLUE	458	375	385	465	178	503	317	348	428	3436		Slope 128
WHITE	447	362	374	450	161	472	309	333	418	3303		
Par	4	4	4	4	3	5	4	4	4	36	WHITE	Rating 69.5
Handicap	1	11	9	5	17	7	15	13	3			Slope 126
RED	393	348	362	383	157	400	263	290	364	2955		
Par	5	4	4	5	3	5	4	4	4	38	RED	Rating 73.0
Handicap	3	11	5	7	17	9	15	13	1			Slope 131
Hole	10	11	12	13	14	15	16	17	18	In		Totals
BLUE	157	379	394	192	542	373	133	369	475	3007	BLUE	6443
WHITE	145	323	375	176	530	359	120	358	462	2789	WHITE	6092
Par	3	4	4	3	5	4	3	4	5	35	Par	71
Handicap	18	12	4	14	2	8	16	10	6			
RED	137	303	356	159	430	345	109	332	384	2531	RED	5486
Par	3	4	4	3	5	4	3	4	5	35	Par	73
Handicap	2	16	14	18	6	4	10	8	12			

Manager: Joe Kuntar   **Pro:** Ron Korn, PGA   **Supt:** Dennis Wrede
Architect: Nicholas Psiahas 1921

CRESTMONT COUNTRY CLUB

750 Eagle Rock Ave, West Orange, NJ 07052   (973) 731-0833

Crestmont is an 18 hole course open from February through December, 6 days a week. Guests may play accompanied by a member. Tee times are by assignment on weekends.

•Driving Range	•Lockers
•Practice Green	•Showers
•Power Carts	•Food
Pull Carts	•Clubhouse
Club Rental	•Outings
•Caddies	•Soft Spikes

Course Description: Crestmont opened in 1912 as a 12 hole layout known as the Newark Athletic Club. This Donald Ross course is known for its small, undulating greens, some two tiered and extremely difficult to putt when fast. Uneven lies are characteristic of hilly Crestmont. The par 5 first hole has an elevated tee ending with an uphill approach shot. The green on the signature par 3 11th is elevated with a back to front slope; landing above the hole would be a big mistake. A carry over water is necessary to reach the 12th hole and the par 3 8th is also over water. A pond has been added to the tenth hole for drainage purposes. The 1997 NJ State Open and the 2000 NJ State Senior Open were held here.

Directions: Essex County, #6 on East Central Map
From GSP or NJTP take Rte. 280 West to Exit 6A, Laurel Ave. Club is about 1/2 mile on the right just before intersection of Eagle Rock Ave.

Hole	1	2	3	4	5	6	7	8	9	Out	BLUE	Rating 72.7
BLUE	489	448	412	162	402	404	307	216	510	3350		·Slope 133
WHITE	478	432	398	148	382	392	295	205	502	3232		
Par	5	4	4	3	4	4	4	3	5	36	WHITE	Rating 71.0
Handicap	11	1	5	17	9	7	15	13	3			Slope 130
RED	467	416	293	132	282	320	292	179	448	2829		
Par	5	5	4	3	4	4	4	3	5	37	RED	Rating 74.2
Handicap	3	5	9	17	11	7	13	15	1			Slope 127
Hole	10	11	12	13	14	15	16	17	18	In		Totals
BLUE	422	163	414	356	521	362	406	230	508	3382	BLUE	6732
WHITE	415	157	402	346	493	353	393	222	494	3275	WHITE	6507
Par	4	3	4	4	5	4	4	3	5	36	Par	72
Handicap	6	18	2	10	14	12	4	16	8			
RED	407	147	327	314	442	308	375	182	384	2886	RED	5715
Par	5	3	4	4	5	4	4	3	5	37	Par	74
Handicap	12	18	2	14	8	6	4	16	10			

Manager: Mark Shan   **Pro:** Peter Famiano, PGA   **Supt:** Peter Pedrazzi, Jr.
Architect: Donald Ross 1912

EAST ORANGE GOLF COURSE `SEMI-PRIVATE`

440 Parsonage Hill Rd., Short Hills, NJ 07078   **(973) 379-7190**

East Orange is a municipal 18 hole course, considered to be semi-private, owned by the City of East Orange and open to the public 7 days a week all year. Memberships are available with the privilege of reserving tee times. No advance tee times available for the public. Irons only for driving range.

• Driving Range	• Lockers
• Practice Green	• Showers
• Power Carts	• Food
• Pull Carts	• Clubhouse
Club Rental	• Outings
• Soft Spikes	

Fees	Weekday	Weekend
Mbrs	$13	$15
Non-mbrs	$35	$35
Power carts	$20	$20

Course Description: This golf course is on the property of the East Orange water Reserve which supplies water to the area. It is adjacent to a wildlife preserve and it sometimes has drainage problems in wet weather. The layout is open and relatively flat. Considerable improvements have been made with the planting of numerous trees and restoration of fairways, greens and cart paths. The clubhouse had work done with the addition of a beautiful patio.

Directions: Essex County, #7 on East Central Map
GSP or NJ Tpke to Rte.78 W. Take Rte.24West to Exit 7C (JFK Pkwy) toward Livingston. Go past Short Hills Mall. Make left onto Parsonage Hill Rd. Club is 1/4 mi on left.

Hole	1	2	3	4	5	6	7	8	9	Out	BLUE	Rating
BLUE												Slope
WHITE	342	396	178	343	500	305	488	204	375	3131		
Par	4	4	3	4	5	4	5	3	4	36	WHITE	Rating 67.6
Handicap	5	1	9	11	15	17	13	3	7			Slope 117
RED	280	355	175	330	419	295	448	199	261	2762		
Par	4	4	3	4	5	4	5	3	4	36	RED	Rating 69.8
Handicap	13	5	17	7	3	9	1	11	15			Slope 122

Hole	10	11	12	13	14	15	16	17	18	In		Totals
BLUE											BLUE	
WHITE	497	344	330	150	419	344	272	149	484	2989	WHITE	6120
Par	5	4	4	3	4	4	4	3	5	36	Par	72
Handicap	8	6	12	16	2	4	18	14	10			
RED	490	334	326	145	409	336	248	144	446	2878	RED	5640
Par	5	4	4	3	5	4	4	3	5	37	Par	73
Handicap	2	8	14	18	6	10	12	16	4			

Manager: Grassella Oliphant   **Supt:** Jeff Krause
Built: Tom Bendelow 1926

ECHO LAKE COUNTRY CLUB

PRIVATE

Springfield Ave., Westfield, NJ 07091   **(908) 232-4288**
www.echolakecc.org

Echo Lake is an 18 hole course open all year 6 days a week. Guests play accompanied by a member. Tee time reservations are not necessary.

- •Driving Range
- •Practice Green
- •Power Carts
- •Pull Carts
- •Club Rental
- •Caddies
- •Lockers
- •Showers
- •Food
- •Clubhouse
- •Outings
- •Soft Spikes

Course Description: Echo Lake is an interesting Donald Ross layout with some hills which result in uneven lies. Many of the greens are small and there are numerous bunkers. The signature par 3 seventh requires a shot over a pond. The 6th and 14th holes have water in play. From the first tee, the scenic view of the Empire State Building is quite dramatic. The club hosted the 1994 US Junior Amateur Championship and the Jr. Girls Amateur Championship in 2002.

Directions: Union County, #8 on East Central Map
GSP North or South to Exit 138 (Kenilworth Blvd.) Turn left onto Kenilworth which becomes Springfield Ave., Go approx. 4 miles to club on left.

Hole	1	2	3	4	5	6	7	8	9	Out	BLUE	Rating 73.0
BLUE	401	247	363	493	365	383	147	418	393	3210		Slope 132
WHITE	391	241	357	489	353	378	138	367	384	3098		
Par	4	4	4	5	4	4	3	4	4	36	WHITE	Rating 71.6
Handicap	10	18	14	2	4	8	16	6	12			Slope 130
RED	365	176	310	483	262	330	126	326	382	2760		
Par	4	4	4	5	4	4	3	4	5	37	RED	Rating 72.8
Handicap	15	5	13	1	7	3	17	11	9			Slope 132
Hole	10	11	12	13	14	15	16	17	18	In		Totals
BLUE	410	546	526	437	214	448	406	170	417	3596	BLUE	6846
WHITE	386	536	521	417	209	433	380	156	398	3436	WHITE	6534
Par	4	5	5	4	3	4	4	3	4	36	Par	72
Handicap	7	1	3	11	15	5	9	17	13			
RED	369	421	422	258	145	428	327	142	279	2791	RED	5551
Par	4	5	5	4	3	5	4	3	4	37	Par	74
Handicap	8	6	2	14	16	4	10	18	12			

Manager: John Gomez   **Pro:** Mike Preston, PGA   **Supt:** Chris Carson
Architect: Donald Ross 1913

ESSEX COUNTY COUNTRY CLUB PRIVATE

350 Mt. Pleasant Ave., West Orange, NJ 07052   **(973) 731-9764**
www.essexcountycc.com

Essex County is an 18 hole course open six days a week all year. Guests may play accompanied by a member. Tee times can be reserved up to one week in advance for weekends and holidays.

• Driving Range	• Lockers
• Practice Green	• Showers
• Power Carts	• Food
Pull Carts	• Clubhouse
• Club Rental	• Outings
• Caddies	• Soft Spikes

Course Description: Essex County CC was established in 1887 on a location which later became a residential community. On subsequently acquired property, Tillinghast and Raynor began developing the new club. Charles Banks was contracted to complete the task and imposed his inimitable style with many steep, deep bunkers and large rolling slick greens The club, which is built on a mountain, is characterized by quite hilly terrain and sprawling fairways. Recently, many trees were removed and wider vistas were acquired. From an elevated tee on the par 3 11th, the golfer needs an accurate shot over a ravine. The beautiful 12th is back over the same ravine. The 18th is a long challenging (455 yds. from the blue) uphill par 4.

Directions: Essex County, #9 on East Central Map
GSP or NJTpke. to Rte. 280West to Exit 8A (Prospect Ave.) At 3rd light, go right onto Mt. Pleasant Ave. Entrance is 300 yards ahead on the left.

Hole	1	2	3	4	5	6	7	8	9	Out	BLUE	Rating 71.8
BLUE	383	298	375	420	460	176	614	524	165	3415		Slope 131
WHITE	377	292	365	414	450	170	560	475	146	3249		
Par	4	4	4	4	4	3	5	5	3	36	WHITE	Rating 69.9
Handicap	11	17	7	5	1	13	3	9	15			Slope 120
RED	320	246	326	360	410	141	452	421	92	2770		
Par	4	4	4	4	5	3	5	5	3	37	RED	Rating 74.3
Handicap	12	14	10	4	8	16	2	6	18			Slope 135

Hole	10	11	12	13	14	15	16	17	18	In		Totals
BLUE	445	192	440	548	336	220	439	390	455	3465	BLUE	6605
WHITE	440	180	405	508	310	203	424	380	440	3290	WHITE	6302
Par	4	3	4	5	4	3	4	4	4	35	Par	71
Handicap	8	12	2	14	18	16	4	10	6			
RED	425	173	379	478	284	166	349	314	367	2935	RED	5714
Par	5	3	4	5	4	3	4	4	4	36	Par	73
Handicap	7	9	1	3	15	17	11	13	5			

Pro: Steve Wilson, PGA   **Supt:** Jason Thompson
Architects: A.W. Tillinghast, Seth Raynor, Charles Banks 1918 **Estab:** 1887

ESSEX FELLS COUNTRY CLUB PRIVATE

219 Devon Rd., Essex Fells, NJ 07021   **(973) 226-5800**
www.essexfellscc.com

Essex Fells is an 18 hole course open 6 days a week all year. Guests play accompanied by a member. Tee time reservations are required for play on Sundays.

•**Driving Range**	•**Lockers**
•**Practice Green**	•**Showers**
•**Power Carts**	•**Food**
Pull Carts	•**Clubhouse**
•**Club Rental**	•**Outings**
•**Caddies**	•**Soft Spikes**

Course Description: Essex Fells is a magnificent, long, and hilly layout with spectacular panoramic views and flowers in abundance. The small, fast greens are mostly elevated with bunkers guarding the front and back of the target areas. Correct club selection is a must for the approach shot. Water is in play on seven holes. The signature #10 is a challenging par 3. The brook on the par 4 fifteenth adds to the course's difficulty. The NJ State Open was held here in 1996.

Directions: Essex County, #10 on East Central Map
From GSP or NJTpke. take Rte. 280West to Laurel Ave Exit 6A. Proceed north on Laurel Ave.and left onto Eagle Rock Ave. Bear right onto Old Eagle Rock. Turn right into Devon Rd. Club is ahead on right.

Hole	1	2	3	4	5	6	7	8	9	Out	BLUE	Rating 71.6
BLUE	452	320	178	396	544	183	357	463	356	3249		Slope 131
WHITE	446	311	149	388	531	168	340	450	308	3091		
Par	4	4	3	4	5	3	4	4	4	35	WHITE	Rating 70.2
Handicap	3	13	17	5	7	15	9	1	11			Slope 128
RED	431	264	119	334	488	149	294	440	269	2788		
Par	5	4	3	4	5	3	4	5	4	37	RED	Rating 72.7
Handicap	7	1	9	6	2	5	8	4	3			Slope 137

Hole	10	11	12	13	14	15	16	17	18	In		Totals
BLUE	208	502	185	385	411	453	439	366	346	3295	BLUE	6544
WHITE	203	491	167	377	404	448	435	340	294	3159	WHITE	6250
Par	3	5	3	4	4	4	4	4	4	35	Par	70
Handicap	12	10	18	8	6	4	2	14	16			
RED	194	476	150	368	401	438	429	302	281	3039	RED	5827
Par	3	5	3	4	5	5	5	4	4	38	Par	75
Handicap	16	2	18	10	8	6	4	12	14			

Manager: Bill Clinton   **Pro:** Russell Helwig, PGA   **Supt:** Richard La Flamme
Estab: 1896   **Architect:** Donald Ross 1918

FOREST HILL FIELD CLUB

9 Belleville Ave., Bloomfield, NJ 07003   (973) 743-9611

Forest Hill is an 18 hole course open 6 days a week and closes for Jan. & Feb. Guests play accompanied by a member. Tee time reservations are not necessary.

- •Driving Range
- •Practice Green
- •Power Carts
- Pull Carts
- •Club Rental
- •Caddies
- •Lockers
- •Showers
- •Food
- •Clubhouse
- •Outings
- •Soft Spikes

Course Description: Mostly narrow fairways, uneven lies and elevated small greens characterize this densely treed challenging course. The par 4 signature #7 is very long and uphill. The shot on the downhill par 3 eighth is to a small well bunkered green, difficult to read, typical of Forest Hill. On the par 4 11th the fairway is three tiered and all uphill. It has an extremely fast bunkered green that requires a delicate touch. The uphill par 3 18th needs an accurate shot to carry over the bunker in front and to avoid another on the side. The course is maintained meticulously.

Directions: Essex County, #12 on East Central Map
GSP to Exit 149. At exit, turn right to traffic light. Then right onto Belleville Ave. Watch carefully for entrance road to club on left at light.

Hole	1	2	3	4	5	6	7	8	9	Out	BLUE	Rating 72.0
BLUE	363	383	518	502	163	374	416	216	399	3337		Slope 129
WHITE	362	368	501	489	147	364	400	209	377	3217		
Par	4	4	5	5	3	4	4	3	4	36	WHITE	Rating 71.0
Handicap	13	7	3	11	17	9	1	15	5			Slope 127
RED	322	317	392	439	125	341	375	187	353	2851		
Par	4	4	5	5	3	4	4	3	4	36	RED	Rating 74.0
Handicap	11	13	5	3	17	9	1	15	7			Slope 131
Hole	10	11	12	13	14	15	16	17	18	In		Totals
BLUE	366	396	303	439	475	362	171	441	200	3153	BLUE	6503
WHITE	361	389	297	434	459	353	161	430	168	3052	WHITE	6274
Par	4	4	4	4	5	4	3	4	3	35	Par	71
Handicap	10	2	16	4	8	18	18	6	14			
RED	340	386	276	400	436	345	148	383	153	2867	RED	5737
Par	4	5	4	4	5	4	3	5	3	37	Par	73
Handicap	12	6	14	4	2	10	18	8	16			

Manager: William Kelly   **Pro:** Charlie Cowell, PGA   **Supt:** Jeff Drake
Estab: 1896 **Architect:** A.W. Tillinghast 1926

FRANCIS BYRNE GOLF COURSE `PUBLIC`

1100 Pleasant Valley Way, West Orange, NJ 07052   **(973) 736-2306**
www.francisbyrne.com

Francis A. Byrne is an 18 hole course, part of the Essex County Dept. of Parks. It is open 7 days a week and closes Jan. & Feb. County residents may purchase an ID. Non ID holders may not make advance tee times, walk-ons only.

Driving Range	Lockers
•**Practice Green**	•**Showers**
•**Power Carts**	•**Food**
•**Pull Carts**	•**Clubhouse**
Club Rental	•**Outings**
•**Soft Spikes**	

Fees	Weekday	Weekend
Res/ID	$14.50	$18
Sr/Jr(res)	$10	$10
NJnon-res.	$29	$36
Jr/Sr(non res) $20		
Power Carts $13pp		

Course Description: Francis Byrne golf course has an interesting history. It was originally the West layout and second 18 of Essex County CC. Purchased by the county for its citizens and the general public, it is lengthy with gently rolling terrain. There are no flat lies here and shot selecttion can be diffi cult for the average golfer. The par 4 15th signature hole is a long sharp dogleg left measuring 442 from the Blues & Whites as well. The 16th, 17th and 18th have a meandering stream in play. This golf facility gets very crowded; it handles about 55,000 rounds annually.

Directions: Essex County, #13 on East Central Map
GSP or NJTpke to Rte. 280 West. Exit at #7 (Pleasant Valley Way). Go south for 1/4 mile. Course is on the left.

Hole	1	2	3	4	5	6	7	8	9	Out	BLUE	Rating 72.0
BLUE	465	230	400	405	140	417	395	385	435	3262		Slope 129
WHITE	456	211	390	365	129	407	360	352	435	3105		
Par	5	3	4	4	3	4	4	4	4	35	WHITE	Rating 71.0
Handicap	16	4	8	6	18	10	12	14	2			Slope 126
RED	427	184	340	210	118	347	246	340	420	2632		
Par	5	3	4	4	3	4	4	4	5	36	RED	Rating 71.0
Handicap	2	6	4	14	16	8	18	12	10			Slope 121
Hole	10	11	12	13	14	15	16	17	18	In		Totals
BLUE	381	405	430	395	160	442	428	360	390	3391	BLUE	6653
WHITE	363	388	430	365	130	442	418	330	367	3233	WHITE	6663
Par	4	4	4	4	3	4	4	4	4	35	Par	70
Handicap	7	9	1	13	17	3	5	15	11			
RED	310	347	350	345	110	346	377	220	347	2752	RED	5384
Par	4	4	4	4	3	4	5	4	4	36	Par	72
Handicap	7	9	1	11	17	3	5	15	13			

Manager: Larry Pallante   **Supt:** Joe Ciccone
Architect: Charles Banks 1920

GALLOPING HILL GOLF COURSE | PUBLIC

Galloping Hill Rd., Union, NJ 07083
www.unioncounty.com

(908) 686-1556

Galloping Hill is a 27 hole Union County facility open 7 days a week all year. Residents purchase IDs and may reserve tee times. Non res. may walk on. A pitch & putt course is on the premises.

Driving Range	
• **Practice Green**	• **Lockers**
• **Power Carts**	• **Showers**
• **Pull Carts**	• **Food**
• **Club Rental**	• **Clubhouse**
• **Soft Spikes**	• **Outings**

Fees	Weekday	Weekend
Res/ID	$22	$24
Sr/Jr(w/ID)	$14	$22
Non-res	$44	$48
Power carts	$26/18	$16/9

Course Description: This very busy, wide open county course is hilly with virtually no flat lies, hence the name. The golfer encounters a variety of uphill and downhill terrain. The well kept undulating greens can be tricky and very hard to read with the more difficult pin placements. A major refurbishment to restore its classic design has been in progress for several years including improved drainage, upgraded cart paths, tees and greens. A new clubhouse is being built as well. An area is available for practice using your own golf balls.

Directions: Union County, #14 on East Central Map
GSP to Exit #138. At light, take jughandle for the U-turn; course is immediately on the west side of the parkway.

Hole	1	2	3	4	5	6	7	8	9	Out	BLUE	Rating 68.5
BLUE	343	338	451	374	146	553	358	224	543	3330		Slope 115
WHITE	336	324	413	339	120	457	326	211	506	3032		
Par	4	4	4	4	3	5	4	3	5	36	WHITE	Rating 65.9
Handicap	15	9	1	7	17	3	13	5	11			Slope 110
RED	312	304	366	293	94	411	318	189	340	2691		
Par	4	4	4	4	3	5	4	3	5	36	RED	Rating 69.4
Handicap	15	9	1	7	17	3	13	5	11			Slope 116
Hole	10	11	12	13	14	15	16	17	18	In		Totals
BLUE	412	186	420	397	406	183	367	378	370	3119	BLUE	6449
WHITE	387	159	376	371	367	166	340	354	342	2862	WHITE	5894
Par	4	3	4	4	4	3	4	4	4	34	Par	70
Handicap	12	16	2	10	4	18	6	14	8			
RED	276	121	265	305	342	152	333	214	286	2294	RED	4985
Par	4	3	4	4	4	3	4	4	4	36	Par	70
Handicap	12	16	2	10	4	18	6	14	9			

Manager: John Richardson   **Pro:** Dominick Micelli, PGA   **Supt:** John Cyran
Architect: Willard Wilkinson 1927   **Redo:** Robert Trent Jones

GLEN RIDGE COUNTRY CLUB

555 Ridgewood Ave., Glen Ridge, NJ 07028   **(973) 744-7803**

Glen Ridge is an 18 hole course open 6 days a week all year. Guests play accompanied by a member. Tee time reservations are not necessary.

•**Driving Range**	•**Lockers**
•**Practice Green**	•**Showers**
•**Power Carts**	•**Food**
Pull Carts	•**Clubhouse**
Club Rental	•**Outings**
•**Caddies**	•**Soft Spikes**

Course Description: Glen Ridge was established in 1894 making it one of the oldest clubs in New Jersey. It was redesigned by A. W. Tillinghast and Robert Trent Jones and it is said to be the "longest 6000 yards you'll ever play." The small, contoured greens have sizeable bunkers guarding them, notably the one on the par 4, 329 yard opening hole. A stone-walled brook must be crossed for the approach shot on four different holes; ponds come into play on several other locations. The uphill, long par 4 18th challenges the golfer with a blind second shot.

Directions: Essex County, #15 on East Central Map
GSP to Exit 151 (Watchung Ave.) Go west on Watchung past Broad St. to Ridgewood Ave. and turn left; club is on the left.

Hole	1	2	3	4	5	6	7	8	9	Out	BLUE	Rating 69.0
BLUE	342	138	519	140	384	474	374	172	364	2907		Slope 130
WHITE	329	132	512	129	377	462	372	152	355	2820		
Par	4	3	5	3	4	5	4	3	4	35	WHITE	Rating 68.8
Handicap	11	17	1	15	3	9	7	13	5			Slope 129
RED	317	128	496	120	359	455	371	134	340	2720		
Par	4	3	5	3	4	5	4	3	4	35	RED	Rating 73.7
Handicap	11	17	1	15	3	7	5	13	9			Slope 132
Hole	10	11	12	13	14	15	16	17	18	In		Totals
BLUE	394	192	488	334	342	330	484	154	405	3123	BLUE	6054
WHITE	384	187	479	321	333	317	477	136	402	3036	WHITE	5892
Par	4	3	5	4	4	4	5	3	4	36	Par	71
Handicap	8	14	2	12	10	16	6	18	4			
RED	379	185	476	320	328	305	474	113	400	2980	RED	5541
Par	4	3	5	4	4	4	5	3	5	37	Par	72
Handicap	10	12	2	16	8	14	6	18	4			

Manager: Cyrus Reitmeyer   **Pro:** Bill Adams, PGA   **Supt:** Mike Vacchiano
Architects: Willie Park, Jr. 1894   **Redesign:** A.W. Tillinghast & Robert Trent Jones

GREEN BROOK COUNTRY CLUB `PRIVATE`

100 W. Green Brook Rd., North Caldwell, NJ 07006   **(973) 226-2406**

Green Brook is an 18 hole course open 6 days a week and closed in February. Guests play accompanied by a member. Tee time reservations are necessary for Fridays and weekends. Caddies are available.

•**Driving Range**	•**Lockers**
•**Practice Green**	•**Showers**
•**Power Carts**	•**Food**
Pull Carts	•**Clubhouse**
•**Club Rental**	•**Outings**
•**Caddies**	•**Soft Spikes**

Course Description: Green Brook is a beautifully maintained course, hilly and tight on the front nine and flatter on the back. The difficult greens add to its character. The par 5 3rd has a spectacular view of western New Jersey from the fairway. The elevated tee of the par 3 5th is the highest point in Essex County. Over the past few years, improvements have been made on the tee boxes, bunkers and greens. Cartpaths are installed throughout. The course is in excellent condition.

Directions: Essex County, #16 on East Central Map
Rte. 80W to Exit 52. Bear right onto Passaic Ave. South. Proceed 1 & 1/2 miles to 6th light, Green Brook Rd. Turn left and club is 1/4mile ahead on the right.

Hole	1	2	3	4	5	6	7	8	9	Out	BLUE	Rating 72.8
BLUE	408	434	513	270	179	380	367	211	390	3152		Slope 133
WHITE	390	423	508	261	170	368	355	204	385	3064		
Par	4	4	5	4	3	4	4	3	4	35	WHITE	Rating 72.4
Handicap	7	3	1	15	17	2	13	11	5			Slope 131
RED	401	379	451	238	152	315	348	175	345	2822		
Par	5	4	5	4	3	4	4	3	4	36	RED	Rating 73.2
Handicap	15	5	1	9	17	11	7	13	3			Slope 128
Hole	10	11	12	13	14	15	16	17	18	In		Totals
BLUE	420	412	441	454	178	528	395	167	401	3396	BLUE	6618
WHITE	399	378	421	440	162	516	385	160	381	3242	WHITE	6353
Par	4	4	4	5	3	5	4	3	4	36	Par	71
Handicap	4	10	2	12	16	6	8	18	14			
RED	401	348	418	420	144	467	324	137	311	2970	RED	5646
Par	5	4	5	5	3	5	4	3	4	38	Par	74
Handicap	14	8	10	4	12	2	6	18	16			

Manager: Michael Frodella   **Pro:** George Sauer, PGA   **Supt:** Patrick Hickey
Architect: Robert White 1923 Hal Purdy

HENDRICKS FIELD GOLF CLUB ■ PUBLIC

Franklin Ave., Belleville, NJ 07109   **(973) 751-0178**

Hendricks Field is an 18 hole Essex County course. It is open 7 days a week all year. County residents purchase an ID and may make tee time reservations through an automated system $2 pp. Non residents $4pp to reserve.

Driving Range	
• **Practice Green**	• **Lockers**
• **Power Carts**	• **Showers**
• **Pull Carts**	• **Food**
• **Club Rental**	• **Clubhouse**
• **Soft Spikes**	• **Outings**

Fees	Weekday	Weekend
Res/ID	$14.50	$18
Sr/Jr Res	$10	$10
NJNon-res	$29	$36
Power cart $13pp		

Course Description: Hendricks Field is wide open with tree lined fairways. It is generally level and thus conducive to walking. No water is in play and few hazards are encountered. Golfers can score well here making it a very popular and busy course in the heart of Essex County. The 400 yard par 4 5th is a difficult dogleg left. The ninth, also a long par 4, is downhill; both give the golfer a challenge.

Directions: Essex County, #17 on East Central Map
GSPSouth to Exit #150 (Hoover Ave.) Turn right at Jeroloman. Make a right onto Franklin Ave; course is ahead on the left. From South, GSP Exit#149 and go right off ramp onto Belleville Ave. At third light make a left onto Franklin Ave. to course.

Hole	1	2	3	4	5	6	7	8	9	Out	BLUE	Rating 69.4
BLUE	386	382	406	372	400	152	437	472	445	3452		Slope 116
WHITE	378	370	402	359	393	140	432	450	406	3330		
Par	4	4	4	4	4	3	4	5	4	36	WHITE	Rating 68.4
Handicap	11	9	3	15	7	13	1	17	5			Slope 114
RED	338	254	398	292	290	132	353	410	366	2833		
Par	4	4	4	4	4	3	4	5	4	36	RED	Rating 68.4
Handicap	11	9	1	15	13	17	5	7	3			Slope 114
Hole	10	11	12	13	14	15	16	17	18	In		Totals
BLUE	475	120	367	295	170	358	377	240	369	2771	BLUE	6223
WHITE	469	112	361	285	161	348	370	222	360	2688	WHITE	6018
Par	5	3	4	3	3	4	4	4	4	34	Par	70
Handicap	10	16	6	12	8	14	4	18	2			
RED	393	103	355	120	153	277	363	213	350	2327	RED	5160
Par	4	3	4	3	3	4	4	4	4	33	Par	69
Handicap	2	18	8	16	14	10	4	12	6			

Manager: Gerard Perilla   **Supt:** Joe Ciccone
Architect: Charles Banks 1929

HYATT HILLS GOLF COURSE

PUBLIC

1300 Raritan Rd., Clark, NJ 07066   **732-669-9100**

www.hyatthills.com

Hyatt Hills is 9 hole course open to the public 7 days a week. Clark/Cranford resident members have reduced fees and preferred tee times. Sr. & Jr rates available. A miniature golf course is on the premises.

• **Driving Range**	• **Lockers**
• **Practice Green**	• **Showers**
• **Power Carts**	• **Food**
• **Pull Carts**	• **Clubhouse**
• **Club Rental**	• **Outings**

Fees	Weekday	Weekend
ResID	$16(9)/25(18)	$30
NJRes	$20/$30	$40
Non NJ	$30/$50	$100
Power Carts $15(9)		$26(18)

Course Description: The Hyatt Hills Golf Complex was formerly an industrial site. After considerable preparation work, the property has become a regulation nine hole course in excellent condition with a driving range, a miniature golf course and a full service clubhouse. Beautifully contoured with bent grass greens, tees and fairways, paved cartpaths throughout, clusters of trees and a 5.4 acre pond, Hyatt Hills has become popular quickly. This 3,216 yard layout, has 2 par fives, 3 par fours and 4 par threes. Holes seven & eight have scenic water in play; the signature 7th, has a green surrounded by a pond. This lovely layout is a remarkable example of imagination and transformation. Hyatt Hills is challenging and definitely worth playing.

Directions: Union County, #18 on East Central Map

GSP to Exit 135. Go right onto Central Ave. At 1st light, go right onto Raritan Rd. Course is on the left immediately over the RR tracks.

Hole	1	2	3	4	5	6	7	8	9	Out	BLUE	Rating 70.4
BLUE	324	500	157	511	331	364	187	444	402	3220		Slope 129
WHITE	298	483	121	476	307	338	140	418	362	2943		
Par	4	5	3	5	4	4	3	4	4	36	WHITE	Rating 68.4
Handicap	15	5	17	3	13	11	7	1	9			Slope 129
RED	280	403	78	426	271	279	115	334	306	2492		
Par	4	5	3	5	4	4	3	4	4	36	RED	Rating 68.8
Handicap	15	1	17	3	13	7	11	9	5			Slope 119

Hole	10	11	12	13	14	15	16	17	18	In		Totals
BLUE	324	500	157	511	331	364	187	444	402	3220	BLUE	6440
WHITE	298	483	121	476	307	338	140	418	362	2943	WHITE	5886
Par	4	5	3	5	4	4	3	4	4	36	Par	72
Handicap	16	6	18	4	14	12	8	2	10			
RED	280	403	78	426	271	279	115	334	306	2492	RED	4984
Par	4	5	3	5	4	4	3	4	4	36	Par	72
Handicap	16	2	18	4	14	8	12	10	6			

Manager & Pro: Dan Hollis, PGA   **Supt:** Joe Flaherty
Architect: Brian Ault 2002

LIBERTY NATIONAL GOLF CLUB PRIVATE

23 Chapel Ave. Jersey City, NJ   (201) 333-0531
www.libertyGolf.shtml

Liberty National Golf Club scheduled to open in 2006. It will be a private 18 hole course open 6 days a week all year. Memberships are by invitation only. Guests play accompanied by a member. Tee time reservations will not be necessary.

- **Driving Range**   • **Lockers**
- **Practice Green**   • **Showers**
- **Power Carts**   • **Food**
-   Pull Carts   • **Clubhouse**
- **Club Rental**   • **Outings**
- **Caddies**   • **Soft Spikes**

Course Description: Liberty National Golf Club is on the western shore of NYBay. It will be accessible by a 12 minute launch ride from Manhattan featuring an on board concierge. The club will encompass a championship layout (7,400 yards, par 70) by the acclaimed team of Tom Kite and Bob Cupp. Directly across from The Statue of Liberty, the views will be spectacular. With a double-ended grass tee practice range, indoor/outdoor video teaching studio and a dramatic 50,000 square foot clubhouse, this promises to be an ultimate experience in golf. Also planned are three high rise luxury condominium towers called the Residences next to the golf course. The rare convergence of the finest golf, luxury and location puts this course in a class of its own. Scorecard not available at press time.

Directions: Hudson County, #11 on East Central Map
NJTPK to Exit #14B (Liberty Park). Go left toward Liberty State Park; then make a right on Caven Pt. Rd; follow to Chapel Ave. and go left on Chapel to Port Liberte.

Architects: Tom Kite & Bob Cupp 2005

MAPLEWOOD COUNTRY CLUB **PRIVATE**

28 Baker St., Maplewood, NJ 07040   **(973) 762-0215**

Maplewood is an 18 hole course open 6 days a week and closed in January & February. Guests play accompanied by a member. Tee time reservations are required for weekends.

•**Driving Range**	•**Lockers**
•**Practice Green**	•**Showers**
•**Power Carts**	•**Food**
Pull Carts	•**Clubhouse**
•**Club Rental**	•**Outings**
•**Caddies**	•**Soft Spikes**

Course Description: Maplewood is a relatively short, very tree-lined course. The small greens are difficult; the golfer must hit straight in order to score well. Water is in play on holes 4, 9, 11, 12 and 18 in the form of a creek meandering through them. Renovations, have included work on bunkers, tee boxes and fairway mounding, and more recently, the driving range has been improved. Maplewood is considered the birthplace of the golf tee. In the 1920s, member Dr. William Lowell, a dentist, was dissatisfied with the tradition of forming a tee by pinching a mound of dirt. He carved out a peg with a rounded cup on top for use on the tee. Some time later, he had the idea patented as the "Reddy Tee".

Directions: Essex County, #19 on East Central Map
GSP or NJTPke to Rte. 78W. Stay on local lanes (Rte24W)to Exit 50B onto Vauxhall Rd. Rt. on Valley St. (light) Turn left onto Baker St. (3rd light) to club entrance on left.

Hole	1	2	3	4	5	6	7	8	9	Out	BLUE	Rating 71.5
BLUE	502	369	324	312	333	393	325	185	406	3149		Slope 131
WHITE	489	361	317	289	320	375	291	168	392	3004		
Par	5	4	4	4	4	4	4	3	4	36	WHITE	Rating 70.4
Handicap	5	9	11	17	15	3	7	13	1			Slope 129
RED	475	333	287	216	292	339	275	148	363	2728		
Par	5	4	4	4	4	4	4	3	5	37	RED	Rating 72.9
Handicap	1	5	9	11	15	3	7	17	13			Slope 130

Hole	10	11	12	13	14	15	16	17	18	In		Totals
BLUE	153	379	334	394	394	509	383	418	149	3113	BLUE	6262
WHITE	140	371	322	383	386	496	376	405	140	3019	WHITE	6023
Par	3	4	4	4	4	5	4	4	3	35	Par	71
Handicap	16	10	14	6	4	8	12	2	18			
RED	127	353	239	330	324	413	338	372	95	2591	RED	5319
Par	3	4	4	4	4	5	4	5	3	36	Par	73
Handicap	16	4	14	6	8	2	12	10	18			

Manager: Michael Lusk   **Pro:** Mickie Gallagher, 3rd, PGA   **Supt:** Josh Kopera
Built: 1911

MILLBURN GOLF COURSE

PUBLIC

White Oak Ridge Rd., Short Hills, NJ 07078   **(973) 379-4156**

Millburn is a 9 hole municipal par 3 course run by the Dept. of Recreation and open 7 days a week from Apr. 1 to Nov. 1. Memberships are available for residents of Millburn and its surrounding communities. Reserved tee times are not necessary.

Driving Range
- **Practice Green**
Power Carts
- **Pull Carts**
- **Club Rental**
- **Soft Spikes**

Lockers
Showers
Food
Clubhouse
- **Outings**

Fees	Weekday	Weekend
Daily	$2.75	$4
Guests	$5.25	$8
Indiv. mbrship $60		

Course Description: Considered to be one of the best par 3 layouts, Millburn gives its residents a good place to practice and play on an interesting Hal Purdy designed short course. There are wooded areas here with an abundance of ditches along the sides and across the fairways adding to the variety and difficulty. The greens are in excellent shape.

Directions: Essex County, #20 on East Central Map
GSP or NJTpke to Rte. 78 West. Take Rte.24 West and exit at Hobart Gap Rd. Bear left onto White Oak Ridge. Entrance to course is through Gero Park Recreational Center for Millburn Township. The sign says "Pool and Golf."

Hole	1	2	3	4	5	6	7	8	9	Out	BLUE	Rating
BLUE												Slope
WHITE	90	125	125	110	150	175	175	125	110	1185		
Par	3	3	3	3	3	3	3	3	3	27	WHITE	Rating
Handicap												Slope
RED												
Par											RED	Rating
Handicap												Slope

Hole	10	11	12	13	14	15	16	17	18	In		Totals
BLUE											BLUE	
WHITE											WHITE	1185
Par											Par	27
Handicap												
RED											RED	
Par											Par	
Handicap												

Director of Recreation: Bob Hogan   **Supt:** Mike Paterno
Architect: Hal Purdy 1970s

MONTCLAIR GOLF CLUB

25 Prospect Ave., West Orange, NJ 07052   **(973) 239-0160**

Montclair is a golf club with 4 separate nines that can be played in various combinations. It is open 6 days a week all year. Guests play accompanied by a member. Reserved tee times are not necessary. The scorecard below is for the first and second nines.

•**Driving Range**	•**Lockers**
•**Practice Green**	•**Showers**
•**Power Carts**	•**Food**
Pull Carts	•**Clubhouse**
•**Club Rental**	•**Outings**
•**Caddies**	•**Soft Spikes**

Course Description: Montclair celebrated its 100th anniversary in 1993. These courses, built by Donald Ross and Charles Banks, have elevation changes up to 500 feet. Each nine starts on a hill and plays into a valley where creeks meander. Grassy hollows with lush greens can be found here. The demanding 454 yard 2nd hole on the 4th nine requires a long approach shot to an elevated green and provides the ultimate in shot-making opportunities. Montclair has beautiful, well-manicured, lightning fast multi-tiered greens and great views. It is not unusual to three putt here. This golf club hosted the 1973 Ladies Amateur and the 1985 Men's Amateur. Caddies are required; players over 55 may ride.

Directions: Essex County, #21 on East Central Map
GSP to Exit #145 or NJTpke to Rte. 280 West. Take Exit 8B (Cedar Grove-Prospect Ave.) Follow Prospect for 1 mile; club is on the left.

Hole	1	2	3	4	5	6	7	8	9	Out	BLUE	Rating 72.2
BLUE	387	386	410	420	181	557	326	160	416	3243		Slope 131
WHITE	361	365	397	411	174	529	315	130	396	3078		
Par	4	4	4	4	3	5	4	3	4	35	WHITE	Rating 71.0
Handicap	9	6	4	1	5	2	7	8	3			Slope 129
RED	340	352	357	402	167	444	304	123	371	2860		
Par	4	4	4	5	3	5	4	3	5	37	RED	Rating 75.1
Handicap	8	6	4	1	7	2	5	8	3			Slope 130
Hole	10	11	12	13	14	15	16	17	18	In		Totals
BLUE	570	163	460	360	207	443	353	324	396	3276	BLUE	6519
WHITE	567	154	440	354	200	387	346	315	383	3146	WHITE	6224
Par	5	3	4	4	3	4	4	4	4	35	Par	70
Handicap	2	9	1	6	8	4	5	7	3			
RED	511	143	405	347	155	367	283	306	368	2885	RED	5700
Par	5	3	5	4	3	4	4	4	5	37	Par	74
Handicap	1	8	2	4	9	6	7	5	3			

Manager: Christian Potthoff   **Pro:** Mike Strlekar, PGA   **Supt:** Gregg Vadala
Architects: Donald Ross, Charles Banks 1893

MOUNTAIN RIDGE CC

713 Passaic Ave., West Caldwell, NJ 07006   **(973) 575-0734**
www.mountainridgecc.org

Mountain Ridge is an 18 hole course open 6 days a week from March through December. Guests play accompanied by a member. Tee time reservations are necessary for weekends. Outings must be member sponsored only.

•**Driving Range**	•**Lockers**
•**Practice Green**	•**Showers**
•**Power Carts**	•**Food**
Pull Carts	•**Clubhouse**
•**Club Rental**	•**Outings**
•**Caddies**	•**Soft Spikes**

Course Description: Mountain Ridge is a traditional meticulously maintained Donald Ross layout with wide fairways, old trees and difficult undulating greens. The course is well watered and plays long. It is nearly 6000 yards from the forward tees with seven par 5s! The par 3 16th requires accuracy in the carry over water to avoid the many bunkers around the green. The long beautiful 8th always seems to have the wind against you. The uphill 18th needs careful placement; the golfer should bear left, but not so much as to go OB. Landing to the right will cause the approach shot to be blocked by a tree. The severely back to front sloped green makes the smart golfer go for a spot below the hole. All new tees boxes have been installed.

Directions: Essex County, #22 on East Central Map
Rte. 80 to Exit 52. Make a right turn onto Passaic Ave.South and go about 3 miles. Club is ahead on the right.

Hole	1	2	3	4	5	6	7	8	9	Out	BLUE	Rating 72.8
BLUE	414	435	338	213	410	498	161	476	491	3436		Slope 137
WHITE	408	425	324	205	395	480	150	463	473	3323		
Par	4	4	4	3	4	5	3	4	5	36	WHITE	Rating 71.7
Handicap	9	3	15	11	5	13	18	1	7			Slope 134
RED	402	416	271	187	326	437	131	442	457	3069		
Par	4	5	4	3	4	5	3	5	5	38	RED	Rating 75.1
Handicap	7	9	15	13	11	3	17	5	1			Slope 138
Hole	10	11	12	13	14	15	16	17	18	In		Totals
BLUE	412	413	370	454	169	392	157	548	452	3367	BLUE	6674
WHITE	401	401	355	441	160	383	130	535	442	3248	WHITE	6432
Par	4	4	4	4	3	4	3	5	4	35	Par	71
Handicap	12	6	14	2	16	10	18	8	4			
RED	390	343	287	399	152	353	107	455	431	2917	RED	5868
Par	4	4	4	5	3	4	3	5	5	37	Par	75
Handicap	8	12	14	4	16	10	18	2	6			

Manager: Stephen Wolsky   **Pro:** Len Siter, PGA   **Supt:** Cliff Moore
Architect: Donald Ross 1929

OAK RIDGE GOLF COURSE

PUBLIC

136 Oak Ridge Rd., Clark, NJ 07066   **(732) 574-0139**

www.unioncounty.com

Oak Ridge is an 18 hole Union County Park System course open 7 days a week all year. Automated tee times with $2 reservation fee. County residents may purchase an ID. Seniors w/ID from Middlesex & Bergen have reciprocity with Union County weekdays.

Driving Range	Lockers
•Practice Green	Showers
•Power Carts	•Food
•Pull Carts	•Clubhouse
•Club Rental	Outings
•Soft Spikes	

Fees	Weekday	Weekend
Res/ID	$22	$24
Sr/ID	$14	$22
Non-res	$44	$48
Power carts	$26/18	$16/9

Course Description: Oak Ridge is a relatively short course with small, fairly fast undulating greens. The course is well-bunkered and carefully maintained. Recent upgrades have made the fairways more narrow and the rough more challenging. Out of bounds right onto the railroad tracks can cause some difficulty. Some water in the form of streams is in play. Oak Ridge is a forgiving course yet has plenty of challenge.

Directions: Union County, #23 on East Central Map
GSP to Exit 135. Go right to Central Ave. At first light, make a left onto Raritan Rd. Go 3 miles on Raritan which becomes Oak Ridge Rd. to club on right.

Hole	1	2	3	4	5	6	7	8	9	Out	BLUE	Rating 70.7
BLUE	391	480	129	405	410	217	432	400	334	3198		Slope 119
WHITE	378	454	111	382	380	182	422	363	317	2989		
Par	4	5	3	4	4	3	4	4	4	35	WHITE	Rating 68.5
Handicap	10	8	18	4	6	16	1	12	14			Slope 114
RED	330	400	93	317	352	151	383	333	227	2586		
Par	4	5	3	4	4	3	5	4	4	36	RED	Rating 70.3
Handicap	4	4	15	4	13	4	5	5	14			Slope 115

Hole	10	11	12	13	14	15	16	17	18	In		Totals
BLUE	422	340	400	155	432	457	348	213	423	3190	BLUE	6392
WHITE	416	320	394	127	378	450	339	192	396	3012	WHITE	6010
Par	4	4	4	3	4	5	4	3	4	35	Par	70
Handicap	5	13	9	17	7	3	11	15	2			
RED	333	285	362	110	343	407	297	168	370	2675	RED	5273
Par	4	4	4	3	4	5	4	3	5	36	Par	72
Handicap	5	11	9	17	7	1	13	15	3			

Manager: Nick Renna   **Pro:** Bill McCluney, PGA   **Supt:** Cormac Hamilton
Architect: Willard Wilkinson 1928

ROCK SPRING CLUB

Rock Spring Rd., West Orange, NJ 07052 **(973) 731-6466**
baker.pga.proshop.com

Rock Spring is an 18 hole course open all year 6 days a week. Guests play accompanied by a member. Reservations may be necessary on weekends.

- •Driving Range
- •Practice Green
- •Power Carts
- Pull Carts
- •Club Rental
- •Caddies
- •Lockers
- •Showers
- •Food
- •Clubhouse
- •Outings
- •Soft Spikes

Course Description: The builder of this course, Charles "Steamshovel" Banks, is responsible for the deep bunkers, characteristic of this architect's style. With narrow fairways and tricky approach shots, the golfer must deal with formidable challenges. Upon reaching the green of the long par 3 third hole, a magnificent view of the New York City skyline can be seen. Cable Lake comes into play on the first and second holes and adds to the picturesque quality of this interesting layout. The course had a major renovation in 2003.

Directions: Essex County, #24 on East Central Map
GSP NorS to Exit 145 to Rte. 280 West Take Exit 8A (Prospect Ave.S) Follow Prospect to end, turn left onto Northfield Ave.; go 100 ft., turn right onto Rock Spring Rd. to club entrance.

Hole	1	2	3	4	5	6	7	8	9	Out	WHITE	Rating 71.2
WHITE	350	380	193	434	398	521	373	313	408	3370		Slope 127
GREEN	346	384	194	443	396	526	374	318	411	3392		
Par	4	4	3	4	4	5	4	4	4	36	GREEN	Rating 68.4
Handicap	15	3	9	1	7	13	11	17	5			Slope 124
GOLD	327	374	177	435	389	520	345	246	397	3232		
Par	4	4	3	5	4	5	4	4	5	38	GOLD	Rating 65.8
Handicap	7	1	9	6	2	5	8	4	3			Slope 118
Hole	10	11	12	13	14	15	16	17	18	In		Totals
WHITE	136	370	408	471	320	418	177	405	337	3042	WHITE	6412
GREEN	140	377	419	467	311	416	178	410	335	3053	GREEN	6445
Par	3	4	4	5	4	4	3	4	4	35	Par	71
Handicap	18	8	2	14	16	6	10	4	12			
GOLD	139	368	402	449	304	405	150	364	322	2894	GOLD	6126
Par	3	4	5	5	4	5	3	4	4	37	Par	75
Handicap	18	6	8	2	12	10	16	4	14			

Mgr: Brian Craig   **Pro:** Baker Maddera, PGA   **Supt:** Jim McNally
Architect: Charles Banks 1925

ROSELLE GOLF CLUB

417 Raritan Rd., Roselle, NJ 07203   **(908) 245-7175**

Roselle is a 9 hole course open 6 days a week and closed for the month of February. Guests may play accompanied by a member. Tee time reservations are necessary for weekends. Call ext. 12 for the pro shop.

•**Driving Range**	•**Lockers**
•**Practice Green**	•**Showers**
•**Power Carts**	•**Food**
•**Pull Carts**	•**Clubhouse**
Club Rental	•**Outings**
Caddies	•**Soft Spikes**

Course Description: Roselle is a fairly level course in excellent condition. The greens are fast and substantially sloped. A pond and two streams affect play on 3 of the holes. There is a separate set of tees for the second nine. Although a short course, it is interesting and challenging enough to demand the golfer's concentration. The clubhouse and irrigation system were recently updated.

Directions: Union County, #25 on East Central Map
GSPNorth to Exit 136. Make a right at exit and left onto Raritan Rd. Club is ahead on right. **OR** GSPSouth to Exit 136. Turn right and go to jughandle for Raritan Rd and turn left. Club is ahead on the right.

Hole	1	2	3	4	5	6	7	8	9	Out	BLUE	Rating
BLUE												Slope
WHITE	358	549	453	426	342	212	291	138	335	3104		
Par	4	5	5	4	4	3	4	3	4	36	WHITE	Rating 70.5
Handicap	9	3	11	1	7	5	17	15	13			Slope 124
RED	320	436	381	395	330	209	217	120	298	2706		
Par	4	5	5	5	4	4	4	3	4	38	RED	Rating 66.9
Handicap	9	3	1	5	7	15	13	17	11			Slope 113

Hole	10	11	12	13	14	15	16	17	18	In		Totals
BLUE											BLUE	
WHITE	371	530	458	404	355	326	150	124	329	3047	WHITE	6151
Par	4	5	5	4	4	4	3	3	4	36	Par	72
Handicap	6	4	10	2	8	12	16	18	14			
RED	328	435	381	395	259	305	144	111	306	2664	RED	5390
Par	4	5	5	5	4	4	3	3	4	37	Par	75
Handicap	10	4	2	6	14	8	16	18	12			

Manager: Sue Glasser   **Pro:** Vincent Harmon, PGA   **Supt:** Mark Burdine
Architect: Seth Raynor 1917

SCOTCH HILLS COUNTRY CLUB PUBLIC

820 Jerusalem Rd., Scotch Plains, NJ 07076   **(908) 232-9748**
www.scotchhills.com

Scotch Hills is a municipally owned, 9 hole course open to the public 7 days a week
from Mar. 15 to Dec. 15. Memberships are available. Tee time reservations are not
necessary. Greens fee is good all day. Irons may be used on the shag field.

Driving Range	
•**Practice Green**	Lockers
•**Power Carts**	Showers
•**Pull Carts**	Food
•**Club Rental**	Clubhouse
•**Soft Spikes**	Outings

Fees	Weekday	Weekend
Mbrs	$12	$14
Sr.	$10	$14
Non-mbrs	$22	$26
Power carts	$10/9	$20/18

Course Description: Scotch Hills, a short, hilly and tight course, is well groomed and
known for its small well conditioned, fast greens. At one time, it was called Shady Rest
CC and was the first black CC in the country. John Shippen, the pro at Scotch Hills in
the late 19th century, was part black and part Shinnecock Indian. He was the first
American born US Pro and played, after some controversy, in the 1896 US Open at
Shinnecock. Cab Calloway, Louis Armstrong and Count Basie golfed here. It is now a
popular golf course for all players in the area. Ratings and totals are based on 18
holes.

Directions: Union County, #26 on East Central Map
Take GSP to Exit 140A to Rte. 22West. Exit at Mountain Ave. in Scotch Plains (not Mtn.
Ave. in Westfield), crossing over Rte. 22 and right on Mtn. Ave for 3 blocks to Jerusalem
Rd. and turn left. Go to the last driveway on the right to club.

Hole	1	2	3	4	5	6	7	8	9	Out	BLUE	Rating
BLUE												Slope
WHITE	298	324	164	309	230	210	166	358	188	2247		
Par	4	4	3	4	4	4	3	4	3	33	WHITE	Rating 61.2
Handicap	7	3	13	5	9	11	15	1	17			Slope 106
RED	287	278	141	280	212	169	148	239	168	2022		
Par	4	5	3	4	4	4	3	5	3	35	RED	Rating 64.6
Handicap	5	3	13	1	9	11	17	7	15			Slope 110
Hole	10	11	12	13	14	15	16	17	18	In		Totals
BLUE											BLUE	
WHITE											WHITE	4494
Par											Par	66
Handicap												
RED											RED	4044
Par											Par	70
Handicap												

Manager: Chris Monahan   **Supt:** Chuck De Francesco
Built: 1889

SHACKAMAXON GOLF & C C

PRIVATE

Shackamaxon Drive, Scotch Plains, NJ 07076   **(908) 233-3989**
www.shackamaxoncc.com

Shackamaxon is an 18 hole course open 6 days a week all year. Guests play accompanied by a member. Tee time reservations are necessary only on weekends and Wednesdays.

> • **Driving Range**   • **Lockers**
> • **Practice Green** • **Showers**
> • **Power Carts**   • **Food**
>   Pull Carts   • **Clubhouse**
> • **Club Rental**   • **Outings**
> • **Caddies**   • **Soft Spikes**

Course Description: Shackamaxon golf course is an example of the classic Tillinghast design characterized by gently rolling fairways, some tree-lined, and small fast greens. The signature par 4 ninth hole is one of the most intimidating in the metropolitan area due in part to its island green and the lake to carry on the tee shot. Five other holes have water in play. In the 1950s, Shackamaxon hosted a PGA tour event known as the "Cavalcade of Golf."

Directions: Union County, #27 on East Central Map
GSPSouth to Exit 135(Central Ave). Go past light & make left onto Terminal Ave. Turn right on Westfield Ave(Rahway Ave on one side) over RR crossing. Take first left onto Lamberts Mill Rd. Go 2 miles and turn left onto Shackamaxon Dr. Club is one block ahead.

Hole	1	2	3	4	5	6	7	8	9	Out	BLUE	Rating 72.2
BLUE	281	401	330	402	205	364	480	449	393	3305		Slope 133
WHITE	274	389	321	387	191	356	469	437	376	3200		-
Par	4	4	4	4	3	4	5	4	4	36	WHITE	Rating 70.9
Handicap	17	7	13	1	15	11	9	3	5			Slope 130
RED	234	372	312	368	169	344	391	401	299	2890		
Par	4	4	4	4	3	4	5	5	4	37	RED	Rating 71.6
Handicap	17	5	15	1	13	9	3	7	11			Slope 126

Hole	10	11	12	13	14	15	16	17	18	In		Totals
BLUE	552	152	422	533	219	403	457	200	349	3287	BLUE	6658
WHITE	540	140	405	520	204	394	454	189	340	3186	WHITE	6369
Par	5	3	4	5	3	4	5	3	4	36	Par	72
Handicap	2	18	6	4	14	8	10	16	12			
RED	440	126	388	445	190	384	386	179	307	2845	RED	5402
Par	5	3	4	5	3	4	5	3	4	36	Par	72
Handicap	2	18	6	4	14	8	10	12	16			

Manager: Jerome Louie   **Pro:** Peter Busch, PGA   **Supt:** Mark De Noble
Architect: A. W. Tillinghast 1916

SUBURBAN GOLF CLUB

1730 Morris Ave., Union, NJ 07083   **(908) 686-0444**

Suburban is an 18 hole course open 6 days a week all year. Guests play accompanied by a member. Tee time reservations are not necessary.

- **•Driving Range**   **•Lockers**
- **•Practice Green**   **•Showers**
- **•Power Carts**   **•Food**
- Pull Carts   **•Clubhouse**
- **•Club Rental**   **•Outings**
- **•Caddies**   **•Soft Spikes**

Course Description: Suburban is relatively short with narrow tree-lined rolling fairways and small, undulating greens. Uneven lies abound; not much water is in play. The bunkering is characteristic of the traditional Tillinghast architectual style. The recent renovation included improving the bunkers, moving some tee boxes to lengthen the holes and redoing some greens. The overgrown trees were culled so that shots on the fairways are not blocked. Originally designed with six holes, it was later expanded to the full 18. A challenging layout, it is particularly picturesque during the fall foliage season. The NJState Golf Ass. Women's Tournament of Club Champions was held in 2004.

Directions: Union County, #28 on East Central Map
GSPSouth to Exit 140A. Take Rte. 82 East (Morris Ave.) towards Elizabeth and Goethals Bridge by bearing right off exit ramp & turning right. Club is ahead on the right.

Hole	1	2	3	4	5	6	7	8	9	Out	BLUE	Rating 71.3
BLUE	361	385	210	430	472	372	339	341	366	3276		Slope 132
WHITE	348	365	196	416	464	355	312	328	354	3138		
Par	4	4	3	4	5	4	4	4	4	36	WHITE	Rating 69.4
Handicap	13	11	15	1	7	3	17	5	9			Slope 131
RED	330	339	180	324	447	337	291	322	345	2915		
Par	4	4	3	4	5	4	4	4	4	36	RED	Rating 74.1
Handicap	11	13	16	9	1	3	15	5	7			Slope 131
Hole	10	11	12	13	14	15	16	17	18	In		Totals
BLUE	314	167	540	403	393	382	160	388	400	3147	BLUE	6423
WHITE	294	157	515	390	377	365	141	369	377	2985	WHITE	6123
Par	4	3	5	4	4	4	3	4	4	35	Par	71
Handicap	16	14	6	4	2	10	18	12	8			
RED	258	130	488	373	361	348	119	349	360	2786	RED	5701
Par	4	3	5	4	5	4	3	4	4	36	Par	72
Handicap	14	17	2	6	4	10	18	12	8			

Manager: Jill Stabile   **Pro:** Mark McCormick, PGA   **Supt:** Tom La Plante
Architect: A. W. Tillinghast 1896

SUMMIT MUNICIPAL GOLF COURSE

River Rd. & Route 24, Summit, NJ 07901   **(908) 277-2932**

Summit Municipal is a nine hole par 3 course open 7 days a week from April to end of November. Memberships are available to residents of Summit. Guests play accompanied by a member.

Driving Range	Lockers
•Practice Green	Showers
Power Carts	Food
•Pull Carts	Clubhouse
•Club Rental	Outings
Caddies	•Soft Spikes

Course Description: This par 3 nine hole course is appreciated by the residents of Summit for its proximity and availability. It affords its townspeople a good place to learn and play inexpensively. Children and seniors can get to play often and practice the basics. The short layout means that the players get good use of their irons. There is even a lake in the middle of the course, on the fourth hole, to give players the opportunity to hit over water.

Directions: Union County, #29 on East Central Map
GSP or NJTpke to Rte. 78 West. At exit #48, take Rte. 24 West to River Rd. Look for Short Hills Mall; go around circle and course is on right on River Rd.

Hole	1	2	3	4	5	6	7	8	9	Out	BLUE	Rating
BLUE												Slope
WHITE	82	106	65	122	100	73	159	142	140	989		
Par	3	3	3	3	3	3	3	3	3	27	WHITE	Rating
Handicap												Slope
RED												
Par											RED	Rating
Handicap												Slope
Hole	10	11	12	13	14	15	16	17	18	In		Totals
BLUE											BLUE	
WHITE											WHITE	
Par											Par	
Handicap												
RED											RED	
Par											Par	
Handicap												

Director of Recreation: Romayne Eaker-Kelly
Built: 1960s

WEEQUAHIC PARK GOLF COURSE

Elizabeth Ave., Newark, NJ 07114   **(973) 923-1838**

Weequahic Park is an 18 hole Essex County course open 7 days a week all year. Through an automated system, ID holders may make tee times up to 7 days in advance for a $2 pp reservation fee.

Driving Range
• **Practice Green**
• **Power Carts**
• **Pull Carts**
  Club Rental
• **Soft Spikes**
• **Lockers**
• **Showers**
• **Food**
• **Clubhouse**
• **Outings**

Fees	Weekday	Weekend
Res/ID	$14.50	$18
Sr/Jr res	$10	$18
Non-res	$29	$36
Power Carts $13pp		

Course Description: Weequahic Park is located in a county park along a lake fed by artesian wells that keep it clean. The fairways are narrow with elevated greens. Few level lies can be found on this hilly layout. The golfer finds little relief when reaching the greens that rarely yield straight putts. The 3rd would be considered the signature hole, a long par 5. Water is in play on a few holes. New tee boxes have been installed and the clubhouse has been renovated recently.

Directions: Essex County, #30 on East Central Map
NJTpke to Exit 14. Take Rte. 78 West to Rte.22 West in Newark. Exit at Frelinghuysen Ave. South. After Meeker Ave, bear right onto Dayton St. and continue into Weequahic Park. Follow signs to golf course.

Hole	1	2	3	4	5	6	7	8	9	Out	BLUE	Rating
BLUE												Slope
WHITE	323	141	490	383	101	477	300	142	326	2683		
Par	4	3	5	4	3	5	4	3	4	35	WHITE	Rating 66.3
Handicap	10	16	1	6	18	2	12	15	9			Slope 108
RED	303	135	410	377	101	462	294	142	321	2542		
Par	4	3	5	4	3	5	4	3	4	35	RED	Rating
Handicap	7	16	2	3	18	1	9	15	6			Slope
Hole	10	11	12	13	14	15	16	17	18	In		Totals
BLUE											BLUE	
WHITE	466	173	372	408	334	285	397	127	364	2926	WHITE	5609
Par	5	3	4	4	4	4	4	3	4	35	Par	70
Handicap	3	13	7	4	11	14	5	17	8			
RED	368	168	302	338	284	255	263	125	274	2377	RED	4922
Par	5	3	4	4	4	4	4	3	4	35	Par	70
Handicap	4	14	8	5	10	13	12	17	11			

Manager: Al Harvey   **Supt:** Joe Capone
Built: 1915 1st nine   1959 2nd nine

WEST CENTRAL REGION

SOMERSET

HUNTERDON

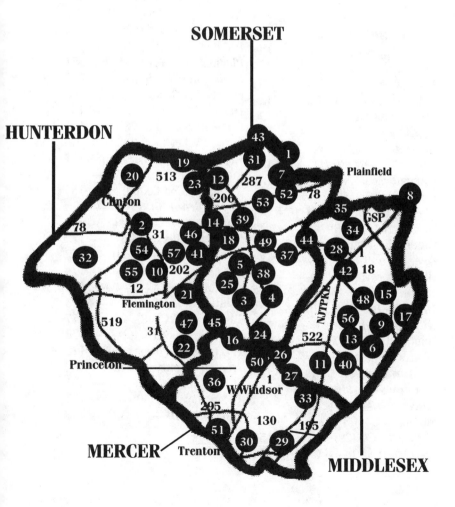

MERCER

MIDDLESEX

125

WEST CENTRAL REGION

Public Courses appear in
bold italics

Map (#)   Page (#)

Basking Ridge CC (1)---------- 127
Beaver Brook CC (2)-------- 128
Bedens Brook Club (3)-------- 129
Bunker Hill GC (4)----------- 130
Cherry Valley CC (5)----------- 131
Clearbrook Golf Club(6)------ 132
Coakley-Russo GC (7)--------- 133
Colonia Country Club (8)----- 134
Concordia Golf Course (9)--- 135
Copper Hill CC (10)------------ 136
Cranbury Golf Club (11)--- 137
Fiddler's Elbow CC (12)------- 138
Forsgate Country Club (13)--- 139
Fox Hollow Golf Club (14)---- 140
Glenwood Country Club (15)- 141
Greenacres CC (16)------------ 142
Greenbriar-Whittingham (17)- 143
Green Knoll GC (18)--------- 144
Hamilton Farm GC (19)------- 145
Heron Glen GC (54)--------- 146
High Bridge Hills (20)------ 147
Hillsborough CC (21)------- 148
Hopewell Valley GC (22)------- 149
Lawrenceville School (24)---- 150
Mattawang Golf Club (25)- 151
Meadows @Middlesex(26)- 152
Mercer Oaks GC (27)-------- 153
Metuchen CC (28)-------------- 154
Miry Run CC (29)------------- 155
Mountain View GC (30)----- 156

Map (#)   Page #

Neshanic Valley GC (55)--- 157
New Jersey National (31)-   158
Oak Hill Golf Club (32)------ 159
Peddie School GC (33)------- 160
Plainfield Country Club (34)- 161
Plainfield CC West (35)---- 162
Princeton CC (36)----------- 163
Quail Brook GC(37)-------- 164
Raritan Landing GC (38)- 165
Raritan Valley CC (39)-------- 166
Regency at Monroe (56)-- 167
Ridge at Back Brook (57)---- 168
Rossmoor Golf Course (40)-- 169
Royce Brook GC (41)------- 170
Rutgers Golf Course (42)- 171
Somerset Hills CC (43)------- 172
Spooky Brook GC (44)----- 173
Springdale GC (45)----------- 174
Stanton Ridge CC(46)-------- 175
Stonybrook GC (47)------- 176
Tamarack GC (48)---------- 177
Tara Greens GC (49)------- 178
TPC at Jasna Polana (50)---- 179
Trenton Country Club (51)-- 180
Trump National (23)--------- 181
Twin Brooks CC (52)--------- 182
Warrenbrook GC (53)------ 183

BASKING RIDGE C C

185 Madisonville Rd., Basking Ridge, NJ 07920   **(908) 766-8200**
www.baskingridgecc.com

Basking Ridge is an 18 hole course that is open from mid-March through Dec. 15, 6 days a week. Guests may play accompanied by a member. Tee time reservations are recommended.

•**Driving Range**	•**Lockers**
•**Practice Green**	•**Showers**
•**Power Carts**	•**Food**
•**Pull Carts**	•**Clubhouse**
•**Club Rental**	•**Outings**
Caddies	•**Soft Spikes**

Course Description: Designed in 1926 by Alexander Findlay, (the architect of over 500 golf courses in various parts of the US), Basking Ridge is relatively long and flat with tight tree-lined fairways and small fast greens. Originally a public course called Pembroke Golf Club, Basking Ridge is set amidst the serene beauty of the neighboring national wildlife refuge. Three holes have elevation changes and water is in play on several holes. The par 3 signature 18th has one of the largest greens in New Jersey; it is three tiered and penalizes the errant shot with a possible 3 putt or chip and two putts. Recently, bunkers have been added, ponds dredged and the course made longer. The entire restaurant, catering and proshop have been redone.

Directions: Somerset County, #1 on West Central Map
Take Rte. 80 West to Rte. 287 South to Exit #30A (North Maple Ave.). Go 1/2 mile to light and turn left onto Madisonville Rd. Club is second driveway on right.

Hole	1	2	3	4	5	6	7	8	9	Out	BLUE	Rating 72.1
BLUE	379	525	127	454	188	533	453	333	377	3369		Slope 133
WHITE	344	496	115	411	170	497	434	309	361	3137		
Par	4	5	3	4	3	5	4	4	4	36	WHITE	Rating 70.0
Handicap	13	1	17	9	15	3	7	11	5			Slope 126
RED	293	392	89	391	116	404	391	280	335	2691		
Par	4	5	3	4	3	5	5	4	4	37	RED	Rating 73.3
Handicap	13	1	17	5	15	7	9	11	3			Slope 121
Hole	10	11	12	13	14	15	16	17	18	In		Totals
BLUE	425	330	367	410	461	449	153	389	190	3174	BLUE	6611
WHITE	402	316	337	400	447	424	137	379	180	3022	WHITE	6200
Par	4	4	4	4	5	4	3	4	3	35	Par	71
Handicap	4	10	12	8	18	2	16	6	14			
RED	325	284	276	396	382	364	114	323	168	2632	RED	5323
Par	4	4	4	5	5	4	3	4	3	36	Par	73
Handicap	8	12	16	2	10	4	18	6	14			

Manager: Bob Adams   **Pro:** Bill Spicer, PGA   **Supt:** Tim Reinagel
Architect: Alexander Findlay 1926

BEAVER BROOK COUNTRY CLUB SEMI-PRIVATE

25 Country Club Dr., Annandale, NJ 08801 **(908) 735-4022**
www.beaverbrookcc.com

Beaver Brook is an 18 hole semi-private course open to the public 7 days a week all year. Memberships are available. Call up to 7 days in advance for tee times; members 14 days in advance.

Driving Range	• **Lockers**
• **Practice Green**	• **Showers**
• **Power Carts**	• **Food**
Pull Carts	• **Clubhouse**
• **Club Rental**	• **Outings**
• **Soft Spikes**	

Fees	**M-Thurs**	**Weekend**
Daily	$69	$89
Fri.		$75
11-3PM		$69
Twi (Mon-Th) $49		$49

Power carts included

Course Description: Formerly a private club, Beaver Brook presents a challenging and interesting layout. It is located in a country setting with an abundance of wildlife, stately oaks, maples and other beautiful trees. Its hilly rolling terrain is a strong test of golf. The large, well contoured greens are difficult to read with some deceptive breaks. The signature par 4 11th has a big tree in the center of the fairway. Water comes into play on the 6th, 7th and 15th holes. The course is now operated by American Golf Corp.

Directions: Hunterdon County, #2 on West Central Map
Take Rte. 80 to Rte. 78 West to Exit #17. Follow signs to Rte. 31 South. Watch for club on right shortly after entering Rte. 31S.

Hole	1	2	3	4	5	6	7	8	9	Out	GOLD	Rating 71.7
GOLD	462	501	400	164	400	399	174	395	290	3256		Slope 125
BLACK	437	478	390	134	371	384	159	380	254	3145		
Par	5	5	4	3	4	4	3	4	4	36	BLACK	Rating 70.4
Handicap	13	11	5	17	7	3	15	1	9			Slope 122
SILVER	407	434	275	101	316	369	144	325	194	2665		
Par	5	5	4	3	4	4	3	4	4	36	SILVER	Rating 71.7
Handicap	9	7	13	17	5	1	11	3	15			Slope 122
Hole	10	11	12	13	14	15	16	17	18	In		Totals
GOLD	354	384	136	380	155	446	467	510	506	3345	GOLD	6601
BLACK	349	361	112	367	143	436	414	482	471	3164	BLACK	6328
Par	4	4	3	4	3	4	4	5	5	36	Par	72
Handicap	10	6	18	4	16	2	8	12	14			
SILVER	277	290	100	341	115	384	349	402	406	2719	SILVER	5384
Par	4	4	3	4	3	4	4	5	5	36	Par	72
Handicap	10	6	18	4	16	2	14	12	8			

Manager: Fred Dobbins, PGA   **Supt:** Jay Long
Architect: Alex Ternyei 1965

THE BEDENS BROOK CLUB

Rolling Hill Rd., Skillman, NJ 08558   **(609) 466-3063**

Bedens Brook is a private 18 hole golf course open 6 days a week between April 15 and Dec. 15. Guests may play accompanied by a member. Reservations for tee times are not necessary.

•**Driving Range**	•**Lockers**
•**Practice Green**	•**Showers**
•**Power Carts**	•**Food**
•**Pull Carts**	•**Clubhouse**
•**Club Rental**	•**Outings**
•**Caddies**	•**Soft Spikes**

Course Description: Excellently maintained and constantly being upgraded, Bedens Brook is a fine example of New Jersey golf. Hilly with well bunkered large greens, accuracy is at a premium here. The 17th, "The Dick Wilson" hole, is 581 yards from the back tees and is a long dogleg right. The two nines are quite different; the front is open while the back is cut through a forest. Bunkers have been rebuilt recently and new tee boxes constructed. The Bedens Brook crosses the signature third hole twice.

Directions: Somerset County, #3 on West Central Map
NJTpke. to Exit #9. Take Rte. 1 South for 6 miles to Finnegan's Lane & turn right. At first light (Rte.27), go left. Proceed for about 3 miles to Rte. 518 (forks to right). Go 3 traffic lights & after 3rd, look for & take 1st left onto Rolling Hill Rd. to club.

Hole	1	2	3	4	5	6	7	8	9	Out	BLUE	Rating 72.8
BLUE	382	149	578	397	331	188	515	388	379	3307		Slope 135
WHITE	367	134	527	382	320	173	507	377	367	3154		
Par	4	3	5	4	4	3	5	4	4	36	WHITE	Rating 71.5
Handicap	7	17	1	3	13	15	11	9	5			Slope 132
RED	337	119	429	322	279	156	440	292	318	2692		
Par	4	3	5	4	4	3	5	4	4	36	RED	Rating 72.6
Handicap	9	17	3	5	11	15	1	13	7			Slope 128
Hole	10	11	12	13	14	15	16	17	18	In		Totals
BLUE	414	395	496	175	317	433	225	581	437	3473	BLUE	6805
WHITE	403	383	466	158	307	417	202	567	427	3330	WHITE	6480
Par	4	4	5	3	4	4	3	5	4	36	Par	72
Handicap	8	6	14	18	16	4	12	10	2			
RED	316	299	400	144	291	352	174	485	418	2879	RED	5571
Par	4	4	5	3	4	4	3	5	5	37	Par	73
Handicap	12	10	8	18	14	6	16	2	4			

Manager: Craig Campbell   **Pro:** Doug Schamback, PGA   **Supt:** Dave Welsh
Architect: Dick Wilson 1965

BUNKER HILL GOLF COURSE

PUBLIC

220 Bunker Hill Rd., Princeton, NJ 08540   **(908) 359-6335**
www.distinctgolf.com

Bunker Hill is a privately owned 18 hole course open to the public 7 days a week all year. Tee times: 7 days in advance. Rates below are walkers/with cart.

Driving Range	Lockers
• **Practice Green**	• **Showers**
• **Power Carts**	• **Food**
• **Pull Carts**	• **Clubhouse**
• **Club Rental**	• **Outings**
• **Soft Spikes**	

Fees	Weekday	Weekend
Daily	$25/$40	$55
Sr.	$21/$35	
Twilight rates available		

Course Description: Bunker Hill is an open hilly course that can get quite busy in season. The signature third is a 489 yard par 5 with an elevated tee box. Its tee shot is over a creek with out of bounds on the right to a tight landing area. This creek comes into play on five holes. The par 3 sixth hole is from an elevated tee to a green surrounded by trees. Numbers 9 and 18 have uphill approach shots to the green.

Directions: Somerset County, #4 on West Central Map
From North: NJTPK to Exit #9. Follow signs to Rte. 1 South and take it to New Rd. Go right and cross Rte. 27 to Bunker Hill Rd. Course is ahead on right.

Hole	1	2	3	4	5	6	7	8	9	Out	BLUE	Rating 68.2
BLUE	368	288	489	149	312	185	491	327	480	3089		Slope 125
WHITE	358	283	483	143	306	179	475	327	348	2902		
Par	4	4	5	3	4	3	5	4	5	37	WHITE	Rating 67.2
Handicap	5	11	1	17	9	13	7	15	3			Slope 120
RED	345	197	393	138	258	150	399	265	333	2478		
Par	4	4	5	3	4	3	5	4	5	37	RED	Rating 68.8
Handicap	6	9	2	8	5	4	1	7	3			Slope 117
Hole	10	11	12	13	14	15	16	17	18	In		Totals
BLUE	335	281	475	182	362	148	344	285	472	2884	BLUE	5973
WHITE	335	281	470	177	357	133	344	279	466	2842	WHITE	5744
Par	4	4	5	3	4	3	4	4	5	36	Par	73
Handicap	4	14	8	16	6	18	10	12	2			
RED	255	218	400	167	283	123	309	214	414	2383	RED	4861
Par	5	4	5	3	4	3	4	4	5	37	Par	74
Handicap	6	12	4	16	8	18	10	14	2			

Manager: Mark McCabe   **Supt:** David Fowler
Architect: Holliss Yarborough 1972

CHERRY VALLEY COUNTRY CLUB `PRIVATE`

133 Country Club Dr., Skillman, NJ 08558   **(609) 466-4464**
www.cherryvalleycc.com

Cherry Valley is an 18 hole golf course that is open 6 days a week from Feb. through December. Guests play accompanied by a member. Tues.-Thurs. guests may play unaccompanied through golf pro courtesy. Tee time reservations are required.

•Driving Range	•Lockers
•Practice Green	•Showers
•Power Carts	•Food
Pull Carts	•Clubhouse
•Club Rental	•Outings
•Caddies	•Soft Spikes

Course Description: Under the creative brilliance of Rees Jones, Cherry Valley was conceived and beautifully designed, the front in 1991 & the wooded back in 1992. This challenging layout is built in a links style on a former farm. The course has bent grass fairways and greens; some creeks and mounds are encountered on the front nine. The large undulating greens are well bunkered and have considerable break. The par 3 eleventh signature hole has a huge cherry tree left of the tee. There are large homes surrounding the property. The pro shop and clubhouse are outstanding.

Directions: Somerset County #5 on West Central Map
NJTPKE South to Exit #9; follow signs to Rte. 18 to Rte.1 South. Take Rte. 1 to the Raymond Rd. exit (approx. 13 miles). Then take Rte.27 thru Princeton to Rte.206 South. Almost immediately, turn right onto Elm Rd. which becomes The Great Road for approx. 4 miles; look for Country Club Dr. on left. Go left to club.

Hole	1	2	3	4	5	6	7	8	9	Out	BLUE	Rating 73.2
BLUE	363	212	513	430	360	441	408	165	555	3447		Slope 132
WHITE	332	187	477	399	330	396	360	137	531	3149		
Par	4	3	5	4	4	4	4	3	5	36	WHITE	Rating 71.2
Handicap	7	15	5	1	13	11	9	17	3			Slope 127
RED	310	100	435	376	310	370	338	115	410	2764		
Par	4	3	5	4	4	4	4	3	5	36	RED	Rating 72.0
Handicap	13	17	3	5	11	7	9	15	1			Slope 122
Hole	10	11	12	13	14	15	16	17	18	In		Totals
BLUE	526	179	393	358	174	466	496	440	451	3483	BLUE	6918
WHITE	490	162	360	335	143	417	452	413	395	3167	WHITE	6480
Par	5	3	4	4	3	4	5	4	4	36	Par	72
Handicap	2	16	6	12	18	14	4	10	8			
RED	420	123	326	283	130	387	412	327	287	2695	RED	5399
Par	5	3	4	4	3	4	5	4	4	36	Par	72
Handicap	2	16	6	12	18	4	8	10	14			

Manager: Tom Hurley   **Dir. of Golf:** Allan Bowman, PGA   **Supt:** Steve Wirth
Architect: Rees Jones 1991

CLEARBROOK GOLF CLUB

PRIVATE

Applegarth Rd., Cranbury, NJ 08512   **(609) 655-3443**

Clearbrook is an adult community with a 9 hole golf course open 7 days a week 10 months a year. Guests play accompanied by a member. Tee times: in advance between 7AM-11AM in season. Associate mbrships are available from outside the community.

•**Driving Range**	Lockers
•**Practice Green**	Showers
•**Power Carts**	Food
•**Pull Carts**	•**Clubhouse**
Club Rental	•**Outings**
Caddies	•**Soft Spikes**

Course Description: Easily walkable and convenient to its community members, Clearbrook is playable almost all year round. With its rolling terrain and water in play on 5 holes, it presents an interesting round of golf without a great degree of difficulty. Changing tee placements on the second nine adds interest when going for a full 18 hole round. The Cranbury area has several adult communities. Clearbrook is one of the earlier ones containing a regulation nine hole course.

Directions: Middlesex County, #6 on West Central Map
NJTPKE South to Exit #8A. Then go East on Rte. 32 (Forsgate) to first light. Turn right on Applegarth Rd. Clearbrook is about 2 miles on the left.

Hole	1	2	3	4	5	6	7	8	9	Out	BLUE	Rating
BLUE												Slope
WHITE	474	147	501	360	173	363	405	371	154	2948		
Par	5	3	5	4	3	4	4/5	4	3	35/36	WHITE	Rating 68.1
Handicap	3	17	1	11	13	9	5	7	15			Slope 116
RED	457	125	442	330	153	326	353	325	125	2636		
Par	5	3	5	4	3	4	4/5	4	3	35/36	RED	Rating 69.7
Handicap	3	17	1	11	13	9	5	7	15			Slope 113

Hole	10	11	12	13	14	15	16	17	18	In		Totals
BLUE											BLUE	
WHITE											WHITE	5902
Par											Par	70/72
Handicap												
RED											RED	5225
Par											Par	70/72
Handicap												

Manager: Tony Wilcenski   **Pro:** Vic Calvaresi, PGA   **Supt:** Dave Lerner
Architect: Hal Purdy 1973

132

COAKLEY-RUSSO GOLF COURSE `PRIVATE`

151 Knollcroft Rd., Lyons, NJ 07939   **(908) 604-2582**

Coakley-Russo is a 9 hole private course for members from Bernard Township and V.A. Hospital affiliated. It is open 7 days a week from April to Nov. Tee times may be made up to 1 week in advance. A separate driving range is open to the general public.

Driving Range	Lockers
•**Practice Green**	Showers
Power Carts	Food
•**Pull Carts**	Clubhouse
Club Rental	Outings
Caddies	•**Soft Spikes**

Course Description: Relatively flat, open, and easy to walk, Coakley-Russo is a course that is on the property of the Lyons V.A. Hospital. There are no bunkers but there are 2 brooks affecting play on three holes; one brook runs across the entire course. The facility was built originally for the patients to utilize for therapeutic purposes. A great layout for practice, a membership waiting list is now in place.

Directions: Somerset County, #7 on West Central Map
Rte. 80 West to Rte. 287 South to Exit #24. Go South on Maple Ave. to Basking Ridge. Make a left onto Finley Ave. (Rte. 527 spur). Road becomes Stonehouse Rd. Turn right onto Valley Rd. Hospital is on right; enter grounds and course is on the left.

Hole	1	2	3	4	5	6	7	8	9	Out	BLUE	Rating
BLUE												Slope
WHITE	495	215	375	127	430	336	370	455	317	3120		
Par	5	3	4	3	4	4	4	4	4	35	WHITE	Rating 34.2
Handicap	7	5	11	17	3	13	9	1	15			Slope 110
RED	436	165	300	127	350	310	320	380	270	2658		
Par	5	3	4	3	4	4	4	4	4	35	RED	Rating 35.4
Handicap	7	5	11	17	3	13	9	1	15			Slope 115
Hole	10	11	12	13	14	15	16	17	18	In		Totals
BLUE											BLUE	
WHITE											WHITE	3005
Par											Par	34
Handicap												
RED											RED	2364
Par											Par	34
Handicap												

Manager: Bill Parkinson   **Supt:** Peter Wright
Architect: Robert Trent Jones, 1946

COLONIA COUNTRY CLUB

PRIVATE

Colonia Blvd., Colonia, NJ 07067   **(732) 381-9500**
www.coloniacc.net

Colonia is an 18 hole private course open all year 6 days a week. Guests may play accompanied by a member. Reserved tee times are suggested.

- •Driving Range
- •Practice Green
- •Power Carts
- Pull Carts
- •Club Rental
- •Caddies

- •Lockers
- •Showers
- •Food
- •Clubhouse
- •Outings
- •Soft Spikes

Course Description: Built in the late 1890s, Colonia is a somewhat short and sporty traditional course offering tight, tree lined fairways and small undulating well bunkered greens that play very fast. There are 4 extremely challenging par 3s which are long and tricky. Water comes into play on several holes. The par five 4th could be considered the signature hole; it is a dogleg left with a pond in front of the green. The course is very well maintained.

Directions: Middlesex County, #8 on West Central Map
GSP to Exit #131. Turn left onto Rte. 27 North. Go approx. 2 miles to traffic light and make a sharp left onto Colonia Blvd. Club is 1 mile on left.

Hole	1	2	3	4	5	6	7	8	9	Out	BLUE	Rating 71.0
BLUE	317	205	304	523	394	171	396	541	347	3198		Slope 124
WHITE	307	200	301	510	381	155	385	528	341	3108		
Par	4	3	4	5	4	3	4	5	4	36	WHITE	Rating 69.7
Handicap	15	11	13	1	5	17	7	3	9			Slope 120
RED	290	122	250	380	370	133	352	426	322	2645		
Par	4	3	4	5	5	3	4	5	4	37	RED	Rating 72.2
Handicap	11	17	13	1	5	15	7	3	9			Slope 127

Hole	10	11	12	13	14	15	16	17	18	In		Totals
BLUE	358	330	313	180	475	576	197	365	360	3154	BLUE	6402
WHITE	339	306	305	162	464	563	184	351	350	3024	WHITE	6132
Par	4	4	4	3	5	5	3	4	4	36	Par	72
Handicap	6	18	16	14	4	2	12	8	10			
RED	333	291	273	143	461	437	153	261	333	2685	RED	5330
Par	4	4	4	3	5	5	3	4	4	36	Par	72
Handicap	6	14	12	18	2	4	16	10	8			

Manager: Salvatore Vigilante   **Pro:** Chris Mazzuchetti, PGA   **Supt:** Lance Rogers
Architects: Tom Bendelow, Robert White, Hal Purdy, Frank Duane   **Built:** 1898

CONCORDIA GOLF COURSE

3 Clubhouse Dr., Monroe Twshp, NJ 08831   **(609) 655-5631**
www.concordiagolf.com

Concordia is a private 18 hole course on the grounds of an adult community. Some non-residents are members. It is open 7 days a week all year. Tee times may be reserved up to 4 days in advance.

• Driving Range	• Lockers
• Practice Green	• Showers
• Power Carts	• Food
• Pull Carts	• Clubhouse
• Club Rental	• Outings
Caddies	• Soft Spikes

Course Description: Narrow fairways, out of bounds on every hole and tricky pin placement contribute to Concordia's challenge. Its signature par 4 fourteenth hole has water off the tee and then again further up the hill. The boomerang shaped green provides various degrees of difficulty depending on the location of the pin. Water affects play on 11 holes; wayward shots do not often get caught in heavy rough. This section of New Jersey is one of the largest retirement areas in the United States.

Directions: Middlesex County, #9 on West Central Map
NJTpke. to Exit #8A. Go East on Forsgate Drive to Applegarth and turn right. Proceed to Prospect Plains Rd. Club is 1 & 1/2 miles on right.

Hole	1	2	3	4	5	6	7	8	9	Out	BLUE	Rating 69.2
BLUE	317	455	315	180	303	386	186	318	350	2810		Slope 120
WHITE	300	438	255	150	275	343	162	298	327	2548		
Par	4	5	4	3	4	4	3	4	4	35	WHITE	Rating 66.7
Handicap	16	10	12	6	8	2	14	18	4			Slope 115
RED	283	421	234	111	249	296	144	268	301	2307		
Par	4	5	4	3	4	4	3	4	4	35	RED	Rating 69.3
Handicap	7	1	9	6	2	5	8	4	3			Slope 116
Hole	10	11	12	13	14	15	16	17	18	In		Totals
BLUE	283	167	511	404	389	166	404	503	386	3213	BLUE	6039
WHITE	270	151	485	393	365	130	375	460	350	2979	WHITE	5527
Par	4	3	5	4	4	3	4	5	4	36	Par	71
Handicap	17	13	11	3	1	15	7	9	5			
RED	257	136	432	371	322	108	349	420	319	2714	RED	5021
Par	4	3	5	4	4	3	4	4	4	36	Par	71
Handicap	13	15	7	3	1	17	9	5	11			

Mgr/Owner: Castle Golf Mgmt.   **Pro:** Raymond Bridy, PGA
Architect: Edmund Ault 1983

COPPER HILL COUNTRY CLUB · PRIVATE

Copper Hill Rd., Flemington, NJ 08822   **(908) 782-4279**
www.copper-hill.com

Copper Hill is an 18 hole private golf course that is open 6 days a week and closed in January Guests may play accompanied by a member. Reserved tee times are not necessary.

•Driving Range	•Lockers
•Practice Green	•Showers
•Power Carts	•Food
•Pull Carts	•Clubhouse
•Club Rental	•Outings
Caddies	•Soft Spikes

Course Description: The meandering stream that runs through Copper Hill affects play on seven holes. The course is characterized by sloping terrain, exceedingly small greens and tight fairways. The signature par 4 18th is the most outstanding hole; it is long with a three tiered elevated green, unusually large for this course. The hole has a downhill lie for the approach shot. In addition, overshooting the green can result in trouble. On many holes, out of bounds on the left awaits an errant shot.

Directions: Hunterdon County, #10 on West Central Map
GSP to Exit 142 OR NJTPK to Exit 14 to I-78 West. Proceed to I-287S to Rte. 202S. Follow signs to Flemington (at Flemington Circle, Rte 202 is joined by Rte. 31S). Go approx. 3 miles South (pass Stewart's Root Beer Stand on right) & turn right at Copper Hill Rd. to club entrance.

Hole	1	2	3	4	5	6	7	8	9	Out	BLUE	Rating 72.3
BLUE	391	235	488	156	366	351	341	416	484	3228		Slope 131
WHITE	372	218	472	132	348	338	307	393	471	3051		
Par	4	3	5	3	4	4	4	4	5	36	WHITE	Rating 71.3
Handicap	3	9	11	17	5	15	13	1	7			Slope 128
RED	337	143	416	100	287	267	250	301	415	2516		
Par	4	3	5	3	4	4	4	4	5	36	RED	Rating 70.9
Handicap	3	17	5	15	7	13	9	11	1			Slope 123
Hole	10	11	12	13	14	15	16	17	18	In		Totals
BLUE	372	165	370	504	165	556	345	384	428	3289	BLUE	6517
WHITE	353	156	352	482	159	532	334	375	410	3153	WHITE	6204
Par	4	3	4	5	3	5	4	4	4	36	Par	72
Handicap	6	18	10	14	16	4	12	8	2			
RED	332	118	289	420	112	416	293	299	401	2680	RED	5196
Par	4	3	4	5	3	5	4	4	5	37	Par	73
Handicap	10	18	6	8	16	2	12	14	4			

Pro: Robert Nicolson, PGA   **Supt:** Robert Mlynarski
Estab: 1928   **Architect:** Michael Hurdzan 1991(Redesign)

CRANBURY GOLF CLUB

SEMI-PRIVATE

49 Southfield Rd., West Windsor, NJ 08550
www.cranburygolf.com

(609) 799-0341

Cranbury Golf Club is a semi-private 18 hole course open to the public 7 days a week all year. Mbrships are available. Tee times: 1 week in advance; 2 weeks for members. Mbrs only until 10:30 on weekend mornings. Sr. & super twi rates available.

•**Driving Range**	•**Lockers**
•**Practice Green**	•**Showers**
•**Power Carts**	•**Food**
•**Pull Carts**	•**Clubhouse**
•**Club Rental**	•**Outings**
•**Soft Spikes**	

Fees	**Weekday**	Fri	**Weekend**
Daily	$34	$43	$60*
1-3PM	$28	$33	$34
Power carts	$16pp		
*incl mandatory cart			

Course Description: The wide open front nine at Cranbury Golf Course was once farmland and is designed around a working farm. Relatively flat with some undulation, the wooded well bunkered back nine is tight. The signature par 3 fifth hole is 211 yards over a pond. There is water in play on three other holes, including the 3rd, known as "Bog Hole" because one must hit over a bog. This busy course draws players from all over, including Staten Island. The restaurant "The Bog" is a major attraction.

Directions: Mercer County, #11 on West Central Map
NJTPKE to Exit #8. Then take Rte. 33 West and at the end of road, make a left at the firehouse. At first light, go right onto Rte. 571 (Stockton St.) Go 3 miles and make a left on Southfield Rd. Course is 1 mi. on right.

Hole	1	2	3	4	5	6	7	8	9	Out	BLUE	Rating 69.5
BLUE	519	333	155	460	211	495	163	419	398	3153		Slope 122
WHITE	506	333	145	420	187	485	142	401	383	3002		
Par	5	4	3	4	3	5	3	4	4	35	WHITE	Rating 68.3
Handicap	11	13	15	3	5	7	17	1	9			Slope 120
RED	470	310	110	310	115	475	115	395	360	2660		
Par	5	4	3	4	3	5	3	5	4	36	RED	Rating 69.1
Handicap	11	13	15	3	5	7	17	1	9			Slope 123

Hole	10	11	12	13	14	15	16	17	18	In		Totals
BLUE	376	175	393	225	347	498	189	371	538	3112	BLUE	6265
WHITE	360	175	378	197	347	490	170	356	529	3002	WHITE	6004
Par	4	3	4	3	4	5	3	4	5	35	Par	70
Handicap	12	14	6	8	18	2	16	10	4			
RED	335	160	335	175	300	460	150	330	490	2735	RED	5395
Par	4	3	4	3	4	5	3	4	5	35	Par	71
Handicap	12	14	6	8	18	2	16	10	4			

Mgr: Colleen Suozzo   **Pro:** Shawn Phillips, PGA   **Supt:** John Alexander
Arch: Garret Renn 1963

FIDDLER'S ELBOW CC

Rattlesnake Bridge Rd., Bedminster, NJ 07921   (908) 439-2513
www.fiddlerselbowcc.com

Fiddler's Elbow is made up of three separate 18 holecourses, Meadow, Forest and River. It is open 7 days a week, March through December. Membership is reserved exclusively for private corporations. Tee times should be reserved in advance.

- •Driving Range
- •Practice Green
- •Power Carts
- Pull Carts
- •Club Rental
- Caddies
- •Lockers
- •Showers
- •Food
- •Clubhouse
- •Outings
- •Soft Spikes

Course Description: Designed and built on former farmland with picturesque views, Fiddler's Elbow was originally named because the land on an old map resembled a crooked arm of a man playing the fiddle. The clubhouse is built in the style of an English Manor House. The Meadows has a links type design on the back nine; the front is tree-lined with water in play on several holes. The 16th hole on the River Course is rated one of the most difficult in New Jersey; its green is on a peninsula. The Rees Jones designed Forest Course has a man made lake and is just as exciting as the other 2 courses. The 1994 NJ Pro & Asst. Pro Tournaments were held here. The scorecard below is for the River Course.

Directions: Somerset County, #12 on West Central Map
NJTPKE or GSP to Rte. 78 West to Exit #26 (Lamington/North Branch). Go left at STOP, cross over Rte. 78 on Rattlesnake Bridge Rd. Club is on right.

Hole	1	2	3	4	5	6	7	8	9	Out	BLUE	Rating 70.8
BLUE	382	514	155	549	158	418	386	148	451	3161		Slope 122
WHITE	336	494	150	506	152	408	375	140	443	3004		
Par	4	5	3	5	3	4	4	3	5	36	WHITE	Rating 69.7
Handicap	8	10	16	4	14	2	6	18	12			Slope 120
RED	305	452	137	460	131	362	307	132	349	2635		
Par	4	5	3	5	3	4	4	3	5	36	RED	Rating 70.7
Handicap	8	10	16	4	14	2	6	18	12			Slope 119

Hole	10	11	12	13	14	15	16	17	18	In		Totals
BLUE	324	168	360	386	200	510	518	184	576	3226	BLUE	6387
WHITE	314	159	352	375	192	499	510	174	569	3144	WHITE	6148
Par	4	3	4	4	3	5	5	3	5	36	Par	72
Handicap	13	17	15	5	11	3	7	9	1			
RED	305	117	346	300	189	378	424	164	498	2721	RED	5356
Par	4	3	4	4	3	5	5	3	5	36	Par	72
Handicap	13	17	15	5	11	3	7	9	1			

Manager: David McGhee   **Pro:** Mike Kallan, PGA   **Supt:** Thomas Breiner
Architects: *River & Meadow*; Hal Purdy, Brian Silva *Forest*; Rees Jones 1994

FORSGATE COUNTRY CLUB

Forsgate Drive, Jamesburg, NJ 08831   (732) 521-0070
www.forsgatecc.com

Forsgate is a private club that has two 18 hole courses open to members and guests all year 7 days a week. Tee times: up to 2 weeks weekdays, 3 days on weekends.

•Driving Range	•Lockers
•Practice Green	•Showers
•Power Carts	•Food
Pull Carts	•Clubhouse
•Club Rental	•Outings
Caddies	•Soft Spikes

Course Description: The "Banks" was originally to be a private personal golf course with the holes replicating the famous golf links of Europe. John Forster, who owned the farmland, commissioned the renowned Charles "Steam Shovel" Banks to design the course on his property which became known as Forsgate. Banks provided his trademark gargantuan deep bunkers and large contoured greens to confront the unwary golfer. The West Course, a more contemporary style, is designed by the Arnold Palmer Group and has smaller bunkers and greens with a multitude of water hazards. The 2nd hole is a long par 5, 623 from the blues. Both courses are beautifully maintained and enjoyable to play. The scorecard below is for the Banks Course.

Directions: Middlesex County, #13 on West Central Map
NJTPKE to Exit #8A. Take Forsgate Drive East to club on left.

Hole	1	2	3	4	5	6	7	8	9	Out	BLUE	Rating 72.9
BLUE	375	403	194	347	417	344	187	570	501	3338		Slope 129
WHITE	367	398	182	332	403	334	179	551	484	3230		
Par	4	4	3	4	4	4	3	5	5	36	WHITE	Rating 71.2
Handicap	9	7	15	13	3	11	17	1	5			Slope 126
RED	350	386	169	317	348	317	165	468	405	2925		
Par	4	4	3	4	4	4	3	5	5	36	RED	Rating 69.1
Handicap	9	5	15	13	3	11	17	1	7			Slope 121

Hole	10	11	12	13	14	15	16	17	18	In		Totals
BLUE	416	357	140	529	411	328	402	235	421	3239	BLUE	6719
WHITE	408	349	140	519	396	318	388	201	398	3117	WHITE	6347
Par	4	4	3	5	4	4	4	3	4	35	Par	71
Handicap	4	12	18	2	10	14	8	16	6			
RED	394	267	133	462	325	313	340	150	369	2753	RED	5678
Par	4	4	3	5	4	4	4	3	4	35	Par	71
Handicap	2	14	18	4	10	12	8	16	6			

Mgr: Dave Wasenda   **Pro:** Rich Hughes, PGA   **Supt:** Robert Ribbans
Architects: Charles Banks 1931 Hal Purdy, Arnold Palmer 1962 *(West Course)*

FOX HOLLOW GOLF CLUB

59 Fox Chase Run, Somerville, NJ 08876   **(908) 526-0010**
www.foxhollowgc.com

Fox Hollow is a private 18 hole course open 7 days a week all year, weather permitting. Guests play accompanied by a member. Tee times should be reserved in advance.

+---+
| •**Driving Range** •**Lockers** |
| •**Practice Green** •**Showers** |
| •**Power Carts**   •**Food** |
| •**Pull Carts**   •**Clubhouse** |
| •**Club Rental**   •**Outings** |
| Caddies   Soft Spikes |
+---+

Course Description: Newly renovated holes number 2 and 3 at Fox Hollow now require a carry over water off the tee. The wooded course is set in the scenic hills of Somerset County. Golfers encounter tree lined fairways with many elevation changes. Water also comes into play on many additonal holes and rather extensively on the signature 18th hole. The 15th is difficult because it is all downhill.

Directions: Somerset County, #14 on West Central Map
NJTPKE or GSP to Rte. 78 West to Exit 26 (Lamington/North Branch); go to traffic light at end of exit & turn left; follow 2 miles to Fox Chase Run on right. Turn right to club.

Hole	1	2	3	4	5	6	7	8	9	Out	BLUE	Rating 71.6
BLUE	350	162	535	179	432	547	395	351	181	3132		Slope 130
WHITE	343	151	525	165	421	540	379	341	155	3020		
Par	4	3	5	3	4	5	4	4	3	35	WHITE	Rating 69.9
Handicap	9	17	3	13	1	5	7	11	15			Slope 124
RED	301	115	495	105	320	490	359	309	108	2602		
Par	4	3	5	3	4	5	4	4	3	35	RED	Rating 65.8
Handicap	9	17	1	15	5	3	7	11	13			Slope 117
Hole	**10**	**11**	**12**	**13**	**14**	**15**	**16**	**17**	**18**	**In**		Totals
BLUE	584	348	189	434	171	565	352	366	185	3194	BLUE	6400
WHITE	565	341	178	421	151	555	344	358	176	3089	WHITE	6135
Par	5	4	3	4	3	5	4	4	3	35	Par	70
Handicap	2	8	10	4	18	6	14	12	16			
RED	480	299	145	415	140	472	326	342	108	2727	RED	5216
Par	5	4	3	5	3	5	4	4	3	36	Par	71
Handicap	4	14	10	6	18	2	12	8	16			

Manager: Mark McAvoy, PGA   **Pro:** Vaughan Abel, PGA   **Supt:** Tim McAvoy
Architect: Hal Purdy 1962

GLENWOOD COUNTRY CLUB

1655 Rte. 9 & Fairway Lane, Old Bridge, NJ 08857   (732) 607-2582
www.njgolfclub.com

Glenwood is an 18 hole course open 6 days a week from Mar.15 to Dec. 15. Guests play accompanied by a member. Reserved tee times are required on weekends only.

- •Driving Range
- •Practice Green
- •Power Carts
- •Pull Carts
- •Club Rental
- Caddies
- •Lockers
- •Showers
- •Food
- •Clubhouse
- •Outings
- •Soft Spikes

Course Description: Glenwood provides a good test of golf; the course offers right and left doglegs, tight fairways and elevated greens and tees. Water is in play on many holes and wind helps make the course challenging and difficult. The signature par 4 seventh, is a slight dogleg left with water in the middle of the fairway coming into play. A NJ State Open qualifying round is held here almost every year.

Directions: Middlesex County, #15 on West Central Map
GSP to Exit #123. Then take Rte. 9 South to Fairway Lane & turn right to club.
From South: GSP to Exit #105 to Rte. 18 North to Rte. 9 North to Fairway Lane.

Hole	1	2	3	4	5	6	7	8	9	Out	BLUE	Rating 74.8
BLUE	539	445	158	406	378	187	396	359	582	3450		Slope 138
WHITE	496	425	138	386	353	167	374	329	552	3220		
Par	5	4	3	4	4	3	4	4	5	36	WHITE	Rating 71.8
Handicap	9	1	17	7	11	15	3	13	5			Slope 133
RED	457	371	117	334	290	115	321	278	489	2767		
Par	5	5	3	4	4	3	4	4	5	37	RED	Rating 71.8
Handicap	2	4	15	7	14	16	8	13	1			Slope 128
Hole	10	11	12	13	14	15	16	17	18	In		Totals
BLUE	410	185	515	414	537	381	395	204	437	3478	BLUE	6943
WHITE	385	162	493	392	470	355	375	179	417	3228	WHITE	6448
Par	4	3	5	4	5	4	4	3	4	36	Par	72
Handicap	14	18	6	2	12	8	10	16	4			
RED	276	115	450	326	369	247	272	124	344	2523	RED	5290
Par	4	3	5	4	5	4	4	3	5	37	Par	74
Handicap	10	17	3	11	5	9	12	18	6			

Manager: Anthony Spirito   **Pro:** Stephen Brown, **PGA**   **Supt:** Frank Tichenor
Architect: Hal Purdy 1967

GREENACRES COUNTRY CLUB **PRIVATE**

2170 Lawrenceville Rd., Lawrenceville, NJ 08648   **(609) 896-0276**

Greenacres is an 18 hole private club that is open 7 days a week from March through December. Reserved tee times are required on weekends. Guests play accompanied by a member.

•Driving Range	•Lockers
•Practice Green	•Showers
•Power Carts	•Food
Pull Carts	•Clubhouse
•Club Rental	•Outings
•Caddies	•Soft Spikes

Course Description: With its difficult, demanding design, Greenacres requires accuracy. There are many tee shots out of chutes on this narrrow tree lined layout. The greens are well bunkered and undulating. Because they are small, fast and in some cases elevated as well, it is tough to get up and down if they are missed on the approach shot. The signature hole is the par 3 fourth; water lurks right of the green. In recent years, the architect, Stephen Kay has made some changes to the course and the driving range has been redone.

Directions: Mercer County, #16 on West Central Map
NJTPKE to Exit #9 and follow signs to Rte.1 South to Lawrenceville. Pass Quaker Bridge Mall on left & take Rte. 295 and 95 (next right turn), sign says "To Pennsylvania." Exit at 7A (Rte. 206 South-Trenton). Greenacres is 1st driveway on left on 206.

Hole	1	2	3	4	5	6	7	8	9	Out	BLUE	Rating 71.6
BLUE	415	368	397	204	510	360	134	334	377	3099		Slope 135
WHITE	395	328	364	173	500	344	120	323	338	2885		
Par	4	5	5	3	5	4	3	4	4	35	WHITE	Rating 69.7
Handicap	1	9	3	15	7	13	17	11	5			Slope 129
RED	375	268	327	130	466	300	110	311	320	2607		
Par	5	4	4	3	5	4	3	4	4	36	RED	Rating 71.0
Handicap	3	11	5	15	1	9	17	13	7			Slope 124
Hole	10	11	12	13	14	15	16	17	18	In		Totals
BLUE	503	377	182	446	181	490	389	413	365	3346	BLUE	6445
WHITE	477	363	160	376	171	475	365	398	333	3118	WHITE	6111
Par	5	4	3	4	3	5	4	4	4	36	Par	71
Handicap	2	6	16	10	18	14	8	4	12			
RED	420	311	129	309	142	423	376	366	291	2767	RED	5424
Par	5	4	3	4	3	5	5	5	4	38	Par	72
Handicap	2	12	18	14	16	4	6	8	10			

Manager: Albert Costatina   **Pro:** Ron Chmura, PGA   **Supt:** Jeff Wetterling
Architects: Devereux Emmet, Alfred Tull, George Fazio   **Built:** 1932

GREENBRIAR @ WHITTINGHAM

101 Whittingham Drive, Jamesburg, NJ 08831   (609) 860-6621

Greenbriar at Whittingham is a 9 hole course that is part of an adult community. Only residents may join here. It is open 7 days a week and closed in Jan. & Feb. Guests play accompanied by a member. Reservations for tee times are necessary.

Driving Range	•Lockers
•Practice Green	•Showers
•Power Carts	•Food
•Pull Carts	•Clubhouse
•Club Rental	Outings
Caddies	•Soft Spikes

Course Description: There are three sets of tees at Greenbriar giving variety to a second nine. Water in play on several holes and the mounding enhance the layout. Many fairway and greenside bunkers add character as well. The signature #5 requires a drive over water, a blind 2nd shot to a rising fairway and then the hole plateaus to the green. Greenbriar offers another opportunity for golfers looking to reside in one of New Jersey's many adult communities. Scorecard below shows totals for a second nine.

Directions: Middlesex County, #17 on West Central Map
NJTPKE to Exit 8A, Go east on Forsgate Drive to 2nd traffic light. Make a right; club is on left about 1 mile.

Hole	1	2	3	4	5	6	7	8	9	Out	BLUE	Rating 70.0
BLUE	350	390	325	135	525	380	200	485	345	3135		Slope 123
WHITE	305	360	315	120	475	355	180	475	300	2885		
Par	4	4	4	3	5	4	3	5	4	36	WHITE	Rating 67.2
Handicap	13	1	11	17	5	3	9	7	15			Slope 119
RED	225	340	265	105	420	325	170	430	275	2555		
Par	4	4	4	3	5	4	3	5	4	36	RED	Rating 69.8
Handicap	13	5	15	17	3	7	9	1	11			Slope 125
Hole	10	11	12	13	14	15	16	17	18	In		Totals
BLUE											BLUE	6270
WHITE											WHITE	5770
Par											Par	72
Handicap												
RED											RED	5710
Par											Par	72
Handicap												

Mgr: Matt Heon   **Pro:** John McDole, PGA   **Supt:** John Cipriano
                          Architect: Brian Ault 1996

GREEN KNOLL GOLF COURSE

PUBLIC

587 Garretson Rd., Bridgewater, NJ 08807   **(908) 722-1301**

Operated by Somerset County Park Çommission, Green Knoll is open all year, 7 days a week. A 9 hole pitch & putt is on the premises. Tee times: 7 days for residents with ID ($30/yr.) Non res. ($60/yr) 5 days in advance. Reservation # is (908)231-1122. Single reserv. fee $10 for 1 day in advance.

Driving Range	Lockers
•Practice Green	Showers
•Power Carts	•Food
•Pull Carts	•Clubhouse
•Club Rental	•Outings
•Soft Spikes	

Fees	Weekday	Weekend
Res/ID	$17	$19
Sr/Jr	$10	$10
Non-res	$34	$38
Power carts $26		

Course Description: Moderately hilly and well maintained, Green Knoll is relatively long, 6443 from the blues. It is known for its tight fairways and rolling contours. On the signature par 4 17th water is encountered three times as a brook meanders through it. Additional trees have been planted recently. Green Knoll is well worth the greens fee, and offers a challenge for the average golfer. The course has cross-country skiing in the winter when snow covered.

Directions: Somerset County, #18 on West Central Map
Rte. 80W to Rte. 287 South to Exit 17 (Rte. 202/206 South). Take 1st exit off 202/206 & watch for sign, Garretson Rd. At light at top of ramp, go right to Commons Way and around Commons Mall to end (several lights). At intersection turn left onto Garretson Rd. Follow signs for course on right opposite the high school.

Hole	1	2	3	4	5	6	7	8	9	Out	BLUE	Rating 70.4
BLUE	531	332	194	397	552	356	178	387	405	3332		Slope 122
WHITE	512	322	174	374	543	332	159	374	387	3177		
Par	5	4	3	4	5	4	3	4	4	36	WHITE	Rating 68.2
Handicap	13	15	7	3	9	11	17	1	5			Slope 116
RED	445	301	150	347	497	306	131	290	286	2753		
Par	5	4	3	4	5	4	3	4	4	36	RED	Rating 69.8
Handicap	3	13	15	7	1	11	17	9	5			Slope 122

Hole	10	11	12	13	14	15	16	17	18	In		Totals
BLUE	404	360	165	346	183	356	427	387	483	3111	BLUE	6443
WHITE	377	347	145	329	160	337	410	370	452	2927	WHITE	6104
Par	4	4	3	4	3	4	4	4	5	35	Par	71
Handicap	6	10	18	4	16	2	8	14	12			
RED	352	333	130	303	131	270	361	345	371	2596	RED	5349
Par	4	4	3	4	3	4	5	4	5	36	Par	72
Handicap	4	8	18	12	16	10	6	14	2			

Manager: Mike Zoda   **Dir. of Golf:** Bill Anderson   **Supt:** John Zujowski
Architect: William F. Gordon 1960

HAMILTON FARM GOLF CLUB PRIVATE

1040 Pottersville Rd., Gladstone, NJ 07934   **(908) 901-4000**
www.hamiltonfarmgolfclub.com

Hamilton Farm Golf Club has an 18 hole championship course with an additional 18
hole executive course on the property. It is open 6 days a week and closed in Jan. A
member must accompany guests. Tee time reservations are optional.

•**Driving Range**	•**Lockers**
•**Practice Green**	•**Showers**
•**Power Carts**	•**Food**
Pull Carts	•**Clubhouse**
Club Rental	Outings
•**Caddies**	•**Soft Spikes**

Course Description: One of the newer courses in NJ is the extraordinary Hamilton
Farm Golf Club in Gladstone. The 36-hole club features the "Highlands,"an impressive
and challenging 7,117 yard championship course with spectacular bunkering, majestic
views, some water in play, a true test of golf skills. It is also the site of the United
States Equestrian Team. The golf courses are surrounded by historic horse jumps and
riding trails. "Hickory" is an equally challenging 18 hole executive course with similar
bunkering and more water, and should not be underestimated. At over 3,000 yards
golfers use every club in their bag. The club features a stately mansion, formerly the
home of James Cox Brady.

Directions: Somerset County, #19 on West Central Map
Take Rte. 80W to Rte. 287 (towards Morristown) to Exit #22. Take Rte. 206 North to
Rte. 512 (Pottersville Rd.) and turn left to club.

Hole	1	2	3	4	5	6	7	8	9	Out	BLACK	Rating 74.7
BLACK	329	568	242	418	406	451	215	367	559	3555		Slope 139
WHITE	293	520	170	374	360	401	187	314	505	3124		
Par	4	5	3	4	4	4	3	4	5	36	WHITE	Rating 70.0
Handicap	17	1	13	7	11	3	15	9	5			Slope 134
RED	285	481	147	312	341	396	155	292	460	2869		
Par	4	5	3	4	4	4	3	4	5	36	RED	Rating 72.8
Handicap	17	1	13	7	11	3	15	9	5			Slope 136
Hole	10	11	12	13	14	15	16	17	18	In		Totals
BLACK	380	519	212	432	545	382	465	196	431	3562	BLACK	7117
WHITE	345	475	184	377	488	343	411	160	370	3153	WHITE	6277
Par	4	5	3	4	5	4	4	3	4	36	Par	72
Handicap	12	6	18	8	2	16	4	14	10			
RED	241	429	159	240	461	296	357	133	360	2676	RED	5545
Par	4	5	3	4	5	4	4	3	4	36	Par	72
Handicap	12	6	18	8	2	16	4	14	10			

Manager: Tom Barbrow   **Pro:** Jeff Diehl, PGA   **Supt:** Paul Ramina
Architects: Dr. Michael Hurdzan & Dana Fry 2000

HERON GLEN GOLF COURSE

PUBLIC

110 Highway 202 & 31, Ringoes, NJ 08551   **(908) 806-6804**
www.heronglen.com

Heron Glen is an 18 hole Hunterdon County public course. It is open 7 days a week and closed in winter. Tee times: residents 7 days in advance, non-res. 3 days. The course is operated by Kemper Sports Management.

- **Driving Range**
- **Practice Green**
- **Power Carts**
- **Pull Carts**
- Club Rental
- **Soft Spikes**

Lockers
Showers
- **Food**
Clubhouse
- **Outings**

NEW

Fees	M-Thurs	Fri-Sun
Res/ID	$26	$38
Non res	$42	$55
Power carts $13pp		

Course Description: Heron Glen, built on a 360 acre former dairy farm, is a fairly wide open links-type course featuring high quality tee boxes and well shaped bunkers. Environmental areas are encountered often; the key to reasonable scoring is avoiding them and the fescue in the rough. The Neshanic River meanders through the course. The rolling terrain produces contoured gently mounded fairways and some elevation changes. There are a number of tempting risk/reward holes that give challenge to the golfer. Although the landscape is somewhat wooded, additional trees have been planted This public facility enforces a pace of play policy.

Directions: Hunterdon County, #54 on West Central Map
Take Rte 31South of Flemington. Make U turn at Everitts Rd. Golf course is ahead on right.

Hole	1	2	3	4	5	6	7	8	9	Out	BLUE	Rating 71.1
BLUE	395	581	424	361	179	371	146	512	378	3347		Slope 125
WHITE	358	539	386	306	160	341	122	488	339	3039		
Par	4	5	4	4	3	4	3	5	4	36	WHITE	Rating 68.6
Handicap	7	1	5	13	15	11	17	3	9			Slope 121
RED	288	474	335	270	139	256	92	444	299	2597		
Par	4	5	4	4	3	4	3	5	4	36	RED	Rating 69.4
Handicap	7	1	5	13	15	11	17	3	9			Slope 119

Hole	10	11	12	13	14	15	16	17	18	In		Totals
BLUE	545	308	155	514	378	204	473	158	449	3184	BLUE	6531
WHITE	530	288	133	490	334	173	449	137	409	2943	WHITE	5982
Par	5	4	3	5	4	3	5	3	4	36	Par	72
Handicap	2	12	18	4	10	14	6	16	8			
RED	466	243	109	429	304	145	407	114	358	2575	RED	5172
Par	5	4	3	5	4	3	5	3	4	36	Par	72
Handicap	2	12	18	4	10	14	6	16	8			

Mgr/Pro: Steve Loomis, PGA   **Supt:** Jason Pierce
Architect: Daniel Schlegel, Ault, Clark & Associates 2002

HIGH BRIDGE HILLS G C

203 Cregar Rd. Highbridge, NJ 08829   **(908) 638-5055**
www. highbridgehills.com

High Bridge Hills Golf Club is an 18 hole course open to the public 7 days a week all year. Memberships are available. Tee times: 10 days for mbrs, 7 days for non-mbrs. Reduced fees for Hunterdon Country residents

•**Driving Range**	Lockers		
•**Practice Green**	Showers		
•**Power Carts**	•**Food**		
•**Pull Carts**	Clubhouse		
•**Club Rental**	•**Outings**		
•**Soft Spikes**			

Fees	Weekday	Weekend
Daily	$58	$73
Twi	$48	$63
Senior	$48	$70
Power carts incl		

Course Description: High Bridge Hills, built in a links design, is a shot-maker's course. The natural fescue gives character and shape. Try not to land in this deep rough; it will require either a strong short iron shot or a drop to get out. The variety of the holes, blind shots, numerous bunkers and the changes in elevation make the course more challenging than its relatively; short length would suggest. The small greens are somewhat fast with slight break. From the "Tournament" tees, it is 6640 yards. Water is in play on the 9th and 14th holes. The 18th, a long uphill par 5, is stunning and difficult. The course, operated by Billy Casper Management, now has GPS on the golf carts.

Directions: Hunterdon County, #20 on West Central Map
Take Rte. 78W to Exit #17. Follow signs to Rte. 31North. Go 3 miles past mile marker #35 and turn right on Cregar Rd. to club on right.

Hole	1	2	3	4	5	6	7	8	9	Out	BLUE	Rating 72.3
BLUE	529	422	495	145	431	100	330	191	420	3063		Slope 128
WHITE	488	392	481	127	407	89	310	152	390	2836		
Par	5	4	5	3	4	3	4	3	4	35	WHITE	Rating 68.8
Handicap	11	3	7	15	1	17	13	9	5			Slope 119
RED	419	346	432	112	313	74	274	98	350	2418		
Par	5	4	5	3	4	3	4	3	4	35	RED	Rating 63.9
Handicap	3	5	1	13	7	17	9	15	11			Slope 107
Hole	10	11	12	13	14	15	16	17	18	In		Totals
BLUE	380	367	120	355	190	474	337	498	405	3126	BLUE	6189
WHITE	366	340	110	338	177	444	317	470	383	2945	WHITE	5781
Par	4	4	3	4	3	5	4	5	4	36	Par	71
Handicap	12	6	18	14	16	10	4	8	2			
RED	317	320	107	249	151	396	211	423	336	2510	RED	4928
Par	4	4	3	4	3	5	4	5	4	36	Par	71
Handicap	14	6	2	10	18	4	12	16	8			

Manager/Dir. of Golf: Jason Lenhart, PGA   **Supt:** Jim Richardson
Architect: Mark Mungeam 1999

HILLSBOROUGH CC

146 Wertsville Rd., Neshanic Station, NJ 08853   **(908) 369-3322**
www.hillsboroughgolf.com

Hillsborough is an 18 hole semi-private course open all year, 7 days a week. Tee times: mbrs. 7 days in advance. Twilight rates available.

- **Driving Range**   Lockers
- **Practice Green** Showers
- **Power Carts**   • **Food**
- **Pull Carts**   • **Clubhouse**
- **Club Rental**   • **Outings**
- **Soft Spikes**

Fees	M-Thurs	Weekend
Daily	$26	$41
Friday	$30	
Sr/Jr	$20	
Power carts	$14pp	

Course Description: Adjacent to a barn and a polo field (which doubles as a driving range), Hillsborough's 450 acres is set on the side of the Sourland Mountains. Spectacular views abound and a constant breeze prevails here. The back nine is tighter and more severely sloped than the front with many sharp doglegs. Many holes have right to left sloping fairways that don't hold drives unless aimed strategically. The uneven lies and out of bounds contribute to the course's difficulty. The signature par 3 11th hole overlooks the entire Amwell Valley. Recently, the greens have been redone and the fairways improved.

Directions: Hunterdon County, #21 on West Central Map
Rte. 80 or 78 West to Rte. 287 South to Exit #13 to Rtes. 202/206S. Take 206S from Somerville Circle for 5.6 mi. then right onto Amwell Rd. Go 4.3 mi. straight thru 3-way STOP to Wertsville Rd. and left to course. See website for more directions.

Hole	1	2	3	4	5	6	7	8	9	Out	BLUE	Rating
BLUE												Slope
WHITE	475	195	360	550	145	305	305	190	510	3035		
Par	5	3	4	5	3	4	4	3	5	36	WHITE	Rating 68.2
Handicap	13	3	15	5	17	11	9	1	7			Slope 117
RED	460	185	345	495	140	300	295	180	475	2875		
Par	5	4	4	5	3	4	4	4	5	38	RED	Rating 74.1
Handicap	3	15	11	5	17	7	9	13	1			Slope 119
Hole	10	11	12	13	14	15	16	17	18	In		Totals
BLUE											BLUE	
WHITE	375	155	295	180	350	530	375	390	155	2805	WHITE	5840
Par	4	3	4	3	4	5	4	4	3	34	Par	70
Handicap	12	16	14	10	4	2	8	6	18			
RED	365	145	285	170	320	440	315	380	150	2570	RED	5445
Par	4	3	4	4	4	5	4	4	3	35	Par	73
Handicap	12	16	6	14	8	2	10	4	18			

Manager: Drew Munro   **Supt:** Craig Kinsey
Architects: Alec Ternyei, George Fazio 1970

HOPEWELL VALLEY GOLF CLUB PRIVATE

114 Pennington-Hopewell Rd., Hopewell, NJ 08525   **(609) 466-9070**

Hopewell Valley is an 18 hole course open 6 days a week and closed for the month of January. Guests play accompanied by a member. Tee time reservations are required for weekends.

•**Driving Range**	•**Lockers**
•**Practice Green**	•**Showers**
•**Power Carts**	•**Food**
•**Pull Carts**	•**Clubhouse**
•**Club Rental**	•**Outings**
Caddies	•**Soft Spikes**

Course Description: Built in 1927, Hopewell Valley is relatively short, tight and about 6500 yards from the blues. The land was formerly a trotter horse farm and is quite picturesque. The Stony Brook meanders through this wooded course affecting play on five holes. Adding to the challenge are the small, fast bent grass greens. The par 3 #13 signature hole is downhill with a carry over a lake. A qualifying round for the NJ State Amateur (Southern Region) was played here. The club hosted the Match Play Championship for the Philadelphia area.

Directions: Mercer County, #22 on West Central Map
(From North)NJTPKE to Exit #9. Take Rte. 1 South and after the Quaker Bridge Mall, take Rte.295/95 on right to Exit #4. Then take Rte. 31North for 5 miles to Rte. 654 and make a right. Club is ahead on right. (Rte. 95 can be reached from the South off of Rte. 295).

Hole	1	2	3	4	5	6	7	8	9	Out	BLUE	Rating 71.5
BLUE	374	381	166	476	432	396	495	400	132	3252		Slope 127
WHITE	357	348	154	457	404	389	469	373	126	3077		
Par	4	4	3	5	4	4	5	4	3	36	WHITE	Rating 70.2
Handicap	9	5	15	13	1	7	11	3	17			Slope 125
RED	316	295	125	414	341	385	426	284	113	2699		
Par	4	4	3	5	4	4	5	4	3	36	RED	Rating 71.3
Handicap	5	11	15	3	7	1	9	13	17			Slope 122

Hole	10	11	12	13	14	15	16	17	18	In		Totals
BLUE	389	404	356	148	352	414	456	209	570	3298	BLUE	6585
WHITE	374	395	344	146	343	383	474	195	550	3204	WHITE	6281
Par	4	4	4	3	4	4	5	3	5	36	Par	72
Handicap												
RED	329	347	331	119	317	298	413	127	455	2736	RED	5435
Par	4	4	4	3	4	4	5	3	5	36	Par	72
Handicap	8	6	12	16	10	14	4	18	2			

Manager: Dominick Guzzo   **Pro:** Duke Kimball, PGA   **Supt:** Steve Bradley
Architect: Thomas Winton 1927

LAWRENCEVILLE SCHOOL GC   PRIVATE

Rte. 206, Lawrenceville, NJ 08648   (609) 896-1481

The Lawrenceville School has a private 9 hole facility open 7 days a week to parents of students and alumni, and a limited number of Lawrence Township residents. Guests may play accompanied by a member. Tee time reservations are not necessary. Current students at the school have playing priority.

•**Driving Range**	Lockers
•**Practice Green**	Showers
Power Carts	Food
•**Pull Carts**	Clubhouse
Club Rental	•**Outings**
Caddies	•**Soft Spikes**

Course Description: Several creeks run through this relatively flat par 70 course. There are double tees usable for the second nine. The eighth and (seventeenth) holes have a pond in play off the tee. Lawrenceville provides an excellent opportunity for short game practice. The facility is open when students are not using it; mornings in Spring and Fall and all day from mid June until Labor Day. An individual or family membership is required for non-current student use. Recently installed are a new putting green and sprinkler system. The scorecard below shows the tees moved back for the second nine.

Directions: Mercer County, #24 on West Central Map
Rte. 1 South thru Princeton to Franklin Corner Rd. Make a right and at 2nd light turn right onto Rte. 206 North. Go past the main entrance of the Lawrenceville School and turn right into the school; pass the tennis courts. Parking lot & golf shack is on left.

Hole	1	2	3	4	5	6	7	8	9	Out	BLUE	Rating
BLUE												Slope
WHITE	309	331	188	358	368	155	336	337	470	2875		
Par	4	4	3	4	4	3	4	4	5	35	WHITE	Rating
Handicap	15	7	13	1	3	17	9	11	5			Slope
RED												
Par											RED	Rating
Handicap												Slope
Hole	10	11	12	13	14	15	16	17	18	In		Totals
BLUE											BLUE	
WHITE	322	306	205	332	425	145	359	312	365	2748	WHITE	5623
Par	4	4	3	4	5	3	4	4	4	35	Par	70
Handicap	8	14	4	10	12	18	2	16	6			
RED											RED	
Par											Par	
Handicap												

Manager/Pro: Ron Kane   Supt: Tim Moore
Built: 1897

MATTAWANG GOLF CLUB

SEMI-PRIVATE

295 Township Line Rd., Belle Mead, NJ 08502   **(908) 281-0778**

Mattawang is an 18 hole semi-private course open to the public 7 days a week all year. Annual memberships available. Members may make tee times 12 days in advance and the public 9 days. Mandatory carts weekends till 12 noon.

•**Driving Range**	•**Lockers**
•**Practice Green**	•**Showers**
•**Power Carts**	•**Food**
•**Pull Carts**	
•**Club Rental**	•**Clubhouse**
•**Soft Spikes**	•**Outings**

Fees	Weekday	Weekend
Daily	$32	$49
Sr/Jr	Discounts weekdays	
Twi rates available		
Power carts $17pp		

Course Description: Hilly, well bunkered with tree lined fairways, Mattawang is not as easy as it appears at first. The traditional layout is well planned with small greens and not much water in play; however those holes that do have water are quite intriguing. Strategically placed sand and grass bunkers guard the greens. The course is constantly being upgraded. A relatively new clubhouse is convenient and attractive. Jack Nicklaus played here some years ago and shot a 66.

Directions: Somerset County, #25 on West Central Map
Rte. 80 West to Rte. 287 South to Rtes. 202/206 South to the Somerville Circle. Follow 206 South for 9 miles into Belle Mead. Bear left at fork; go over bridge and pass RR sign that says "Mattawang." Make a left onto Township Line Rd. Club is 1 & 1/2 miles on right.

Hole	1	2	3	4	5	6	7	8	9	Out	BLUE	Rating 72.8
BLUE	333	323	182	328	528	198	492	400	390	3174		Slope 134
WHITE	292	318	170	320	498	150	440	381	320	2889		
Par	4	4	3	4	5	3	5	4	4	36	WHITE	Rating 70.9
Handicap	11	15	17	13	3	9	5	1	7			Slope 127
RED	283	315	114	323	446	139	395	342	311	2668		
Par	4	4	3	4	5	3	5	5	4	37	RED	Rating 71.8
Handicap	11	13	15	9	1	17	3	7	5			Slope 123
Hole	10	11	12	13	14	15	16	17	18	In		Totals
BLUE	388	142	540	221	407	486	437	287	426	3334	BLUE	6803
WHITE	313	135	490	157	377	464	375	285	394	2990	WHITE	6508
Par	4	3	5	3	4	5	4	4	4	36	Par	72
Handicap	14	18	8	12	2	10	6	16	4			
RED	306	122	484	153	313	410	372	273	366	2301	RED	5469
Par	4	3	5	3	4	5	5	4	5	38	Par	75
Handicap	6	18	2	16	4	8	12	14	10			

Manager/Pro: Mahlon Dow, PGA   **Supt:** Dave Gilette
Architect: Mike Myles 1960

THE MEADOWS AT MIDDLESEX   PUBLIC

70 Hunters Glen Dr., Plainsboro, NJ 08536   **(609) 799-4000**
www.imiddlesex.e-golf.net

The Meadows @ Middlesex is an 18 hole course open to the public 7 days a week all year. Part of the Middlesex Cty. system, residents w/ID may call for tee times up to 6 days in advance at (732) 951-8920. Non residents may play as walk ons.

Driving Range	
• Practice Green	• Lockers
• Power Carts	• Showers
• Pull Carts	• Food
• Club Rental	• Clubhouse
• Soft Spikes	• Outings

Fees	Weekday	Weekend
Res/ID	$20	$28
Non-res	$32	$40
Sr/ID	$12	
Power carts	$28	Sr $17/2

Course Description: Formerly Princeton Meadows, the course is flat, open, easy to walk with greens that are small with some break. The back nine is much more difficult than the front. There is an abundance of water available to help keep the course green even during hot dry summers. The par 3 17th signature hole requires a shot over a pond and is considered most picturesque. The course is maintained in excellent shape with a state-of-the-art irrigation system.

Directions: Middlesex County, #26 on West Central Map
NJTPKE to Exit #8. Make a right and bear left to 2nd light to Rte. 130 South(Georges Rd.) Turn left to 2nd light & turn right onto Dey Rd. At 2nd light turn left onto Scudders Mill Rd. After 2 lights & 300 yards turn left onto Hunters Glen Rd. (part of a condo dev.) Proceed 3/8 mile to course on left.

Hole	1	2	3	4	5	6	7	8	9	Out	BLUE	Rating 70.3
BLUE	525	155	350	390	410	160	515	160	325	2990		Slope 121
WHITE	495	131	323	369	398	150	502	147	300	2817		
Par	5	3	4	4	4	3	5	3	4	35	WHITE	Rating 68.7
Handicap	4	12	14	8	2	18	10	16	6			Slope 118
RED	475	120	290	360	388	139	472	135	290	2669		
Par	5	3	4	4	4	3	5	3	4	35	RED	Rating 71.5
Handicap	4	12	14	8	2	18	10	16	6			Slope 122

Hole	10	11	12	13	14	15	16	17	18	In		Totals
BLUE	195	430	510	452	400	220	435	148	510	3300	BLUE	6290
WHITE	185	326	498	442	392	208	426	137	500	3114	WHITE	5931
Par	3	4	5	4	4	3	4	3	5	35	Par	70
Handicap	15	9	11	1	13	5	3	17	7			
RED	150	270	450	395	385	165	390	130	465	2800	RED	5469
Par	3	4	5	4	4	3	4	3	5	35	Par	70
Handicap	15	9	11	1	13	5	3	17	7			

Mgr: Susan Desario   **Pro:** Randy Luberecki, PGA   **Supt:** Ewan Macauley
Architect: Joe Finger 1978

MERCER OAKS GOLF COURSE

PUBLIC

Village Rd. West, West Windsor, NJ 08561
www.usegolf.com

(609) 936-9603

Operated by Mercer County, Mercer Oaks has 2 18 hole courses open between Mar. 15 & Dec., 7 days a week. ID cards are available: Tee time policy: registered with ID, call **(609) 989-7398** 7 days in advance. Greens fees are $5 higher pp on the East Course.

- Driving Range
- Practice Green
- Power Carts
- Pull Carts
- Club Rental
- Soft Spikes
- Lockers
- Showers
- Food
- Clubhouse
- Outings

Fees	Weekday	Weekend
ReswID	$18	$20
No ID	$35	$39
Power carts	$26	
Twi, Jr/Sr discounts		

Course Description: Many old trees have been preserved on the relatively flat and tree lined West course. Large undulating greens with sizeable steep moguls protecting them and well placed bunkers affect play. The par 4 signature 17th, 405 yards from the back tees, has an elevated tee and a lake alongside of it requiring a forced carry on the approach shot to the green. The facility has a new state of the art clubhouse with facilities for large banquets.. The East Course, opened in 2003, is a links type, 7200 yards from the tips. The scorecard below is for the West Course.

Directions: Mercer County, #27 on West Central Map
Rte. 295 to Exit#65A, Sloan Ave. Go East on Sloan to 1st light and make a left on Quakerbridge Rd. At third light go right on Village Rd. West. Course is 1 mile on right.

Hole	1	2	3	4	5	6	7	8	9	Out	BLUE	Rating 73.5
BLUE	395	365	445	535	213	454	600	165	380	3552		Slope 129
WHITE	360	335	375	505	160	400	535	155	350	3175		
Par	4	4	4	5	3	4	5	3	4	36	WHITE	Rating 70.3
Handicap	15	13	5	7	9	1	3	17	11			Slope 121
RED	320	310	340	445	110	360	460	110	275	2730		
Par	4	4	4	5	3	4	5	3	4	36	RED	Rating 70.2
Handicap	15	13	5	7	9	1	3	17	11			Slope 120
Hole	10	11	12	13	14	15	16	17	18	In		Totals
BLUE	390	450	425	160	355	505	240	405	535	3465	BLUE	7053
WHITE	360	410	380	130	325	465	185	365	510	3130	WHITE	6305
Par	4	4	4	3	4	5	3	4	5	36	Par	72
Handicap	14	2	6	18	12	10	4	8	16			
RED	325	340	340	115	300	415	155	300	335	2625	RED	5355
Par	4	4	4	3	4	5	3	4	5	36	Par	72
Handicap	14	2	6	18	16	12	10	4	8			

Manager/Pro: Bobby Kauth, PGA   **Supt:** Bob Bishop
Architect: Brian Ault 1990

METUCHEN GOLF & CC

Plainfield Rd., Edison, NJ 08818   **(732) 548-3003**

Metuchen is an 18 hole golf course open 6 days a week and closed in January. Guests may play accompanied by a member. Tee time reservations are required for weekends. Pull carts permitted after 3PM.

> Driving Range   •**Lockers**
> •**Practice Green**   •**Showers**
> •**Power Carts**   •**Food**
> •**Pull Carts**   •**Clubhouse**
> •**Club Rental**   •**Outings**
> •**Caddies**   •**Soft Spikes**

Course Description: With its rolling land, amply bunkered greens and heavily treed terrain, Metuchen presents a challenge to all golfers. A feature of this well conditioned relatively flat course is the variety of its greens; each has a different shape and contour. Water is not a major factor. The seventh and twelfth holes have a double green. The signature #14 par 4 has a tree in the middle of the fairway and requires a shot over a pond to the green.

Directions: Middlesex County, #28 on West Central Map
GSP to Exit #131. Go right to Rte. 27 South. At 6th traffic light, make a right onto Central Ave. which becomes Plainfield Rd. Club is about 1 & 1/2 miles on right.

Hole	1	2	3	4	5	6	7	8	9	Out	BLUE	Rating 71.9
BLUE	398	199	387	376	353	522	457	446	376	3514		Slope 130
WHITE	387	178	365	350	331	478	441	402	364	3296		
Par	4	3	4	4	4	5	4	4	4	36	WHITE	Rating 70.3
Handicap	5	11	17	9	15	7	1	3	13			Slope 127
RED	375	156	352	329	319	412	378	391	345	3057		
Par	4	3	4	4	4	5	4	5	4	37	RED	Rating 74.1
Handicap	3	17	15	9	11	1	5	7	13			Slope 133
Hole	10	11	12	13	14	15	16	17	18	In		Totals
BLUE	281	555	292	542	408	314	156	394	167	3109	BLUE	6623
WHITE	262	521	284	534	400	287	144	381	147	2960	WHITE	6256
Par	4	5	4	5	4	4	3	4	3	36	Par	72
Handicap	14	4	12	6	2	10	18	8	16			
RED	257	454	276	459	376	270	126	317	133	2668	RED	5725
Par	4	5	4	5	5	4	3	4	3	37	Par	74
Handicap	14	6	10	2	4	12	18	8	16			

Manager: Tod Pierce   **Pro:** Andy Brock, PGA   **Supt:** Brett Price
Architects: Marty O'Loughlin, Charles Laing   **Built:** 1915

SEMI-PRIVATE

106 B Sharon Rd., Robbinsville, NJ 08691   **(609) 259-1010**

Miry Run is an 18 hole course open to the public all year, 7 days a week. Memberships are available. Tee times: mbrs. up to 14 days in advance /non-mbrs 7 days. Driving range/irons only. Carts are mandatory until 1PM on weekends.

•Driving Range	•Lockers
•Practice Green	•Showers
•Power Carts	•Food
•Pull Carts	•Clubhouse
•Club Rental	•Outings
•Soft Spikes	

Fees	Weekday	Weekend
Daily	$22	$30
Twi.	$18	$25
Power carts $15pp		
M-Fri $60/2 w cart & food		

Course Description: Originally known as Skyview CC, Miry Run was later named for the Miry Run Creek that runs through the course. It is well maintained and relatively flat with fast greens that vary in size. The front is somewhat open; the back more so. The signature third hole has a lake and creek in front of the green. The 18th, a dogleg left, features a horseshoe shaped bunker that protects the rear and both sides of the green.

Directions: Mercer County, #29 on West Central Map
From North: NJTPKE to Exit 7A. Take Rte. I-95 West; exit at #5B to Rte. 130 North. Go to 4th light and make a right onto Sharon Rd. Club is ahead on right. From South: NJTPKE to Exit 7 to Rte. 206 North which goes into Rte. 130 N. Go 3 lights past I-95 interchange to Sharon Rd.

Hole	1	2	3	4	5	6	7	8	9	Out	BLUE	Rating 71.9
BLUE	543	166	386	382	520	385	394	197	405	3378		Slope 116
WHITE	528	151	371	367	505	370	379	182	389	3242		
Par	5	3	4	4	5	4	4	3	4	36	WHITE	Rating 70.7
Handicap	15	13	1	9	17	7	5	11	3			Slope 114
RED	463	122	330	300	460	305	341	167	354	2842		
Par	5	3	4	4	5	4	4	3	4	36	RED	Rating 70.7
Handicap	6	12	2	14	8	16	10	18	4			Slope 114

Hole	10	11	12	13	14	15	16	17	18	In		Totals
BLUE	221	405	403	345	377	552	434	231	503	3471	BLUE	6849
WHITE	206	390	388	330	362	537	419	216	488	3336	WHITE	6578
Par	3	4	4	4	4	5	4	3	5	36	Par	72
Handicap	10	4	6	18	12	8	2	14	16			
RED	141	355	375	315	347	422	400	170	435	2960	RED	5802
Par	3	4	4	4	4	5	5	3	5	37	Par	73
Handicap	17	5	1	15	9	11	3	13	7			

Manager: Heidi Matisa   **Pro:** Mike Beal, PGA   **Supt:** Richard Potts
Architect: Fred Lambert 1966

MOUNTAIN VIEW GOLF COURSE

PUBLIC

Bear Tavern Rd., West Trenton, NJ 08628   **(609) 882-4093**
www.usegolf.com

Mountain View is a Mercer County public course open 7 days a week, all year. Tee times: up to 7 days in advance for Mercer Cty residents w/ID.

- •Driving Range
- •Practice Green
- •Power Carts
- •Pull Carts
- •Club Rental
- •Soft Spikes

- •Lockers
- •Showers
- •Food
- •Clubhouse
- •Outings

Fees	Weekday	Weekend
Daily/ID	$13	$15
Non-res	$26	$30
Jr/Sr	$9	
Power carts	$26	

Course Description: Well maintained with beautiful high vistas, Mountain View is a relatively flat public course. The back nine is more hilly than the front. The layout has mostly wide fairways with some holes tree-lined. Water affects play on two holes. The par 4 twelfth, uphill over a pond, is the most difficult. A new sprinkler system has recently been installed. There are golf leagues that play here making the course very busy in summer.

Directions: Mercer County, #30 on West Central Map
NJTPKE to Exit #9, then take Rte. 1 South. At Lawrenceville, watch for exit to Rtes. I-95 & 295. Take Exit #2 at Bear Tavern Rd. (Rte. 579)& left off exit ramp. Go right on Nursery which becomes Mountain View Rd.; course is ahead on right.

Hole	1	2	3	4	5	6	7	8	9	Out	BLUE	Rating 72.6
BLUE	390	375	350	235	545	410	145	420	425	3295		Slope 127
WHITE	365	350	335	190	450	380	135	395	405	3005		
Par	4	4	4	3	5	4	3	4	4	35	WHITE	Rating 69.8
Handicap	13	15	16	11	5	8	18	1	3			Slope 122
RED	330	300	290	165	410	340	125	300	330	2590		
Par	4	4	4	3	5	4	3	4	4	35	RED	Rating 70.8
Handicap	13	15	16	11	5	8	18	1	3			Slope 118

Hole	10	11	12	13	14	15	16	17	18	In		Totals
BLUE	530	470	440	165	375	345	430	210	515	3480	BLUE	6775
WHITE	490	440	405	140	340	330	390	190	490	3215	WHITE	6220
Par	5	5	4	3	4	4	4	3	5	37	Par	72
Handicap	9	7	2	17	10	12	4	6	14			
RED	460	375	350	110	320	310	380	155	450	2910	RED	5500
Par	5	5	4	3	4	4	5	3	5	38	Par	73
Handicap	9	7	2	17	10	12	4	6	14			

Manager: Richard Hills   **Pro:** Steve Bowers, PGA   **Supt:** Robert Bishop
Built: 1958

NESHANIC VALLEY GOLF COURSE

PUBLIC

2301 South Branch Rd., Neshanic Station, NJ 08853 (908) 369-8200

Neshanic Valley has 27 regulation holes plus a 9 hole executive course. Operated by the Somerset County Park Commission 7 days a week and closed in the winter, residents with an ID call automated tee time @ (908)231-1122. Memberships are available. Clubhouse will be ready in 2005.

- •Driving Range
- •Practice Green
- •Power Carts
- •Pull Carts
- Club Rental
- •Soft Spikes

Lockers
Showers
•Food
•Clubhouse
•Outings

NEW

Fees	Weekday	Weekend
Res/ID	$65	$65
non res	$42	$55
Sr/Jr.	$39	$39

Course Description: How lucky are the residents of Somerset County to have this wonderful golf course that includes a Callaway Performance Center. Formerly 2 large farms on 350 acres, the rolling topography has 4 man-made ponds and sensitively handled wetlands running throughout. The prevailing wind adds to the difficulty as well as the fescue grass and the subtle, undulating medium to large greens. The learning facility offers areas for pitching and chipping, a 2 sided driving range and 2 practice holes. The Scorecard below is for the Meadow and Lake nines.

Directions: Somerset County, #31 on West Central Map
Take Rte 287S to Exit 17. From Somerville circle, take 202 South and left on W. County Drive which becomes So. Branch Rd. to course on left.

Hole	1	2	3	4	5	6	7	8	9	Out	BLACK	Rating 73.8
BLACK	419	391	197	523	458	175	336	444	577	3520		Slope 130
BLUE	374	338	145	468	401	137	295	392	520	3070		
Par	4	4	3	5	4	3	4	4	5	36	BLUE	Rating 69.3
Handicap	5	6	8	2	3	9	7	4	1			Slope 121
GREEN	303	272	97	408	335	83	232	327	467	2524		
Par	4	4	3	5	4	3	4	4	5	36	GREEN	Rating 69.4
Handicap	5	6	8	2	3	9	7	4	1			Slope 119

Hole	10	11	12	13	14	15	16	17	18	In		Totals
BLACK	434	362	174	458	588	422	382	204	525	3549	BLACK	7059
BLUE	387	316	132	404	533	361	330	170	471	3104	BLUE	6174
Par	4	4	3	4	5	4	4	3	5	36	Par	72
Handicap	4	7	9	3	1	5	6	8	2			
GREEN	332	244	82	357	464	300	259	117	417	2572	GREEN	5096
Par	4	4	3	4	5	4	4	3	5	36	Par	72
Handicap	4	7	9	3	1	5	6	8	2			

Mgr: Alan Conover   **Pro:** Fred Glass, PGA   **Supt:** Darrell Marcinek
Architect: Hurdzan/Fry 2004

NEW JERSEY NATIONAL GOLF CLUB

PRIVATE

579 Allen Rd. Basking Ridge, NJ 07920   **(908) 781-9400**
www.newjerseynational.com

New Jersey National is an 18 hole private course open 6 days a week all year, weather permitting. It is part of Empire Golf Clubmax and entitles members privileges at Pine Hill, Pine Barrens, Branton Woods, Hollow Brook and Minisceongo.

•**Driving Range**	•**Lockers**
•**Practice Green**	•**Showers**
•**Power Carts**	•**Food**
Pull Carts	•**Clubhouse**
•**Club Rental**	•**Outings**
•**Caddies**	•**Soft Spikes**

Course Description: New Jersey National, formerly a public course that has gone private, is carved out of heavily treed terrain and natural wetlands. It is an impressive and beautiful layout having virtually no parallel fairways. The holes are each memorable; differing lengths, unique topography and level changes add interest. The large bent grass greens are fast and well bunkered. The signature par 4 #17 requires a long carry over a catch basin from the back tees. The 8th is a double dogleg with a lengthy carry over a ditch. The 5 sets of tees make the course playable for golfers of every skill level.

Directions: Somerset County, #32 on West Central Map
Rte.287South to Exit 22. Bear right at exit and then make an immediate U turn onto Rtes.202/206South. Get in left lane, go under Rte.287 and turn left onto Schley Mt. Rd. Proceed through Hills development. Course is about 2 miles ahead on left.

Hole	1	2	3	4	5	6	7	8	9	Out	BLUE	Rating 72.1
BLUE	400	495	388	165	395	387	140	539	369	3278		Slope 130
WHITE	365	471	367	145	380	371	131	515	361	3106		
Par	4	5	4	3	4	4	3	5	4	36	WHITE	Rating 70.5
Handicap	8	4	10	16	14	6	18	2	12			Slope 127
RED	298	412	281	118	257	288	107	405	235	2401		
Par	4	5	4	3	4	4	3	5	4	36	RED	Rating 68.8
Handicap	10	2	8	16	12	6	18	4	14			Slope 121
Hole	10	11	12	13	14	15	16	17	18	In		Totals
BLUE	450	202	367	546	431	182	341	375	553	3447	BLUE	6725
WHITE	423	184	355	521	409	170	335	335	535	3267	WHITE	6373
Par	4	3	4	5	4	3	4	4	5	36	Par	72
Handicap	1	13	9	7	5	15	17	11	3			
RED	325	130	310	468	345	122	270	219	429	2618	RED	5019
Par	4	3	4	5	4	3	4	4	5	36	Par	72
Handicap	7	17	9	3	5	15	13	11	1			

Manager: Ed Scott   **Pro:** Mark Mahon   **Supt:** Brad Fox
Architect: Roy Case 1997

OAK HILL GOLF CLUB

15 Fernwood Rd., Milford, NJ 08848   **(908) 995-2285**

Oak Hill is an 18 hole private club open 7 days a week and closed Jan. and Feb. Guests may play accompanied by a member or during the week, unaccompanied per member's request. Tee time reservations are not necessary.

•**Driving Range**   •**Lockers**   •**Practice Green**   •**Showers**   •**Power Carts**   •**Food**   •**Pull Carts**   •**Clubhouse**   •**Club Rental**   •**Outings**   Caddies   •**Soft Spikes**

Course Description: A hilly layout, Oak Hill is a challenge for all: its severely sloped greens make three putting commonplace. The picturesque property offers panoramic views, including the entire Delaware Valley. The course is very well maintained and has excellent drainage. Its signature 15th hole, which is considered a very difficult par 3, is tight and features a dramatically contoured green. In the past, Oak Hill has hosted several MGA and NJSGA tournaments as well as Trenton District events.

Directions: Hunterdon County, #33 on West Central Map
NJTPKE or GSP to Rte. 78 West to Exit 11. Follow signs to Pattenburg and take bridge over Rte. 78 & bear right onto Rte. 614. Stay on 614 for about 6 miles: follow signs carefully for Rte. 614 W. Go right onto Rte. 519 for 1 mile; at Fernwood, go right to club.

Hole	1	2	3	4	5	6	7	8	9	Out	BLUE	Rating 71.3
BLUE	388	373	182	418	167	535	400	515	396	3374		Slope 125
WHITE	377	362	171	385	154	520	387	510	360	3226		
Par	4	4	3	4	3	5	4	5	4	36	WHITE	Rating 69.9
Handicap	9	11	17	7	15	3	13	1	5			Slope 123
RED	365	351	160	368	119	446	360	420	321	2910		
Par	4	4	3	4	3	5	4	5	4	36	RED	Rating 74.1
Handicap	11	7	15	13	17	1	9	3	5			Slope 130
Hole	10	11	12	13	14	15	16	17	18	In		Totals
BLUE	541	146	418	387	369	228	355	356	528	3328	BLUE	6702
WHITE	530	119	407	371	358	215	325	345	513	3183	WHITE	6409
Par	5	3	4	4	4	3	4	4	5	36	Par	72
Handicap	4	18	2	12	8	6	10	16	14			
RED	475	102	320	360	347	153	291	334	443	2825	RED	5735
Par	5	3	4	4	4	3	4	4	5	36	Par	72
Handicap	2	18	8	16	6	10	14	12	4			

Pro: Michael P. Knight, PGA   **Supt:** David McGhee
Architect: William Gordon 1963

PEDDIE SCHOOL GOLF COURSE `PRIVATE`

S.Main St. (PO Box A), Hightstown, NJ 08520   **(609) 490-7542**

Peddie School Golf Course is an 18 hole private club open 7 days a week, all year. Guests may play accompanied by a member. Students have privileges while school is in session. There is a waiting list to get into this club.

> •**Driving Range**   •**Lockers**
> •**Practice Green**   •**Showers**
> •**Power Carts**   •**Food**
> •**Pull Carts**   •**Clubhouse**
> •**Club Rental**   •**Outings**
>   Caddies   •**Soft Spikes**

Course Description: The European style golf course at the Peddie School is tight with many old trees lining the fairways. There are small greens that play hard and fast; well placed approach shots are necessary to score well. Some consider the par 4 fourth the signature hole because of its picturesque tree lined fairway and water to carry in front of the green.

Directions: Mercer County, #34 on West Central Map
NJTPKE to Exit #8. Take Rte. 33 West to first light, then go left. Make right turn at STOP sign onto Ward St. Make the next left at STOP sign onto S. Main St. Course is 1 mile on left.

Hole	1	2	3	4	5	6	7	8	9	Out	BLUE	Rating
BLUE												Slope
WHITE	523	352	115	380	121	381	492	350	413	3127		
Par	5	4	3	4	3	4	5	4	4	36	WHITE	Rating 69.8
Handicap	7	13	17	3	15	5	9	11	1			Slope 119
RED	485	306	115	334	109	333	441	350	413	2886		
Par	5	4	3	4	3	4	5	4	5	37	RED	Rating 71.6
Handicap	5	11	15	1	17	9	3	7	13			Slope 124
Hole	10	11	12	13	14	15	16	17	18	In		Totals
BLUE											BLUE	
WHITE	385	307	560	135	485	360	157	177	550	3151	WHITE	6278
Par	4	4	5	3	5	4	3	3	5	36	Par	72
Handicap	2	18	6	12	14	8	16	10	4			
RED	320	307	471	105	412	301	157	130	470	2673	RED	5559
Par	4	4	5	3	5	4	3	3	5	36	Par	73
Handicap	10	12	2	18	6	8	14	16	4			

Manager/Pro: Mike Bechsel, PGA   **Supt:** Bill Greene
Built: 1st nine 1920s, 2nd nine 1950s

PLAINFIELD COUNTRY CLUB

PRIVATE

Box 311 Woodland Ave., Plainfield, NJ 07061   **(908) 769-3666**
www.plainfieldcc.com

Plainfield CC is an 18 hole private course open all year, 6 days a week.   Guests may play accompanied by a member. Tee time reservations are advisable. Outings are held on Mondays.

- •Driving Range
- •Practice Green
- •Power Carts
- Pull Carts
- •Club Rental
- •Caddies
- •Lockers
- •Showers
- •Food
- •Clubhouse
- •Outings
- •Soft Spikes

Course Description: A true Donald Ross gem, Plainfield ranks as one of the finest and most difficult courses in the US and has an illustrious history. Over 100 years old, it has hosted the 1978 US Amateur Tournament won by John Cook and the 1987 Ladies US Open won by Laura Davies. The course is hilly, scenic and very well maintained. Even the driving range has a spectacular view of the Watchung Mountains. The dogleg par 4 seventeenth is a most outstanding hole. The par 3 third hole requires a 160 yard carry over water from the blue tees. A ravine comes into play on the 2nd shot of the par 5 twelfth hole.

Directions: Middlesex County, #35 on West Central Map
GSP South to Exit #131, Iselin-Metuchen. Keep right to 1st light. Turn right onto Wood Ave. At 1st light go left onto Oak Tree Rd. for 3 & 1/2 mi. to Woodland Ave. Turn right and club is 1 mile on right.

Hole	1	2	3	4	5	6	7	8	9	Out	BLUE	Rating 74.2
BLUE	431	450	179	331	525	141	458	510	367	3392		Slope 140
WHITE	421	445	160	312	509	130	400	482	356	3215		
Par	4	4	3	4	5	3	4	5	4	36	WHITE	Rating 72.1
Handicap	5	1	13	15	11	17	3	9	7			Slope 135
RED	404	423	151	265	486	102	327	450	310	2918		
Par	5	5	3	4	5	3	4	5	4	38	RED	Rating 75.4
Handicap	13	5	15	7	1	17	11	3	9			Slope 141
Hole	10	11	12	13	14	15	16	17	18	In		Totals
BLUE	360	147	585	447	224	371	554	423	384	3495	BLUE	6887
WHITE	349	139	555	394	188	357	537	404	366	3289	WHITE	6504
Par	4	3	5	4	3	4	5	4	4	36	Par	72
Handicap	16	18	6	4	12	10	8	2	14			
RED	274	132	512	313	136	320	490	313	321	2811	RED	5729
Par	4	3	5	4	3	4	5	4	4	36	Par	74
Handicap	14	18	2	12	16	6	4	8	10			

Manager: Manny Gugliuzza   **Pro:** Scott Paris, PGA   **Supt:** Greg James
Architect: Donald Ross 1890

PLAINFIELD CC - WEST NINE

PUBLIC

Corner Woodland & Maple Ave., Edison, NJ 08818   **(908) 769-3672**

Plainfield West Country Club is a 9 hole golf course open to the public 7 days a week all year. Memberships are available with discounts for seniors and juniors. Tee time reservations are not necessary.

Driving Range	Lockers
•Practice Green	Showers
•Power Carts	•Food
•Pull Carts	Clubhouse
•Club Rental	Outings
•Soft Spikes	

Fees	Weekday	Weekend
Member	$13	$15
Non-Mbr	$24	$29
Sr	$10	$13
Power carts	$22/18	$11/9

Course Description: This well maintained nine hole course is ideal for seniors and beginners. Plainfield West has wide open undulating fairways, rolling terrain and small greens, some of which are a punch-bowl type. The first and second holes are long and challenging with difficult rough. The property is owned by Plainfield Country Club which can be seen across the field. Green fees are for all day play. A second nine may be played changing the tee position.

Directions: Middlesex County, #36 on West Central Map
GSP to Exit #131. Keep right to 1st traffic light and turn right onto Wood Ave. At 1st light, make a left onto Oak Tree Ave. Go approx. 3 & 1/2 miles to Woodland Ave. and turn right. Club is 1 mile on right.

Hole	1	2	3	4	5	6	7	8	9	Out	BLUE	Rating
BLUE												Slope
WHITE	409	413	151	241	179	339	189	274	308	2503		
Par	4	4	3	4	3	4	3	4	4	33	WHITE	Rating 63.7
Handicap	1	3	9	15	7	5	13	17	11			Slope 108
RED												
Par	5	5	3	4	3	4	3	4	4	35	RED	Rating 68.5
Handicap												Slope 111

Hole	10	11	12	13	14	15	16	17	18	In		Totals
BLUE											BLUE	
WHITE											WHITE	5006
Par											Par	66
Handicap												
RED											RED	4986
Par											Par	70
Handicap												

Manager: Kumi Inoue   **Pro:** Babe Lechardus, PGA   **Supt:** Greg James
Architect: Tom Bendelow 1932   **Estab:** 1898

PRINCETON COUNTRY CLUB

PUBLIC

1 Wheeler Way, Princeton, NJ 08540   **(609) 452-9382**
www.thegolfnetwork.com

Princeton Country Club is an 18 hole public golf course operated by the Mercer County Park Commission and open 7 days a week, all year. Residents obtain ID ($22). Tee time reservations are not necessary. Walk ons are encouraged.

Driving Range	• Lockers
• Practice Green	Showers
• Power Carts	• Food
• Pull Carts	• Clubhouse
• Club Rental	• Outings
• Soft Spikes	

Fees	Weekday	Weekend
Res w/ID	$13	$15
Non-res	$26	$30
Sr/Jr	$9	
Power carts	$26	

Course Description: This popular county course is short, well bunkered and tightly wooded. Seniors like Princeton Country Club because it is flat and easy to walk. Several of the greens are elevated and water comes into play from the 13th hole through the 17th. The most challenging hole is the par 5 second, a dogleg right, 220 yards to the corner. This course gets quite busy in summer.

Directions: Mercer County, #37 on West Central Map
From North: NJTPKE to Exit #9 to Rte. 1 South. In Princeton, from Rte. 1 go right on Emmons Drive, then left on Wheeler Way to club on right.
From South: Take Rte. 1 North, make a left from the Meadow Rd. jughandle back onto Rte. 1 South, then right onto Emmons Drive as above.

Hole	1	2	3	4	5	6	7	8	9	Out	BLUE	Rating 68.8
BLUE	345	515	420	150	370	360	180	355	325	3020		Slope 123
WHITE	335	500	410	140	355	345	170	340	310	2905		
Par	4	5	4	3	4	4	3	4	4	35	WHITE	Rating 67.6
Handicap	11	1	3	17	5	9	13	7	15			Slope 121
RED	300	470	380	110	325	320	145	315	290	2655		
Par	4	5	5	3	4	4	3	4	4	36	RED	Rating 70.7
Handicap	11	1	3	17	5	9	13	7	15			Slope 122
Hole	10	11	12	13	14	15	16	17	18	In		Totals
BLUE	370	335	355	175	395	300	170	510	430	3040	BLUE	6060
WHITE	360	325	345	165	385	290	160	490	420	2940	WHITE	5845
Par	4	4	4	3	4	4	3	5	4	35	Par	70
Handicap	10	14	12	8	4	18	16	2	6			
RED	335	300	320	110	360	280	135	465	400	2705	RED	5360
Par	4	4	4	3	4	4	3	5	5	36	Par	72
Handicap	10	14	12	8	4	18	16	2	6			

Managers: Various   **Pro:** Steve Bowers, PGA   **Supt:** Frank Caravella
Architects: William & David Gordon 1964

QUAIL BROOK GOLF COURSE   PUBLIC

625 New Brunswick Rd., Somerset, NJ 08873   **(732) 560-9199**

Quail Brook is operated by the Somerset County Park Commission. It has 18 holes and is open to the public all year, 7 days a week. Registered residents call up to 7 days in advance @ (908) 231-1122. Special weekday cart rates for seniors.

•**Driving Range**	Lockers
•**Practice Green**	Showers
•**Power Carts**	•**Food**
•**Pull Carts**	•**Clubhouse**
•**Club Rental**	•**Outings**
•**Soft Spikes**	

Fees	Weekday	Weekend
Resw/ID	$17	$19
Non-res	$34	$38
Sr/Jr	$10	
Power carts	$26	Srs. $20

Course Description: Quail Brook can be proud of two of what is considered the best holes on a public course in New Jersey; numbers 17 & 18. The lengthy 17th hole has a tree blocking the tee shot, and needs super accuracy to a green surrounded by traps. The eighteenth is equally difficult. Water comes into play only on holes one and two with an errant shot likely to land in Quail Brook Lake. This course is very busy on weekends and draws players from Staten Island and Middlesex County, as well as Somerset.

Directions: Somerset County, #38 on West Central Map
Rte. 287 to Exit #10. Exit off ramp and take a right at 2nd light onto Cedar Grove Lane. Go to New Brunswick Rd. and turn left. Course is on right.

Hole	1	2	3	4	5	6	7	8	9	Out	BLUE	Rating 71.4
BLUE	519	359	352	191	398	538	404	166	346	3273		Slope 123
WHITE	456	315	324	163	355	500	357	145	313	2928		
Par	5	4	4	3	4	5	4	3	4	36	WHITE	Rating 68.9
Handicap	5	11	9	15	3	1	7	17	13			Slope 118
RED	436	298	296	135	337	413	312	124	287	2638		
Par	5	4	4	3	4	5	4	3	4	36	RED	Rating 70.9
Handicap	1	9	11	15	5	3	7	17	13			Slope 119

Hole	10	11	12	13	14	15	16	17	18	In		Totals
BLUE	353	151	407	384	525	151	336	470	424	3201	BLUE	6614
WHITE	308	133	356	344	486	128	323	435	394	2907	WHITE	6058
Par	4	3	4	4	5	3	4	4	4	35	Par	71
Handicap	12	16	8	10	6	18	14	2	4			
RED	292	123	301	327	462	105	298	401	327	2636	RED	5385
Par	4	3	4	4	5	3	4	5	4	36	Par	72
Handicap	14	16	10	8	2	18	12	4	6			

Manager: Joe Bozzomo   **Pro:** Fred Glass, PGA   **Supt:** Thomas Grigal
Architect: Edmund Ault 1982

RARITAN LANDING GOLF COURSE PUBLIC

491 Sidney Road, Piscataway, NJ 08854   **(732) 885-9600**
www.imiddlesex.e-golf.net

Raritan Landing Golf Course is a Middlesex County 18 hole executive par 58 course open 7 days a week, all year. Registered golfers with ID may make tee times by calling (732 951-8920). Discounts for Jrs. & Srs.

Driving Range	Lockers
•**Practice Green**	Showers
•**Power Carts**	•**Food**
•**Pull Carts**	•**Clubhouse**
•**Club Rental**	•**Outings**
•**Soft Spikes**	

Fees	Weekday	Weekend
Reg w ID	$16	$18
Non-reg cty	$24	$26
Non res.	$28	$30
Power carts	$26	

Course Description: Built on 103 acres of county owned land, Raritan Landing is an 18 hole executive style 3400 yard par 58 public course with 14 par 3s and 4 par 4s. Environmentally friendly in design, the builders have preserved trees, natural rolling terrain and vegetation. Creeks are present resulting in the need to hit over water many times. Some of the undulating greens are two-tiered giving such contour that the golfer can often get on in one only to putt in three. The course is a great place to practice the short game.

Directions: Middlesex County, #38 on West Central Map
NJTPKE North to Exit #9, bear right to Rte. 18N. Proceed on Rte. 18 thru N.Bruns, over Lynch Bridge & go left at River Rd. to 2nd light; on top of hill go right onto Hoes Lane West to end of road & at light go left onto Hoes Lane. At 4th light make a right at Sidney Rd. to course on right.

Hole	1	2	3	4	5	6	7	8	9	Out	BLUE	Rating
BLUE												Slope
WHITE	139	144	264	144	170	139	342	158	160	1660		
Par	3	3	4	3	3	3	4	3	3	29	WHITE	Rating 57.8
Handicap												Slope 88
RED	105	114	226	103	132	96	234	117	126	1253		
Par	3	3	4	3	3	3	4	3	3	29	RED	Rating 54.6
Handicap												Slope 80
Hole	10	11	12	13	14	15	16	17	18	In		Totals
BLUE											BLUE	
WHITE	108	108	121	138	173	329	341	148	170	1636	WHITE	3296
Par	3	3	3	3	3	4	4	3	3	29	Par	58
Handicap												
RED	72	87	90	98	143	296	291	120	133	1330	RED	2583
Par	3	3	3	3	3	4	4	3	3	29	Par	58
Handicap												

Manager: Rick Dalina   **Supt:** Charles McMonagle
Architect: Stephen Kay 1999

RARITAN VALLEY COUNTRY CLUB | PRIVATE

747 Route 28 Bridgewater, NJ 08807   (908) 722-2000

Raritan Valley is a private 18 hole course open 6 days a week and closed for the month of February. Guests may play accompanied by a member. Tee time reservations are required after 11:30 AM on weekends.

•Driving Range	•Lockers
•Practice Green	•Showers
•Power Carts	•Food
Pull Carts	•Clubhouse
•Club Rental	•Outings
•Caddies	•Soft Spikes

Course Description: The extremely well-maintained Raritan Valley seems cool on hot days due to the winds from the west. With its gently rolling and well bunkered fairways, it is a deceivingly difficult layout. Well placed shots are rewarded on this generously wide course. The par 3 seventh signature hole requires a shot over a pond; a stone wall guards that green. Water also affects play on the 4th, 15th and 16th holes. Qualifying rounds for State Match Play championships were held here.

Directions: Somerset County, #39 on West Central Map
NJTPKE to Exit #10. Then take Rte. 287 North to Somerville. Exit at Rte. 22. Go west and take Rtes. 202/206 South towards Princeton. At 1st traffic circle take 1st right to Rte. 28. Raritan Valley is immediately after circle on right.

Hole	1	2	3	4	5	6	7	8	9	Out	BLUE	Rating 72.2
BLUE	570	414	424	337	343	205	173	432	493	3390		Slope 131
WHITE	563	401	418	332	334	198	135	424	480	3285		
Par	5	4	4	4	4	3	3	4	5	36	WHITE	Rating 71.1
Handicap	3	5	7	11	13	15	17	1	9			Slope 129
RED	444	301	310	252	295	167	79	328	440	2616		
Par	5	4	4	4	4	3	3	4	5	36	RED	Rating 71.3
Handicap	3	11	9	13	7	15	17	5	1			Slope 124
Hole	10	11	12	13	14	15	16	17	18	In		Totals
BLUE	151	530	528	390	381	205	427	405	400	3417	BLUE	6808
WHITE	147	524	511	353	361	190	417	390	388	3281	WHITE	6566
Par	3	5	5	4	4	3	4	4	4	36	Par	72
Handicap	18	6	4	14	12	16	2	8	10			
RED	127	462	417	307	287	138	366	310	315	2729	RED	5345
Par	3	5	5	4	4	3	4	4	4	36	Par	72
Handicap	18	4	2	12	14	16	6	10	8			

Manager: Robert Osborne   **Pro:** John Fagan, PGA   **Supt:** Al Rathjens
Architect: Herbert Barker 1911

REGENCY AT MONROE

51 County Club Dr, Monroe Twp, NJ 08831   **(732) 605-9057**

Regency at Monroe is a 9 hole par 3 course within a gated adult community. Residents have golf memberships but it is also open to the public. Open 6 days a week, it is closed Jan & Feb. Tee times may be made up to 7 days in advance

•**Driving Range**	Lockers
•**Practice Green**	Showers
•**Power Carts**	
Pull Carts	•**Food**
•Club Rental	Clubhouse
•**Soft Spikes**	•**Outings**

Fees	Weekday	Weekend
Daily 9hole	$15	$15
Power carts $10pp		

Course Description: Regency at Monroe is a well maintained 9 hole par 3 course that offers a variety of holes. The greens are hand cut and in great condition. The first six holes are over the natural lakes that were formed from a former quarry. 5 sets of tees are planned as well as some lengthening which will result in a total yardage of 1562. The signature 3rd is a traditional Palmer design with a bulkhead protecting an almost island green. Arnold Palmer actually visited here in 2003 when he held a clinic, played the 9 holes and attended a luncheon.

Directions: Hunterdon County, #56 on West Central Map
NJ Tpke to Exit 8A. Go east on Forsgate Drive about 3 miles and then right on Rte. 522. Make left into Regency development.

Hole	1	2	3	4	5	6	7	8	9	Out	BLUE	Rating
BLUE	145	168	133	166	135	148	139	114	183	1331		Slope
WHITE	130	95	93	153	110	135	125	104	148	1093		
Par	3	3	3	3	3	3	3	3	3	27	WHITE	Rating
Handicap												Slope
RED	112	85	89	86	80	112	92	81	109	846		
Par	3	3	3	3	3	3	3	3	3	27	RED	Rating
Handicap												Slope
Hole	10	11	12	13	14	15	16	17	18	In		Totals
BLUE	545	308	155	514	378	204	473	158	449	3184	BLUE	6531
WHITE	530	288	133	490	334	173	449	137	409	2943	WHITE	5982
Par	5	4	3	5	4	3	5	3	4	36	Par	72
Handicap	2	12	18	4	10	14	6	16	8			
RED	466	243	109	429	304	145	407	114	358	2575	RED	5172
Par	5	4	3	5	4	3	5	3	4	36	Par	72
Handicap	2	12	18	4	10	14	6	16	8			

Manager/Pro: Bill Olear, PGA   **Sup't:** Tod Jackson
Architect: Arnold Palmer Design, 2002

THE RIDGE AT BACK BROOK

1211 Wertsville Rd., Ringoes, NJ 08551   **(609) 466-7702**
www.theridgegc.com

The Ridge is a private 18 hole course open 6 days a week and closed in Jan & Feb.
Guests play accompanied by a member. Reservations may be made in advance.

- **Driving Range**
- **Practice Green**
- **Power Carts**
- Pull Carts
- Club Rental
- **Caddies**
- **Lockers**
- **Showers**
- **Food**
- **Clubhouse**
- **Outings**
- **Soft Spikes**

Course Description: Chosen by Golf Digest as the #6 best new private course in
2003, The Ridge is an outstanding example of utilizing the natural beauty of the land
in creating a dramatic and spectacular layout. No 2 holes are alike; on this expansive
wooded routing, there are no homes to be seen. The actual ridge, which results in an
80 to 100 foot vertical wall, is part of the property and the back brook can be found on
many of the holes. The land was formerly used for farming and hunting. The course
is 7160 yards from the back tees. On the back, there are 3 par 3s and 3 par 5s. Some
of the interest here comes from the variety, the elevation changes, the water and the
ubiquitous fescue. A magnificent clubhouse adds to the attraction.

Directions: Somerset County, #57 on West Central Map
Take Rte. 80W to Rte. 287 (towards Morristown) to Exit #17. Take Rte. 202/32South
and make a left on Wertsville Rd. Course is 2 miles ahead on the left.

Hole	1	2	3	4	5	6	7	8	9	Out	BLUE	Rating 72.7
BLUE	359	168	396	410	528	394	568	169	381	3373		Slope 1379
SILVER	336	120	358	382	496	368	550	124	351	3085		
Par	4	3	4	4	5	4	5	3	4	36	SILVER	Rating 70.2
Handicap	15	13	1	7	3	11	5	17	9			Slope 133
GREEN	277	102	327	268	449	264	500	119	301	2607		
Par	4	3	4	4	5	4	5	3	4	36	GREEN	Rating 71.0
Handicap	13	17	5	7	1	9	3	15	11			Slope 131
Hole	10	11	12	13	14	15	16	17	18	In		Totals
BLUE	392	516	181	387	544	201	433	163	520	3313	BLUE	6686
SILVER	363	463	147	347	517	183	369	135	503	3027	SILVER	6112
Par	4	5	3	4	5	3	4	3	5	36	Par	72
Handicap	6	8	10	12	16	14	2	18	4			
GREEN	262	408	118	285	451	153	339	96	474	2586	GREEN	5193
Par	4	5	3	4	5	3	4	3	5	36	Par	72
Handicap	8	4	10	12	6	14	16	18	2			

Manager: Pam Moore   **Pro:** Joey Rassett, PGA   **Supt:** Todd Bunte
Architects: Tom Fazio 2002

ROSSMOOR GOLF COURSE

10 Clubhouse Drive, Jamesburg, NJ 08831   **(609) 655-3182**

Rossmoor is an 18 hole course open 7 days a week all year. Guests may play accompanied by a member. Outside memberships are available to relatives and friends of the residents. Tee time reservations are necessary on weekends.

•**Driving Range**	Lockers
•**Practice Green**	Showers
•**Power Carts**	Food
•**Pull Carts**	•**Clubhouse**
•**Club Rental**	•**Outings**
Caddies	•**Soft Spikes**

Course Description: Located within an adult community, Rossmoor is characterized by tree lined fairways and large elevated bent grass greens. The latter are well protected by bunkers making this short layout somewhat difficult. The course record here is a 65. Rossmoor is comfortable for walkers as it is relatively flat. Ponds come into play on 7 of the holes. The signature par 3 12th requires a substantial carry over water.

Directions: Middlesex County, #40 on West Central Map
NJTPKE to Exit #8A. Proceed to Forsgate Drive towards Jamesburg. Club is ahead on right before Applegarth Road.

Hole	1	2	3	4	5	6	7	8	9	Out	BLUE	Rating 70.2
BLUE	410	425	360	125	340	160	310	435	510	3075		Slope 122
WHITE	395	420	340	115	305	150	280	410	425	2840		
Par	4	5	4	3	4	3	4	4	5	36	WHITE	Rating 67.7
Handicap	1	3	5	17	13	7	15	11	9			Slope 118
RED	375	335	320	105	290	140	270	330	405	2570		
Par	4	5	4	3	4	3	4	4	5	36	RED	Rating 70.5
Handicap	5	1	7	17	11	15	13	9	3			Slope 116
Hole	10	11	12	13	14	15	16	17	18	In		Totals
BLUE	410	285	185	520	385	150	525	350	420	3230	BLUE	6305
WHITE	375	275	145	475	375	120	500	340	355	2960	WHITE	5800
Par	4	4	3	5	4	3	5	4	4	36	Par	72
Handicap	2	16	14	8	4	18	12	6	10			
RED	355	265	135	460	365	105	435	330	275	2725	RED	5295
Par	4	4	3	5	4	3	5	4	4	36	Par	72
Handicap	8	16	12	2	6	18	4	10	14			

Pros: Tony Wilcenski, PGA, Ted Servis, PGA   **Supt:** Tom Tucci
Architect: Desmond Muirhead 1967

ROYCE BROOK GOLF CLUB

201 Hamilton Rd., Somerville, NJ 08876
www.roycebrook.com

(908) 904-0499

Royce Brook offers 2 18 hole courses, East open to public 7 days a week, closed Jan. & Feb.and West with memberships and tee times up to 30 days in advance. The East course recently reversed the nines. Tee times: 7 days in advance.

•Driving Range	•Lockers
•Practice Green	•Showers
•Power Carts	•Food
•Pull Carts(elec)	•Clubhouse
•Club Rental	•Outings
•Soft Spikes	•Caddies

Fees	M-Thurs	Fri-Sun
Daily	$75	$105
Twi	$60	$75
Power carts included		

Course Description: The West is links style featuring numerous and severe bunkers along the fairways and around the greens as well as fescue grass in the rough. Strategically placed bunkers and a more traditional, somewhat wooded terrain characterize the East Course. Both have bent grass tees, greens and fairways. The architect, Steve Smyers, is known for enhancing the natural landscape by following the gently rolling topography and leaving the land relatively undisturbed except to incorporate interesting challenges. The setting is made more beautiful by the absence of residential or commercial development within view. Scorecard is for East Course.

Directions: Somerset County, #41 on West Central Map
Rte. 287 South to Exit #17. Follow signs carefully for Rte. 206S. At the Somerville Circle, continue on 206S. Approx. 5 mi. from circle, look for Hamilton Rd. & take jughandle left onto Hamilton Rd. Club is 1.5 mi. on left.

Hole	1	2	3	4	5	6	7	8	9	Out	GREEN	Rating 71.3
GREEN	437	374	155	524	320	360	475	172	430	3247		Slope 127
WHITE	387	356	125	475	292	331	443	160	390	2959		
Par	4	4	3	5	4	4	5	3	4	36	WHITE	Rating 69.0
Handicap	3	13	17	7	11	5	15	9	1			Slope 122
RED	332	334	88	433	240	300	393	81	345	2536		
Par	4	4	3	5	4	4	5	3	4	36	RED	Rating 69.4
Handicap	3	13	17	7	11	5	15	9	1			Slope 115
Hole	10	11	12	13	14	15	16	17	18	In		Totals
GREEN	401	359	479	352	389	182	415	141	482	3200	GREEN	6447
WHITE	347	343	450	310	367	172	389	131	467	2976	WHITE	5935
Par	4	4	5	4	4	3	4	3	5	36	Par	72
Handicap	16	14	8	10	4	6	12	18	2			
RED	300	314	357	274	352	119	298	87	415	2526	RED	5062
Par	4	4	5	4	4	3	4	3	5	36	Par	72
Handicap	16	14	8	10	4	6	12	18	2			

Manager: David Karner   **Dir of Golf:** Michael Sparks, PGA   **Supt:** Mike Gonnert
Architect: Steve Smyers 1998

RUTGERS GOLF COURSE

777 Hoes Lane, Piscataway, NJ 08854
www.teemaster.com

(732) 445-2637

Rutgers is an 18 hole course located on the Rutgers University campus, open 7 days a week from March through December. Call (888) 950-6728 or go to website for tee times.

- **Driving Range**
- **Practice Green**
- **Power Carts**
- **Pull Carts**
- Club Rental
- **Soft Spikes**

Lockers
Showers
- **Food**
Clubhouse
Outings

Fees	Weekday	Weekend
Daily	$29	$40
Twi	$20	$20
Sr (registered at Rutgers) $24		
Power carts $30		

Course Description: Noted for its impressive evergreen trees and its fair test of skill, Rutgers is an interesting layout. Each hole is named for a tree that can be found on the course. The many fairway bunkers are an obstacle for golfers of all levels. Water is not a major factor although there is some in play on several holes. The par 3 eleventh is both picturesque and challenging with an elevated tee that requires a shot over a stream and a ravine to an uphill well bunkered green. This hole, the signature, also has the oldest Japanese sour gum tree in the state.

Directions: Middlesex County, #42 on West Central Map
NJTPKE to Exit #9. Take Rte. 18 North to River Rd. and make a left. At 2nd light, make a right onto Hoes Lane to course up ahead on the right.

Hole	1	2	3	4	5	6	7	8	9	Out	BLUE	Rating 70.5
BLUE	353	381	178	483	349	369	531	201	448	3293		Slope 130
WHITE	335	365	155	469	323	350	522	184	434	3137		
Par	4	4	3	5	4	4	5	3	4	36	WHITE	Rating 68.7
Handicap	9	5	17	7	15	13	3	11	1			Slope 125
RED	308	307	127	453	284	308	466	172	405	2830		
Par	4	4	3	5	4	4	5	3	5	37	RED	Rating 70.5
Handicap	5	13	17	3	11	7	1	15	9			Slope 123

Hole	10	11	12	13	14	15	16	17	18	In		Totals
BLUE	381	158	539	382	160	363	352	197	512	3044	BLUE	6337
WHITE	361	140	520	367	143	348	338	184	496	2897	WHITE	6034
Par	4	3	5	4	3	4	4	3	5	35	Par	71
Handicap	4	18	2	8	16	14	10	12	6			
RED	318	128	401	355	122	314	314	149	428	2529	RED	5359
Par	4	3	5	4	3	4	4	3	5	35	Par	72
Handicap	2	16	8	6	18	12	4	14	10			

Manager/Pro: Jill Jerauld, PGA   **Supt:** Terry Sedon
Architect: Hal Purdy 1963

SOMERSET HILLS CC

Mine Mount Rd., Bernardsville, NJ 07924   **(908) 766-0044**

Somerset Hills is an 18 hole course that is open 6 days a week and closed Jan - March. Guests may play accompanied by a member. Tee time reservations are not necessary.

- •**Driving Range** •**Lockers**
- •**Practice Green** •**Showers**
- •**Power Carts** •**Food**
- •**Pull Carts** •**Clubhouse**
- •**Club Rental** •**Outings**
- •**Caddies** •**Soft Spikes**

Course Description: The back nine of Somerset Hills is tight and cut out of the woods, while the front is built in an open links design. Golf is taken very seriously at this truly spectacular Tillinghast course. Each hole is named after a well known Scottish hole. There are 109 bunkers around the undulating greens. The signature par 3 2nd hole, "Redan" (meaning a fortress guarded by bunkers), has beautiful views and is well protected. Some say the "Happy Valley" hole, a favorite of the late Duke of Windsor, is the most appealing requiring a carry over a creek and a waterfall. The "Racetrack" used to be an actual racetrack and its grooves and paddock can still be seen. The 12th, "Despair" is all water and an island green.

Directions: Somerset County, #43 on West Central Map
Rte. 80 West towards Morristown to Rte. 287S; exit at Mt. Airy-Bernardsville #26B. Go 2.1 mi. on Rte. 202S to Claremont Rd. & turn right for 0.3 mi. to Mine Mt. Rd. At church turn left. Club is 1/4 mile on left.

Hole	1	2	3	4	5	6	7	8	9	Out	BLUE	Rating 72.2
BLUE	448	175	375	427	343	484	445	230	514	3416		Slope 132
WHITE	408	175	358	418	329	465	402	194	514	3263		
Par	4	3	4	4	4	5	4	3	5	36	WHITE	Rating 70.1
Handicap	5	15	11	3	17	9	1	13	7			Slope 127
RED	440	148	324	353	285	448	360	186	465	3009		
Par	5	3	4	4	4	5	4	3	5	37	RED	Rating 67.5
Handicap	7	17	5	11	15	3	9	13	1			Slope 122
Hole	10	11	12	13	14	15	16	17	18	In		Totals
BLUE	496	411	144	409	414	394	167	387	319	3123	BLUE	6659
WHITE	480	388	130	391	372	375	162	362	295	2955	WHITE	6235
Par	5	4	3	4	4	4	3	4	4	35	Par	71
Handicap	10	4	18	2	12	6	16	8	14			
RED	417	370	107	360	352	301	132	324	271	2634	RED	5648
Par	5	4	3	4	4	4	3	4	4	35	Par	72
Handicap	8	2	18	4	10	12	16	6	14			

Manager: Elizabeth Grant   **Pro:** Adam Machala, PGA   **Supt:** Bob Dwyer
Architect: A.W. Tillinghast 1917

SPOOKY BROOK GOLF COURSE   PUBLIC

Elizabeth Ave., Franklin Township, NJ 08734   **(732) 873-2242**

Spooky Brook, operated by Somerset County Park Commission, is 18 holes and open to the public all year, 7 days a week. Registered residents call 7 days in advance; 5 days for others at (908) 231-1122.

•**Driving Range**	Lockers
•**Practice Green**	Showers
•**Power Carts**	•**Food**
•**Pull Carts**	•**Clubhouse**
•**Club Rental**	•**Outings**
•**Soft Spikes**	

Fees	Weekday	Weekend
Res/ID	$17	$19
Sr/Jr	$10	$19
Non-res	$34	$38
Power carts $26		

Course Description: Considered easy to walk, Spooky Brook is a relatively flat course offering spacious greens and tees and wide open fairways. The signature par 4 17th, a dogleg left, requires an approach shot over a pond. The first, second and fourteenth are the most difficult holes. Upgrading goes on here regularly. It gets quite busy on weekends. The other Somerset County courses are Green Knoll, Warrenbrook, Quail Brook and the new Neshanic Valley.

Directions: Somerset County, #44 on West Central Map
NJTPKE to Exit #10. Take Rte. 287 North to Exit #12. At Weston Canal Rd. make a right. Proceed about 100 yds. & go right onto Edgewood Terrace. At light, turn right onto Elizabeth Ave. Course is on right just past Colonial Park entrance.

Hole	1	2	3	4	5	6	7	8	9	Out	BLUE	Rating 71.2
BLUE	458	424	148	438	536	404	358	196	375	3337		Slope 124
WHITE	422	405	134	418	531	384	339	178	358	3169		
Par	4	4	3	4	5	4	4	3	4	35	WHITE	Rating 69.6
Handicap	1	3	17	7	5	11	13	15	9			Slope 119
RED	349	284	118	319	526	361	321	158	258	2694		
Par	4	4	3	4	5	5	4	3	4	36	RED	Rating 69.0
Handicap	5	11	17	9	1	3	7	15	13			Slope 116

Hole	10	11	12	13	14	15	16	17	18	In		Totals
BLUE	363	188	373	525	409	364	167	379	507	3275	BLUE	6612
WHITE	347	169	356	503	383	340	155	366	492	3111	WHITE	6280
Par	4	3	4	5	4	4	3	4	5	36	Par	71
Handicap	12	16	14	8	2	10	18	4	6			
RED	336	159	339	483	288	257	142	281	402	2687	RED	5381
Par	4	3	4	5	4	4	3	4	5	36	Par	72
Handicap	10	18	6	2	12	14	16	8	4			

Manager: Jaynee Mahnken   **Pro:** Fred Glass, PGA   **Supt:** Billy Martin
Architect: Edmund B. Ault 1970

SPRINGDALE GOLF CLUB

26 College Road West, Princeton, NJ 08540   **(609) 924-3198**

Springdale is an 18 hole private course open 7 days a week and closed for January. Guests may play accompanied by a member. Tee time reservations are necessary.

- •**Driving Range**
- •**Practice Green**
- •**Power Carts**
- •**Pull Carts**
- •**Club Rental**
- Caddies

- •**Lockers**
- •**Showers**
- •**Food**
- •**Clubhouse**
- •**Outings**
- •**Soft Spikes**

Course Description: Situated on the grounds of Princeton University, Springdale Golf Club was expanded to its present 18 holes in the early part of the 20th century. It is a mature course with narrow fairways. The small bent grass greens have subtle breaks and are tightly bunkered. The seventeenth, a difficult par 4 starts from an elevated tee, then curves and slopes to the right to a fairway bordered by a brook. The par 3s are very challenging as well. Garden State Women's Golf association holds tournaments here.

Directions: Mercer County, #45 on West Central Map
From North: NJTPKE to Exit #9, then Rte. 1 South to Princeton. Make a right onto Alexander Rd.West in Princeton. Go 3 lights; at College Rd. turn left. Club is on left. From South: Rte. 1 North and go left at Alexander Rd; follow as above.

Hole	1	2	3	4	5	6	7	8	9	Out	BLUE	Rating 70.7
BLUE	296	180	424	405	364	343	442	526	193	3173		Slope 129
WHITE	275	168	369	388	359	331	430	502	186	3008		
Par	4	3	4	4	4	4	4	5	3	35	WHITE	Rating 69.0
Handicap	15	17	3	7	9	11	1	5	13			Slope 126
RED	271	130	360	372	324	325	423	445	147	2798		
Par	4	3	4	4	4	4	5	5	3	36	RED	Rating 72.5
Handicap	15	17	9	3	7	5	11	1	13			Slope 125
Hole	10	11	12	13	14	15	16	17	18	In		Totals
BLUE	572	318	413	185	470	126	336	404	383	3207	BLUE	6380
WHITE	525	300	397	156	453	122	322	374	360	3009	WHITE	6017
Par	5	4	4	3	5	3	4	4	4	36	Par	71
Handicap	2	16	4	12	10	18	14	6	8			
RED	497	293	386	148	432	116	306	351	328	2857	RED	5655
Par	5	4	4	3	5	3	4	4	4	36	Par	72
Handicap	2	14	4	12	8	18	16	6	10			

Manager: Donna DiLorenzo   **Pro:** Dan McCarthy, PGA   **Supt:** Charles Dey
Built: 1895   **Architects:** William Dunn, Howard Toomey & William Flynn

STANTON RIDGE GOLF & CC

Clubhouse Drive, Stanton, NJ 08885   (908) 534-1234
www.stantonridgecc.com

Stanton Ridge is an 18 hole course that is open 6 days a week and closed in Jan. & Feb. Guests may play accompanied by a member. Tee time reservations are not necessary.

•**Driving Range**	•**Lockers**
•**Practice Green**	•**Showers**
•**Power Carts**	•**Food**
Pull Carts	•**Clubhouse**
•**Club Rental**	•**Outings**
Caddies	•**Soft Spikes**

Course Description: Built on spectacular terrain, Stanton Ridge is a Scottish style layout located in the Cushetunk Mountains. As its architect Stephen Kay said, "it is old style elegance that is at one with the land, a modern course that looks seventy years old." The 555 acre property is surrounded by about 150 residences. The lush fairways are cut through virgin woods, the latter a haven for deer and pheasant. The elevated tees, strategically placed bunkers and fine bent grass greens add beauty and interest. The difficult and picturesque #10 is considered the signature hole. Water is in play on a few holes. The State Head Pro Championship is held here.

Directions: Hunterdon County, #46 on West Central Map
GSP to Exit #142 or NJTPKE to Exit #14 to I-78 West. Proceed to Exit 24 (Rte. 523 South). Proceed on Rte. 523S approx. 6.4 miles to club on right.

Hole	1	2	3	4	5	6	7	8	9	Out	GOLD	Rating 71.1
GOLD	365	407	371	310	119	527	207	504	378	3188		Slope 133
SILVER	345	373	352	297	111	491	195	481	365	3010		
Par	4	4	4	4	3	5	3	5	4	36	SILVER	Rating 69.5
Handicap	15	11	7	13	17	1	5	3	9			Slope 130
RED	287	335	251	245	95	425	110	423	335	2506		
Par	4	4	4	4	3	5	3	5	4	36	RED	Rating 69.4
Handicap	15	11	7	13	17	1	5	3	9			Slope 125
Hole	10	11	12	13	14	15	16	17	18	In		Totals
GOLD	445	407	192	322	542	450	351	196	412	3317	GOLD	6362
SILVER	410	380	170	310	525	412	315	185	385	3092	SILVER	6036
Par	4	4	3	4	5	4	4	3	4	35	Par	71
Handicap	4	8	18	16	6	2	14	12	10			
RED	351	333	75	269	485	328	282	135	320	2578	RED	5084
Par	4	4	3	4	5	4	4	3	4	35	Par	71
Handicap	4	8	18	16	6	2	14	12	10			

Manager: Jeff Miller   **Pro:** Jeffrey Rickenbach, PGA   **Supt:** Fred Riedel
Architect: Stephen Kay 1993

STONYBROOK GOLF CLUB

PUBLIC

Stonybrook Rd., Hopewell, NJ 08525   **(609) 466-2215**

Stonybrook is an 18 hole par 62 executive course that is open 7 days a week and closed from the end of Oct. until April. Tee time reservations are not necessary; walk ons only. Call for specials such as Ladies Day and extra senior discounts.

Driving Range	Lockers
•**Practice Green**	Showers
•**Power Carts**	Food
•**Pull Carts**	Clubhouse
•**Club Rental**	Outings
Soft Spikes	

Fees	Weekday	Weekend
Daily	$21	$24
Sr(60+)	$16	$18
Twi(4PM)	$14	
Power carts	$20	

Course Description: Stonybrook is a short tree lined, well bunkered layout. Although an executive course, it has 2 par 5s. A stream runs throughout. The signature par 3 first hole, is 223 yards from the back tees and is quite difficult. Rounds can be played in less than three hours making the course perfect for seniors, women, beginners and those whose golfing time is limited.

Directions: Mercer County, #47 on West Central Map
Rte. 295 to Exit #14, then take Rte. 31 North toward Pennington. Make a right onto Rte. 654. Follow road and make a left onto Stonybrook.

Hole	1	2	3	4	5	6	7	8	9	Out	BLUE	Rating
BLUE												Slope
WHITE	223	240	81	310	182	505	82	125	101	1849		
Par	3	4	3	4	3	5	3	3	3	31	WHITE	Rating 57.3
Handicap	3	7	17	5	9	1	13	11	16			Slope 91
RED	212	233	76	300	172	490	77	115	91	1766		
Par	4	4	3	4	3	5	3	3	3	32	RED	Rating 59.2
Handicap	11	5	9	3	7	1	15	13	16			Slope 93
Hole	10	11	12	13	14	15	16	17	18	In		Totals
BLUE											BLUE	
WHITE	273	72	142	235	201	468	160	135	68	1754	WHITE	3603
Par	4	3	3	4	3	5	3	3	3	31	Par	62
Handicap	6	18	12	8	4	2	10	14	15			
RED	263	65	132	225	188	458	150	125	63	1669	RED	3435
Par	4	3	3	4	4	5	3	3	3	32	Par	64
Handicap	4	18	12	6	10	2	8	14	17			

Manager: Leo Hughs   **Supt:** Willard Cruiser
Architect: Robert Kraeger 1964

TAMARACK GOLF COURSE

PUBLIC

97 Hardenburg Lane, East Brunswick, NJ 08816   **(732) 821-8881**
www.imiddlesex.e-golf.net

Tamarack has 2 18 hole courses, East and West. Operated by Middlesex County, it is open 7 days a week, all year. Residents can obtain an ID for $35/year. Tee times may be made by calling (732) 951-8920 $3 reservation fee, Srs. $1.

•Driving Range	•Lockers
•Practice Green	•Showers
•Power Carts	•Food
•Pull Carts	•Clubhouse
•Club Rental	Outings
•Soft Spikes	

Fees	Weekday	Weekend
Res w/ID	$16	$22
Sr/Jr	$10	
Non res.	$28	$34
Power carts	$26	

Course Description: Middlesex County residents have a choice of two courses to play here. The Meadows at Middlesex and Raritan Landing have been added to the county system fairly recently. The dogleg right par 5 third on the West course is long and uphill. The 7th is 589 yards from the championship tees; even a low handicapper must put together two long shots to land within a reasonable distance for the approach shot. Tamarack gets very busy and has earned its popularity. Scorecard below is for the West Course.

Directions: Middlesex County, #48 on West Central Map
NJTPKE to Exit #9, then take Rte. 18 North to Rte. 1South to second Milltown exit. Continue on Main St. in Milltown. At Riva Ave., make a right; then a left at 2nd light to Hardenburg Lane to course.

Hole	1	2	3	4	5	6	7	8	9	Out	BLUE	Rating 73.8
BLUE	375	385	531	376	168	452	589	397	192	3465		Slope 130
WHITE	350	362	496	335	134	420	546	364	159	3166		
Par	4	4	5	4	3	4	5	4	3	36	WHITE	Rating 70.3
Handicap	7	4	3	5	9	2	1	6	8			Slope 128
RED	336	340	476	310	111	400	517	340	139	2969		
Par	4	4	5	4	3	4	5	4	3	36	RED	Rating 72.5
Handicap	7	4	3	5	9	2	1	6	8	3		Slope 122
Hole	10	11	12	13	14	15	16	17	18	In		Totals
BLUE	403	225	515	442	205	423	367	510	470	3560	BLUE	7025
WHITE	364	178	473	404	161	385	318	456	435	3174	WHITE	6340
Par	4	3	5	4	3	4	4	5	4	36	Par	72
Handicap	6	9	5	2	7	4	8	3	1			
RED	322	152	452	379	130	357	285	437	327	2841	RED	5810
Par	4	3	5	4	3	4	4	5	4	36	Par	72
Handicap	6	9	4	1	7	3	8	2	5			

Manager: Tom Brush   **Pro:** Randy Luberecki, PGA   **Supt:** Rod Brennan
Architect: Hal Purdy 1976

TARA GREENS GOLF CENTER

PUBLIC

955 Somerset St., Somerset, NJ 08873   **(732) 247-8284**
www.taragreensgolf.com

Tara Greens is a regulation 9 hole course open 7 days a week all year, weather permitting. Tee time reservations are not required. Reduced fees for Srs after 3PM. A 9 hole "Pitch & Putt" is adjacent as well as a miniature golf course & a full driving range.

•**Driving Range**	Lockers
•**Practice Green**	Showers
•**Power Carts**	Food
•**Pull Carts**	Clubhouse
•**Club Rental**	Outings
Soft Spikes	

Fees	Weekday	Weekend
Daily(18 holes)	$15	$20
Sr(over 65)	$10 (until 3PM)	
Power carts	$18	$25

Course Description: Maintained immaculately, Tara Greens is owned by the Cleary Chemical Co. and was originally built to test turf chemicals. The company continues to do so which helps the greens stay in excellent condition. The 615 yard par 5 7th is one of the longest holes in the state; it is a dogleg right with a big tree in the fairway. The course is flat and tree lined; some water is in play. The dogleg left par 4 6th is wooded and picturesque. The pitch & putt course has real greens. The full length driving range affords the golfer great practice opportunities.

Directions: Somerset County, #49 on West Central Map
NJTPKE to Exit 9, then take Rte. 18 North to Rte. 27 South towards Princeton. Go 3 & 1/2 miles south to club on right (Somerset St.)

Hole	1	2	3	4	5	6	7	8	9	Out	BLUE	Rating
BLUE												Slope
WHITE	213	238	417	455	352	465	615	247	137	3139		
Par	3	4	4	4	4	5	5	4	3	36	WHITE	Rating 70.0
Handicap	8	7	4	3	5	2	1	6	9			Slope 119
RED	203	228	400	440	342	460	515	237	130	2955		
Par	3	4	4	5	4	5	6	4	3	38	RED	Rating 74.0
Handicap	6	9	2	8	5	4	1	7	3			Slope 124

Hole	10	11	12	13	14	15	16	17	18	In		Totals
BLUE											BLUE	
WHITE											WHITE	3139
Par											Par	36
Handicap												
RED											RED	2955
Par											Par	38
Handicap												

Manager: John Christman   **Pros:** Brendan Boyle, PGA & Maura Waters
Supt: Robert Harris **Built:** 1950s

TPC AT JASNA POLANA

8 Lawrenceville Rd., Princeton, NJ 08540   **(609) 688-0500**
www.tpcatjasnapolana.com

The Tournament Player's Club (TPC) is an 18 hole course open 6 days a week all year. Guests play accompanied by a member. Tee time reservations may be made up to 14 days in advance. Corporate mbrs. 14-30 days.

•**Driving Range**	•**Lockers**
•**Practice Green**	•**Showers**
•**Power Carts**	•**Food**
•**Pull Carts(elec)**	•**Clubhouse**
•**Club Rental**	•**Outings**
Caddies	•**Soft Spikes**

Course Description: With its gently rolling terrain, natural creeks and mature hardwood trees, Jasna Polana's golf course as well as The Tournament Player's Club is another venue that adds to NJ's array of excellent golf opportunities. Gary Player, the architect here, is well known for creating golf courses that preserve and enhance the natural environment. The 230 acre property is designated exclusively for the 18 hole layout, over 7,000 yards from the back tees. Hole #18, the signature, is downhill, then over water for the approach. The clubhouse utilizes the neo-classical country villa, Jasna Polana, the elegant home of the late Seward Johnson and his widow, Barbara.

Directions: Mercer County, #50 on West Central Map
NJTPKE to Exit #9; then take Rte. 1 South through Princeton to Province Line Rd. and turn right carefully following signs. Go past Rte. 206 (Lawrenceville Rd.) and turn right into main gate of Jasna Polana.

Hole	1	2	3	4	5	6	7	8	9	Out	BLUE	Rating 71.8
BLUE	378	127	480	304	361	427	558	193	441	3269		Slope 138
WHITE	359	101	474	277	351	395	508	162	414	3041		
Par	4	3	5	4	4	4	5	3	4	36	WHITE	Rating 69.2
Handicap	13	17	9	15	7	1	11	5	3			Slope 130
RED	267	53	401	198	309	290	402	115	188	2223		
Par	4	3	5	4	4	4	5	3	4	36	RED	Rating 65.7
Handicap	13	17	9	15	7	1	11	5	3			Slope 107
Hole	10	11	12	13	14	15	16	17	18	In		Totals
BLUE	414	152	517	411	380	419	293	165	515	3266	BLUE	6535
WHITE	400	135	480	364	325	356	281	128	494	2963	WHITE	6004
Par	4	3	5	4	4	4	4	3	5	36	Par	72
Handicap	2	18	14	6	12	4	16	10	8			
RED	242	115	345	291	221	267	182	95	437	2195	RED	4418
Par	4	3	5	4	4	4	4	3	5	36	Par	72
Handicap	2	18	14	6	12	4	16	10	8			

Manager: John Buser   **Pro:** Ben Moore, PGA   **Supt:** Roger Stewart, Jr.
Architect: Gary Player 1998

TRENTON COUNTRY CLUB

PRIVATE

201 Sullivan Way, Trenton, NJ 08628   **(609) 883-3800**

Trenton Country Club is an 18 hole course open 6 days a week and closed for 3 weeks in the beginning of Jan. Guests play accompanied by a member. Tee time reservations are required on weekends.

```
•Driving Range    •Lockers
•Practice Green   •Showers
•Power Carts      •Food
 Pull Carts       •Clubhouse
 Club Rental      •Outings
•Caddies          •Soft Spikes
```

Course Description: A traditional course built in the late 19th century, Trenton has tight fairways and small, fast well bunkered greens. There are a number of tricky doglegs and blind shots on this relatively hilly course. Reasonable accuracy is needed due to the out of bounds on the right on 13 of the holes. The par 3 third, 195 yards from the whites is considered the signature hole; it is uphill with a sloped green. Almost all the tees and some greens were rebuilt recently. Trenton CC hosted a Mid Amateur Qualifying round. A fine new Pro Shop was cconstructed as a small replica of the Clubhouse's architectural style.

Directions: Mercer County, #51 on West Central Map
NJTPKE to Exit #9. Take Rte. 1 South and at Lawrenceville, take I-95/295 South; exit at Bear Tavern Rd. Follow exit south. Road becomes Sullivan Way; course is on right.

Hole	1	2	3	4	5	6	7	8	9	Out	BLUE	Rating 71.0
BLUE	286	450	212	448	196	315	452	366	475	3200		Slope 130
WHITE	275	441	195	419	182	303	440	355	461	3071		
Par	4	4	3	4	3	4	5	4	5	36	WHITE	Rating 69.9
Handicap	17	3	5	1	11	9	15	13	7			Slope 128
RED	266	433	178	408	148	284	429	305	447	2898		
Par	4	5	3	4	3	4	5	4	5	37	RED	Rating 67.5
Handicap	17	7	11	9	15	5	1	13	3			Slope 122
Hole	10	11	12	13	14	15	16	17	18	In		Totals
BLUE	162	437	565	150	422	114	351	529	392	3122	BLUE	6358
WHITE	152	429	560	134	407	102	344	521	382	3031	WHITE	6127
Par	3	4	5	3	4	3	4	5	4	35	Par	71
Handicap	16	2	6	14	4	18	12	8	10			
RED	132	420	555	110	353	86	304	455	315	2730	RED	5628
Par	3	4	5	3	4	3	4	5	4	35	Par	72
Handicap	14	10	2	16	8	18	4	6	12			

Manager: John Case   **Pro:** Dennis Milne, PGA   **Supt:** Tom Tuttle
Built: 1897

TRUMP NATIONAL GOLF CLUB

567 Lamington Rd., Bedminster, NJ 07921   **(908) 470-4400**
www.trumpnational.com

Trump National is an 18 hole private club open 6 days a week and closed in Feb. Guests play accompanied by a member. A second 18 hole course is proposed with the permit process ongoing as we go to press.

- •Driving Range   •Lockers
- •Practice Green   •Showers
- •Power Carts   •Food
- Pull Carts   •Clubhouse
- •Club Rental   •Outings
- •Caddies   •Soft Spikes

Course Description: Trump National is another spectacular achievment augmenting the superlative vision of its owner. Built on the DeLorean estate, the former Lamington Farm, it may host in the future not only a PGA tour event but possibly a major. There is ample space for onsite parking! 7560 yards from the Championship tees, the course is a test for every level of golfer. The magnificent rural setting provides the backdrop for an environmentally sensitive and dramatic layout. The densely wooded property of varying topography was a wonderful challenge for the architect to create a world class golf venue. No expense was spared. A high quality equestion center will be found on the extensive grounds as well as tennis courts and swimming pool. The existing Georgian manor house has been converted into the distinctive clubhouse.

Directions: Somerset County, #23 on West Central Map
Take Rte. 78W to Exit #26. Go right on Rattlesnake Bridge Rd. At dead end, make a right on Lamington Rd. to club on right.

Hole	1	2	3	4	5	6	7	8	9	Out	BLUE	Rating 72.7
BLUE	537	355	435	170	425	381	168	535	428	3434		Slope 139
WHITE	483	328	410	143	384	351	158	440	384	3081		
Par	5	4	4	3	4	4	3	5	4	36	WHITE	Rating 69.8
Handicap	3.	9	5	17	7	11	15	1	13			Slope 128
RED	440	290	270	130	325	306	118	384	342	2605		
Par	5	4	4	3	4	4	3	5	4	36	RED	Rating 70.4
Handicap	3	7	13	17	9	11	15	1	5			Slope 129
Hole	**10**	**11**	**12**	**13**	**14**	**15**	**16**	**17**	**18**	**In**		Totals
BLUE	165	312	524	397	380	392	405	167	540	3282	BLUE	6716
WHITE	150	295	502	358	320	350	337	160	510	2982	WHITE	6063
Par	3	4	5	4	4	4	4	3	5	36	Par	72
Handicap	16	12	2	14	8	10	6	18	4			
RED	100	269	400	313	290	274	268	122	460	2496	RED	5101
Par	3	4	5	4	4	4	4	3	5	36	Par	72
Handicap	16	8	2	6	12	10	14	18	4			

Pro: Mike Fisher, PGA   **Supt:** Greg Nicoll
Architect: Tom Fazio 2004

600 Mountain Blvd., Watchung, NJ 07060   **(908) 561-8858**

Twin Brooks is an 18 hole course open 6 days a week from March through December, Guests may play accompanied by a member. Tee time reservations are necessary on weekends when caddies are available.

> • **Driving Range** • **Lockers**
> • **Practice Green** • **Showers**
> • **Power Carts** • **Food**
>   Pull Carts   • **Clubhouse**
> • **Club Rental** • **Outings**
> • **Caddies**   • **Soft Spikes**

Course Description: The Watchung Mountain setting at Twin Brooks provides its members with majestic views. Two brooks run through the course, hence the name. The course is secluded so that no homes or roads are in sight. Hilly with rolling fairways, the layout features many uneven lies and small, fast difficult greens. The par 4 eighth has a green set on a peninsula. Work has been done on the 1st and third holes. The unique par 3 19th brings an extraordinary aspect to many events here; it is used as an alternate hole or in some cases tournaments are played with a 19 hole format.

Directions: Somerset County, #52 on West Central Map
GSP to Exit #141. Go west on Rte. 78 to Exit 40. Make a left over Rte.78 to STOP and turn right to Watchung circle. Go 1/2 way around onto Mountain Blvd. Club is one mile up on the right.

Hole	1	2	3	4	5	6	7	8	9	Out	BLUE	Rating 72.5
BLUE	370	450	490	135	520	365	435	365	210	3340		Slope 135
WHITE	360	420	475	120	505	355	410	355	185	3185		
Par	4	4	5	3	5	4	4	4	3	36	WHITE	Rating 70.6
Handicap	7	1	9	17	11	3	5	13	15			Slope 130
RED	290	400	405	110	485	300	385	285	135	2795		
Par	4	5	5	3	5	4	4	4	3	37	RED	Rating 72.6
Handicap	13	9	7	15	1	5	3	11	17			Slope 136

Hole	10	11	12	13	14	15	16	17	18	In		Totals
BLUE	350	195	420	145	380	320	510	380	580	3280	BLUE	6715
WHITE	335	170	385	135	375	300	500	355	530	3085	WHITE	6260
Par	4	3	4	3	4	4	5	4	5	36	Par	72
Handicap	8	14	6	18	2	16	12	10	4			
RED	330	150	330	125	365	290	450	310	445	2775	RED	5515
Par	4	3	4	3	5	4	5	4	5	37	Par	74
Handicap	4	16	6	18	8	14	10	12	2			

Manager: Jim Sampson   **Pro:** Ralph Romano, PGA   **Supt:** Tom Crump
Built: Tom Bendelow 1898

WARRENBROOK GOLF COURSE PUBLIC

500 Warrenville Rd., Warren Township, NJ 07060   **(908) 754-8402**

Warrenbrook is an 18 hole public course operated by Somerset County Park Commission 7 days a week from April through Nov. Tee times: 7 days in advance for res./ID. For $60/year non-residents may reserve tee times 5 days in advance. Reservation # is (908) 231-1122. For $10, non-registered may reserve 1 day ahead.

Driving Range	
• **Practice Green**	Lockers
• **Power Carts**	Showers
• **Pull Carts**	• **Food**
• **Club Rental**	• **Clubhouse**
• **Soft Spikes**	• **Outings**

Fees	Weekday	Weekend
Res/ID	$17	$19
Sr/Jr	$10	
Non-res	$34	$38
Power carts $26		

Course Description: Originally 2 holes on the private estate of a golf enthusiast, Warrenbrook was subsequently increased to the present 18 holes and eventually purchased by Somerset County in 1978. It is very hilly, heavily wooded and gets quite busy. The fairways are tight with water affecting play on 3 holes. The signature third is the toughest; out of bounds lurks on the left. The contours provide plenty of uphill and downhill lies. The most picturesque hole is the 17th where a large pond confronts the golfer on the approach shot and out of bounds encroaches on the right. Cartpaths have recently been installed throughout.

Directions: Somerset County, #53 on West Central Map
NJTPKE or GSP to Rte. 78 West to Exit #36. Take King George Rd. South. At light, it becomes Bethel Rd. Continue and road becomes Warrenville Rd. Course is on left.

Hole	1	2	3	4	5	6	7	8	9	Out	BLUE	Rating 70.8
BLUE	378	369	407	186	561	213	365	473	145	3097		Slope 124
WHITE	355	349	391	165	558	199	355	455	125	2952		
Par	4	4	4	3	5	3	4	5	3	35	WHITE	Rating 69.5
Handicap	5	13	1	9	11	7	3	15	17			Slope 122
RED	305	298	315	152	449	170	345	407	85	2526		
Par	4	4	4	3	5	3	4	5	3	35	RED	Rating 69.2
Handicap	3	13	5	15	9	11	1	7	17			Slope 117

Hole	10	11	12	13	14	15	16	17	18	In		Totals
BLUE	393	364	174	406	326	522	345	376	369	3275	BLUE	6372
WHITE	371	350	157	390	311	510	331	355	347	3122	WHITE	6074
Par	4	4	3	4	4	5	4	4	4	36	Par	71
Handicap	8	6	10	2	16	14	12	4	18			
RED	321	280	130	334	260	407	287	304	246	2569	RED	5095
Par	4	4	3	4	4	4	4	4	4	35	Par	70
Handicap	10	12	16	4	18	8	14	2	6			

Manager: County Park Commission   **Supt:** Dave Richards
Architect: Hal Purdy 1966

Under the wide and open sky,

Dig the grave and let me lie

Gladly I've lived and gladly die

Away from this world of strife;

This be the epitaph for me

"Here he lies where he longed to be

Lies in death by the nineteenth tee,

Where he lied all through his life."

(Blackbeard's Castle 1889)

I only play golf on days that end with a "y".

Golf is a test of temper, a trial of honor,

a revealer of character.

(Tom's River)

UPPER SHORE REGION

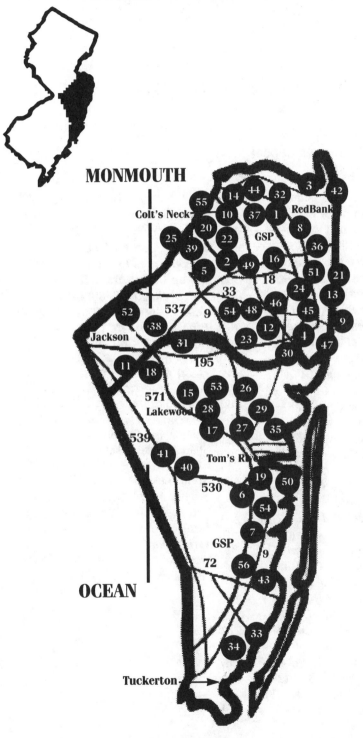

UPPER SHORE

Public Courses appear in
bold italics

Map (#)	Page #
Bamm Hollow CC (1)--------	187
Battleground CC (2)----------	188
Beacon Hill CC (3)-----------	189
Bel Aire Golf Club (4)-----	190
Bella Vista CC (5)------------	191
Bey Lea Golf Course (6)--	192
Cedar Creek GC (7) -------	193
Charleston Springs (8)---	194
Colonial Terrace GC (9)--	195
Colts Neck GC(10)---------	196
Cream Ridge GC (11)-----	197
Cruz Farm CC (12)--------	198
Deal Golf Club (13)-----------	199
Due Process Stables (14)---	200
Eagle Oaks GC (46)----------	201
Eagle Ridge GC (15)-------	202
Fairway Mews GC (16)------	203
Forge Pond GC (35)--------	204
Four Seasons CC (17)--------	205
Gambler Ridge GC (18)---	206
Greenbriar Oceanaire (56)--	207
Greenbriar Woodlands(19)	208
Hole in One GC (20)-------	209
Hollywood Golf Club (21)---	210
Hominy Hill GC (22)-------	211
Howell Park GC (23)-------	212
Jumping Brook CC (24)------	213
Knob Hill GC (25)-----------	214
Lakewood CC (26)----------	215
Leisure Village East (27)----	216
Leisure Village West (28)----	217
Lions Head CC (29)----------	218

Map (#)	Page #
Manasquan River (30)-------	219
Metedeconk National (31)----	220
Navesink Country Club (32)--	221
Ocean Acres CC (33)--------	222
Ocean Cty at Atlantis (34)-	223
Old Orchard CC (36)--------	224
Pebble Creek GC (37)-------	225
Pine Barrens GC (38)-------	226
Pine Brook GC (39) ---------	227
Pine Ridge* (40)----------------	228
Quail Ridge GC (54)---------	229
Renaissance GC (41)-----------	230
Rumson CC (42)----------------	231
Sea Oaks GC (43)------------	232
Shadow Isle GC (55)-----------	233
Shadow Lake Village (44)-----	234
Shark River GC (45)---------	235
Spring Lake Golf Club (47)----	236
Spring Meadow GC (48)----	237
Sun Eagles @Ft. Mnmth(49)*	238
Tom's River CC (50)------------	239
Twin Brook GC (51)---------	240
Westlake GC (52)---------------	241
Woodlake CC (53)-------------	242

BAMM HOLLOW COUNTRY CLUB

215 Sunnyside Rd., Lincroft, NJ 07738   **(732) 741-4774**

Bamm Hollow is a 27 hole private course open 6 days a week all year. Guests play accompanied by a member. Tee time reservations are necessary on weekends. Pull carts are only permitted weekdays.

•**Driving Range**	•**Lockers**
•**Practice Green**	•**Showers**
•**Power Carts**	•**Food**
•**Pull Carts**	•**Clubhouse**
•**Club Rental**	•**Outings**
Caddies	•**Soft Spikes**

Course Description: The three nines at Bamm Hollow offer a variety of playing combinations. The narrow, rolling fairways have changes in elevation that result in a number of blind shots challenging the golfer. On the signature 6th hole, a 90 degree dogleg left, a huge oak tree in the middle of the fairway must be negotiated; water in play adds to the difficulty. An LPGA tournament was played here in 1989. The scorecard below shows the Blue and White nines.

Directions: Monmouth County, #1 on Upper Shore Map
GSP to Exit #114. Go right at first light onto Red Hill Road. Turn left at the next light onto Everett. Pass through 1 traffic light to Sunnyside Rd. and turn left to club 1/2 m. on the left.

Hole	1	2	3	4	5	6	7	8	9	Out	BLUE	Rating 71.2
BLUE	551	372	174	387	391	218	426	466	397	3382		Slope 121
WHITE	513	348	157	361	375	192	412	450	367	3175		
Par	5	4	3	4	4	3	4	5	4	36	WHITE	Rating 73.0
Handicap	3	5	9	2	4	8	1	7	6			Slope 125
RED	480	296	142	338	322	171	401	402	342	2896		
Par	5	4	3	4	4	3	5	5	4	37	RED	Rating 74.4
Handicap	1	7	9	2	4	8	3	6	5			Slope 131
Hole	10	11	12	13	14	15	16	17	18	In		Totals
BLUE	576	186	429	418	506	461	192	479	340	3687	BLUE	6669
WHITE	530	164	413	389	486	438	182	429	322	3354	WHITE	6529
Par	5	3	4	4	5	4	3	4	4	36	Par	72
Handicap	5	9	3	4	6	2	8	1	7			
RED	489	149	266	341	410	422	174	383	307	2961	RED	5857
Par	5	3	4	4	5	5	3	4	4	37	Par	74
Handicap	1	8	9	2	4	5	7	3	6			

Manager: Tom Yoshida   **Pro:** Bob Pedrazzi, PGA   **Supt:** Matt Dobbie
Architect: Hal Purdy 1959

BATTLEGROUND COUNTRY CLUB `PRIVATE`

100 Millhurst Rd., Tennent, NJ 07763   **(732) 462-7466**
www.battlegroundcc.com

Battleground is an 18 hole course open 6 days a week and closed for the months of Jan. and Feb. Guests play accompanied by a member. Reservations for tee times up to one week in advance.

•Driving Range	•Lockers
•Practice Green	•Showers
•Power Carts	•Food
Pull Carts	•Clubhouse
•Club Rental	•Outings
Caddies	•Soft Spikes

Course Description: Built on the site of the Battle of Monmouth, fought during the War of Independence, Battleground is on open country farmland with apple orchards adjoining Battlefield Park. Golfers may spot deer at dusk among the beautiful oak, pine, cedar and apple trees that line the fairways. Water is in play on several holes. Most greens are elevated and slope from back to front. The long par 3 signature tenth offers both a pond to hit over and a stream to avoid. The 12th requires a long shot over a picturesque pond. The well maintained greens are receptive though fast.

Directions: Monmouth County, #2 on Upper Shore Map
NJTpke to Exit 8. Proceed east on Rte.33 for approximately 9 miles to Millhurst Mills Rd. (Rte.527North). Go through light and use jughandle. Club is 1/2 mile on right.

Hole	1	2	3	4	5	6	7	8	9	Out	BLUE	Rating 73.8
BLUE	527	372	370	502	360	195	379	405	392	3502		Slope 129
WHITE	499	350	360	420	330	175	373	398	359	3264		
Par	5	4	4	5	4	3	4	4	4	37	WHITE	Rating 72.1
Handicap	3	9	17	13	5	11	15	1	7			Slope 125
RED	459	272	302	415	325	155	302	347	317	2894		
Par	5	4	4	5	4	3	4	4	4	37	RED	Rating 71.9
Handicap	1	17	15	7	9	11	13	5	3			Slope 121
Hole	10	11	12	13	14	15	16	17	18	In		Totals
BLUE	190	377	427	142	172	421	575	330	434	3068	BLUE	6570
WHITE	175	334	332	122	150	401	450	314	417	2695	WHITE	5959
Par	3	4	4	3	3	4	5	4	4	34	Par	71
Handicap	10	12	2	18	16	4	8	14	6			
RED	166	300	327	105	140	390	443	296	338	2505	RED	5399
Par	3	4	4	3	3	4	5	4	4	34	Par	71
Handicap	10	14	6	18	16	4	2	12	8			

Manager: Michael Rutkin   **Pro:** Sal Silverstrone, PGA   **Supt:** Mark Martini
Architect: Hal Purdy 1961

BEACON HILL COUNTRY CLUB

Beacon Hill Rd., Atlantic Highlands, NJ 07716   (732) 291-3344

Beacon Hill is an 18 hole course open 6 days a week and closed in January. Guests play accompanied by a member. Tee time reservations are not necessary.

•Driving Range	•Lockers
•Practice Green	•Showers
•Power Carts	•Food
Pull Carts	•Clubhouse
Club Rental	•Outings
•Caddies	•Soft Spikes

Course Description: The tricky and rather challenging Beacon Hill features narrow, tight fairways, extremely small well-bunkered greens and water in play on three holes. On clear days the views of the New York City skyline and Sandy Hook are spectacular. From the elevated tee on the par 5 5th, the best views are seen before hitting the difficult and hopefully straight tee shot. This location has been the site of the Mid-Amateur and the NJ State Open qualifyers. A major renovation by Stephen Kay was completed in 2003, making the course even tougher. Caddies are available upon advance notice.

Directions: Monmouth County, #3 on Upper Shore Map
GSP to Exit #117. Take Rte. 36 East for 10 miles. Exit at Avenue D. Bear right to stop sign. Club is directly across the road.

Hole	1	2	3	4	5	6	7	8	9	Out	BLUE	Rating 70.1
BLUE	403	381	318	386	538	184	500	178	161	3049		Slope 132
WHITE	387	343	290	346	516	177	485	170	140	2854	WHITE	Rating 68.3
Par	4	4	4	4	5	3	5	3	3	35		Slope 126
Handicap	5	3	15	1	11	13	7	9	17			
RED	367	315	270	316	465	138	465	160	120	2616	RED	Rating 72.6
Par	4	4	4	4	5	3	5	3	3	35		Slope 131
Handicap	5	7	11	3	9	15	1	13	17			
Hole	10	11	12	13	14	15	16	17	18	In		Totals
BLUE	389	412	513	511	171	324	272	331	161	3084	BLUE	6133
WHITE	364	389	508	501	164	321	262	326	158	2993	WHITE	5847
Par	4	4	5	5	3	4	4	4	3	36	Par	71
Handicap	6	2	4	8	12	10	18	16	14			
RED	304	369	468	482	155	310	252	260	155	2755	RED	5371
Par	4	4	5	5	3	4	4	4	3	36	Par	71
Handicap	10	2	6	4	16	8	12	18	14			

Manager: Roger Bremekamp   **Pro:** Chuck Edwards, PGA   **Supt:** Michael Hocko
Architect: Seymour Dunn 1899

BEL-AIRE GOLF COURSE

Route 34 & Allaire Rd., Wall, NJ 07719   **(732) 449-6024**
www.monmouth.e/golfnet

Bel-Aire is part of the Monmouth County Park System. The 27 holes consist of one 18 hole executive and one 9 hole par 3 course. It is open to the public 7 days a week all year. Golfers play first come, first served. Discounts are available for Srs. & Jrs.

Driving Range	Lockers
•**Practice Green**	Showers
•**Power Carts**	•**Food**
•**Pull Carts**	•**Clubhouse**
•**Club Rental**	Outings
•**Soft Spikes**	

Fees	Weekday	Weekend
Res/ID	$15.25	$18.25
Non-res	$21.50	$30
9 holes	$8.75	$9.75
Power carts $23 (18)		$17 (9)

Course Description: The par 60 18 hole executive layout at Bel-Aire has amply wide well bunkered fairways and medium sized greens kept in excellent condition. Since purchased by Monmouth County, the two courses have been upgraded to its high standards. Water comes into play on 4 holes. For a short non-regulation layout, Bel-Aire can be quite interesting. The 9 hole course has no water and is easy to walk. The par 3 17th plays to a kidney shaped green. This facility is quite busy on weekends.

Directions: Monmouth County, #4 on Upper Shore Map
GSP to Exit 98. Follow signs to Rte. 34S and take it for 1/2 mile. Go left at circle and into Bel-Aire parking lot.

Hole	1	2	3	4	5	6	7	8	9	Out	BLUE	Rating
BLUE												Slope
WHITE	141	116	157	275	118	335	110	298	138	1688		
Par	3	3	3	4	3	4	3	4	3	30	WHITE	Rating 55.6
Handicap	11	13	9	5	15	1	17	3	7			Slope 72
RED	101	116	115	255	118	290	110	255	138	1498		
Par	3	3	3	4	3	4	3	4	3	30	RED	Rating
Handicap	11	13	9	3	15	1	17	5	7			Slope

Hole	10	11	12	13	14	15	16	17	18	In		Totals
BLUE											BLUE	
WHITE	285	138	170	312	148	375	141	178	188	1935	WHITE	3623
Par	4	3	3	4	3	4	3	3	3	30	Par	60
Handicap	12	16	8	10	14	2	18	4	6			
RED	260	138	130	238	148	345	141	151	170	1721	RED	3219
Par	4	3	3	4	3	4	3	3	3	30	Par	60
Handicap	8	16	12	10	14	2	18	6	4			

Manager: Tom Ketchum   **Golf Dir./Pro:** Alan Roberts, PGA   **Supt:** Gary Stedman
Architect: Mort Hansen 1964

BELLA VISTA COUNTRY CLUB   PRIVATE

100 School Road East, Marlboro, NJ 07746   (732) 308-4600
www.bellavistacc.com

Bella Vista is an 18 hole course open 6 days a week, and is closed in Jan. & Feb. Guests play accompanied by a member. Tee time reservations may be made in advance.

•Driving Range	•Lockers
•Practice Green	•Showers
•Power Carts	•Food
•Pull Carts	•Clubhouse
•Club Rental	•Outings
Caddies	•Soft Spikes

Course Description: Bella Vista had undergone a major reconstruction and expansion recently. Twelve holes were redone and designed in a links style with rolling mounds and a variety of grasses. The 8th is the signature, a par 3 out of a chute, featuring heavy mounds and fescue grass. Ponds may be encountered on 5 of the holes and wind can affect play. The front nine is more open; the back is tree-lined, cut out of the woods. The driving range and clubhouse were also improved.

Directions: Monmouth County, #5 on Upper Shore Map
NJ Tpke to Exit #9. Follow signs and take Rte. 18 East over Rte. 9 to a left onto Rte. 79North. At first light, turn right onto School Rd. Club is ahead on right.

Hole	1	2	3	4	5	6	7	8	9	Out	BLUE	Rating
BLUE												Slope
WHITE	358	166	304	316	332	395	169	215	321	2576		
Par	4	3	4	4	4	4	3	3	4	33	WHITE	Rating 67.8
Handicap	4	16	14	12	8	2	18	10	6			Slope 122
RED	334	136	252	276	281	359	110	164	260	2172		
Par	4	3	4	4	4	4	3	3	4	33	RED	Rating 67.0
Handicap	4	16	10	12	8	2	18	14	6			Slope 116
Hole	10	11	12	13	14	15	16	17	18	In		Totals
BLUE											BLUE	
WHITE	183	391	344	135	402	534	509	318	331	3147	WHITE	5723
Par	3	4	4	3	4	5	5	4	4	36	Par	69
Handicap	9	7	13	17	5	1	3	15	11			
RED	162	306	319	112	369	434	416	278	306	2702	RED	4874
Par	3	4	4	3	4	5	5	4	4	36	Par	69
Handicap	9	7	13	17	5	1	3	15	11			

Manager: Anhony Beshara   **Pro:** Chris Dzergoski, PGA   **Supt:** Kerry Boyer
Architect: Harvey Holland 1970's   **Redesign:** Stephen Kay 2000

BEY LEA GOLF COURSE

PUBLIC

1536 North Bay Ave., Toms River, NJ 08753   **(732) 349-0566**
www.usegolf.com
Bey Lea is an 18 hole municipal course for Dover Township open to the public 7 days
a week all year. Special rates for seniors & students. Memberships are available for
residents. Tee time reservations are req; call 732-736-8889 or use web (see above).

Driving Range
- Practice Green
- Power Carts
- Pull Carts
- Club Rental
- Soft Spikes

- Lockers
- Showers
- Food
- Clubhouse
- Outings

Fees	Weekday	Weekend
Res/ID	$14	$16
Non-resNJ	$28	$32
Power carts	$26/18	$16/9

Course Description: Bey Lea is an open, well-maintained somewhat hilly course.
Water is in play on several holes and bunkers are placed along some of the fairways.
The greens are large and undulating. The signature par 5 #18 is long and requires a
shot over a picturesque lake. Water lurks on both sides of the 16th hole. The course
is very busy in season.

Directions: Ocean County, #6 on Upper Shore Map
GSP to Exit 82 (Seaside Hgts.) Take Rte. 37 East for 2 traffic lights. Take jughandle to
Hooper Ave. North (Rte.549) past the Ocean Cty. Mall. Proceed 6 lights to jughandle
for Oak St. and into parking lot.

Hole	1	2	3	4	5	6	7	8	9	Out	BLUE	Rating 71.5
BLUE	370	490	377	170	455	342	553	203	383	3343		Slope 126
WHITE	345	469	354	150	430	322	530	173	366	3139		
Par	4	5	4	3	4	4	5	3	4	36	WHITE	Rating 69.2
Handicap	10	6	8	18	4	14	2	16	12			Slope 121
RED	320	419	331	130	410	298	509	146	351	2914		
Par	4	5	4	3	4	4	5	3	4	36	RED	Rating 71.4
Handicap	10	6	8	18	4	14	2	16	12			Slope 120
Hole	10	11	12	13	14	15	16	17	18	In		Totals
BLUE	397	336	207	362	434	516	390	187	505	3334	BLUE	6677
WHITE	375	314	182	344	412	490	368	142	485	3112	WHITE	6251
Par	4	4	3	4	4	5	4	3	5	36	Par	72
Handicap	9	13	15	11	7	3	5	17	1			
RED	353	291	159	322	391	465	332	134	432	2879	RED	5793
Par	4	4	3	4	4	5	4	3	5	36	Par	72
Handicap	9	13	15	11	7	3	5	17	1			

Manager: Gloria Pieretti   **Supt:** Gary Nokes
Architect: Hal Purdy 1969

CEDAR CREEK GOLF COURSE

PUBLIC

Tilton Blvd., Bayville, NJ 08721   **(732) 269-4460**

Cedar Creek is an 18 hole Berkeley Township course open 7 days a week all year. Annual memberships are available. Tee time reservations are necessary weekends & holidays. Power carts are priced per person.

•Driving Range	Lockers
•Practice Green	Showers
•Power Carts	•Food
•Pull Carts	•Clubhouse
•Club Rental	•Outings
•Soft Spikes	

Fees	Weekday	Weekend
Res.	$14	$16
Sr	$10	
Non-res	$27	$31
Power carts res.	$11/(18)	$8/(9)
Non-res.	$14/18	$10/9

Course Description: This well maintained and popular course draws players from Staten Island and Long Island as well as from New Jersey. With narrow fairways and hilly terrain the course offers golfers an enjoyable round. The front nine is links style, and the back is hilly having three lakes in play on holes 10, 12, 13 and 14. The par 5 18th is lined with pine trees, oaks and dogwood and has a beautiful view, making it the signature hole.

Directions: Ocean County, #7 on Upper Shore Map
GSP N or S to Exit 77. Go left onto Double Trouble Rd. to end. At "T" make a left onto Pinewall-Keswick which becomes Forest Hills Parkway. Go past high school on right. Make a right onto Tilton Blvd. and go into Veteran's Park & Cedar Creek Golf Course.

Hole	1	2	3	4	5	6	7	8	9	Out	BLUE	Rating 70.5
BLUE	499	161	385	453	372	339	130	367	359	3065		Slope 120
WHITE	494	144	355	440	346	330	121	333	332	2895		
Par	5	3	4	5	4	4	3	4	4	36	WHITE	Rating 68.9
Handicap	6	18	4	16	8	12	14	10	2			Slope 117
RED	415	119	312	369	300	285	113	291	280	2484		
Par	5	3	4	5	4	4	3	4	4	36	RED	Rating 69.5
Handicap	6	18	4	16	8	12	14	10	2			Slope 118
Hole	10	11	12	13	14	15	16	17	18	In		Totals
BLUE	529	234	441	380	368	326	308	127	547	3260	BLUE	6325
WHITE	520	220	418	368	340	320	282	115	525	3108	WHITE	6003
Par	5	3	4	4	4	4	4	3	5	36	Par	72
Handicap	5	1	3	7	11	13	15	17	9			
RED	468	164	365	307	303	285	219	95	464	2670	RED	5154
Par	5	3	4	4	4	4	4	3	5	36	Par	72
Handicap	7	5	1	3	11	13	15	17	9			

Manager: Kathleen Seidler   **Supt:** Roger Kelly
Architect: Nicholas Psiahas 1981

CHARLESTON SPRINGS GC

PUBLIC

101 Woodville Rd., Millstone Twp., NJ 07726   **(732) 409-7227**
www.monmouthcountyparks.com

Charleston Springs consists of two 18 hole Monmouth County Parks System courses, open 7 days a week and closed bet. Dec. 23-Mar. 15. Only ID card holders (res. or non res.) may make advance tee times. Walk-ons allowed. Tee time res: (732) 758-8383.

•**Driving Range**   •**Lockers**
•**Practice Green**   •**Showers**
•**Power Carts**   •**Food**
•**Pull Carts**   •**Clubhouse**
•**Club Rental**   Outings
•**Soft Spikes**

Fees	Weekday	Weekend
Res/ID	$31	$31
Non-res	$62	$62
Discounts for Sr, Jr, & Twi.		
Power carts $33 per cart		

Course Description: Charleston Springs is a 619 acre property with a few smalll rolling hills and relatively flat terrain. Ecological considerations were taken into account to enhance this recreational facility. The North course is built in an open links style using a wide variety of native and fescue grasses. The South 18 hole layout is built in a parkland style retaining many more trees. Five sets of tees provide ample options for.golfers. Wind and some water affect play. The greens are slick and in great condition. Both golf courses continue the high quality tradition that Monmouth County has set for its golf facilities. The driving range is a wonderful facility; it is two tiered with yardages posted and target greens. Scorecard below is the North Course.

Directions: Monmouth County, #8 on Upper Shore Map
NJTPKE to Exit 8. Proceed East on Rte. 33 for about 9 miles to Rte. 527 South (Woodville Rd.) Straight thru 4 way STOP sign to course ahead on left.

Hole	1	2	3	4	5	6	7	8	9	Out	BLUE	Rating 73.4
BLUE	522	430	441	498	203	360	413	160	432	3459		Slope 126
WHITE	442	363	358	433	157	295	317	116	353	2834		
Par	5	4	4	5	3	4	4	3	4	36	WHITE	Rating 67.6
Handicap	1	3	9	13	15	11	5	17	7			Slope 117
RED	418	321	329	382	136	258	292	96	318	2550		
Par	5	4	4	5	3	4	4	3	4	36	RED	Rating 69.4
Handicap	1	3	9	13	15	11	5	17	7			Slope 119

Hole	10	11	12	13	14	15	16	17	18	In		Totals
BLUE	419	519	172	397	420	569	450	196	410	3552	BLUE	7011
WHITE	356	434	135	323	333	497	363	147	336	2924	WHITE	5758
Par	4	5	3	4	4	5	4	3	4	36	Par	72
Handicap	4	10	18	14	12	8	2	16	6			
RED	317	400	100	290	310	358	339	113	294	2521	RED	5017
Par	4	5	3	4	4	5	4	3	4	36	Par	72
Handicap	4	10	18	14	12	8	2	16	6			

Dir. of Golf: Alan Roberts, PGA   **Pros:** Lloyd Monroe & David Laudien, PGA
Supt: Ron Luepke   **Manager:** Bill O'Shaughnessy   **Architect:** Mark Mungeam 1998

COLONIAL TERRACE GOLF CLUB **PUBLIC**

1005 Wickapecko Drive, Wanamassa, NJ 07712   **(732) 775-3636**

Colonial Terrace is a 9 hole course open to the public 7 days a week all year. Tee time reservations are not necessary.

Driving Range	Lockers
•**Practice Green**	Showers
•**Power Carts**	•**Food**
•**Pull Carts**	•**Clubhouse**
•**Club Rental**	•**Outings**
•**Soft Spikes**	

Fees	Weekday	Weekend
Daily	$17	$20
Sr.	$12	
Power carts	$27/18	$15/9

Course Description: Colonial Terrace is a regulation 9 hole course with different tees for the 2nd nine. It has been steadily improved. The first hole is a drivable par 4. On the 3rd, a "lake" is in play; (environmentalists now consider this area marshland). The signature 463 yard par 4 second features woods and water surrounding the small fast green. Colonial Terrace is a good facility for iron practice and is easy to walk. The course has become "geese free".

Directions: Monmouth County, #9 on Upper Shore Map
GSP to Exit #102. Bear right off the exit to Asbury Park traffic circle. Take Rte.35 North to Sunset Ave. (2nd light after circle) and turn right. At 2nd light, go right onto Wickapecko Drive; course is 1 and 1/2 blocks on right.

Hole	1	2	3	4	5	6	7	8	9	Out	BLUE	Rating
BLUE												Slope
WHITE	271	463	162	433	127	349	431	157	311	2704		
Par	4	4	3	5	3	4	5	3	4	35	WHITE	Rating 69.0
Handicap	7	1	5	4	9	2	3	8	6			Slope 115
RED	243	347	124	382	112	236	358	126	247	2175		
Par										35	RED	Rating 67.0
Handicap												Slope 114

Hole	10	11	12	13	14	15	16	17	18	In		Totals
BLUE											BLUE	
WHITE											WHITE	2704
Par											Par	35
Handicap												
RED											RED	2175
Par											Par	35
Handicap												

Manager: Regina Savage   **Supt:** Anthony Savage
Built: 1925

COLTS NECK GOLF CLUB

50 Flock Rd., Colt's Neck, NJ 07722   **(732) 303-9330**
www.coltsneckgolfclub.com

Colts Neck is an 18 hole semi-private course open to the public 7 days a week all year. Memberships are available that offer a variety of amenities. Tee times may be made 7 days in advance. Call for off season rates.

- **Driving Range**
- **Practice Green**
- **Power Carts**
- **Pull Carts**
- **Club Rental**
- **Soft Spikes**
- **Lockers**
- **Showers**
- **Food**
- **Clubhouse**
- **Outings**

Fees	Weekday	Weekend
Daily	$60	$80

Power carts $20pp
Twi, Jr & Sr rates available
Seasonal discounts

Course Description: Scottish links style on the front nine and wooded pinelands in the back, Colts Neck offers golfers an interesting golf experience on a well conditioned course with breathtaking views of the natural landscape. Featuring penalizing thick rough, high fescue grass off the fairways, ample bunkering and water in play on several holes, the layout is a challenge for all levels of golfers. The secondary rough is equally troublesome. The difficult ninth is a long heavily bunkered par 4; water appears along the right side. The greens are large and undulating, many surrounded by more bunkers of a Scottish style.

Directions: Monmouth County, #10 on Upper Shore Map
GSP to Exit 109. Go west on Rte. 520. At third light, make a left onto Phalanx Rd. (Phalanx becomes Flock). Cross over Rte. 34. Course is 1/4 mile on right.

Hole	1	2	3	4	5	6	7	8	9	Out	BLUE	Rating 70.2
BLUE	340	385	486	170	316	583	133	560	365	3338		Slope 126
WHITE	318	347	439	150	283	546	105	505	330	3023		
Par	4	4	5	3	4	5	3	5	4	37	WHITE	Rating 67.3
Handicap	17	11	3	9	7	1	15	5	13			Slope 123
RED	271	322	380	125	230	485	80	445	303	2641		
Par	4	4	5	3	4	5	3	5	4	37	RED	Rating 67.6
Handicap	17	11	3	9	7	1	15	5	13			Slope 117
Hole	10	11	12	13	14	15	16	17	18	In		Totals
BLUE	183	431	224	378	352	496	151	464	233	2912	BLUE	6250
WHITE	162	400	205	347	323	470	135	437	187	2666	WHITE	5689
Par	3	4	3	4	4	5	3	5	3	34	Par	71
Handicap	10	2	6	12	14	8	16	18	4			
RED	160	283	255	415	108	378	140	271	322	2332	RED	4862
Par	3	4	3	4	4	5	3	5	3	34	Par	71
Handicap	10	2	6	12	14	8	16	18	4			

Manager: Rich Wasko   **Dir. of Instruction:** Bob Gartner, PGA   **Supt:** Ed Mellor
Architect: Mark Mungeam, 2000

CREAM RIDGE GOLF CLUB

SEMI-PRIVATE

181 Route 539, Cream Ridge, NJ 08514   **(609) 259-2849**
www.creamridgegolfclub.com

Cream Ridge is an 18 hole semi-private club open to the public 7 days a week all year. Tee times may be reserved up to one week in advance. Alternate phone # (800) 345-4957. Carts are mandatory until 3PM weekends in season.

- Driving Range
- Practice Green
- Power Carts
- Pull Carts
- Club Rental
- Soft Spikes
- Lockers
- Showers
- Food
- Clubhouse
- Outings

Fees	Weekday	Weekend
Daily	$45	$57
Twi (12PM)	$38	(5PM)$21.50
Sr	$29	
Power carts included		

Course Description: Golfers travel from all over (Staten Island, PA., Jersey Shore) to enjoy Cream Ridge. The course is well-maintained and features rolling hills, mid-sized undulating greens, bumpy terrain and many water hazards. The signature par 5 18th, 488 yards from the whites, demands strategy to deal with the double dogleg and the water that comes into play along one side and again on the approach shot. The greens are constantly being upgraded. The clubhouse is a comfortable place to relax after a round of golf.

Directions: Monmouth County, #11 on Upper Shore Map
NJTPKE to Exit 7A. Take Rte.195E to Exit #7. Follow signs to Allentown. At first STOP sign, turn right onto Main St. (Rte. 539S). Club is 4 miles ahead on right.

Hole	1	2	3	4	5	6	7	8	9	Out	BLUE	Rating 71.6
BLUE	530	165	263	162	385	403	414	426	580	3328		Slope 129
WHITE	520	138	258	145	343	307	408	401	573	3093		
Par	5	3	4	3	4	4	4	4	5	36	WHITE	Rating 69.4
Handicap	5	15	9	11	13	17	7	3	1			Slope 124
RED	432	128	250	116	308	295	337	317	433	2616		
Par	5	3	4	3	4	4	4	4	5	36	RED	Rating 69.6
Handicap	4	12	10	14	16	18	8	2	6			Slope 119

Hole	10	11	12	13	14	15	16	17	18	In		Totals
BLUE	418	396	340	180	440	367	331	191	500	3163	BLUE	6483
WHITE	352	380	334	172	430	362	316	154	488	2988	WHITE	6040
Par	4	4	4	3	4	4	4	3	5	35	Par	71
Handicap	6	12	18	8	2	10	16	14	4			
RED	332	334	297	151	321	328	293	145	333	2534	RED	5110
Par	4	4	4	3	4	4	4	3	4	34	Par	70
Handicap	3	11	15	13	7	5	17	9	1			

Manager: Bill Miscoski   **Pro:** Bill Marine, PGA   **Supt:** Ken Horner
Architect: Frank Miscoski 1958

CRUZ FARM COUNTRY CLUB

PUBLIC

55 Birdsall Rd., Farmingdale, NJ 07727   **(732) 938-3378**

Cruz Farm is an 18 hole course open 7 days a week, all year. Reserved tee times are not necessary. Prices vary by season.

Driving Range	
•**Practice Green**	Lockers
•**Power Carts**	Showers
•**Pull Carts**	•**Food**
•**Club Rental**	Clubhouse
•**Soft Spikes**	•**Outings**

Fees	**Weekday**	**Weekend**
Daily	$24	$29
Twi (after 4)	$20	23
Power carts	$28/cart	

Course Description: Easily walkable, Cruz Farm Country Club is a short, level layout with wide fairways. Many holes have water in play making it more interesting. The course is well bunkered, and has medium sized greens which are relatively slow. It is a popular course in summer.

Directions: Monmouth County, #12 on Upper Shore Map
GSP to Exit 100A. Go west on Rte. 33 for 1 mile to circle. Proceed south on Rte. 34 for 2 lights. Turn right onto Belmar Blvd. and continue for 1 mile; turn left onto Birdsall Rd to club on left.

Hole	1	2	3	4	5	6	7	8	9	Out	BLUE	Rating
BLUE												Slope
WHITE	132	288	441	286	170	496	286	135	281	2515		
Par	3	4	5	4	3	5	4	3	4	35	WHITE	Rating 64.3
Handicap	18	12	8	4	6	2	10	16	14			Slope 114
RED	102	264	398	235	140	430	258	120	234	2181		
Par	3	4	5	4	3	5	4	3	4	35	RED	Rating 64.4
Handicap	18	12	8	4	6	2	10	16	14			Slope 109

Hole	10	11	12	13	14	15	16	17	18	In		Totals
BLUE											BLUE	
WHITE	114	250	401	303	312	195	150	340	482	2547	WHITE	5062
Par	3	4	5	4	4	3	3	4	5	35	Par	70
Handicap	17	15	5	9	13	3	11	7	1			
RED	110	204	320	261	243	154	122	270	405	2089	RED	4270
Par	3	4	5	4	4	3	3	4	5	35	Par	70
Handicap	17	15	5	9	13	3	11	7	1			

Manager: Lee Cruz   **Dir. of Golf:** Acacio Froes   **Supt:** Ronald Simpson
Architect: Evaristo Cruz, Sr. 1976

DEAL GOLF CLUB

Roseld Ave., Deal, NJ 07723   ·   **(732) 531-1198**

Deal is an 18 hole course open 6 days a week and closed in February. Guests play accompanied by a member. Tee time reservations are not necessary.

•**Driving Range**	•**Lockers**
•**Practice Green**	•**Showers**
•**Power Carts**	•**Food**
Pull Carts	•**Clubhouse**
Club Rental	•**Outings**
•**Caddies**	•**Soft Spikes**

Course Description: Deal Golf Club is over 100 years old and was recently refurbished. Narrow tree lined fairways and deep rough present a challenge. Water is in play on two holes. An errant shot on this course can land deep in the woods from which it is difficult to extricate oneself. The tee shot on the picturesque signature par 4 5th is out of a chute with water along the right side. The approach is daunting; the green is protected by a bunker and a creek. The course becomes even more challenging when a strong ocean wind is blowing. The clubhouse is beautiful and stately.

Directions: Monmouth County, #13 on Upper Shore Map
GSP to Exit 105. Go east for 2 miles to traffic circle and take Rte. 35S for about 3 miles to jughandle for Deal Rd. Continue on Deal to end and turn right onto Monmouth Rd. Turn left onto Roseld Ave. Club is ahead on right.

Hole	1	2	3	4	5	6	7	8	9	Out	BLUE	Rating 69.5
BLUE												Slope 126
WHITE	325	431	348	351	366	194	393	180	478	3066		
Par	4	4	4	4	4	3	4	3	5	35	WHITE	Rating 70.5
Handicap	15	1	11	7	3	13	5	17	9			Slope 126
RED	315	380	322	320	360	173	350	163	460	2843		
Par	4	5	4	4	5	3	4	3	5	37	RED	Rating 73.7
Handicap	17	7	11	3	5	13	9	15	1			Slope 128
Hole	10	11	12	13	14	15	16	17	18	In		Totals
BLUE											BLUE	
WHITE	355	332	554	139	478	413	408	388	170	3237	WHITE	6303
Par	4	4	5	3	5	4	4	4	3	36	Par	71
Handicap	12	10	2	18	8	6	4	14	16			
RED	343	320	472	118	427	402	375	372	160	2989	RED	5832
Par	4	4	5	3	5	5	4	4	3	37	Par	74
Handicap	14	12	2	18	8	6	4	10	16			

Manager: Jozsef de Kovacs   **Pro:** Jason Lamp, PGA   **Supt:** Angelo Petraglia
Architects: Donald Ross, Lawrence Van Etten   **Estab:** 1898

DUE PROCESS STABLES

 **PRIVATE**

Route 537, Colt's Neck, NJ 07722   **(732) 542-0317**

Due Process Stables is an 18 hole course open 6 days a week and closed in winter.
Guests play accompanied by a member. Tee times can be reserved 1 day in advance.

•**Driving Range**	•**Lockers**
•**Practice Green**	•**Showers**
•**Power Carts**	•**Food**
Pull Carts	•**Clubhouse**
Club Rental	Outings
•**Caddies**	•**Soft Spikes**

Course Description: Formerly a working stable, Due Process was conceived of by
Robert Brennan and designed in an equine motif by Johnny Miller and Gene Bates. The
clubhouse is a converted barn with statues of racing horses all around. There are
shamrocks on the entrance gates. The tees are designated as Derby, Preakness &
Belmont, instead of the usual colors. The course features stacked sod bunkers, long
fescue grass in the rough, considerable mounding and rolling terrain. Two holes have
double fairways; some sections are in a links style. Opportunities abound for bump
and run shots. Caddies are mandatory.

Directions: Monmouth County, #14 on Upper Shore Map
GSP to Exit 109, Lincroft. Make a right off the ramp to Rte. 520 West. At 2nd light,
turn left onto Swimming River Road. Go for about 2 miles and bear right at fork onto
Rte. 537 West. Club entrance is at third driveway on left.

Hole	1	2	3	4	5	6	7	8	9	Out	BLUE	Rating 74.6
BLUE	417	458	435	158	529	403	182	508	336	3476		Slope 142
WHITE	360	416	384	150	503	336	175	480	362	3166		
Par	4	4	4	3	5	4	3	5	4	36	WHITE	Rating 72.1
Handicap	10	4	2	18	8	12	14	6	16			Slope 136
RED	347	351	357	134	479	319	142	435	338	2902		
Par	4	4	4	3	5	4	3	5	4	36	RED	Rating 70.0
Handicap	10	4	2	18	8	12	14	6	16			Slope 129
Hole	10	11	12	13	14	15	16	17	18	In		Totals
BLUE	437	209	540	451	398	216	413	427	521	3612	BLUE	7138
WHITE	407	182	524	423	363	179	385	402	496	3361	WHITE	6570
Par	4	3	5	4	4	3	4	4	5	36	Par	72
Handicap	3	15	5	1	13	17	7	9	11			
RED	376	364	450	302	127	435	387	141	344	2926	RED	5966
Par	4	3	5	4	4	3	4	4	5	36	Par	72
Handicap	3	15	5	1	13	17	7	9	11			

Pro: Wayne Warms, PGA   **Supt:** Tim Kwiat
Architect: Johnny Miller & Gene Bates   1996

EAGLE OAKS GOLF CLUB

20 Shore Oaks Dr., Farmingdale, NJ 07727   **(732) 938-9696**
www.eagleoaks.com

Eagle Oaks Golf Club is a private 18 hole course open 6 days a week and closed in Jan. and Feb. Guests play accompanied by a member. For pro shop, call ext. 28.

•Driving Range	•Lockers
•Practice Green	•Showers
•Power Carts	•Food
Pull Carts	•Clubhouse
•Club Rental	•Outings
•Caddies	•Soft Spikes

Course Description: Eagle Oaks Golf Club (formerly called Shore Oaks) is the first designed by Johnny Miller and considered his signature effort. This generally flat, open course is well bunkered and has tricky mounding to negotiate. Beautifully maintained and landscaped, there are hazards on 13 holes. Nearly all the holes are separated from each other giving it a links-style feel. The greens are relatively shallow making it a great test for iron play. The signature par 4 fifteenth is picturesque, long and demanding; water is found left and short of the green. The 1992 State PGA was held here as well as the NJ State Amateur.

Directions: Monmouth County, #46 on Upper Shore Map
GSPSouth to Exit 100A or from south Exit 100B. Take Rte. 33 west to Rte. 547 South which merges with Asbury Ave. Take 1st right onto Shore Oaks Drive.

Hole	1	2	3	4	5	6	7	8	9	Out	BLUE	Rating 73.5
BLUE	427	351	558	412	192	391	456	167	557	3511		Slope 132
WHITE	365	310	520	368	141	353	386	135	515	3093		
Par	4	4	5	4	3	4	4	3	5	36	WHITE	Rating 71.6
Handicap	9	13	5	3	15	11	1	17	7			Slope 128
RED	365	310	363	280	141	302	352	118	445	2676		
Par	4	4	4	4	3	4	4	3	5	35	RED	Rating 71.2
Handicap	1	11	5	7	15	13	9	17	3			Slope 121

Hole	10	11	12	13	14	15	16	17	18	In		Totals
BLUE	422	171	438	397	399	453	207	494	427	3408	BLUE	6919
WHITE	377	138	364	342	315	396	157	461	376	2926	WHITE	6505
Par	4	3	4	4	4	4	3	5	4	35	Par	71
Handicap	8	16	6	14	10	2	18	12	4			
RED	413	110	364	342	315	339	157	416	320	2776	RED	5452
Par	5	3	4	4	4	4	3	5	4	36	Par	71
Handicap	8	18	6	12	14	4	16	2	10			

Manager: Joe Callahan   **Pro:** Wendell Dix, PGA   **Supt:** Marty Sommerfeld
Architect: Johnny Miller 1990

EAGLE RIDGE GOLF CLUB

SEMI-PRIVATE

2 Augusta Blvd., Lakewood, NJ 08701　　　**(732) 901-4900**
www.eagleridgegolf.com

Eagle Ridge is an 18 hole course open 7 days a week all year. Memberships are available. Special discounts ($10 off) for residents of the Fairways & Meadows at Lake Ridge adult communities. Tee times: 14 days members, 7 days non-members. Sr. member discount available.

- •**Driving Range**
- •**Practice Green**
- •**Power Carts**
- Pull Carts
- •**Club Rental**
- •**Soft Spikes**
- •**Lockers**
- •**Showers**
- •**Food**
- •**Clubhouse**
- •**Outings**

Fees	Mon-Thur	Fri-Sun
Daily(non-mbr)	$80	$95
Power carts included		
Members pay only cart fees		
GPS on all carts		

Course Description: Built on a former sand quarry, the links style Eagle Ridge is a major attraction for Monmouth and Ocean County residents. With scenic views substantial elevation changes, sloping fairways, natural grasses and scrub pines in the heavier rough, the course offers challenge and variety. Water is in play on 5 holes. The greens are contoured, some two-tiered, and many guarded by strategically placed bunkers. The signature par 5 5th has a pond confronting the golfer on the approach shot. Waste areas, sand and grass bunkers are encountered here along with elevated greens and tees. The beautiful 18th hole finishes at the magnificent new clubhouse and "The View" restaurant overlooking this unique property.

Directions: Ocean County, #15 on Upper Shore Map
From North: GSP to Exit 88. Take Rte. 70 West for 3.3 mi. Go right onto Massachusetts Ave. At Cross St., turn left and course is on the left 1 mile ahead.

Hole	1	2	3	4	5	6	7	8	9	Out	WHITE	Rating 70.3
WHITE	368	389	207	315	510	392	551	151	320	3203		Slope 128
GOLD	342	358	131	280	475	368	520	132	300	2906		
Par	4	4	3	4	5	4	5	3	4	36	GOLD	Rating 67.8
Handicap	11	7	9	13	3	5	1	17	15			Slope 122
RED	293	315	105	230	383	315	439	114	260	2454		
Par	4	4	3	4	5	4	5	3	4	36	RED	Rating 68.3
Handicap	9	5	13	15	3	7	1	17	11			Slope 125

Hole	10	11	12	13	14	15	16	17	18	In		Totals
WHITE	330	135	381	368	395	505	114	360	350	2938	WHITE	6141
GOLD	308	110	340	338	360	475	106	325	318	2680	GOLD	5586
Par	4	3	4	4	4	5	3	4	4	35	Par	71
Handicap	14	16	6	12	4	2	18	10	8			
RED	282	88	298	276	289	449	85	288	283	2338	RED	4792
Par	4	3	4	4	4	5	3	4	4	35	Par	71
Handicap	10	16	8	12	6	2	18	14	4			

Manager: Kokes Enterprise　　**Dir. of Golf:** Mike Attara, PGA　　**Supt:** Dennis Parker
Architects: Ault, Clark & Associates, Ltd. 1999

FAIRWAY MEWS GOLF CLUB

1 Clubhouse Dr., Spring Lake Heights, NJ 07762   **(732) 449-8883**

Fairway Mews Golf & Racquet Club is an 18 hole executive course for residents of the adult community where it is located. It is open 6 days a week from Mar. 15th through Dec. 15th. Tee time reservations are advisable.

Driving Range	Lockers
•Practice Green	•Showers
•Power Carts	Food
•Pull Carts	•Clubhouse
Club Rental	Outings
Caddies	•Soft Spikes

Course Description: Fairway Mews is an executive layout, par 60 from the whites and playing to a par 65 from the Reds. Winding through the housing development, the course is narrow, flat and easy to walk. Most members own their golf carts. Water is in play on six holes. The fast greens are of medium size; some putts necessitate a careful read.

Directions: Monmouth County, #16 on Upper Shore Map
GSP to Exit 98. Take Rte. 138 East to Rte. 35 South for 1 mile to Warren Ave. Make a left on Warren. Entrance to club is 1/2 mile on left.

Hole	1	2	3	4	5	6	7	8	9	Out	BLUE	Rating
BLUE												Slope
WHITE	142	180	238	307	166	160	157	150	300	1800		
Par	3	3	4	4	3	3	3	3	4	30	WHITE	Rating 59.4
Handicap	12	8	6	2	10	14	15	18	4			Slope 95
RED	134	140	201	263	157	133	146	141	285	1600		
Par	3	3	4	5	3	3	3	3	5	32	RED	Rating 59.3
Handicap	16	6	8	4	10	12	14	18	2			Slope 95

Hole	10	11	12	13	14	15	16	17	18	In		Totals
BLUE											BLUE	
WHITE	141	267	220	159	391	200	139	197	181	1895	WHITE	3695
Par	3	4	4	3	4	3	3	3	3	30	Par	60
Handicap	15	3	9	11	1	7	17	5	13			
RED	85	254	193	141	308	170	134	147	131	1563	RED	3230
Par	3	4	4	3	5	4	3	3	3	32	Par	65
Handicap	17	1	7	13	3	11	15	5	9			

Manager: Brian O'Gibney   **Pro:** Kevin Kenny, PGA   **Supt:** Joseph Beaudoin
                               Built: Late 1970s

FORGE POND GOLF COURSE

PUBLIC

301 Chambers Bridge Rd., Brick, NJ 08723   **(732) 920-8899**
www.oceancountygolf.com

Forge Pond is an 18 hole executive par 60 Ocean County course open all year. Tee time reservations may be made up to 1 week in advance. Reduced rates after 1PM.

Driving Range	Lockers
•**Practice Green**	Showers
•**Power Carts**	•**Food**
•**Pull Carts**	Clubhouse
•**Club Rental**	Outings
•**Soft Spikes**	

Fees	Weekday	Weekend
Res/ID	$18	$16
Non-res	$24	$28
Sr/Jr	$10	
Power carts $18 per cart		

Course Description: A retiree haven, Forge Pond is a very busy course, excellent for working on your game. It has narrow fairways and small greens. With only 6 par 4s and no par 5s, it is advisable to leave your woods at home unless you hit very straight. The signature par 3 12th requires a shot over a pond with a beckoning bunker at the green.

Directions: Ocean County, #35 on Upper Shore Map
GSP South to Exit 91. Bear right onto Lanes Mills Rd. which becomes Chambers Bridge Rd. Take jughandle and course is just past the high school. From South, take GSP to Exit 90, make right onto Chambers Bridge and proceed as above.

Hole	1	2	3	4	5	6	7	8	9	Out	BLUE	Rating 59.4
BLUE	340	113	118	219	339	146	308	161	172	1916		Slope 98
WHITE	325	100	102	206	322	133	301	144	153	1786		
Par	4	3	3	3	4	3	4	3	3	30	WHITE	Rating 58.3
Handicap	3	16	18	8	5	12	1	13	10			Slope 95
RED	315	91	95	196	314	122	292	136	144	1705		
Par	4	3	3	3	4	3	4	3	3	30	RED	Rating 60.5
Handicap	3	16	18	8	5	12	1	13	10			Slope 97
Hole	10	11	12	13	14	15	16	17	18	In		Totals
BLUE	191	182	144	291	172	235	309	153	323	2000	BLUE	3916
WHITE	168	169	122	274	156	218	293	139	313	1852	WHITE	3638
Par	3	3	3	4	3	3	4	3	4	30	Par	60
Handicap	9	14	17	2	11	7	4	15	6			
RED	159	157	93	266	147	208	282	129	302	1743	RED	3448
Par	3	3	3	4	3	3	3	3	4	30	Par	60
Handicap	9	14	17	2	11	7	4	15	6			

Manager: Dan O'Connor   **Supt:** Scott Binkley
Architect: Hal Purdy 1990

FOUR SEASONS SPA & CC

1600 Spring Meadow Dr., Lakewood, NJ 08701   732-477-2730

Four Seasons Spa & Country Club has a 9 hole golf course available to residents of this adult community. It is open 6 days a week (closed Tuesdays), from Mar. 15 to Dec. 15. Guests play accompanied by members.

Driving Range	•Lockers
•Practice Green	•Showers
•Power Carts	Food
•Pull Carts	•Clubhouse
•Club Rental	Outings
Caddies	•Soft Spikes

Course Description: The Tom Fazio executive course at Four Seasons has 6 par 3s and 3 par 4s. Many homes are situated on the left or right of every hole. Some water is in play; the signature 4th has three quarters of the green surrounded by water and is a replica of the par 3 fourth hole at Baltusrol. The tees and greens are well conditioned. For variety, golfers play Blue for front and White for the second nine to make 18. Residents of this adult community are fortunate to have this attractive amenity along with the other activities offered here.

Directions: Ocean County, #17 on Upper Shore Map
GSP to Exit 88. Go east on Rte. 70 and make a right at first light, Shorrock St. Pass Lions Head Woods, another adult community, and turn right onto Four Seasons Drive into development. Make right onto Spring Meadow Drive to clubhouse.

Hole	1	2	3	4	5	6	7	8	9	Out	BLUE	Rating 29.8
BLUE	150	145	360	143	300	180	130	330	96	1834		Slope 105
WHITE	140	135	320	130	266	146	120	300	92	1649		
Par	3	3	4	3	4	3	3	4	3	30	WHITE	Rating 29.0
Handicap	8	7	2	3	4	5	6	1	9			Slope 100
RED	129	115	295	127	229	132	110	272	94	1503		
Par	3	3	4	3	4	3	3	4	3	30	RED	Rating 28.9
Handicap	8	7	2	3	4	5	6	1	9			Slope 99
Hole	10	11	12	13	14	15	16	17	18	In		Totals
BLUE											BLUE	1834
WHITE											WHITE	1649
Par											Par	30
Handicap												
RED											RED	1503
Par											Par	30
Handicap												

Pro: Ron Henefer, PGA   **Supt:** Harry Leonard
Architect: Tom Fazio 1997

GAMBLER RIDGE GOLF CLUB

PUBLIC

Burlington Path Rd., Cream Ridge, NJ 08514   **(609) 758-3588**
www.gamblerridge.com

Gambler Ridge is an 18 hole course open 7 days a week all year. Tee times may be reserved 7 days in advance. Carts are required before 11 AM on weekends. For more info call (800) 427-8463. There are reduced rates for Srs. and early birds.

•**Driving Range**	Lockers
•**Practice Green**	Showers
•**Power Carts**	•**Food**
•**Pull Carts**	•**Clubhouse**
•**Club Rental**	•**Outings**
•**Soft Spikes**	

Fees	Weekday	Weekend
Prime Time	$38	$50
Midday	$28	$34
Twilight	$20	$29
Power carts	included	

Course Description: Built on 120 acres, Gambler Ridge is constantly being improved. It is a good challenge for the average golfer, fairly open with somewhat rolling terrain and scattered maturing trees along the fairways. Built on a former farm deep in race horse country, it is relatively level; the bent grass greens are mid-sized and fast. Water is in play on 12 holes. The par 3 twelfth requires a tee shot over two ponds. The 15th and 17th holes share a green.

Directions: Monmouth County, #18 on Upper Shore Map
NJTPKE to Exit 7A. Take Rte. 195 East to Exit 16. Take Rte. 537W (past Great Adventure); go about 5 miles to the first light. Turn right onto Rte. 539 North. Travel 2 miles to Burlington Path Rd. and turn right. Course is 1 mile ahead on the right.

Hole	1	2	3	4	5	6	7	8	9	Out	BLUE	Rating 70.6
BLUE	358	369	171	534	275	335	166	540	381	3129		Slope 125
WHITE	349	359	105	521	270	325	148	531	375	2983		
Par	4	4	3	5	4	4	3	5	4	36	WHITE	Rating 68.9
Handicap	16	8	12	2	18	10	14	4	6			Slope 122
RED	282	286	80	434	244	295	125	435	323	2504		
Par	4	4	3	5	4	4	3	5	4	36	RED	Rating 69.5
Handicap	16	8	12	2	18	10	14	4	6			Slope 114
Hole	10	11	12	13	14	15	16	17	18	In		Totals
BLUE	378	233	365	321	211	416	525	402	390	3241	BLUE	6342
WHITE	360	198	356	317	201	401	513	390	383	3119	WHITE	6089
Par	4	3	4	4	3	4	5	4	4	35	Par	71
Handicap	9	7	11	17	15	3	13	1	5			
RED	303	142	295	258	161	353	459	332	318	2621	RED	5140
Par	4	3	4	4	3	4	5	4	4	35	Par	71
Handicap	9	7	11	17	15	3	13	1	5			

Supt: Gary Cameron
Architects: Jason Nickelson, Brian Rockhill 1985

GREENBRIAR OCEANAIRE GC

PRIVATE

3 Beach Haven Way, Waretown, NJ 08758   **(609) 242-7100**
www.ushome.com

Greenbriar Oceanaire is an 18 hole course open 7 days a week all year. It is situated within a private gated community. Memberships are available. Guests may play accompanied by a member. Tee times are not necessary.

- •**Driving Range**
- •**Practice Green**
- •**Power Carts**
- •**Pull Carts**
- •**Club Rental**
- Caddies

- •**Lockers**
- •**Showers**
- •**Food**
- •**Clubhouse**
- •**Outings**
- •**Soft Spikes**

NEW

Course Description: The rolling terrain and heavily wooded 18 holes at Greenbriar Oceanaire are an outstanding amenity offered to the residents here. Despite the lovely homes surrounding the golf course, beautiful views of the natural surroundings are apparent. Several holes are up for consideration as the signature. The spectacularly scenic starting hole contains a foot bridge and a man made spring within its layout. The 38,000 square foot clubhouse is the largest recreational facility in a private NJ adult community.

Directions: Ocean County, #56 on Upper Shore Map
GSP southbound take Exit #67: go left onto Bay Blvd. Make an immediate left onto the northbound lane of the GSP. Take Exit #69 and go right onto 532 (Wells Mill Rd.) Go 7/10 mile to club on right.

Hole	1	2	3	4	5	6	7	8	9	Out	BLUE	Rating
BLUE												Slope
WHITE	563	372	154	433	363	537	158	467	427	3474		
Par	5	4	3	4	4	5	3	4	4	36	WHITE	Rating
Handicap												Slope
RED												
Par											RED	Rating
Handicap												Slope

Hole	10	11	12	13	14	15	16	17	18	In		Totals
BLUE											BLUE	
WHITE	355	332	175	380	543	555	213	374	360	3287	WHITE	6761
Par	4	4	3	4	5	5	3	4	4	36	Par	72
Handicap												
RED											RED	
Par											Par	
Handicap												

Manager: Ocean Golf Mgmt.
Architect: Arthur Hills 2003

GREENBRIAR WOODLANDS GC `PRIVATE`

1 Kensington Circle, Toms River, NJ 08755　　　**(732) 286-6889**

Greenbriar is an 18 hole executive course. Residents of this adult community may take a yearly membership or may play on a daily basis. It is open 7 days a week and is closed for Jan. & Feb. Reserved tee times are not necessary.

•**Driving Range**	Lockers
•**Practice Green**	Showers
•**Power Carts**	Food
•**Pull Carts**	•**Clubhouse**
•**Club Rental**	Outings
•**Soft Spikes**	Caddies

Course Description: This lovely golf course may be found amidst the 1,000 housing units of Greenbriar Woodlands. The front nine is short consisting of all par 3s with the longest hole 120 yards. The more challenging back has longer par 3s and a par 4. The fairways are narrow and well bunkered. The small greens are elevated, hard and fast often sloping away from the pin. The most picturesque hole is the 18th; it features a pond to carry in front of the green.

Directions: Ocean County, #19 on Upper Shore Map
GSP to Exit 83 (Seaside Heights). At the first jughandle, take Rte. 37E. Go to the next light and turn right onto Old Freehold Road. Continue until it becomes New Hampshire Ave. Make a right into Greenbriar Woodlands to the gatehouse and go straight ahead to clubhouse parking.

Hole	1	2	3	4	5	6	7	8	9	Out	BLUE	Rating
BLUE												Slope
WHITE	117	60	98	102	87	110	115	65	120	874		
Par	3	3	3	3	3	3	3	3	3	27	WHITE	Rating 58.6
Handicap	4	9	6	7	5	1	2	8	3			Slope 96
RED												
Par											RED	Rating 59.2
Handicap												Slope 98
Hole	10	11	12	13	14	15	16	17	18	In		Totals
BLUE											BLUE	
WHITE	131	110	121	167	381	111	182	146	156	1505	WHITE	2379
Par	3	3	3	3	4	3	3	3	3	28	Par	58
Handicap	6	16	12	10	2	18	8	14	4			
RED	152	95	143	145	403	94	196	135	172	1535	RED	2409
Par	3	3	3	3	4	3	3	3	3	28	Par	58
Handicap	5	15	11	9	1	17	7	13	3			

Manager: Carol Magretto　　**Pro:** Mike Harris,PGA　　**Supt:** Thomas McConnell
Architects: Smith Assoc. & Harry Harsin 1987

HOLE IN ONE GOLF CENTER

PUBLIC

530 Route 33 West, Englishtown, NJ 07726   **(732) 792-2818**

Hole in One Golf Center is a 9 hole par 3 course open 7 days a week all year. All holes are between 98 and 160 yards. A miniature golf facility is on the premises.

•**Driving Range**	Lockers
•**Practice Green**	Showers
Power Carts ·	•**Food**
•**Pull Carts**	•**Clubhouse**
•**Club Rental**	•**Outings**
•**Soft Spikes**	

Fees	Weekday	Weekend
Daily	$12/9 holes	$14/9
Children	$10	$12
2nd round is 1/2 price		

Course Description: This par 3 course is a good place to practice one's short game. Two holes require shots over water. The bent grass greens are large as are the tee areas. There is a chipping green, sand bunker and an 8200 square foot putting green.

Directions: Monmouth County, #20 on Upper Shore Map
NJTPKE to Exit #8. Go east on Rte. 33 (towards Freehold) approx. 5 miles and make U turn. Course is on right.

Hole	1	2	3	4	5	6	7	8	9	Out	BLUE	Rating
BLUE	102	88	121	101	124	136	98	118	160	1048		Slope
WHITE	84	88	104	86	78	122	84	112	117	875		
Par	3	3	3	3	3	3	3	3	3		WHITE	Rating
Handicap												Slope
RED	51	67	84	63	51	87	76	102	102	683		
Par											RED	Rating
Handicap												Slope
Hole	10	11	12	13	14	15	16	17	18	In		Totals
BLUE											BLUE	1048
WHITE											WHITE	875
Par											Par	
Handicap												
RED											RED	683
Par											Par	
Handicap												

Manager/Supt: Ming C. Kong
Architects: Scott Monn & Lisa Maki 2000

HOLLYWOOD GOLF CLUB

510 Roseld Avenue, Deal, NJ 07723   **(732) 531-8950**
www.hollywoodgolfclub.org

Hollywood is an 18 hole course open 6 days a week between Mar. 15 and Dec. 1.
Guests may play accompanied by a member. Tee times are required for weekends.

•**Driving Range**	•**Lockers**
•**Practice Green**	•**Showers**
•**Power Carts**	•**Food**
Pull Carts	•**Clubhouse**
Club Rental	•**Outings**
•**Caddies**	•**Soft Spikes**

Course Description: Hollywood Golf Club has been rated as one of the top 8 courses
in NJ by Golf Digest. With gently rolling terrain in a links style layout, accuracy off the
tee is extremely important. The well-guarded, small greens are fast with some break.
The signature par 3 4th is rated one of the best short par 3s in the world. Mounding
and bunkering confront the golfer most of the time. Too short a shot and the ball rolls
back off the green; if hit over the target area, it rolls down a slope. The bunkers and
tees have been re-designed by Rees Jones. The NJ state PGA was held here in 1998.

Directions: Monmouth County, #21 on Upper Shore Map
GSP to Exit 105. Proceed east on Rte. 36 to light (about 2 miles.) Turn right onto Rte.
35S for about 3 miles to Deal Rd. (jughandle left). Go east on Deal Rd. to end and turn
right onto Monmouth Rd. Go 4 blocks to Roseld Ave. & turn right. Club is on right.

Hole	1	2	3	4	5	6	7	8	9	Out	BLUE	Rating 73.9
BLUE	419	359	456	149	392	391	539	392	384	3481		Slope 138
WHITE	404	347	394	143	351	366	523	360	369	3257		
Par	4	4	4	3	4	4	5	4	4	36	WHITE	Rating 71.9
Handicap	4	16	6	18	14	10	2	12	8			Slope 136
RED	388	335	342	130	330	321	463	341	335	2985		
Par	5	4	4	3	4	4	5	4	4	37	RED	Rating 73.4
Handicap	5	13	3	17	15	11	1	7	9			Slope 132
Hole	10	11	12	13	14	15	16	17	18	In		Totals
BLUE	512	382	452	315	378	167	459	230	396	3291	BLUE	6812
WHITE	491	375	432	310	352	158	454	210	392	3174	WHITE	6386
Par	5	4	4	4	4	3	5	3	4	36	Par	72
Handicap	7	3	1	13	9	17	15	11	5			
RED	407	307	418	275	314	133	390	183	354	2718	RED	5766
Par	5	4	5	4	4	3	5	3	4	37	Par	74
Handicap	8	10	2	16	12	18	4	14	6			

Manager: Ralph Strivelli   **Pro:** Ron MacDougal, PGA   **Supt:** Jan Kasyjanski
Architects: Walter Travis 1898   **Redesign:** Dick Wilson, Rees Jones

HOMINY HILL GOLF COURSE

PUBLIC

92 Mercer Rd., Colt's Neck, NJ 07722
www.imonmouth.e-golf.net

(732) 462-9222

Hominy Hill is an 18 hole Monmouth County course open 7 days a week from March 15 to Dec. 23. Residents reserve up to 7 days in advance for $3.00, non res. 7 days $6.00 pp. Must have res. or non-res. ID card to use system; call (732) 758-8383.

- •Driving Range
- •Practice Green
- •Power Carts
- •Pull Carts
- •Club Rental
- •Soft Spikes

- •Lockers
- •Showers
- •Food
- •Clubhouse
- Outings

Fees	Weekday	Weekend
Daily(res)	$29	$33
Non-res	$58	$66
Res. Seniors 20% discount		
Carts $33 per cart		

Course Description: Designed by Robert Trent Jones and originally built as a private golf course, Hominy Hill is long and well designed with rolling fairways and deep Kentucky Blue Grass always cut to tournament height. Large, contoured well bunkered greens, many doglegs in both directions and long tee boxes are prevalent here. The par 3 signature eleventh requires considerable carry over water to a sloping green. This highly reputed course is very popular and players from all over try to obtain the few starting times that the county residents leave open. Hominy Hill os considered one of New Jersey's best public courses.

Directions: Monmouth County, #22 on Upper Shore Map
GSP south to Exit 123. Take Rte. 9South (approx 5 mi.) to Rte. 18S Go (9 mi.)to Rte. 537East & turn right. Course is one mile on the right on Mercer Rd. **OR** NJTPKE to Exit 7A. Then take Rte. 195E to Rte. 537E past Rte. 18 to course.

Hole	1	2	3	4	5	6	7	8	9	Out	BLUE	Rating 74.2
BLUE	426	396	211	542	341	406	195	435	513	3465		Slope 131
WHITE	390	328	181	498	312	374	175	390	475	3123		
Par	4	4	3	5	4	4	3	4	5	36	WHITE	Rating 71.5
Handicap	6	12	14	2	10	16	18	4	8			Slope 126
RED	356	298	141	458	288	337	130	366	430	2804		
Par	4	4	3	5	4	4	3	4	5	36	RED	Rating 73.6
Handicap	6	12	14	2	10	16	18	4	8			Slope 129

Hole	10	11	12	13	14	15	16	17	18	In		Totals
BLUE	458	207	441	393	535	397	209	537	417	3594	BLUE	7049
WHITE	430	176	419	370	504	375	188	501	384	3347	WHITE	6456
Par	4	3	4	4	5	4	3	5	4	36	Par	72
Handicap	11	13	5	15	1	17	9	3	7			
RED	397	123	378	320	473	344	160	464	331	2990	RED	5793
Par	4	3	4	4	5	4	3	5	4	36	Par	72
Handicap	11	13	5	15	1	17	9	3	7			

Manager: Brian Corrigan   **Pro:** Alan Roberts, PGA   **Supt:** Tim Mariner
Architect: Robert Trent Jones 1964

HOWELL PARK GOLF COURSE

PUBLIC

Preventorium Rd., Farmingdale, NJ 07727   **(732) 938-4771**

Howell Park is an 18 hole Monmouth County course open 7 days a week between Mar. 15 and Dec. 23. Reservations: 7 days in advance @$1.50pp, for residents with ID; non-res with ID, 7 days @ $3pp. Call 1-888-435-3613 for automated tee times. Walk ons allowed.

•**Driving Range**	Lockers
•**Practice Green**	Showers
•**Power Carts**	•**Food**
•**Pull Carts**	•**Clubhouse**
•**Club Rental**	Outings
•**Soft Spikes**	

Fees	Weekday	Weekend
Res/ID	$23	$28
Sr.	20% off	
Non-res	$46	$56
Power carts $33		

Course Description: Howell Park is an exceptional facility for the fortunate Monmouth County residents to enjoy. The medium to large sized greens are fast and have considerable break. The terrain is fairly flat and not much water is in play although some creeks run along the bent grass tree-lined fairways. The 8th hole was redesigned and has a "Pete Dye" look with 5 teeing areas. It plays 190-200 yards from the Blues. A good teaching program is available here. With its outstanding reputation, this excellently maintained course gets very busy.

Directions: Monmouth County, #23 on Upper Shore Map
GSP to Exit 98. Take Rte. 195 West to exit 31B. At light, take a left onto Rte. 524A (Squamgum-Yellowbrook Rd.) Course is on left just before the high school.

Hole	1	2	3	4	5	6	7	8	9	Out	BLUE	Rating 73.0
BLUE	425	557	382	202	401	541	336	175	410	3429		Slope 126
WHITE	387	522	363	172	372	505	313	137	393	3164		
Par	4	5	4	3	4	5	4	3	4	36	WHITE	Rating 70.2
Handicap	11	1	13	15	9	3	7	17	5			Slope 120
RED	376	476	308	132	343	416	290	105	369	2815		
Par	4	5	4	3	4	5	4	3	4	36	RED	Rating 72.5
Handicap	11	1	13	15	9	3	7	17	5			Slope 125
Hole	10	11	12	13	14	15	16	17	18	In		Totals
BLUE	415	513	391	222	387	539	381	157	451	3456	BLUE	6916
WHITE	391	470	373	150	364	475	342	135	412	3112	WHITE	6302
Par	4	5	4	3	4	5	4	3	4	36	Par	72
Handicap	4	2	8	18	12	16	6	14	10			
RED	360	408	355	140	332	457	300	112	384	2878	RED	5725
Par	4	5	4	3	4	5	4	3	4	36	Par	72
Handicap	4	2	8	18	12	16	6	14	10			

Manager: Vern Hasselbrock   **Pro:** David Laudien, PGA   **Supt:** Bob Duncan
Architect: Frank Duane 1972

JUMPING BROOK GOLF & CC

PRIVATE

210 Jumping Brook Rd., Neptune, NJ 07753   **(732) 922-6140**
www.jumpingbrookcc.com

Jumping Brook is a private 18 hole course open 7 days a week all year. Tee time reservations are recommended. Guests may play accompanied by a member.

- **•Driving Range** • **Lockers**
- **•Practice Green** • **Showers**
- **•Power Carts** • **Food**
- Pull Carts • **Clubhouse**
- **•Club Rental** • **Outings**
- Caddies • **Soft Spikes**

Course Description: Jumping Brook is classic in design and hillier than most shore courses. Open, with small undulating greens, it has a brook running through it that affects play on 4 holes. The front nine is more difficult than the back. The third hole is 598 yards from the Blue tees requiring a thoughtful layup second or a gallant effort over the brook to set up a shorter approach to an elevated green. The NJ State Open was played here in the 1930s and the State PGA in 1951. Recently renovated, it is now more interesting and challenging than before. A unique feature of this course is that you can see the entire layout from both the first tee and the clubhouse.

Directions: Monmouth County, #24 on Upper Shore Map
GSP South to Exit 100B. Take Rte. 33 east and at 2nd light make a left onto Jumping Brook Rd. to course 1/2 mile on the right.

Hole	1	2	3	4	5	6	7	8	9	Out	BLUE	Rating 73.0
BLUE	292	342	598	434	210	362	357	364	537	3496		Slope 139
WHITE	277	332	546	416	199	338	347	357	513	3325		
Par	4	4	5	4	3	4	4	4	5	37	WHITE	Rating 70.6
Handicap	17	9	1	3	15	7	11	13	5			Slope 133
RED	235	315	479	364	188	278	293	319	392	2863		
Par	4	4	5	4	3	4	4	4	5	37	RED	Rating 72.4
Handicap	17	9	1	3	13	7	11	15	5			Slope 130
Hole	10	11	12	13	14	15	16	17	18	In		Totals
BLUE	416	180	482	212	497	147	407	323	409	3073	BLUE	6569
WHITE	356	155	421	206	448	132	381	314	394	2807	WHITE	6132
Par	4	3	5	3	5	3	4	4	4	35	Par	72
Handicap	12	16	6	14	10	18	4	8	2			
RED	342	138	384	154	416	108	307	271	305	2425	RED	5288
Par	4	3	5	3	5	3	4	4	4	35	Par	72
Handicap	10	16	8	14	4	18	6	12	2			

Manager: Stu Owens   **Dir. of Golf:** Tom McCarthy, PGA   **Supt:** Eric Cadenelli
Architects: Willard Wilkinson 1925   **Restored:** 1999 Ian Scott Taylor

KNOB HILL GOLF CLUB

SEMI-PRIVATE

1 Shinnecock Drive, Manalapan, NJ 07726   **(732) 792-8118**
www.knobhillgolf.com

Knob Hill is an 18 hole semi-private course open 6 days a week all year (closed Mondays). Memberships are available. Tee times: public 3 days in advance; members 7 days. Carts mandatory until 2PM weekends. Info: (732) 792-7722.

Driving Range
- **Practice Green**
- **Power Carts**

Pull Carts
- **Club Rental**
- **Soft Spikes**

- **Lockers**
- **Showers**
- **Food**
- **Clubhouse**
- **Outings**

Fees	Weekday	Weekend
Daily	$55	$70
Twi	$35	$45
Power carts $20 pp		

Course Description: Great care has been taken to protect the environment by keeping the original trees intact on this 140 acre layout. A completely automated double line irrigation system guarantees exceptional conditioning. The signature par 3 15th overlooks a horse farm with a pond behind the green enhancing the scenic view. Several carries over water and wetlands add challenge exemplified by the approach shot to a peninsula green on #8. Bent grass fairways, 15 ponds & lakes and elevation changes make this a very interesting course indeed. Knob Hill is the first course to be designed by Mark McCumber in the Northeast. The pro, Mark Schaare was the State PGA player of the year 2000.

Directions: Monmouth County, #25 on Upper Shore Map
NJTPKE to Exit 8. Go east for 7 miles on Rte. 33 to Woodward Rd. and make U-turn. Club is on the right on Rte. 33 West.

Hole	1	2	3	4	5	6	7	8	9	Out	BLUE	Rating 71.6
BLUE	429	419	142	476	345	196	495	386	157	3045		Slope 132
WHITE	389	319	131	439	331	176	455	372	133	2745		
Par	4	4	3	4	4	3	5	4	3	34	WHITE	Rating 68.7
Handicap	11	9	13	1	7	15	3	5	17			Slope 119
RED	338	282	107	333	295	124	404	275	114	2272		
Par	4	4	3	4	4	3	5	4	3	34	RED	Rating 68.8
Handicap	11	9	13	1	7	15	3	5	17			Slope 120

Hole	10	11	12	13	14	15	16	17	18	In		Totals
BLUE	447	463	125	422	510	194	489	346	472	3468	BLUE	6513
WHITE	410	369	110	388	485	154	458	312	445	3131	WHITE	5876
Par	4	4	3	4	5	3	5	4	4	36	Par	70
Handicap	12	8	18	4	10	16	6	14	2			
RED	339	327	96	352	344	113	415	257	402	2645	RED	4917
Par	4	4	3	4	5	3	5	4	4	36	Par	70
Handicap	12	8	18	4	10	16	6	14	2			

Manager: Bob Elliot   **Pro:** Mark Schaare, PGA   **Supt:** Mike King
Architect: Mark McCumber 1998

LAKEWOOD COUNTRY CLUB   PUBLIC

145 Country Club Drive, Lakewood, NJ 08701   **(732) 364-8899**
www.lakewoodcountryclub.com

Lakewood is an 18 hole course open to the public 7 days a week all year. Memberships are available. Reservations for tee times up to 1 week in advance for weekends till 1PM, weekdays call 12 noon the day before.

•Driving Range	•Lockers
•Practice Green	•Showers
•Power Carts	•Food
•Pull Carts	•Clubhouse
•Club Rental	•Outings
•Soft Spikes	

Fees	Weekday	Weekend
Daily*	$42	$47
Twilight(walk)	$20	$22
*Including cart		
Power carts $15pp		

Course Description: Lakewood, nestled in the Pinelands of New Jersey, is a short, wooded scenic course featuring small undulating greens. The front is flat and the back nine has elevated tees and greens. The signature par 3 15th has both a pond and a stream in play. The 16th has been redesigned as a par 5 of 512 yards. Holes 4, 5, 6 & 7 have been altered adding challenge to the course. The substantially increased slopes indicate the result of this upgrade. Interesting pictures of people dressed in old fashioned clothing decorate the clubhouse. Theodore Roosevelt and Babe Ruth played here early in the past century.

Directions: Ocean County, #26 on Upper Shore Map
GSP to Exit 91. Go straight thru light at end of ramp and proceed 1/2 mile to next light. Turn left onto Rte. 526 West. Golf course is 6 miles on the left on Country Club Dr.

Hole	1	2	3	4	5	6	7	8	9	Out	BLUE	Rating 71.7
BLUE	385	184	362	387	372	187	340	375	522	3114		Slope 133
WHITE	369	150	332	333	332	164	324	334	482	2820		
Par	4	3	4	4	3	4	4	4	5	35	WHITE	Rating 68.9
Handicap	13	15	11	1	5	3	9	17	7			Slope 127
RED	330	129	281	280	252	107	283	317	440	2419		
Par	4	3	4	5	3	4	4	4	5	35	RED	Rating 65.9
Handicap	15	17	11	1	5	3	7	13	9			Slope 116

Hole	10	11	12	13	14	15	16	17	18	In		Totals
BLUE	219	539	332	493	382	223	512	354	398	3452	BLUE	6566
WHITE	204	506	307	460	347	185	492	323	376	3200	WHITE	6020
Par	4	5	3	5	4	3	5	4	4	37	Par	72
Handicap	13	2	15	5	17	1	11	7	9			
RED	165	451	196	360	318	120	447	301	358	2716	RED	5135
Par	4	5	4	5	5	3	4	4	5	37	Par	72
Handicap	12	2	10	18	6	16	4	14	8			

Manager: Michael Smith   **Pro:** Tom Hilliard, PGA   **Supt:** Fran Owsik
Architect: Willie Dunn 1892

LEISURE VILLAGE EAST

PRIVATE

1 Dumbarton Dr., Lakewood, NJ 08701   **(732) 477-6150**

Leisure Village East is a private residential adult community with a 9 hole par 3 golf course. It is open 7 days a week from April to the end of December. Reservations for tee times are not necessary.

Driving Range	Lockers
•**Practice Green**	Showers
Power Carts	Food
•**Pull Carts**	Clubhouse
Club Rental	Outings
Caddies	•**Soft Spikes**

Course Description: This meticulously maintained course is generally flat with narrow fairways and undulating greens. The signature 117 yard 3rd hole, the longest on the course, is heavily bunkered and out of bounds on the left can catch a wayward shot. The 6th, considered the most picturesque, is deceptively bunkered and features a slightly elevated green that slopes toward the right.

Directions: Ocean County, #27 on Upper Shore Map
GSP to Exit 88. Take Rte. 70 East and go right on Shorrock St. Go one mile to Leisure Village community and to course on the right.

Hole	1	2	3	4	5	6	7	8	9	Out	BLUE	Rating
BLUE												Slope
WHITE	77	92	117	102	50	72	62	83	76	731		
Par	3	3	3	3	3	3	3	3	3	27	WHITE	Rating
Handicap	6	2	1	3	5	8	9	4	7			Slope
RED	72	87	102	95	45	67	55	77	70	670		
Par											RED	Rating
Handicap												Slope

Hole	10	11	12	13	14	15	16	17	18	In		Totals
BLUE											BLUE	
WHITE											WHITE	731
Par											Par	27
Handicap												
RED											RED	670
Par											Par	27
Handicap												

Manager: John Cunnius
Built: Leisure Technology 1960s

LEISURE VILLAGE WEST

1 Buckingham Drive, Manchester, NJ 08759   **(732) 657-9109**
www.lvwa.net

Leisure Village West has 2 nine hole par 3 golf courses, the Pines and the Willows open 7 days a week all year, weather permitting. They are within a private residential adult community. Tee time reservations are not necessary.

Driving Range	Lockers
•**Practice Green**	Showers
Power Carts	Food
•**Pull Carts**	Clubhouse
Club Rental	Outings
Caddies	Soft Spikes

Course Description: There are homes on all sides of the holes here on both of these short, flat and walkable courses. No water confronts the golfer, but there are some bunkers to negotiate. Due to its short yardage, long hitters may opt to just use irons here. The longest hole is on the Willows course, 118 yards.

Directions: Ocean County, #28 on Upper Shore Map
GSP to Exit 88. Take Rte 70 West past Leisure Village West sign, then take the jughandle and stay straight on Buckingham to gatehouse.

Hole	1	2	3	4	5	6	7	8	9	Out	BLUE	Rating
												Slope
WILLOW	60	97	118	75	103	63	80	57	70	723		
Par	3	3	3	3	3	3	3	3	3	27	WHITE	Rating
Handicap												Slope
PINES	63	92	57	105	63	88	77	50	93	688		
Par	3	3	3	3	3	3	3	3	3	27	RED	Rating
Handicap												Slope
Hole	10	11	12	13	14	15	16	17	18	In		Totals
WHITE											WILLOW	723
Par											Par	27
Handicap												
RED											PINES	688
Par											Par	27
Handicap												

Manager: Ed Kenney   **Supt:** Keith Fallon

LION'S HEAD COUNTRY CLUB `PRIVATE`

251 Lion's Head Blvd. S., Brick, NJ 08723   **(732) 477-7277**

Lion's Head, a private residential adult community, has a 9 hole executive course open 6 days a week from Mar. 15 to Dec. 30. Guests play accompanied by a member. Tee time reservations are not necessary.

Driving Range	Lockers
•**Practice Green**	Showers
Power Carts	Food
•**Pull Carts**	•**Clubhouse**
Club Rental	Outings
Caddies	•**Soft Spikes**

Course Description: Within this community of approximately 900 units is an easily walkable, flat course with a natural wildlife area in the center. In some cases, golfers need to use a boardwalk to go from one hole to another. The fairways are tree lined and a second set of tees may be used for a second nine. The oversized greens get faster as the day progresses. The signature par 4 5th is surrounded by trees adding to the scenic terrain. A stream crosses the ninth hole.

Directions: Ocean County, #29 on Upper Shore Map
GSP to Exit 88. Take Rte. 70 East, turn right at light onto Shorrock St. At "T", turn left onto Beaverson Blvd. Make a right into Lionshead South Blvd. Club is on the right in the Lions Head community.

Hole	1	2	3	4	5	6	7	8	9	Out	BLUE	Rating
BLUE												Slope
WHITE	75	125	155	75	280	95	100	120	125	1150		
Par	3	3	3	3	4	3	3	3	3	28	WHITE	Rating
Handicap	8	4	2	9	1	7	6	5	3			Slope
RED												
Par											RED	Rating
Handicap												Slope
Hole	10	11	12	13	14	15	16	17	18	In		Totals
BLUE											BLUE	
WHITE	115	165	185	105	305	125	130	155	160	1445	WHITE	2595
Par	3	3	3	3	4	3	3	3	3	28	Par	56
Handicap	17	13	11	18	10	16	15	14	12			
RED											RED	
Par											Par	
Handicap												

Director: Art Beaver   **Supt:** H & L Landscaping
Architect: Hal Purdy 1963

MANASQUAN RIVER GOLF CLUB `PRIVATE`

Riverview Drive, Brielle, NJ 08730   **(732) 528-9678**
www.mrgc.com

Manasquan River Golf Club is an 18 hole course open 6 days a week, all year. Guests play accompanied by a member. Tee time reservations are not necessary.

•**Driving Range**	•**Lockers**
•**Practice Green**	•**Showers**
•**Power Carts**	•**Food**
Pull Carts	•**Clubhouse**
•**Club Rental**	•**Outings**
•**Caddies**	•**Soft Spikes**

Course Description: The beautiful Manasquan River golf course is set in the woods with river views from many holes. Hillier than one would expect in this locale, water comes into play a great deal on the back nine. Being so near the river, wind is usually a factor; however, during most normal winters, the course is playable due to the moderate shore climate. The small greens are fast and undulating. The par 5 7th hole, known as Horizon, requires a daunting drive over a ravine to land in the fairway, a high point from which the ocean is visible. US Open qualifying rounds have been played here.

Directions: Monmouth County, #30 on Upper Shore Map
GSP to Exit 98. Follow signs to Pt. Pleasant-Brielle and Rte. 34 South. At the 2nd traffic circle on Rte. 34, take Rte. 70 West for 1 mile to Riverview Drive and turn left. The club is on the left in about 1 mile.

Hole	1	2	3	4	5	6	7	8	9	Out	BLUE	Rating 73.3
BLUE	320	371	162	345	467	209	594	379	418	3265		Slope 141
WHITE	311	355	154	340	450	202	584	370	399	3165		
Par	4	4	3	4	5	3	5	4	4	36	WHITE	Rating 72.1
Handicap	15	3	17	11	9	13	1	5	7			Slope 133
RED	302	314	137	327	392	164	480	354	324	2794		
Par	4	4	3	4	5	3	5	4	4	36	RED	Rating 74.7
Handicap	13	3	17	9	7	15	1	5	11			Slope 131
Hole	10	11	12	13	14	15	16	17	18	In		Totals
BLUE	426	527	357	419	321	222	361	461	344	3438	BLUE	6703
WHITE	415	521	352	381	312	204	350	447	333	3315	WHITE	6480
Par	4	5	4	4	4	3	4	4	4	36	Par	72
Handicap	4	8	16	6	18	10	12	2	14			
RED	402	443	339	313	312	177	340	431	231	2988	RED	5782
Par	5	5	4	4	4	3	4	5	4	38	Par	74
Handicap	2	8	12	14	16	10	6	4	18			

Manager: Mike Zusack   **Pro:** Brent Studer, PGA   **Supt:** Glenn Miller
Architect: Robert White 1922

METEDECONK NATIONAL GC `PRIVATE`

Hannah Hill Rd., Jackson, NJ 08527   **(732) 928-0111**
www.metedeconk.org

Metedeconk National Golf Club offers 27 holes and is open 6 days a week from Mar. 15 to Dec. 1. Guests play accompanied by a member. Tee times may be made in advance.

•**Driving Range**	•**Lockers**
•**Practice Green**	•**Showers**
•**Power Carts**	•**Food**
Pull Carts	•**Clubhouse**
•**Club Rental**	•**Outings**
•**Caddies**	•**Soft Spikes**

Course Description: Metedeconk is hidden on a rolling piece of wooded property. Following the contours of the pinelands, each hole is distinct. The layout features high fescue grass in the rough and small, fast well guarded greens. The very special signature hole, the 6th, crosses over the Metedeconk River and is a 150 yard carry from the blues. Opened in the summer of 1998, the 3rd nine is sculpted out of the woods and traverses natural wetlands. This nine, along with the original upgraded 18, provide 27 of the most interesting and rugged holes in NJ. A stunning new clubhouse completes this elegant club. The scorecard below is for the front and the third nine.

Directions: Ocean County, #31 on Upper Shore Map
NJTPKE to Exit #7A. Take Rte. 195 East to Exit #21. Make a left turn at exit. Hannah Hill Rd. is 300 yards up on the right. Take this road through woods to club.

Hole	1	2	3	4	5	6	7	8	9	Out	BLUE	Rating 72.6
BLUE	392	195	551	397	505	176	386	408	406	3416		Slope 137
WHITE	362	170	517	364	465	156	364	387	370	3155		
Par	4	3	5	4	5	3	4	4	4	36	WHITE	Rating 73.2
Handicap	5	7	1	3	9	8	6	4	2			Slope 139
RED	316	124	467	288	416	124	304	318	316	2673		
Par	4	3	5	4	5	3	4	4	4	36	RED	Rating 72.4
Handicap	4	9	2	7	3	8	6	5	1			Slope 139
Hole	10	11	12	13	14	15	16	17	18	In		Totals
BLUE	369	392	534	404	169	502	165	410	419	3364	BLUE	6780
WHITE	347	363	500	387	140	467	152	366	377	3099	WHITE	6254
Par	4	4	5	4	3	5	3	4	4	36	Par	72
Handicap	8	4	1	3	7	6	9	5	2			
RED	329	339	467	320	91	435	92	339	341	2753	RED	5426
Par	4	4	5	4	3	5	3	4	4	36	Par	72
Handicap	7	6	3	5	8	4	9	2	1			

Manager: Michael Pollack   **Pro:** Jay Davis, PGA   **Supt:** Tim Christ
Architects: Robert Trent Jones 1988   Roger Rulewich 1998

NAVESINK COUNTRY CLUB

50 Luffburrow Lane, Middletown, NJ 07748   **(732) 842-3366**
navgolfshop@aol.com*

Navesink is an 18 hole course open 6 days a week all year. Guests play accompanied
by a member. Tee time reservations may be made one week in advance for weekends.
*EMail

•**Driving Range**	•**Lockers**
•**Practice Green**	•**Showers**
•**Power Carts**	•**Food**
Pull Carts	•**Clubhouse**
•**Club Rental**	•**Outings**
•**Caddies**	•**Soft Spikes**

Course Description: The drive on Navesink River Rd. is scenic with magnificent views
of the hilly terrain, the Atlantic Ocean and nearby Sandy Hook. The course is kept in
excellent condition and is known for its fast greens and uneven lies. Water in play on
both the 5th and the 15th, two difficult par 5s, provides some of the challenge here.
The NJ State Open has been held here twice as well as LPGA tournaments. There is a
regulation ice hockey rink on the premises.

Directions: Monmouth County, #32 on Upper Shore Map
GSP to Exit 109. Turn left onto Rte. 520 E & go under the pkwy. Take jughandle onto
Half Mile Rd. At end, turn right onto W. Front St. Turn left onto Hubbard Ave at light.
Go 1 mi, passing school, to Navesink Rd., and turn right. Proceed, crossing Rte. 35, to
Luffburrow Lane and turn left. Club is ahead on left.

Hole	1	2	3	4	5	6	7	8	9	Out	BLUE	Rating 73.2
BLUE	330	574	388	227	484	372	359	190	375	3299		Slope 131
WHITE	321	557	374	214	461	367	353	176	365	3196		
Par	4	5	4	3	5	4	4	3	4	36	WHITE	Rating 72.0
Handicap	15	3	11	13	1	5	7	17	9			Slope 126
RED	301	492	302	165	409	347	319	160	325	2781		
Par	4	5	4	3	5	4	4	3	4	36	RED	Rating 74.6
Handicap	11	3	13	15	1	5	7	17	9			Slope 131
Hole	10	11	12	13	14	15	16	17	18	In		Totals
BLUE	404	466	166	419	397	547	184	502	310	3416	BLUE	6715
WHITE	395	457	149	399	377	525	172	493	310	3277	WHITE	6173
Par	4	4	3	4	4	5	3	5	4	36	Par	72
Handicap	8	4	18	6	10	2	16	12	14			
RED	372	429	132	376	359	446	158	459	275	2996	RED	5777
Par	4	5	3	4	4	5	3	5	4	37	Par	73
Handicap	6	12	18	4	8	2	16	10	14			

Manager: David Schutzenhofer   **Pro:** Steve Sieg, PGA   **Supt:** Pat O'Neill
Architect: Hal Purdy 1963

OCEAN ACRES COUNTRY CLUB **PUBLIC**

925 Buccaneer Lane, Manahawkin, NJ 08050   **(609) 597-9393**
www.allforeclub.com

Ocean Acres is an 18 hole course open to the public 7 days a week all year. Various membership plans are available. Reservations for tee times: 7 days in advance for members, 5 days for non-members.

Driving Range	
•Practice Green	•Lockers
•Power Carts	•Showers
•Pull Carts	•Food
•Club Rental	•Clubhouse
•Soft Spikes	•Outings

Fees	Weekday	Weekend
Daily	$45	$49
Fees include cart		
After 4 PM, reduced rates		
Variable off season rates		

Course Description: The friendly atmosphere is quite pervasive at Ocean Acres, conveniently located just minutes off the GSP in Manahawkin. The front nine is comfortably open while the back is tight and wooded with ponds affecting play on several holes. Generally flat, the course is in excellent shape. The view of the lake from the clubhouse is spectacular overlooking the signature par 3 10th. This hole requires a shot over a man made lake to an island green.

Directions: Ocean County, #33 on Upper Shore Map
GSP South to Exit 67 (Barnegat). Go right off the ramp onto Bay Ave. Make a left onto Lighthouse Dr. then left onto Buccaneer Lane to club. **OR** GSP North to Exit 63A to Rte. 72. Make a right onto Lighthouse, then right on Buccaneer to club.

Hole	1	2	3	4	5	6	7	8	9	Out	BLUE	Rating 70.8
BLUE	490	328	401	192	518	382	362	156	422	3251		Slope 124
WHITE	475	311	381	181	487	364	352	144	409	3104		
Par	5	4	4	3	5	4	4	3	4	36	WHITE	Rating 69.7
Handicap	8	14	4	16	2	12	10	18	6			Slope 117
RED	440	266	347	171	458	329	323	128	338	2820		
Par	5	4	4	3	5	4	4	3	4	36	RED	Rating 70.4
Handicap	8	14	4	16	2	12	10	18	6			Slope 117
Hole	10	11	12	13	14	15	16	17	18	In		Totals
BLUE	183	342	415	205	328	518	360	411	550	3312	BLUE	6563
WHITE	150	325	407	180	313	501	325	400	541	3142	WHITE	6246
Par	3	4	4	3	4	5	4	4	5	36	Par	72
Handicap	17	9	1	15	11	5	13	3	7			
RED	125	232	347	142	229	415	291	343	468	2592	RED	5412
Par	3	4	4	3	4	5	4	4	5	36	Par	72
Handicap	17	9	1	15	11	5	13	3	7			

Manager/Pro: Richard Taylor, PGA   **Supt:** Matt Szumski
Built: 1960s

OCEAN COUNTY @ ATLANTIS

Country Club Boulevard, Tuckerton, NJ 08087   **(609) 296-2444**

This 18 hole Ocean County course is open to the public 7 days a week all year. For county residents w/ID, reservations are necessary for play between 7AM-2PM up to 7 days in advance. Walk-ons permitted. Driving range is for irons only.

•**Driving Range**	Lockers
•**Practice Green**	Showers
•**Power Carts**	•**Food**
•**Pull Carts**	•**Clubhouse**
•**Club Rental**	•**Outings**
•**Soft Spikes**	

Fees	Weekday	Weekend
Res/ID	$18	$24
Non-res	$35	$42
Jr/Sr	$15	
Power carts	$24/18	$14/9

Course Description: Formerly a privately owned country club, Ocean County bought this course in 1989 and made improvements. Automatic sprinklers were installed, a modern clubhouse was built and the facility was generally upgraded. The par 3 6th is considered the most picturesque; from an elevated tee, the shot is over a lake. The par 5 7th hole features a blind tee shot that necessitates intelligent club selection, too long and straight will end up in the woods on this dogleg right. There is a pond to cross on the par 3 11th. The generally narrow fairways provide challenge for the golfer at this busy facility.

Directions: Ocean County, #34 on Upper Shore Map
GSP to Exit 58. Take Rte. 539S (North Green St.) Go right on West Main Street (Rte. 9S). At fork, bear left and go 2 blocks to Radio Rd. & turn right. Follow signs to club.

Hole	1	2	3	4	5	6	7	8	9	Out	BLUE	Rating 73.0
BLUE	373	411	526	392	376	200	517	168	438	3401		Slope 134
WHITE	360	383	508	382	343	150	490	153	423	3192		
Par	4	4	5	4	4	3	5	3	4	36	WHITE	Rating 71.0
Handicap	15	5	3	9	11	13	7	17	1			Slope 130
RED	341	353	428	312	305	98	447	136	393	2813		
Par	4	4	5	4	4	3	5	3	4	36	RED	Rating 71.0
Handicap	13	9	2	11	7	17	4	15	1			Slope 124

Hole	10	11	12	13	14	15	16	17	18	In		Totals
BLUE	420	191	406	372	492	384	206	574	402	3447	BLUE	6848
WHITE	387	179	390	358	470	338	195	536	387	3240	WHITE	6432
Par	4	3	4	4	5	4	3	5	4	36	Par	72
Handicap	4	18	10	14	12	8	16	2	6			
RED	326	120	336	341	435	287	158	455	308	2766	RED	5579
Par	4	3	4	4	5	4	3	5	4	36	Par	72
Handicap	8	18	12	6	5	10	16	3	14			

Manager: Dan O'Connor   **Supt:** Barry Cox
Architect: George Fazio 1962

OLD ORCHARD COUNTRY CLUB `SEMI-PRIVATE`

54 Monmouth Rd., Eatontown, NJ 07724 **(732) 542-7666**

Old Orchard is an 18 hole semi-private course open to the public 7 days a week all year. Memberships are available. For tee times, call up to 30 days in advance.

Driving Range	
•Practice Green	•**Lockers**
•**Power Carts**	•**Showers**
•**Pull Carts**	•**Food**
•**Club Rental**	•**Clubhouse**
•**Soft Spikes**	•**Outings**

Fees	M-Thurs	Fri-Sun
Daily	$42	$48
After 2PM	$35	$40
After 4	$30	$35
Sr.	$30	
Power cart	$17pp	

Course Description: Old Orchard is a mostly flat, wide open layout. The poana grass sloped greens are small and get fast in dry weather. A creek crosses 8 holes. The signature par 5 seventh features an island green. This scenic well maintained course has been upgraded with 10 new bunkers. The distances from the forward tees have been made considerably longer and more challenging.

Directions: Monmouth County, #36 on Upper Shore Map
GSP to Exit #105. After toll, take Rte. 36 East for 6 traffic lights to the jughandle for Rte. 71North (Monmouth Rd.) Course is on the left on Monmouth.

Hole	1	2	3	4	5	6	7	8	9	Out	BLUE	Rating 72.1
BLUE	441	497	158	423	404	205	480	345	392	3345		Slope 127
WHITE	421	457	143	397	390	175	450	325	372	3130		
Par	4	5	3	4	4	3	5	4	4	36	WHITE	Rating 69.1
Handicap	1	9	17	5	3	13	7	15	11			Slope 122
RED	400	442	438	387	375	455	440	250	360	2947		
Par	4	5	3	4	4	3	5	4	4	36	RED	Rating 73.0
Handicap	1	9	17	5	3	13	7	15	11			Slope 121

Hole	10	11	12	13	14	15	16	17	18	In		Totals
BLUE	442	420	435	360	170	360	365	195	532	3279	BLUE	6624
WHITE	425	390	390	320	140	348	350	175	500	3038	WHITE	6168
Par	5	4	4	4	3	4	4	3	5	36	Par	72
Handicap	8	4	2	14	18	16	10	12	6			
RED	420	375	375	265	122	346	335	155	470	2860	RED	5807
Par	5	4	4	4	3	4	4	3	5	36	Par	72
Handicap	8	4	2	14	18	16	10	12	6			

Manager/Pro: George Craig, PGA　　　　**Supt:** John Hutchison
Architect: A. W. Tillinghast 1929

PEBBLE CREEK GOLF COURSE

40 Route 537 East, Colt's Neck, NJ 07722   **(732) 303-9090**
www.pebblecreekgolfclub.com

Pebble Creek is an 18 hole course open all year 7 days a week, weather permitting.
Tee times may be made up to 7 days in advance. Carts are mandatory until 1PM on
Sat. & Sun.

Driving Range	
•**Practice Green**	Lockers
•**Power Carts** ·	Showers
•**Pull Carts**	•**Food**
•**Club Rental**	•**Clubhouse**
•**Soft Spikes**	•**Outings**

Fees	**Weekday**	**Weekend**
Daily	$57	$68
After 3PM reduced rates		
Carts included		
Seasonal rates available		

Course Description: Pebble Creek offers a picturesque natural atmosphere. The
front nine holes are surrounded by mature woods; the second nine is more of an open
links type. Water in the form of lakes and ponds is in play on six holes of the more difficult back nine. The greens are large, undulating and true. The par 4 16th, a 344 yard
dogleg with water in play on both the tee and approach shots, has birdie potential. The
cart paths are totally paved and some remodeling has taken place recently. Golfers
have an opportunity for an enjoyable round of golf on this beautifully maintained
course.

Directions: Monmouth County, #37 on Upper Shore Map
GSP to Exit 109 (Lincroft). Go west on Rte. 520 to 2nd light and turn left onto
Swimming River Rd. to the end. Turn right on Rte. 537 West. Course is 3 & 1/2 miles
on the left.

Hole	1	2	3	4	5	6	7	8	9	Out	BLUE	Rating 70.0
BLUE	330	405	177	411	197	341	350	540	352	3103		Slope 121
WHITE	322	387	162	394	172	325	274	530	345	2911		
Par	4	4	3	4	3	4	4	5	4	35	WHITE	Rating 68.8
Handicap	9	5	17	3	15	7	13	1	11			Slope 119
RED	230	365	126	370	157	297	245	480	305	2575		
Par	4	4	3	4	3	4	4	5	4	35	RED	Rating 71.0
Handicap	9	5	17	3	15	7	13	1	11			Slope 119
Hole	10	11	12	13	14	15	16	17	18	In		Totals
BLUE	380	218	320	298	585	366	344	527	184	3222	BLUE	6325
WHITE	370	200	301	291	570	361	329	502	167	3091	WHITE	6002
Par	4	3	4	4	5	4	4	5	3	36	Par	71
Handicap	12	14	8	16	2	6	10	4	18			
RED	334	182	263	251	540	341	295	442	133	2761	RED	5356
Par	4	3	4	4	5	4	4	5	3	36	Par	71
Handicap	12	14	8	16	2	6	10	4	18			

Manager/Pro: David Melody, PGA   **Supt:** Jim Cadott
Architect: Hal Purdy 1996

PINE BARRENS GOLF CLUB

SEMI-PRIVATE

540 S. Hope Chapel Rd., Jackson, NJ 08527   **(877) 746-3227**
www.pinebarrensgolf.com

Pine Barrens is an 18 hole course open to the public all year 7 days a week. Memberships are available that are affiliated with other Empire Golf courses. Tee times may be made up to 7 days in advance. Call (732) 408-1154 for tee times.

- •**Driving Range**
- •**Practice Green**
- •**Power Carts**
- Pull Carts
- •**Club Rental**
- •**Soft Spikes**
- •**Lockers**
- •**Showers**
- •**Food**
- •**Clubhouse**
- •**Outings**

Fees	M-Thurs	Fri-Sun
Daily	$97	$115

Fees include cart
Twi. rates available
Prices reduced off season

Course Description: Carved from the sandy soil of NJ, Pine Barrens is one of the finest courses in the state. Over 7100 yards from the championship tees, it features large waste bunkers, native grass vegetation in the rough and large undulating bent grass greens. It is a pinelands layout winding through the woods with 5 sets of tees. Water is in play on holes 10 and 18; on the latter a considerable carry is required off the tee. The course is in immaculate condition. An impressive double-ended practice facility with bunkers and target greens, provides a chance for the golfer to warm up. Pine Barrens was ranked as #1by *Golf Week Magazine* for NJ Public Courses in 2004.

Directions: Ocean County, #38 on Upper Shore Map
GSPSouth to Exit 88. Make a right onto Rte. 70 West. Go 3.5 miles and turn right onto Whitesville Rd. (Rte. 527.) After 3 miles, turn left at light onto S. Hope Chapel Rd. Club is 1 mile ahead on the right. *Check website for particulars.*

Hole	1	2	3	4	5	6	7	8	9	Out	BLUE	Rating 72.7
BLUE	365	383	183	427	174	546	293	415	534	3320		Slope 130
WHITE	333	354	156	391	161	521	271	390	495	3072		
Par	4	4	3	4	3	5	4	4	5	36	WHITE	Rating 70.6
Handicap	12	6	14	2	8	16	18	4	10			Slope 129
RED	263	276	124	320	112	450	213	333	409	2500		
Par	4	4	3	4	3	5	4	4	5	36	RED	Rating 69.7
Handicap	12	6	14	2	8	16	18	4	10			Slope 123

Hole	10	11	12	13	14	15	16	17	18	In		Totals
BLUE	424	362	169	378	208	501	391	456	572	3461	BLUE	6781
WHITE	384	339	150	359	195	488	365	406	556	3252	WHITE	6324
Par	4	4	3	4	3	5	4	4	5	36	Par	72
Handicap	9	17	11	15	3	7	13	1	5			
RED	282	298	104	310	150	414	316	349	486	2709	RED	5209
Par	4	4	3	4	3	5	4	4	5	36	Par	72
Handicap	9	17	11	15	3	7	13	1	5			

Genl. Mgr/Dir of Golf: Rudy Virga,PGA   **Pro:** Michael Yevchak, PGA
Supt: Jeremy Daubert   **Architect:** Eric Bergstol 1999

PINE BROOK GOLF COURSE

1 Covered Bridge Blvd., Englishtown, NJ 07726   **(732) 536-7272**
www.monmouthcountyparks.com

Pine Brook is an 18 hole Monmouth County executive course open 7 days a week. It closes Dec. 23 & reopens Mar. 15. With a county ID, automated tee times may be reserved up to 7 days in advance, call (732) 758-8383. Walk-ons are allowed as well.

Driving Range	Lockers		**Fees**	**Weekday**	**Weekend**
•**Practice Green**	Showers		Res/ID	$15.75	$19
•**Power Carts**	Food		Non-res	$31.50	$38
•**Pull Carts**	Clubhouse		Sr.	$11	
•**Club Rental**	Outings		Carts	$23 per cart	
•**Soft Spikes**					

Course Description: Excellently maintained, Pine Brook is a good place for iron practice. It is a generally flat, well shrubbed course with water occasionally in play. The signature par 3 9th has water surrounding the green. The par 4 16th, 380 yards from the whites, can be an interesting hole. This facility gets quite busy in season.

Directions: Monmouth County, #39 on Upper Shore Map
GSP to Exit 123. Take Rte. 9 South and after the light for Union Hill Rd., watch carefully for Covered Bridge Blvd. and make right to course on right..

Hole	1	2	3	4	5	6	7	8	9	Out	BLUE	Rating
BLUE												Slope
WHITE	343	167	143	333	195	163	499	156	157	2156		
Par	4	3	3	4	3	3	5	3	3	31	WHITE	Rating 59.8
Handicap	1	13	17	9	7	11	5	15	3			Slope 93
RED	315	125	111	313	151	121	463	121	136	1856		
Par	4	3	3	4	3	3	5	3	3	31	RED	Rating 59.3
Handicap	1	13	17	9	7	11	5	15	3			Slope 90

Hole	10	11	12	13	14	15	16	17	18	In		Totals
BLUE											BLUE	
WHITE	150	194	333	317	154	134	380	158	192	2012	WHITE	4168
Par	3	3	4	4	3	3	4	3	3	30	Par	61
Handicap	14	4	8	10	16	18	6	12	2			
RED	112	157	288	275	117	92	266	105	153	1585	RED	3441
Par	3	3	4	4	3	3	4	3	3	30	Par	61
Handicap	14	4	8	10	16	18	6	12	2			

Manager: Eric Kaplan   **Supt:** Dave Miskin

PINE RIDGE GOLF COURSE

Lakehurst Naval Base, Lakehurst, NJ 08733   **(732) 323-7483**

Lakehurst has a 9 hole course open to the active duty military, Dept. of Defense employees and retired career military. It is open all year 7 days a week. Guests may play accompanied by members or at the discretion of the manager. Reservations may be made up to 3 days in advance and are necessary in season.

> - **Driving Range** • **Lockers**
> - **Practice Green** • **Showers**
> - **Power Carts** • **Food**
> - **Pull Carts** • **Clubhouse**
> - **Club Rental** • **Outings**
>   Caddies • **Soft Spikes**

Course Description: Formerly called Navy Golf Course, Pine Ridge is a short, resort type layout. The rolling fairways are planted in rye. The easy to read greens are of bent grass and the many seniors that golf here find the course wide open and very playable. The signature par 4 9th features an elevated tee, a dogleg right and a 70 yard long fairway bunker. There are different tee boxes for the second nine. The course recently had upgrades consisting of contouring the fairways, improving some tee boxes and greens, rebuilding the waste bunkers and installing more sprinkler heads.

Directions: Ocean County, #40 on Upper Shore Map
GSP to Exit 88. Take Rte. 70 West to Rte. 547 North. Enter Lakehurst Naval Base and get pass at office to go through gate to golf course.

Hole	1	2	3	4	5	6	7	8	9	Out	BLUE	Rating 68.8
BLUE	336	310	338	185	535	501	372	160	360	3098		Slope 116
WHITE	331	286	322	160	445	467	355	158	330	2854		
Par	4	4	4	3	5	5	4	3	4	36	WHITE	Rating 68.6
Handicap	9	13	7	15	1	3	11	17	5			Slope 116
RED	216	287	237	80	353	338	386	86	263	2064		
Par	4	4	4	3	4	4	4	3	4	34	RED	Rating 70.6
Handicap	13	15	9	11	1	3	7	17	5			Slope 119
Hole	10	11	12	13	14	15	16	17	18	In		Totals
BLUE	340	330	341	202	515	530	391	217	401	3267	BLUE	6365
WHITE	337	325	329	179	509	490	364	195	353	3081	WHITE	5935
Par	4	4	4	3	5	5	4	3	4	36	Par	72
Handicap	10	12	8	16	4	2	14	18	6			
RED	280	283	311	155	435	460	349	150	322	2745	RED	4809
Par	4	4	4	3	4	5	4	3	4	35	Par	69
Handicap	14	16	10	12	2	4	8	18	6			

Manager/Pro: Todd Toohey, PGA   **Supt:** Keith Bunell
Built: 1956

QUAIL RIDGE GOLF COURSE

PUBLIC

1770 Rte. 34 North, Wall Township, NJ 07719
www.quailridgegolf.com

(732) 681-1800

Quail Ridge is an 9 hole executive course open to the public 7 days a week from Mar. 15 thru Dec.1. Tee times are not necessary. There is a miniature golf and pitch & putt available.

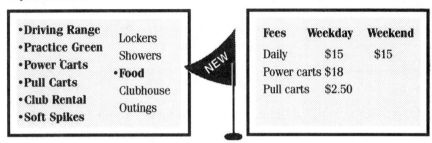

- **Driving Range**
- **Practice Green**
- **Power Carts**
- **Pull Carts**
- **Club Rental**
- **Soft Spikes**

Lockers
Showers
•**Food**
Clubhouse
Outings

Fees	Weekday	Weekend
Daily	$15	$15
Power carts $18		
Pull carts $2.50		

Course Description: Level and easy to walk, this short par 28 executive course is an excellent choice for beginners. The course has a few hazards and sand traps. Golfers can practice the short game with no obstacles to traverse. Four of the holes have grass mats a distance behind the tee box for those who prefer to hit longer shots.

Directions: Monmouth County, # 54 on Upper Shore Map
GSP to Exit 98. Take Rte. 34N; course on right.

Hole	1	2	3	4	5	6	7	8	9	Out	BLUE	Rating
BLUE												Slope
WHITE	93	124	148	121	237	148	178	159	87	1295		
Par	3	3	3	3	4	3	3	3	3	28	WHITE	Rating
Handicap	5	3	9	8	1	7	4	2	6			Slope
RED												
Par											RED	Rating
Handicap												Slope

Hole	10	11	12	13	14	15	16	17	18	In		Totals
BLUE											BLUE	
											WHITE	
Par											Par	
Handicap												
RED											RED	
Par											Par	
Handicap												

Manager: Richard & Robert Mueller   **Pros:** Ted Graygor & Tom Jaeger
Architect: Bob Mueller 2001

RENAISSANCE GOLF COURSE

3 Renaissance Blvd. East, Lakehurst, NJ 08733   (732) 657-8900

A private adult community with an executive 18 hole golf course, Renaissance is open 6 days a week & closed Dec. through March. Guests play accompanied by a member. The residents may take an annual golf membership or walk on and pay as daily fee.

Driving Range	•**Lockers**
•**Practice Green**	•**Showers**
•**Power Carts**	•**Food**
•**Pull Carts**	•**Clubhouse**
•**Club Rental**	•**Outings**
Caddies	•**Soft Spikes**

Course Description: Renaissance Golf is considered an upscale executive golf course with manicured greens and a great layout. Having four to five tees on each hole and some modest undulation, the course is an interesting experience for the golfing residents of this private country club community. The magnificent clubhouse adds to ambience here. The 19 man-made lakes affect play and provide beautiful views.

Directions: Ocean County, #41on Upper Shore Map
GSP to Exit 88. At bottom of exit ramp, turn right onto Rte. 70West. Go about 6 miles and turn right onto Rte. 571North. Entrance is on the right.

Hole	1	2	3	4	5	6	7	8	9	Out	BLUE	Rating 59.4
BLUE	334	319	158	297	140	352	130	106	192	1970		Slope 98
WHITE	298	251	133	277	124	337	114	97	170	1801		
Par	4	4	3	4	3	4	3	3	3	31	WHITE	Rating 58.0
Handicap												Slope 95
RED	277	292	113	265	114	325	110	82	154	1645		
Par	4	4	3	4	3	4	3	3	3	31	RED	Rating 58.5
Handicap												Slope 96

Hole	10	11	12	13	14	15	16	17	18	In		Totals
BLUE	252	245	104	354	179	353	138	130	221	1992	BLUE	3962
WHITE	232	175	91	341	157	343	109	117	228	1793	WHITE	3594
Par	4/3	4/3	3	4	3	4	3	3	4/3		Par	63/60
Handicap												
RED	140	150	76	269	132	293	92	98	200	1448	RED	3093
Par											Par	60
Handicap												

Manager/Pro: Art Robidoux, PGA   **Supt:** Harry Leonard
Architect: J. Christopher Commins 1999

RUMSON COUNTRY CLUB

Rumson Rd., Rumson, NJ 07760   (732) 842-2885

Rumson is a private 18 hole course open 6 days a week all year, weather permitting. Guests play accompanied by a member. Tee time reservations are not necessary.

```
• Driving Range    • Lockers
• Practice Green   • Showers
• Power Carts      • Food
• Pull Carts       • Clubhouse
• Club Rental       Outings
• Caddies          • Soft Spikes
```

Course Description: Rumson is a typical seashore layout, flat and low lying with a moderate amount of water in play in the form of ponds or creeks. The Shrewsbury River can be seen from some areas of the course; the highest point is 6 feet above sea level. The most difficult hole is the par 4 7th, 433 yards from the blues. On the drive, the landing area is guarded by bunkers The 2nd shot, using a long iron or a fairway wood, is to a green protected in front by a pond. Some upgrading of the course has been done recently.

Directions: Monmouth County, #42 on Upper Shore Map
GSP to Exit 109. Follow signs and take Rte. 520 East. Continue to Broad St. and at end of road, turn left over RR tracks. Turn right onto Pinckney Rd. and then right onto Branch Ave. At light, turn left onto Rumson Rd. Club is ahead on right.

Hole	1	2	3	4	5	6	7	8	9	Out	BLUE	Rating 71.5
BLUE	399	551	145	493	433	388	433	408	396	3646		Slope 124
WHITE	389	503	134	463	421	377	425	358	385	3455		
Par	4	5	3	5	4	4	4	4	4	37	WHITE	Rating 70.1
Handicap	10	5	18	7	3	13	1	12	9			Slope 121
RED	339	460	117	436	375	339	400	329	320	3115		
Par	4	5	3	5	4	4	5	4	4	38	RED	Rating 73.7
Handicap	9	1	17	7	3	13	11	5	15			Slope 133
Hole	10	11	12	13	14	15	16	17	18	In		Totals
BLUE	299	400	443	380	163	429	307	180	370	2971	BLUE	6617
WHITE	283	381	434	364	146	417	301	169	352	2847	WHITE	6302
Par	4	4	4	4	3	4	4	3	4	34	Par	71
Handicap	16	6	2	8	17	4	14	15	11			
RED	267	317	401	332	113	409	273	147	308	2567	RED	5682
Par	4	4	5	4	3	5	4	3	4	34	Par	74
Handicap	16	4	8	2	18	10	12	14	6			

Manager: Joe Turner   **Pro:** Don Brigham, PGA   **Supt:** Jim Cross
Architect: Herbert W. Barker 1908

SEA OAKS GOLF CLUB

SEMI-PRIVATE

99 Golf View Dr., Little Egg Harbor Twp, NJ 08087
www.seaoaksgolf.com

(609) 296-2656

Sea Oaks is an 18 hole course open to the public 7 days a week all year. Memberships are available with privileged tee times and rates. Tee times may be made 5 days in advance for the public.

- **Driving Range**
- **Practice Green**
- **Power Carts**
- Pull Carts
- **Club Rental**
- **Soft Spikes**

- **Lockers**
- **Showers**
- **Food**
- **Clubhouse**
- **Outings**

Fees	M-Thurs	Fri-Sun
Daily	$95*	$105*

Reduced rates off season & for members & associate members. *Carts included

Course Description: Views of Atlantic City to the South and Long Beach Island nearby are apparent from this fine links style golf club. More than the usual Jersey Shore courses, Sea Oaks has 75 feet of elevation changes. Some of the property is tree lined and other parts are wide open with extensive waste bunkers. Water is in play on six holes. The signature 560 yard par 5 16th is a double dogleg; its green is surrounded by a pond on three sides and protected by a stone wall. The greens are generally large and contoured. The architect was able to take advantage of the site's natural rugged beauty incorporating the fescue grass, oak and pine woods while making the course playable for the beginner and challenging for the more experienced.

Directions: Ocean County, #43 on Upper Shore Map
GSP to Exit 58. Take Rte.539 South. Main entrance is 2 and 1/2 miles on the left.

Hole	1	2	3	4	5	6	7	8	9	Out	BLUE	Rating 71.9
BLUE	565	365	340	175	405	410	165	370	550	3345		Slope 128
WHITE	520	325	310	155	370	375	145	345	500	3045		
Par	5	4	4	3	4	4	3	4	5	36	WHITE	Rating 69.6
Handicap	5	7	11	15	3	9	17	13	1			Slope 123
RED	425	270	255	125	305	310	115	280	410	2495		
Par	5	4	4	3	4	4	3	4	5	36	RED	Rating 68.9
Handicap	5	7	11	15	3	9	17	13	1			Slope 119
Hole	10	11	12	13	14	15	16	17	18	In		Totals
BLUE	545	395	235	405	200	410	540	465	410	3605	BLUE	6635
WHITE	495	365	195	370	180	375	495	435	375	3285	WHITE	6330
Par	5	4	3	4	3	4	5	4	4	36	Par	72
Handicap	10	14	6	16	18	12	8	2	4			
RED	405	295	160	355	165	360	475	415	355	2655	RED	5150
Par	5	4	3	4	3	4	5	4	4	36	Par	72
Handicap	10	14	6	16	18	12	8	2	4			

Manager/Dir. of Golf: Jeff Bonicky PGA   **Supt:** Rolf Strobel
Architect: Raymond Hearn 2000

SHADOW ISLE GOLF CLUB

81 Route 34 South, Colts Neck, NJ 07722   **(732) 625-9211**
www.shadowisle.com

Shadow Isle is an 18 hole course open 6 days a week all year. It is a private club with limited memberships. Guests may play accompanied by a member. Tee times are not necessary.

- •Driving Range
- •Practice Green
- •Power Carts
- •Pull Carts
- •Club Rental
- •Caddies
- •Lockers
- •Showers
- •Food
- •Clubhouse
- •Outings
- •Soft Spikes

Course Description: Shadow Isle is a 7100 yard new private club welcome in Monmouth County. The "disappearing" cart paths which wind through swales and mounds are an interesting feature. Formerly an airport, 2 million cubic yards of earth was moved to build the course. Multiple tee boxes, generous landing areas and large softly contoured greens challenge both experienced and new golfers alike. In addition to the 4 sets of tees there are Pate bonus tees which are beyond the blacks and are only for the best players. The sixth is up for consideration as the signature hole. It is a long par 4 with an approach over water, then a land route around the right side to avoid a forced carry. Beautiful homes surround the course.

Directions: Monmouth County, #55 on Upper Shore Map
GSP (from South) to Exit 105. Merge onto Rte. 18 toward N.Brunswick. Merge onto Rte.34 at exit 19A toward Matawan. Left turn onto 537 for 1/2 mi. then turn left onto Hominy Hill Rd. Golf course on left.

Hole	1	2	3	4	5	6	7	8	9	Out	BLUE	Rating 71.4
BLUE	377	481	158	287	432	406	516	170	353	3180		Slope 130
WHITE	347	441	140	255	399	366	476	132	310	2866		
Par	4	5	3	4	4/5	4	5	3	4	36/37	WHITE	Rating 68.3
Handicap	13	11	17	15	3	1	5	9	7			Slope 124
RED	273	412	114	207	372	278	414	102	274	2466		
Par	4	5	3	4	4/5	4	5	3	4	36/37	RED	Rating 70.8
Handicap	5	13	3	17	15	11	1	7	9			Slope 126

Hole	10	11	12	13	14	15	16	17	18	In		Totals
BLUE	403	129	371	504	404	199	345	402	512	3269	BLUE	6449
WHITE	343	121	346	457	387	166	303	365	479	2967	WHITE	5833
Par	4	3	4	5	4/5	3	4	4	5	36/37	Par	72/74
Handicap	12	16	8	6	2	14	18	10	4			
RED	299	104	316	430	363	151	268	312	448	2691	RED	5137
Par	4	3	4	5	4/5	3	4	4	5	36/37	Par	72/74
Handicap	12	14	8	6	4	16	18	10	2			

Owners: O'Neill family   **Mgr:** Connie Newton   **Pro:** TBA   **Supt:** Robert Kedziora
                Architect: Jerry Pate   2004

SHADOW LAKE VILLAGE

1 Loch Arbor Way, Red Bank, NJ 07701
www.shadowlakevillage.com

(732) 842-9580

Shadow Lake Village is an adult community with a 9 hole par 3 golf course. It is open 6 days a week and is open all year depending on the weather. Tee time reservations are not necessary.

Driving Range	Lockers
Practice Green	•**Showers**
*Power Carts	Food
•**Pull Carts**	•**Clubhouse**
Club Rental	Outings
Caddies	•**Soft Spikes**

Course Description: Shadow Lake golf course is open only for residents of the adult community of 952 units. The mostly flat course is easy to walk. No water is in play. * Two power carts are available for those with physical limitations. With three sets of tees, the golfers have the option of going around twice using different yardages.

Directions: Monmouth County, #44 on Upper Shore Map
GSP to Exit 114 (Holmdel-Middletown). Turn left at exit toward Middletown. Pass two traffic lights and turn right at Dwight. Pass a light and a school on the left. The road becomes Nut Swamp Rd. Go 1.5 miles to sign on right for Shadow Lake Village. The community has a security gate. An appointment is necessary to enter.

Hole	1	2	3	4	5	6	7	8	9	Out	BLUE	Rating
BLUE	191	188	133	130	164	193	141	123	175	1438		Slope
WHITE	186	176	127	124	161	183	137	113	171	1378		
Par	3	3	3	3	3	3	3	3	3	27	WHITE	Rating
Handicap	1	7	15	17	5	3	9	11	13			Slope
RED	161	161	122	115	143	121	122	105	167	1217		
Par	3	3	3	3	3	3	3	3	3	27	RED	Rating
Handicap	2	4	16	18	8	14	10	12	6			Slope

Hole	10	11	12	13	14	15	16	17	18	In		Totals
BLUE											BLUE	
WHITE											WHITE	
Par											Par	
Handicap												
RED											RED	
Par											Par	
Handicap												

Manager: Richard Carpenter   **Supt:** Robert Donofrio
Built: 1972

SHARK RIVER GOLF COURSE

PUBLIC

320 Old Corlies Ave., Neptune, NJ 07753　　**(732) 922-4141**
www.monmouthcountyparks.com

Shark River is an 18 hole Monmouth County course open to the public 7 days a week all year. Tee times for residents may be made 7 days in advance with ID. Call (732) 758-8383.

Driving Range	Lockers
•**Practice Green**	Showers
•**Power Carts**	•**Food**
•**Pull Carts**	•**Clubhouse**
•**Club Rental**	Outings
•**Soft Spikes**	

Fees	Weekday	Weekend
Res/ID	$21	$25
Sr/Jr	$14.70	
Non-res	$42	$50
Power Carts $33 per cart		

Course Description: Shark River was originally called Asbury Park Golf & CC and changed names in 1936. Rates were $1 weekdays, $2 weekends! It closed for a while and reopened after World War II. Well maintained, it is an old style, fairly flat course with narrow fairways and greens that are medium sized and fast in summer. Many old trees and a few hills dot this well bunkered layout. The rough is of fescue grass; very little water is in play. The signature par 5 9th is a long, difficult double dogleg. Plans for upgrading the course are in progress.

Directions: Monmouth County, #45 on Upper Shore Map
GSP to Exit 100B from north or south. Take Rte. 33 East for 4 lights. Then turn right on Green Grove Rd. Make left onto Old Corlies. Course is on right before Rte. 18 overpass.

Hole	1	2	3	4	5	6	7	8	9	Out	BLUE	Rating 70.3
BLUE	358	525	182	290	185	417	441	169	586	3153		Slope 130
WHITE	348	490	172	280	180	407	431	159	578	3045		
Par	4	5	3	4	3	4	4	3	5	35	WHITE	Rating 69.1
Handicap	12	9	13	14	6	5	4	8	1			Slope 127
RED	323	475	162	265	171	393	413	145	566	2913		
Par	4	5	3	4	3	4	4	3	5	35	RED	Rating 72.0
Handicap	12	9	13	14	6	5	4	8	1			Slope 130
Hole	10	11	12	13	14	15	16	17	18	In		Totals
BLUE	424	386	123	291	328	533	152	451	353	3041	BLUE	6284
WHITE	417	381	113	281	316	526	142	446	343	2965	WHITE	6033
Par	4	4	3	4	4	5	3	5	4	36	Par	71
Handicap	2	7	18	15	11	3	17	16	10			
RED	342	311	101	261	294	505	120	388	320	2642	RED	5417
Par	4	4	3	4	4	5	3	5	4	36	Par	71
Handicap	2	7	18	15	11	3	17	16	10			

Manager: Gregg Wolff　　　**Supt:** John Paddock
Architect: Hal Purdy 1967

SPRING LAKE GOLF CLUB

Warren Ave., Spring Lake, NJ 07762   **(732) 449-7185**
www.springlakegolfclub.com

Spring Lake is an 18 hole course open 6 days a week all year.   Guests play accompanied by a member.

•**Driving Range**	•**Lockers**
•**Practice Green**	•**Showers**
•**Power Carts**	•**Food**
Pull Carts	•**Clubhouse**
Club Rental	•**Outings**
•**Caddies**	•**Soft Spikes**

Course Description: Spring Lake, an excellently maintained golf course, has interesting contours to challenge the golfer. It is considered a pleasant test of golf requiring the use of every club in the bag. The long uphill par 5 3rd deserves to be the number one handicap hole. It has out of bounds on the right, usually plays into the wind, and includes a gully to get over on the approach shot to the plateau green. Some of the holes have been lengthened recently adding to the challenge here. The NJ State Open has been played here in the past as well as the US Women's Amateur. In 1998, Spring Lake again hosted the State Open.

Directions: Monmouth County, #47 on Upper Shore Map
GSP to Exit 98. Take Rte. 138East to Rte. 35South and make right turn. Go three lights and turn left onto Warren Ave. Club is ahead on right.

Hole	1	2	3	4	5	6	7	8	9	Out	BLUE	Rating 72.0
BLUE	408	392	542	345	311	218	354	136	476	3182		Slope 128
WHITE	399	384	534	339	301	214	341	125	465	3102		
Par	4	4	5	4	4	3	4	3	5	36	WHITE	Rating 70.4
Handicap	3	7	1	13	15	11	9	17	5			Slope 125
RED	337	330	484	288	212	165	302	123	440	2681		
Par	4	4	5	4	4	3	4	3	5	36	RED	Rating 72.9
Handicap	7	3	1	13	11	15	9	18	5			Slope 130
Hole	10	11	12	13	14	15	16	17	18	In		Totals
BLUE	162	334	536	462	330	387	196	402	373	3182	BLUE	6364
WHITE	155	319	527	442	320	376	189	389	359	3076	WHITE	6178
Par	3	4	5	5	4	4	3	4	4	36	Par	72
Handicap	18	14	2	10	12	6	16	4	8			
RED	142	286	477	422	294	364	183	354	341	2863	RED	5544
Par	3	4	5	5	4	4	3	4	4	36	Par	72
Handicap	17	14	2	10	12	4	16	6	8			

Manager: Karl Habib   **Pro:** Bill King, PGA   **Supt:** Bruce Peeples
Architects: George Thomas Jr. 1898 (Renovations A. W. Tillinghast)

SPRING MEADOW GOLF COURSE

PUBLIC

4181 Atlantic Ave. Farmingdale, NJ 07727   (732) 449-0806

Spring Meadow is an 18 hole course open 7 days a week all year. It is the only facility owned and operated by the State of New Jersey. Tee time reservations may be made 7 days in adance. Cart prices are reduced after 2 PM.

•Driving Range	•Lockers
•Practice Green	•Showers
•Power Carts	•Food
•Pull Carts	•Clubhouse
•Club Rental	•Outings
•Soft Spikes	

Fees	Weekday	Weekend
Daily	$23	$28
Twi (2PM)	$19	$23
Srs.	$13	
Power Carts $30 per cart		

Course Description: A tributory of the Manasquan River runs through this golf course; water affects play on 5 holes. Adjacent to Allaire State Park, woods surround much of the property. From the the 14th tee, a beautiful view of the golf course can be seen. Spring Meadow is well maintained and has good drainage. It is a very popular and consequently busy facility with friendly and helpful personnel.

Directions: Monmouth County, #48 on Upper Shore Map
GSP to Exit 98. Take Rte. 34 South. At jughandle make right onto Allenwood; take it to the end, then right onto Rte. 524 West (Atlantic Ave.). Course is 1 mile on left.

Hole	1	2	3	4	5	6	7	8	9	Out	BLUE	Rating 70.4
BLUE	458	385	420	110	399	376	197	394	165	2914		Slope 125
WHITE	442	368	375	96	383	353	165	377	146	2705		
Par	5	4	4	3	4	4	3	5	3	35	WHITE	Rating 69.0
Handicap	14	2	4	18	6	12	8	10	16			Slope 120
RED	398	343	337	83	354	271	149	359	127	2421		
Par	5	5	4	3	5	4	3	5	3	37	RED	Rating 70.6
Handicap	4	6	10	18	8	12	14	2	16			Slope 121
Hole	10	11	12	13	14	15	16	17	18	In		Totals
BLUE	429	510	166	480	428	325	153	465	374	3310	BLUE	6224
WHITE	412	476	140	432	403	268	144	453	336	3064	WHITE	5769
Par	4	5	3	5	4	4	3	5	4	37	Par	72
Handicap	1	11	17	7	5	13	15	3	9			
RED	369	428	126	379	360	208	194	396	256	2653	RED	5074
Par	5	5	3	5	5	4	3	5	4	39	Par	72
Handicap	3	7	17	1	13	5	11	9	15			

Supt: Joseph Gunson
Built: 1920

SUN EAGLES @ MONMOUTH GC `MILITARY`

Building 2067, Fort Monmouth, NJ 07703   **(732) 532-4307**
www.USAG.monmouth.com

Sun Eagles at Fort Monmouth is an 18 hole course open to active duty personnel, 20 yr. retirees and civilian Fort employees who may make tee time reservations. It is open all year, 6 days a week. Guests play accompanied by a member.

•Driving Range	•Lockers
•Practice Green	•Showers
•Power Carts	•Food
•Pull Carts	•Clubhouse
•Club Rental	•Outings
Caddies	•Soft Spikes

Course Description: Built originally for private use, this course was bought by the Fort in 1942 and is now called Sun Eagles at Fort Monmouth. Characteristic of a Tillinghast championship course, it has numerous treacherous bunkers and small, undulating greens. The demanding par 3 14th is well-bunkered and has beautiful views from both the tee and the slightly lower green. The 15th is a dogleg left and then another dogleg depending on the tee box location; it also features a bunker in mid fair-way. The course is being restored with every effort to keep to the original Tillnghast design. At this site was the first professional victory in 1935 for Byron Nelson who later won the NJ State Open when he was the assistant pro at Ridgewood County Club.

Directions: Monmouth County, #49 on Upper Shore Map
GSP to Exit 105(Eatontown). Take Hope Road and go north to 4th traffic light and make a right. Fort Monmouth is the 1st driveway on the right.

Hole	1	2	3	4	5	6	7	8	9	Out	BLUE	Rating 70.9
BLUE	365	212	460	433	350	260	113	392	437	3022		Slope 128
WHITE	338	169	428	411	333	237	110	374	421	2821		
Par	4	3	5	4	4	4	3	4	4	35	WHITE	Rating 69.2
Handicap	9	13	11	3	7	15	17	5	1			Slope 123
RED	317	147	400	370	319	215	85	330	403	2586		
Par	4	3	5	4	4	4	3	4	5	36	RED	Rating 72.0
Handicap	11	13	5	1	9	15	17	7	3			Slope 121

Hole	10	11	12	13	14	15	16	17	18	In		Totals
BLUE	365	470	355	378	204	575	341	165	509	3363	BLUE	6385
WHITE	343	453	336	357	196	558	323	144	490	3200	WHITE	6021
Par	4	5	4	4	3	5	4	3	5	37	Par	72
Handicap	12	18	16	6	4	2	10	8	14			
RED	259	410	311	307	170	489	293	120	440	2794	RED	5380
Par	4	5	4	4	3	5	4	3	5.	37	Par	72
Handicap	14	6	8	10	12	2	18	16	4			

Manager: Chip Dayton   **Pro:** Bryan Carey, PGA   **Supt:** Duncan Bowie
Architect: A. W. Tillinghast 1926

TOMS RIVER COUNTRY CLUB

419 Washington St., Tom's River, NJ 08753   **(732) 349-8867**

Toms River is a 9 hole course open 7 days a week and closed in January. Guests play accompanied by a member. Tee time reservations are suggested.

Driving Range	•Lockers
•Practice Green	•Showers
•Power Carts	•Food
•Pull Carts	•Clubhouse
Club Rental	•Outings
Caddies	•Soft Spikes

Course Description: The layout at Toms River was originally 18 holes. During the Depression, 9 holes were sold off. It became a member owned club in 1983. This picturesque course is noted for its small, elevated greens that offer subtle breaks. The signature par 3 6th sits on the Toms River; its green is virtually an island. Some ditches on other holes confront the golfer. Players can watch the boats go by. The fairways and tee boxes are maintained very well. Golfers have the choice of a different set of tees for the second nine.

Directions: Ocean County, #50 on Upper Shore Map
GSP to Exit 81. Take Water St. east and turn left on Dock St. Make a right on Washington St. Club is ahead on right.

Hole	1	2	3	4	5	6	7	8	9	Out	BLUE	Rating
BLUE												Slope
WHITE	401	171	360	409	461	144	368	312	455	3092		
Par	4	3	4	4	5	3	4	4	5	36	WHITE	Rating 70.2
Handicap	3	15	11	1	7	17	5	13	9			Slope 125
RED	333	166	290	384	345	138	361	308	416	2802		
Par	4	3	4	4	5	3	4	4	5	36	RED	Rating 72.6
Handicap	13	15	11	1	7	17	3	9	5			Slope 130

Hole	10	11	12	13	14	15	16	17	18	In		Totals
BLUE											BLUE	
WHITE										3014	WHITE	6106
Par											Par	36
Handicap												
RED										2734	RED	5536
Par											Par	36
Handicap												

Manager: Andy Maglione   **Pro:** Tony Bruno, PGA   **Supt:** Ed McSeaman
Built: 1930's

TWIN BROOK GOLF CENTER

PUBLIC

1251 Jumping Brook Rd., Tinton Falls, NJ 07724   **(732) 922-1600**

Twin Brook is a 9 hole regulation par 3 golf course open to the public 7 days a week all year. The golf center also has a driving range, a miniature golf course and a full service health club on the property. Tee time reservations are not necessary.

•**Driving Range**	Lockers
•**Practice Green**	Showers
•**Power Carts**	•**Food**
•**Pull Carts**	•**Clubhouse**
•**Club Rental**	•**Outings**
•**Soft Spikes**	

Fees	Weekday	Weekend
9 holes	$12	$14
18 holes	$18	$20
Sr/Jr	$10	
Power carts $10pp		

Course Description: Twin Brook is an open, flat course with moderate sized fairly slow greens giving the golfer a good place to practice his game. A small pond is in play on the 6th and a ditch runs across holes #s 3, 4 and 5. A lake on the side of the ninth hole and its length make it the #1 handicap. All the holes have been renovated and several lengthened.

Directions: Monmouth County, #51 on Upper Shore Map
GSP to Exit 102. Stay right proceeding east on Asbury Ave. Turn right at 1st light. Twin Brook is on the right. From South: GSP to exit 100A. Go east on Rte. 66. Make a left at 1st light onto Jumping Brook Rd. Center is on the left.

Hole	1	2	3	4	5	6	7	8	9	Out	BLUE	Rating
BLUE	150	135	145	165	165	140	135	90	180	1305		Slope
WHITE	135	110	130	120	155	135	75	70	160	1090		
Par	3	3	3	3	3	3	3	3	3	27	WHITE	Rating
Handicap	7	6	8	3	2	4	5	9	1			Slope
RED	90	110	105	130	130	75	75	70	130	915		
Par	3	3	3	3	3	3	3	3	3	27	RED	Rating
Handicap	7	6	8	3	2	4	5	9	1			Slope

Hole	10	11	12	13	14	15	16	17	18	In		Totals
BLUE											BLUE	1305
WHITE											WHITE	1090
Par											Par	27
Handicap												
RED											RED	915
Par											Par	27
Handicap												

Pro: Pat Jordan, LPGA   **Supt:** Ken Miller
Architect: Harry Harsin 1992

WESTLAKE GOLF & CC

1 Pine Lakes Circle., Jackson, NJ 08527   **(732) 833-7274**
www.geocities.com

Westlake is an 18 hole private course open to residents 6 days a week from 3/15-12/31*(weather permitting)*. Guests may play accompanied by a member. Tee time reservations are recommended 3 days in advance.

Driving Range	•**Lockers**
•**Practice Green**	•**Showers**
•**Power Carts**	•**Food**
Pull Carts	•**Clubhouse**
•**Club Rental**	Outings
Caddies	•**Soft Spikes**

Course Description: Westlake Golf & Country Club is a well maintained 6330 yard 18 hole course. It is within an adult community that has about 1400 homes. Water comes into play on 15 holes on this tree lined wide open layout. Featured are rolling fairways, generous landing areas and considerable mounding. The signature par 5 tenth is aesthetically the most picturesque and photographed hole. The greens are over sized and undulating. Westlake offers another great choice for a golf and country club life style in New Jersey.

Directions: Ocean County, #52 on Upper Shore Map
GSP to Exit 98. Take Rte 195West to Exit 28A and take Rte. 9 South for .5 mi. Then turn right into Aldrich Rd. Go 3.8 miles and turn left onto Manhattan St. At STOP, turn left onto Cooks Bridge Rd. to Club on right.

Hole	1	2	3	4	5	6	7	8	9	Out	BLUE	Rating
BLUE	405	458	134	366	424	141	332	404	317	2981		Slope
WHITE	370	443	120	356	408	135	303	358	287	2780		
Par	4	5	3	4	4	3	4	4	4	35	WHITE	Rating
Handicap	7	3	17	1	5	15	11	9	13			Slope
RED	296	367	80	270	314	95	244	294	220	2180		
Par	4	5	3	4	4	3	4	4	4	35	RED	Rating
Handicap	3	5	15	1	7	17	9	11	13			Slope
Hole	10	11	12	13	14	15	16	17	18	In		Totals
BLUE	491	356	331	155	477	372	387	158	298	3025	BLUE	6006
WHITE	468	346	309	140	460	359	378	144	288	2892	WHITE	5672
Par	5	4	4	3	5	4	4	3	4	36	Par	71
Handicap	2	12	10	16	4	8	6	18	14			
RED	401	268	217	68	386	264	276	92	188	2160	RED	4340
Par	5	4	4	3	5	4	4	3	4	36	Par	71
Handicap	2	8	6	18	4	12	10	16	14			

Mgr: Ocean Golf Mgmt.   **Pro:** Paul Findlow, PGA   **Supt:** John Boyer
Architect: Arthur Hills, 2001

WOODLAKE GOLF & CC

25 New Hampshire Ave., Lakewood, NJ 08701

www.woodlakecountryclub.com

(732) 370-1002

Woodlake Country Club is an 18 hole course open 7 days a week all year. Members may reserve up to 15 days in advance. Carts are mandatory on weekends until 2PM. Guests play accompanied by a member.

•Driving Range	•Lockers
•Practice Green	•Showers
•Power Carts	•Food
Pull Carts	•Clubhouse
•Club Rental	•Outings
Caddies	•Soft Spikes

Course Description: Woodlake is long and fairly flat with narrow fairways in a parkland setting. Water comes into play on 12 holes. The medium sized greens are fast and very undulating. The signature 16th is a difficult par 4; water can be encountered on the tee shot, along the fairway and on the approach shot as well. The private club atmosphere is apparent here. The course is very well maintained and is run by Matrix Golf & Hospitality.

Directions: Ocean County, #53 on Upper Shore Map
GSP to Exit 91. Stay to the right at fork. Go straight for 3 lights to Rte. 88. Turn right and then right at light onto New Hampshire Ave. Go right to 2nd entrance on right.

Hole	1	2	3	4	5	6	7	8	9	Out	BLUE	Rating 72.8
BLUE	394	525	422	165	360	515	375	217	412	3385		Slope 132
WHITE	380	510	407	150	340	496	356	202	395	3236		
Par	4	5	4	3	4	5	4	3	4	36	WHITE	Rating 70.9
Handicap	10	8	2	18	14	6	12	16	4			Slope 125
RED	340	460	369	98	300	430	313	181	345	2836		
Par	4	5	5	3	4	5	4	3	4	37	RED	Rating 72.3
Handicap	8	2	16	18	14	4	12	10	6			Slope 123
Hole	10	11	12	13	14	15	16	17	18	In		Totals
BLUE	380	422	498	205	346	566	391	183	390	3381	BLUE	6766
WHITE	363	410	485	193	324	542	378	168	339	3202	WHITE	6438
Par	4	4	5	3	4	5	4	3	4	36	Par	72
Handicap	7	3	11	15	13	1	5	17	9			
RED	306	374	427	148	262	450	340	115	299	2721	RED	5557
Par	4	5	5	3	4	5	4	3	4	36	Par	74
Handicap	7	13	5	15	11	1	3	17	9			

Manager: Stewart Owens   **Pro:** Rick Durham, PGA   **Supt:** Gene Stiles
Architect: Edward Packard 1972

SOUTHWEST REGION

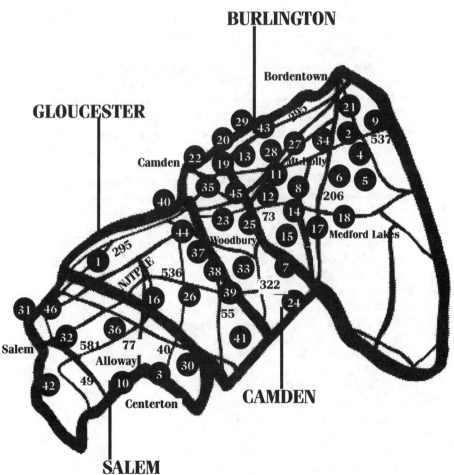

BURLINGTON

Bordentown

GLOUCESTER

295

21
9
29
43
20
28
27
34
2
537
Camden 22
19
13
4
Mt. Holly
11
6
5
35
45
8
40
12
206
23
73
14
44
25
18
Woodbury
15
17
Medford Lakes
1
295
37
536
38
33
7
16
26
39
322
31
46
55
24
32
36
41
Salem 581
77
40
Alloway
30
42
49
10
3
CAMDEN
Centerton

SALEM

SOUTHWEST REGION

Public Courses appear in *bold italics*

Map (#)   Page #

Beckett CC (1)--------------- 245
Burlington CC (2) ------------ 246
Centerton Golf Club (3)--- 247
Deerwood CC (4)------------ 248
Falcon Creek GC* (5)--------- 249
Fountain Green* (6)---------- 250
Freeway Golf Course (7)-- 251
Golden Pheasant GC (8)-- 252
Hanover CC (9)-------------- 253
Holly Hills Golf Club (10)- 254
Indian Spring GC (11)----- 255
Kresson Golf Course (12)- 256
Laurel Creek CC (13)--------- 257
Links Golf Club (14) --------- 258
Little Mill CC (15)------------ 259
Maple Ridge GC (16)------- 260
Medford Lakes CC (17)------ 261
Medford Village CC (18)------ 262
Merchantville CC (19)-------- 263
Moorestown Field Club (20)- 264
Olde York CC (21)------------ 265
Pennsauken CC (22)-------- 266
Pine Hill CC (23)------------ 267
Pinelands Golf Club (24)-- 268
Pine Valley Golf Club (25)---- 269
Pitman Golf Club (26)----- 270
Ramblewood CC (27)------- 271
Rancocas Golf Club (28)-- 272
Riverton Country Club (29)-- 273
River Winds (46)-------------- 274

Map (#)   Page #

Running Deer (30)--------- 275
Sakima CC (31---------------- 276
Salem CC (32)--------------- 277
Scotland Run Nat. (33)--- 278
Springfield GC (34)-------- 279
Tavistock Country Club (35) 280
Town & Country (36)------ 281
Valleybrook GC (37)------- 282
Washington Twnshp (38)- 283
Wedgewood CC (39)------- 284
Westwood Golf Club (40)- 285
White Oaks CC (41)-------- 286
Wild Oaks GC (42)--------- 287
Willow Brook CC (43)----- 288
Woodbury CC (44)----------- 289
Woodcrest CC (45)----------- 290

*Military Course

244

BECKETT GOLF CLUB

PUBLIC

Box 47A, Old King's Highway, Swedesboro, NJ 08085 **(856) 467-4700**
www.beckettgc.com

Beckett is a 27 hole semi-private club open to the public 7 days a week, all year.
Memberships are available. For weekend tee times: members call 1 week in advance;
general public, 5 days.

•Driving Range	•Lockers
•Practice Green	•Showers
•Power Carts	•Food
•Pull Carts	•Clubhouse
•Club Rental	•Outings
Soft Spikes	

Fees	Weekday	Weekend
Daily	$15	$19
Twi	$12	$15
Power carts	$15pp	
Midweek $48/cart/lunch/for2		

Course Description: The three nines that make up this 27 hole relatively hilly layout become progressively more difficult in the order of Red, White and Blue. The par 5 fifth on the Blue is heavily treed, boomerang shaped and the tee shot has water to carry. It is justifiably called the "monster hole." On the Red nine, the 8th is a par 3 over water with a slight dogleg left and the 6th has a severe dogleg right. Scorecard below is for Blue and Red nines.

Directions: Gloucester County, #1 on Southwest Map
Rte. 295 to Exit #10. From the top of the ramp going north, take a right, going south take a left. Proceed 4.5 miles & at the 2nd STOP go right onto Old Kings Highway. Course is 1.5 mi. on right. OR NJTPKE to Exit #2; get onto Rte. 322 W to Kings Hwy. (Rte. 620); follow to Swedesboro. Bear left then right to 2nd fork to club.

Hole	1	2	3	4	5	6	7	8	9	Out	BLUE	Rating 69.9
BLUE	513	173	386	157	488	472	348	342	377	3256		Slope 116
WHITE	502	162	375	146	477	371	337	331	366	3067		
Par	3	3	4	3	5	4	4	4	4	36	WHITE	Rating 69.0
Handicap	4	6	3	9	1	2	8	7	5			Slope 114
RED	500	152	365	116	467	361	327	321	356	2965		
Par	3	3	4	3	5	4	4	4	4	36	RED	Rating 72.3
Handicap	3	8	2	9	1	4	7	6	5			Slope 117
Hole	10	11	12	13	14	15	16	17	18	In		Totals
BLUE	498	199	338	387	313	465	378	358	226	3162	BLUE	6418
WHITE	488	189	328	377	303	455	368	348	216	3072	WHITE	6139
Par	5	3	4	4	4	5	4	4	3	36	Par	72
Handicap	1	8	3	5	6	9	7	2	4			
RED	488	150	318	367	286	373	278	259	206	2725	RED	5690
Par	5	3	4	4	4	5	4	4	3	36	Par	72
Handicap	1	9	6	5	7	2	3	4	8			

Manager/Pro: Steve DeVito, PGA   **Supt:** Wally Miller
Architects: Dick & Loretta Kidder 1964

BURLINGTON COUNTRY CLUB PRIVATE

Burrs Road, (Box 170), Mt. Holly, NJ 08060   (609) 267-1887

Burlington is an 18 hole course open 6 days a week all year. Guests play accompanied by a member. Tee time reservations are not necessary. Players may not use pull carts on Sat. or Sun. before 1 PM.

```
• Driving Range    • Lockers
• Practice Green   • Showers
• Power Carts      • Food
• Pull Carts       • Clubhouse
  Club Rental      • Outings
  Caddies          • Soft Spikes
```

Course Description: The traditionally styled and well maintained Burlington is a demanding course with narrow tree lined fairways and high rough. Out of bounds lurks on twelve holes; a meandering creek on the back nine may catch an errant shot. The small bent grass greens are firm and fast. The par 3 #12 signature hole with carry over water, has a Pete Dye type of bulkhead which is more modern looking than the rest of the course. Bunkers have been added recently on the back nine. The 2 day Burlington Classic Pro Am event is held here.

Directions: Burlington County, #2 on Southwest Map
NJTPKE to Exit #5. Make a right onto Rte. 541 South. At first light, make a left onto Burrs Rd. Course is 1 mile ahead on left.

Hole	1	2	3	4	5	6	7	8	9	Out	BLUE	Rating 70.9
BLUE	420	215	396	501	115	392	480	413	432	3364		Slope 126
WHITE	409	203	383	461	106	376	461	408	399	3206		
Par	4	3	4	5	3	4	5	4	4	36	WHITE	Rating 69.0
Handicap	1	11	9	13	17	7	15	3	5			Slope 123
RED	335	165	340	432	98	310	425	399	311	2815		
Par	4	3	4	5	3	4	5	5	4	37	RED	Rating 65.2
Handicap	5	15	1	3	17	11	7	13	9			Slope 113
Hole	10	11	12	13	14	15	16	17	18	In		Totals
BLUE	143	333	177	412	371	379	361	350	318	2844	BLUE	6410
WHITE	135	320	141	398	365	358	355	344	280	2696	WHITE	6006
Par	3	4	3	4	4	4	4	4	4	34	Par	70
Handicap	18	14	6	2	10	4	12	16	8			
RED	127	304	78	354	356	293	334	336	247	2429	RED	5263
Par	3	4	3	4	4	4	4	4	4	34	Par	71
Handicap	16	14	18	2	4	10	6	12	8			

Pro: Mike Mack, PGA   **Supt:** Brian Minemiar
Architect: Alexander Findlay 1929

CENTERTON GOLF CLUB

PUBLIC

1016 Almond Rd., Pittsgrove, NJ 08318   **(856) 358-2220**
www.centerton.com

Centerton is a semi-private course that is open to the public 7 days a week all year. Memberships are available. Tee times may be made 7 days in advance. Carts req'd until 11AM on weekends.

•**Driving Range**	•**Lockers**
•**Practice Green**	•**Showers**
•**Power Carts**	•**Food**
•**Pull Carts**	•**Clubhouse**
•**Club Rental**	•**Outings**
Soft Spikes	

Fees	Weekday	Weekend
Daily	$24	$47/cart
After 11		$37/cart
Srs.	$30/cart	
Power Carts	$13pp	

Course Description: Easily accessible from both Philadelphia and Atlantic City, Centerton offers some test of skill and an enjoyable experience for both beginners and more advanced players. It is gently rolling and tree lined with large greens and no parallel fairways. Water is in play on three holes. The most difficult hole, the 410 yard 16th, is a dogleg left; its green is small, undulating and tricky to read. The 14th, designed in a links style, is open with some mounding.

Directions: Salem County, #3 on Southwest Map
NJTPKE to Exit #2. Then take Rte. 322 East to Rte 55 South. to Exit # 45 (Centerton). At top of ramp, go right onto Rte. 553. for 9 miles to light at Rte 553 & Rte. 540 (Almond Rd.) Go left onto 540. Club is 1/2 mile on right.

Hole	1	2	3	4	5	6	7	8	9	Out	BLUE	Rating 70.5
BLUE	369	360	200	515	360	420	184	405	365	3178		Slope 119
WHITE	355	328	188	490	335	390	150	385	350	2971		
Par	4	4	3	5	4	4	3	4	4	35	WHITE	Rating 68.6
Handicap	6	16	4	14	8	10	18	2	12			Slope 114
RED	342	305	180	463	308	353	134	370	307	2762		
Par	4	4	3	5	4	4	3	4	4	35	RED	Rating 71.8
Handicap	6	16	14	4	10	12	18	2	8			Slope 123
Hole	10	11	12	13	14	15	16	17	18	In		Totals
BLUE	397	585	160	405	520	320	410	175	450	3422	BLUE	6600
WHITE	343	565	155	370	450	300	400	165	423	3171	WHITE	6142
Par	4	5	3	4	5	4	4	3	4	36	Par	71
Handicap	9	5	15	7	17	13	1	11	3			
RED	332	518	137	348	405	280	383	145	406	2954	RED	5716
Par	4	5	3	4	5	4	4	3	5	37	Par	72
Handicap	13	1	15	5	7	11	3	17	9			

Pro: Pat Sweetra, PGA   **Supt:** Alan Bewley
Architect: Ed Carman 1962

DEERWOOD COUNTRY CLUB   SEMI-PRIVATE

845 Woodlane Rd., Westampton, NJ 08060   **(609) 265-1800**
www.deerwoodcc.com

Deerwood is an 18 hole semi-private course open 6 days a week all year (closed Mondays). Memberships are available. Tee times are required: may be made 24 hours in advance.

•**Driving Range**	•**Lockers**
•**Practice Green**	•**Showers**
•**Power Carts**	•**Food**
Pull Carts	•**Clubhouse**
•**Club Rental**	•**Outings**
•**Soft Spikes**	

Fees	Weekday	Weekend
Daily	$75	$87
Power carts included		

Course Description: Shot selection is critical at Deerwood which was constructed in a "Figure 8" pattern to provide a variety of wind and sun orientation. With five sets of tees, the golfers skill is tested by its five man made ponds, three tiered greens and naturally preserved hit overs. The par 4 465 yard fifth is known as the "there goes my score" hole. It has a tee shot over a pond and then goes uphill to a well trapped green. The fourteenth plays longer than its 398 yards indicate with westerly winds and water confronting the golfer. Putting is quite a challenge on the contoured bent grass greens. Deerwood no longer requires cart paths only. The Ladies Championship tees have been rated 72.5 with a 130 slope.

Directions: Burlington County, #4 on Southwest Map
NJTPKE to Exit #5. Go South on Rte. 541 then left at jughandle onto Woodlane Rd. (Rte. 630 East). Club is ahead on left.

Hole	1	2	3	4	5	6	7	8	9	Out	BLUE	Rating 69.6
BLUE	380	383	365	136	465	350	513	209	334	3135		Slope 124
WHITE	371	369	349	130	436	325	481	197	323	2981		
Par	4	4	4	3	4	4	5	3	4	35	WHITE	Rating 68.3
Handicap	7	11	9	17	1	13	5	3	15			Slope 121
RED	316	273	294	114	367	294	405	131	267	2461		
Par	4	4	4	3	4	4	5	3	4	35	RED	Rating 67.2
Handicap	7	11	9	17	1	13	5	3	15			Slope 111

Hole	10	11	12	13	14	15	16	17	18	In		Totals
BLUE	375	368	176	139	398	310	398	556	376	3096	BLUE	6231
WHITE	364	330	164	130	380	287	383	546	363	2947	WHITE	5928
Par	4	4	3	3	4	4	4	5	4	35	Par	70
Handicap	10	12	16	18	4	14	8	2	6			
RED	300	303	137	118	221	224	311	441	291	2346	RED	4807
Par	4	4	3	3	4	4	4	5	4	35	Par	70
Handicap	10	12	16	18	4	14	8	2	6			

Manager: Terry Mulligan   **Pro:** Greg Farrow, PGA   **Supt:** Joel Collura
Architects: Dick Alaimo, Jim Blaukovitch 1996

FALCON CREEK GOLF COURSE `MILITARY`

McGuire Air Force Base, Wrightstown, NJ 08641   (609) 754-3330

Falcon Creek is an 18 hole course open to active duty military, career retirees, Dept. of Defense, reservists and their guests. It is open 7 days a week all year. Memberships are available. Tee times are necessary for weekends and holidays.

- •Driving Range
- •Practice Green
- •Power Carts
- •Pull Carts
- •Club Rental
- •Soft Spikes

- •Lockers
- •Showers
- •Food
- •Clubhouse
- •Outings

Fees	Weekday	Weekend
Daily	$11-$25*	
*Varies with rank & season		
Power carts	$22/18	$12/9
Single cart	$14	

Course Description: Relatively flat, Falcon Creek offers a good test of golf with as many as 52 bunkers clustered around the mid-sized bent grass greens. Nine holes are affected by water. The signature thirteenth hole, the #1 handicap, is lined with trees and has a ditch running across it. The cart paths are asphalt.

Directions: Burlington County, #5 on Southwest Map
NJTPKE to Exit #7. Then take Rte. 206S briefly to Fort Dix Access Highway #68 to Rte. 537 East (Monmouth Rd.) Follow signs to McGuire Air Force Base and ask at gate for directions to golf course.

Hole	1	2	3	4	5	6	7	8	9	Out	BLUE	Rating 72.6
BLUE	320	145	527	349	280	429	239	378	550	3217		Slope 122
WHITE	300	140	507	339	275	409	185	368	535	3058		
Par	4	3	5	4	4	4	3	4	5	36	WHITE	Rating 70.6
Handicap	10	16	8	12	18	4	2	14	6			Slope 118
RED	280	135	343	329	270	320	242	348	429	2696		
Par	4	3	4	4	4	4	4	3	5	35	RED	Rating 70.7
Handicap	11	15	1	5	13	7	17	3	9			Slope 118
Hole	10	11	12	13	14	15	16	17	18	In		Totals
BLUE	437	162	468	430	419	596	200	402	498	3612	BLUE	6764
WHITE	407	126	448	410	399	586	188	382	478	3424	WHITE	6434
Par	4	3	4	4	4	5	3	4	5	36	Par	72
Handicap	11	17	5	1	3	7	9	13	15			
RED	261	122	428	390	369	443	160	283	458	2914	RED	5384
Par	4	3	5	4	4	5	3	4	5	37	Par	72
Handicap	14	16	6	12	10	2	18	8	4			

Manager: Val Mendoza   **Pro**: John Green   **Supt**: Dan Mears
Built: 1960s

FOUNTAIN GREEN GOLF COURSE ▮MILITARY▮

Fort Dix, NJ 08640   **(609) 562-5443**

Fountain Green is an 18 hole course available for Dep't. of Defense employees with I.D., active military personnel & dependents & retired career military. It is open 7 days a week all year. Memberships are available. Tee times are necessary on weekends.

•**Driving Range**	•**Lockers**
•**Practice Green**	•**Showers**
•**Power Carts**	•**Food**
•**Pull Carts**	•**Clubhouse**
•**Club Rental**	•**Outings**
•**Soft Spikes**	

Fees	Weekday	Weekend
Daily w/ID	$11-15	$11-15
Twi/9hole	$9	Guest $14
Guest	$28	$28
Power carts	$15/1, $24/2	

Course Description: The regulation sized Fountain Green is short featuring small, very fast bent grass greens. It is a walkable layout with water affecting play on 3 holes. The tree lined fairways are somewhat hilly. Drainage here is excellent; even after a heavy rainfall, the course is playable. The maintenance is outstanding due to the talents of the superintendent, John Huda, who is himself a scratch golfer. It hardly ever gets crowded at Fountain Green because strict eligibility criteria are enforced.

Directions: Burlington County, #6 on Southwest Map
NJTPKE to Exit 7; then take Rte. 206 South to Rte. 68 East to end into Fort Dix. Go around circle and straight to clubhouse on left.

Hole	1	2	3	4	5	6	7	8	9	Out	BLUE	Rating 70.6
BLUE	505	413	114	430	313	550	373	423	218	3339		Slope 118
WHITE	485	397	104	313	302	535	357	413	210	3116		
Par	5	4	3	4	4	5	4	4	3	36	WHITE	Rating 68.7
Handicap	9	5	17	7	15	1	11	3	13			Slope 115
RED	423	380	87	245	292	401	339	404	201	2772		
Par	5	4	3	4	4	5	4	5	3	37	RED	Rating 71.8
Handicap	9	5	17	7	15	1	11	3	13			Slope 123

Hole	10	11	12	13	14	15	16	17	18	In		Totals
BLUE	400	388	356	219	401	311	210	295	470	3050	BLUE	6389
WHITE	383	378	334	176	380	301	200	284	437	2873	WHITE	5989
Par	4	4	4	3	4	4	3	4	4/5	34/35	Par	70/71
Handicap	4	6	10	14	2	16	8	18	12			
RED	361	368	311	115	364	291	187	272	425	2694	RED	5466
Par	4	4	4	3	4	4	3	4	5	35	Par	72
Handicap	4	6	10	14	2	16	8	18	12			

Manager/Pro: Bill Lyons, PGA   **Supt:** John Huda
Built: 1st stage early 50s   2nd stage late 50s

FREEWAY GOLF COURSE

PUBLIC

1858 Sicklerville, Rd., Sicklerville, NJ 08081   **(856) 227-1115**
www.freewaygolfcourse.com

Freeway is an 18 hole course open to the public 7 days a week all year. Memberships are available with preferred tee times and pre-paid green fees.   Tee times: members/10 days, non-mbrs. 7 days. Power carts required morning weekends.

•**Driving Range**	•**Lockers**
•**Practice Green**	•**Showers**
•**Power Carts**	•**Food**
•**Pull Carts**	•**Clubhouse**
Club Rental	•**Outings**
•**Soft Spikes**	

Fees	Weekday	Weekend
Daily	$32	$48
Twi(3PM)	$28	$32
Sr	$29	
Power Carts included		

Course Description: Freeway is a well maintained layout that is flat and wide open on the front nine while the back is shorter and narrower. Water affects play on four holes. The par 3 14th signature hole is long, narrow and requires an accurate tee shot. Many golfers drive up from Philadelphia to play here making it quite busy in season. Improvements have been made recently; a new irrigation system, tee boxes & grasses have been installed and the fairways made wider. The course is in better condition than ever and a lot more challenging.

Directions: Camden County, #7 on Southwest Map
NJTPKE to Exit #3. Exit at Rte. 168 South; then to Rte. 42 South to Exit 168 North. At first light go right on Sicklerville Rd; club is 2 miles on left.

Hole	1	2	3	4	5	6	7	8	9	Out	BLUE	Rating 71.0
BLUE	587	182	394	349	368	409	408	389	580	3666		Slope 121
WHITE	562	169	382	325	342	394	387	379	557	3497		
Par	5	3	4	4	4	4	4	4	5	37	WHITE	Rating 69.7
Handicap	2	7	8	11	12	5	6	9	1			Slope 119
RED	497	142	365	249	301	336	326	341	502	3059		
Par	5	3	5	4	4	5	4	4	5	39	RED	Rating 70.3
Handicap	2	7	9	11	12	5	6	9	1			Slope 118

Hole	10	11	12	13	14	15	16	17	18	In		Totals
BLUE	318	195	316	415	232	472	346	161	415	2870	BLUE	6536
WHITE	309	169	305	395	212	442	278	144	400	2654	WHITE	6151
Par	4	3	4	5	3	5	4	3	4	35	Par	72
Handicap	15	17	14	10	16	4	18	13	3			
RED	299	145	285	307	185	409	223	128	345	2336	RED	5395
Par	4	3	4	5	3	5	4	3	5	36	Par	75
Handicap	15	17	14	10	16	4	18	13	3			

Manager: Karlon Hickman   **Pro:** William Bishop, PGA   **Supt:** David Hunt
Built: 1968

GOLDEN PHEASANT GOLF CLUB

141 Country Club Dr., Medford, NJ 08055   **(609) 267-4276**
www.golfgoldenpheasant.com

Golden Pheasant is an 18 hole course open 7 days a week all year. Memberships are available. Tee time reservations are required for weekends & holidays in season. Power carts are required before noon on weekends.

Driving Range	•**Lockers**
•**Practice Green**	•**Showers**
•**Power Carts**	•**Food**
•**Pull Carts**	•**Clubhouse**
•**Club Rental**	•**Outings**
Soft Spikes	

Fees	Weekday	Weekend
Daily	$32	$54/cart
Sr.	$31/cart	
Twi rates available		
Power carts $12pp		

Course Description: As the golfer moves along the well maintained somewhat hilly Golden Pheasant course, the holes become more challenging. Starting with open fairways, it progresses gradually to more demanding, rolling terrain and elevated greens. Other features that pique one's interest are the ravines, streams and valleys. The 450 yard par 4 fourth has a tough downhill approach shot to a small undulating green. New bunkers have been added on 9 and 18.

Directions: Burlington County, #8 on Southwest Map
NJTPKE to Exit #5, Mt. Holly. Take Rte. 541 South to Mt. Holly. Then take Mt. Holly bypass to Rte. 38 and turn left. Go right at 2nd light, Eayrestown Rd. As road dead ends, make a sharp right and then a quick left onto Country Club Drive to club on right.

Hole	1	2	3	4	5	6	7	8	9	Out	BLUE	Rating 68.7
BLUE	555	153	365	450	423	354	302	183	471	3256		Slope 121
WHITE	550	143	360	420	409	336	289	173	453	3133		
Par	5	3	4	4	4	4	4	3	5	36	WHITE	Rating 67.0
Handicap	3	11	5	1	7	17	13	9	15			Slope 115
RED	409	120	340	375	348	326	279	140	388	2725		
Par	5	3	4	4	4	4	4	3	5	36	RED	Rating 68.7
Handicap	3	11	5	1	7	17	13	9	15			Slope 112
Hole	**10**	**11**	**12**	**13**	**14**	**15**	**16**	**17**	**18**	**In**		Totals
BLUE	540	179	298	371	518	149	331	288	343	3017	BLUE	6273
WHITE	526	170	283	346	487	138	315	277	327	2869	WHITE	6002
Par	5	3	4	4	5	3	4	4	4	36	Par	72
Handicap	2	10	16	8	4	14	6	12	18			
RED	478	123	198	268	423	97	284	196	313	2380	RED	5105
Par	5	3	4	4	5	3	4	4	4	36	Par	72
Handicap	2	10	16	8	4	14	6	12	18			

Manager/Supt: Paul Capri   **Pro: Jim Bergen**
Architect: Richard Kidder 1964

HANOVER GOLF CLUB

133 Larrison Rd., North Hanover, NJ 08562   **(609) 758-0300**

Hanover is an 18 hole public course open 7 days a week all year. Memberships are available which may include green fees and set weekend tee times for the season. Tee times may be made 1 week ahead for daily fee and up to 30 days for members.

•**Driving Range**	Lockers
•**Practice Green**	•**Showers**
•**Power Carts**	•**Food**
•**Pull Carts**	•**Clubhouse**
•**Club Rental**	•**Outings**
•**Soft Spikes**	

Fees	Weekday	Weekend
Daily(bef 12)	$32	$45
12-4PM	$20	$32
Sr.	$18	
Power carts included		
Twilight rates available		

Course Description: Hanover is a well groomed, fair course with tree lined fairways, large greens that hold well and a hilly back nine. Although a small creek runs through the entire course, water is actually in play on four holes. From the elevated tee on the signature 621 yard par 5 eighteenth, the drive is to an open fairway. The second shot is over water, or the less confident can lay up for an approach to a contoured green. New fairway and greenside bunkering have been added and some tee boxes have been reconditioned. In addition, drainage has been improved and the cart paths upgraded.

Directions: Burlington County, #9 on Southwest Map
NJTPKE to Exit 7A. Take Rte. 195 East to Exit #16. Then take Rte. 537 West for 8 miles to Larrison Rd. Hanover CC is on the right.

Hole	1	2	3	4	5	6	7	8	9	Out	GOLD	Rating 71.6
GOLD	423	437	494	161	369	350	146	577	363	3320		Slope 125
BLUE	384	422	480	147	355	330	132	559	348	3157		
Par	4	4	5	3	4	4	3	5	4	36	BLUE	Rating 69.8
Handicap	6	2	8	16	12	10	18	4	14			Slope 121
RED	363	394	436	96	318	269	94	415	323	2708		
Par	4	4	5	3	4	4	3	5	4	36	RED	Rating 65.8
Handicap	4	8	6	16	10	12	18	2	14			Slope 115
Hole	10	11	12	13	14	15	16	17	18	In		Totals
GOLD	379	303	418	403	397	192	442	156	621	3311	GOLD	6612
BLUE	366	290	399	375	375	178	416	145	599	3143	BLUE	6288
Par	4	4	4	4	4	3	4	3	5	35	Par	71
Handicap	9	13	3	11	5	15	7	17	1			
RED	344	273	296	321	316	145	356	133	405	2629	RED	5286
Par	4	4	4	4	4	3	4	3	5	35	Par	71
Handicap	5	13	3	9	7	15	11	17	1			

Manager/Pro: Kevin Kriews, PGA   **Supt:** Dan Tewes
Built: 1960s

HOLLY HILLS GOLF CLUB

SEMI-PRIVATE

Friesburg Road, Alloway, NJ 08001 **(856) 935-2412**

Holly Hills is an 18 hole semi-private course open to the public 7 days a week all year.
Memberships are available (inc. annual green fees & preferred starting times.) Tee
times: mbrs. 10 days, non-mbrs. 7 days. Coupon specials during season.

•Driving Range	•Lockers
•Practice Green	•Showers
•Power Carts	•Food
•Pull Carts	•Clubhouse
•Club Rental	•Outings
Soft Spikes	

Fees	Weekday	Weekend
Daily	$30	$40
Twi (2PM)	$25	$25
9 holes	$13	$15
Power carts included		

Course Description: Not far from the Delaware River is Holly Hills, an appealing and
well maintained golf course. Almost half of the holes are affected by water in the form
of ponds and streams that cross the fairways. Additional bunkers and ponds have
been added. It is a nature lover's delight with its rolling hills, variety of wildlife and
rustic scenery. The signature par 5 10th hole has a narrow fairway and plays downhill
into a valley and then up to a large undulating green. This course was rated #1 by the
Courier-Post for public golf courses in the past.

Directions: Salem County, #10 on Southwest Map
NJTPKE to Exit #2. Then take Rte. 322 East toward Mullica Hill. Turn right at Rte. 45
which becomes Rte. 77S. At traffic circle take Rte. 635W for 7 miles to Friesburg Rd.
and turn right. Course is 1 mile on right.

Hole	1	2	3	4	5	6	7	8	9	Out	BLUE	Rating 71.4
BLUE	556	198	284	418	166	180	247	381	483	2913		Slope 124
WHITE	546	175	274	400	160	170	236	373	475	2809		
Par	5	3	4	4	3	3	4	4	5	35	WHITE	Rating 70.0
Handicap	7	5	17	1	13	11	15	3	9			Slope 123
RED	522	96	223	255	98	143	221	292	429	2279		
Par	5	3	4	4	3	3	4	4	5	35	RED	Rating 68.6
Handicap	1	17	15	9	7	13	11	5	3			Slope 118
Hole	10	11	12	13	14	15	16	17	18	In		Totals
BLUE	567	158	490	420	354	376	201	411	487	3464	BLUE	6377
WHITE	557	149	481	400	335	349	175	401	457	3304	WHITE	6113
Par	5	5	5	4	4	4	3	4	5	37	Par	72
Handicap	2	18	8	10	14	6	16	12	4			
RED	500	126	423	340	240	332	138	247	431	2777	RED	5056
Par	5	5	5	4	4	4	3	4	5	37	Par	72
Handicap	2	18	8	10	14	6	16	12	4			

Manager/Pro: Scott Kompo   **Supt:** Mike Farino
Architect: Horace Smith 1970

INDIAN SPRING GOLF CLUB

115 S.Elmwood Rd., Marlton, NJ 08053   **(856) 983-0222**
www.evesham-nj.gov

Indian Spring is an 18 hole municipal course open 7 days a week all year. Memberships are available with reduced rates for Evesham Township residents. Tee times may be made 6 days in advance.

•**Driving Range**	•**Lockers**
•**Practice Green**	•**Showers**
•**Power Carts**	•**Food**
•**Pull Carts**	
Club Rental	•**Clubhouse**
•**Soft Spikes**	•**Outings**

Fees	Weekday	Weekend
Daily	$30	$35
Twi	$25	$30
Sr	$29/cart	
Power carts	$14/pp	

Course Description: Originally farmland, Indian Spring is relatively flat, walkable and quite busy. Creeks and ponds come into play on on a few holes. The long par 5 fifth hole has an approach shot over water or the more prudent lay up as an alternative to arrive at the large undulating green. The scorecard is helpful with yardages provided to the center of the green from strategic locations on the fairways. There is a driving range nearby. A beautiful clubhouse providing catering and a pro shop have recently been completed.

Directions: Burlington County, #11 on Southwest Map
NJTPKE to Exit #4. Take Rte. 73 South to Rte. 70 East (Olga's Diner). When Rte. 70 becomes 2 lanes from 4, at next set of lights, turn right onto Elmwood Rd. Club is 1/4 mile ahead.

Hole	1	2	3	4	5	6	7	8	9	Out	BLUE	Rating 68.9
BLUE	404	406	355	294	500	143	442	224	374	3142		Slope 113
WHITE	387	388	338	281	482	119	420	205	357	2977		
Par	4	4	4	4	5	3	4	3	4	35	WHITE	Rating 67.8
Handicap	7	5	9	13	1	17	3	11	15			Slope 111
RED	370	370	321	268	456	105	398	185	340	2813		
Par	4	4	4	4	5	3	4	3	4	35	RED	Rating 70.8
Handicap	7	5	9	13	1	17	3	11	15			Slope 116
Hole	10	11	12	13	14	15	16	17	18	In		Totals
BLUE	404	379	368	152	423	414	194	351	549	3234	BLUE	6409
WHITE	379	368	348	130	405	390	174	333	514	3041	WHITE	6047
Par	4	4	4	3	4	4	3	4	5	35	Par	70
Handicap	4	10	12	18	2	6	16	14	8			
RED	355	357	327	108	349	366	154	315	440	2771	RED	5590
Par	4	4	4	3	4	4	3	4	5	35	Par	70
Handicap	4	10	12	18	2	6	16	14	8			

Manager/Pro: Bill Torlucci, PGA   **Supt:** Tom Arlotta
Architects: Burt Jaggard 1960s   **Redesign:** Ron Forsch 1998

KRESSON GOLF COURSE

PUBLIC

298 Kresson-Gibbsboro Rd., Voorhees, NJ 08043   **(856) 435-3355**

Kresson is an 18 hole course open 7 days a week, all year. Tee time reservations are not necessary.

Driving Range	Lockers
•**Practice Green**	Showers
•**Power Carts**	•**Food**
•**Pull Carts**	Clubhouse
•**Club Rental**	Outings
Soft Spikes	

Fees	Weekday	Weekend
Daily	$23	$27
Twi(after 3)	$15	$15
Sr	$19	
Power carts	$24	

Course Description: The well maintained Kresson is a relatively flat, scenic public course good for beginners and those wanting to practice iron shots. The greens have some bunkering and are relatively slow. Four ponds bring water into play on five holes. The front nine is longer than the back on this par 68 short scenic course.

Directions: Camden County, #12 on Southwest Map
Rte. 295 to the Haddonfield Exit #32. Then take Rte. 561 South (Haddonfield-Berlin Rd.) for 10 miles & turn left on Kresson-Gibbsboro Rd. Golf course is on the right.

Hole	1	2	3	4	5	6	7	8	9	Out	BLUE	Rating
BLUE												Slope
WHITE	253	300	480	105	122	210	500	250	485	2705		
Par	4	4	5	3	3	3	5	4	5	36	WHITE	Rating
Handicap												Slope
RED												
Par	4	4	5	3	3	4	5	4	5	37	RED	Rating
Handicap												Slope
Hole	10	11	12	13	14	15	16	17	18	In		Totals
BLUE											BLUE	
WHITE	120	260	360	175	160	220	340	160	300	2095	WHITE	4800
Par	3	4	4	3	3	4	4	3	4	32	Par	68
Handicap												
RED											RED	4800
Par	3	4	4	4	3	4	4	3	4	33	Par	70
Handicap												

Manager/Supt: John Aducat   **Built:** 1960s

LAUREL CREEK COUNTRY CLUB   PRIVATE

701 Moorestown-Centerton Rd., Mt. Laurel, NJ 08054   **(856) 778-1342**
www.laurelcreek.org

Laurel Creek is an 18 hole course open all year 6 days a week.   Guests may play accompanied by a member. Tee time reservations are not required.

•**Driving Range**	•**Lockers**
•**Practice Green**	•**Showers**
•**Power Carts**	•**Food**
Pull Carts	•**Clubhouse**
Club Rental	•**Outings**
Caddies	•**Soft Spikes**

Course Description: The excellently maintained Laurel Creek is considered a haven for the golf purist; it is Irish links type with tees, fairways and greens of bent grass. The course abounds with high fescue grass in the secondary roughs. There are 14 man-made lakes, many unique, special holes and five sets of tees. Laurel Creek is dotted with bunkers that can trap the unwary golfer. This layout was carved out of a defunct clay mining operation, a farm and orchards. Great care was taken not to disturb the wetlands. From the tips, the course measures close to 7,000 yards. The Mid-Amateur Invitational and the Patterson Cup are held here..

Directions: Burlington County, #13 on Southwest Map
NJTPKE to Exit #5 and turn left. Go 2 miles to Rte. 295 South to Exit #43B, Delran-Rancocas Woods (Exit 43 from South). Bear right on exit ramp to Delran. At first light, turn left to Centerton Rd. Club is 1/2 mile up ahead.

Hole	1	2	3	4	5	6	7	8	9	Out	BLUE	Rating 71.9
BLUE	417	376	166	405	514	451	215	365	555	3232		Slope 143
WHITE	390	349	135	355	482	357	168	311	495	3042		
Par	4	4	3	4	5	4	3	4	5	36	WHITE	Rating 70.4
Handicap	6	16	18	14	4	2	12	8	10			Slope 132
RED	371	244	119	331	437	342	142	283	452	2721		
Par	4	4	3	4	5	4	3	4	5	36	RED	Rating 72.5
Handicap	2	18	16	12	4	8	14	10	6			Slope 130

Hole	10	11	12	13	14	15	16	17	18	In		Totals
BLUE	409	405	459	384	169	520	435	227	445	3353	BLUE	6564
WHITE	398	342	420	360	146	466	405	196	407	3140	WHITE	6180
Par	4	4	4	4	3	5	4	3	4	35	Par	71
Handicap	7	11	5	13	17	15	3	9	1			
RED	398	329	357	336	138	444	358	135	376	2871	RED	5551
Par	5	4	4	4	3	5	4	3	4	36	Par	72
Handicap	13	11	3	5	15	17	7	9	1			

Manager: Ron Dunn   **Pro:** John Tyrell, PGA   **Supt:** John Slade
Architect: Arnold Palmer 1990

LINKS GOLF CLUB

100 Majestic Way, Marlton, NJ 08053   (856) 983-2000

Links is an 18 hole private course open 7 days a week all year. Guests may play accompanied by a member. Tee time reservations are not required.

•**Driving Range**	•**Lockers**
•**Practice Green**	•**Showers**
•**Power Carts**	•**Food**
Pull Carts	•**Clubhouse**
Club Rental	Outings
•**Caddies**	Soft Spikes

Course Description: Beautiful homes surround this golf course designed strictly for the dedicated golfer; it is not a typical country club. Most of its members come from Cherry Hill and Philadelphia and only a few from the development of 5000 homes. The layout is in a links style, particularly obvious on the back nine. The well groomed and narrow fairways make the golfer think about placement strategy on the way to the small greens. New tee boxes have been installed and the yardages have been increased to make 2 additional par 5s. Driving areas are contoured and give way to lots of bunkers making this course one that demands accuracy and patience.

Directions: Burlington County, #14 on Southwest Map
NJTPKE to Exit #4. Take Rte. 73 South to Marlton Pkwy. and turn left. Follow to Crown Royal Pkwy. and turn right. Go 7/10 mile on left to Majestic Way and entrance.

Hole	1	2	3	4	5	6	7	8	9	Out	BLACK	Rating 71.3
BLACK	320	334	377	203	343	440	450	325	400	2892		Slope 135
GREEN	310	323	359	187	329	422	126	309	380	2745		
Par	4	4	4	3	4	4	3	4	4	34	GREEN	Rating 69.9
Handicap	15	9	5	11	7	1	17	13	3			Slope 131
WHITE	294	312	300	174	316	364	110	296	355	2521		
Par	4	4	4	3	4	4	3	4	4	34	WHITE	Rating 71.2
Handicap	15	9	5	11	7	1	17	13	3			Slope 121
Hole	10	11	12	13	14	15	16	17	18	In		Totals
BLACK	382	350	489	524	178	428	430	158	392	3331	BLACK	6577
GREEN	366	337	469	509	158	417	415	144	376	3191	GREEN	6247
Par	4	4	5	5	3	4	4	3	4	36	Par	72
Handicap	10	8	14	12	16	2	4	18	6			
WHITE	296	307	426	457	126	364	384	135	341	2836	WHITE	5448
Par	4	4	5	5	3	4	4	3	4	36	Par	72
Handicap	10	8	14	12	16	2	4	18	6			

Dir. of Golf: David Quinn,PGA   **Pro:** James Shukdinas,PGA
Supt: James Acheson   **Architect:** Frederick Hawtree 1971

LITTLE MILL COUNTRY CLUB PRIVATE

104 Borton's Rd., Marlton, NJ 08053 (856) 767-0559
www.littlemillcc.com

Little Mill is a 27 hole course open 6 days a week all year. Guests play accompanied by a member. Tee time reservations are required on weekends and holidays in season.

- •Driving Range
- •Practice Green
- •Power Carts
- •Pull Carts
- •Club Rental
- Caddies
- •Lockers
- •Showers
- •Food
- •Clubhouse
- •Outings
- •Soft Spikes

Course Description: An abundance of trees can be found at Little Mill, a course cut out of a forest. The fairways are tree lined and relatively wide. There are 3 nines, Devil's Glen, Stoney Mt. and Little Mill; varying the combinations adds interest for members. Water comes into play on every nine. The signature par 3 eighth on the Stoney Mt. Blue nine, offers the highest elevation in Burlington County, 118 feet above sea level. On clear days, the amazing view goes as far as Philadelphia to the west and Atlantic City to the east. The scorecard below is for Little Mill and Stoney Mt. Power carts are required on weekends.

Directions: Burlington County, #15 on Southwest Map
NJTPKE to Exit #4. Take Rte. 73 South toward Atlantic City. Go left on Marlton Pkwy. to Hopewell Rd. and take it for 2 miles to club on right.

Hole	1	2	3	4	5	6	7	8	9	Out	BLUE	Rating 73.2
BLUE	307	164	436	510	456	419	564	218	411	3485		Slope 135
WHITE	287	148	410	490	440	399	542	198	385	3299		
Par	4	3	4	5	4	4	5	3	4	36	WHITE	Rating 71.2
Handicap	8	9	5	4	1	3	2	7	6			Slope 131
RED	242	117	312	390	334	344	415	145	313	2612		
Par	4	3	4	5	4	4	5	3	4	36	RED	Rating 66.2
Handicap	7	9	6	4	1	3	2	8	5			Slope 131
Hole	10	11	12	13	14	15	16	17	18	In		Totals
BLUE	514	377	383	391	161	514	372	159	419	3290	BLUE	6840
WHITE	494	364	371	378	141	502	360	143	400	3153	WHITE	6452
Par	5	4	4	4	3	5	4	3	4	36	Par	72
Handicap	2	7	6	5	9	1	4	8	3			
RED	429	329	317	325	124	416	306	143	419	2802	RED	5438
Par	5	4	4	4	3	5	4	3	5	36	Par	72
Handicap	2	6	7	4	8	1	3	9	5			

Manager: Peter Lange   **Pro:** George Frake 2nd, PGA   **Supt:** Ray Pasold
Architect: Garrett Wren 1967

MAPLE RIDGE GOLF CLUB

PUBLIC

1705 Glassboro Road, Sewell, NJ 08080   **(856) 468-3542**
www.championshipgolfmanagement.com

Maple Ridge is an 18 hole course open 7 days a week all year. Memberships are available. Tee time reservations: members 10 days, non-members 7 days.

•**Driving Range**   Lockers
•**Practice Green**   Showers
•**Power Carts**
•**Pull Carts**   •**Food**
•**Club Rental**   •**Clubhouse**
•**Soft Spikes**   •**Outings**

Fees	Weekday	Weekend
Daily	$28	$38
Twi(2PM)	$23	$28
Power carts included		

Course Description: Tough, challenging and well maintained, Maple Ridge (formerly Eagle's Nest) is relatively flat on the front nine but very hilly, tree lined and narrow on the back offering many uneven lies. The par 3 16th is the signature hole requiring a tee shot over a big pond that features a little waterfall; its green is large and sloping. A creek meanders through the course making it interesting for golfers on the par 5s, #7 and #15.

Directions: Gloucester County, #16 on Southwest Map
Rte. 55S (accessible from the Atlantic City Xway or NJTPKE Exit #3) to Exit 53B. Take Rte. 553 for 1 & 1/2 miles; course is on the left.

Hole	1	2	3	4	5	6	7	8	9	Out	BLUE	Rating 71.3
BLUE	351	324	211	378	353	360	503	140	557	3177		Slope 130
WHITE	343	311	199	361	343	354	485	130	544	3070		
Par	4	4	3	4	4	4	5	3	5	36	WHITE	Rating 70.0
Handicap	11	16	15	13	12	8	2	18	3			Slope 128
RED	341	299	167	345	333	222	445	120	414	2686		
Par	4	4	3	4	4	4	5	3	5	36	RED	Rating 71.2
Handicap	9	13	7	5	11	17	3	15	1			Slope 125
Hole	10	11	12	13	14	15	16	17	18	In		Totals
BLUE	391	211	401	408	424	494	172	497	205	3203	BLUE	6380
WHITE	366	170	385	395	408	484	117	471	192	2988	WHITE	6058
Par	4	3	4	4	4	5	3	5	3	35	Par	71
Handicap	7	10	5	1	4	6	17	9	14			
RED	333	142	372	382	293	328	102	393	179	2524	RED	5210
Par	4	3	4	4	4	5	3	5	3	35	Par	71
Handicap	8	12	2	4	16	6	18	10	14			

Owners: Championship Golf Mgmt   **Pro:** Kevin Martino   **Supt:** Darren Watofski
Architects: William & David Gordon 1964

MEDFORD LAKES COUNTRY CLUB

P.O.Box 600 Oak Dr., Medford Lakes, NJ 08055   (609) 654-5109

Medford Lakes is an 18 hole private course open 6 days a week all year. Guests may play accompanied by a member. Tee time reservations are not necessary.

•**Driving Range**	•**Lockers**
•**Practice Green**	•**Showers**
•**Power Carts**	•**Food**
•**Pull Carts**	•**Clubhouse**
Club Rental	•**Outings**
Caddies	•**Soft Spikes**

Course Description: Narrow wooded fairways are prevalent at Medford Lakes, a short tight course with bent grass greens. The front nine has two holes over water, while the back nine is surrounded by an abundance of water. The par 4 second is considered the signature hole, beautiful yet difficult requiring a carry over a large lake.

Directions: Burlington County, #17 on Southwest Map
NJTPKE to Exit #4 to Rte. 73 South to Rte. 70 East to Rte. 541South (Stokes Rd.) Go 3 miles to Settler's Inn & make a left on Tabernacle to course.

Hole	1	2	3	4	5	6	7	8	9	Out	BLUE	Rating
BLUE												Slope
WHITE	341	362	392	322	330	159	267	307	488	2968		
Par	4	4	4	4	4	3	4	4	5	36	WHITE	Rating 69.8
Handicap	11	1	3	9	5	15	17	13	7			Slope 121
RED	330	339	370	299	322	129	219	295	466	2769		
Par	4	4	4	4	4	3	4	4	5	36	RED	Rating 73.3
Handicap	11	1	3	9	7	15	17	13	5			Slope 125

Hole	10	11	12	13	14	15	16	17	18	In		Totals
BLUE											BLUE	
WHITE	305	162	361	316	497	416	163	403	512	3135	WHITE	6103
Par	4	3	4	4	5	5	3	4	5	36	Par	72
Handicap	12	18	4	14	8	2	16	6	10			
RED	297	141	344	302	482	403	148	382	498	2997	RED	5766
Par	4	3	4	4	5	4	3	4	5	37	Par	73
Handicap	14	18	8	12	2	10	16	4	6			

Manager/Pro: Dan Haskell, PGA   **Supt:** Gregg Armbruster
Architects: William Findlay (1st nine) 1929   Hal Purdy (back nine)

MEDFORD VILLAGE COUNTRY CLUB `PRIVATE`

Golf View Drive, Medford, NJ 08055　　　　　　**(609) 654-8211**
www.medfordvillage.com

Medford Village is an 18 hole private golf course open all year, 6 days a week. Guests may play accompanied by a member. Tee time reservations are not necessary.

- •Driving Range
- •Practice Green
- •Power Carts
- Pull Carts
- Club Rental
- Caddies
- •Lockers
- •Showers
- •Food
- •Clubhouse
- •Outings
- •Soft Spikes

Course Description: Designed with Pine Valley as an inspiration, Medford Village is heavily wooded; pine and oak trees encroach on the fairways. A long course (7100 yds. from the blues), the fairways are tighter on the back nine and more open on the front. Constructed on property known as Sunny Jim's Farm, it originally was called Sunny Jim GC. The course is laid out so that no one can be hit by a stray shot from another hole. The #1 handicap from the back tees is the first with water in play off the tee and again near the green. This club has hosted the South Jersey Open and other professional events.

Directions: Burlington County, #18 on Southwest Map
NJTPKE South to Exit #15. Turn right onto Rte. 541 S through Mt. Holly and Medford Circle (Rte.70.) Approx. 1mile after circle, go right onto Himmelein Rd. Then take the 2nd left onto Golf View Dr. Club is at end of street.

Hole	1	2	3	4	5	6	7	8	9	Out	BLUE	Rating 71.8
BLUE	420	415	536	230	545	166	380	375	440	3507		Slope 135
WHITE	402	411	490	205	485	150	360	350	408	3261		
Par	4	4	5	3	5	3	4	4	4	36	WHITE	Rating 70.2
Handicap	1	3	11	13	15	17	9	7	5			Slope 131
RED	320	335	342	140	412	96	305	285	367	2602		
Par	4	4	5	3	5	3	4	4	4	36	RED	Rating 70.4
Handicap	5	7	13	15	1	17	11	9	3			Slope 124
Hole	10	11	12	13	14	15	16	17	18	In		Totals
BLUE	590	215	415	400	550	385	213	385	440	3593	BLUE	7100
WHITE	520	163	397	340	510	362	200	355	395	3242	WHITE	6503
Par	5	3	4	4	5	4	3	4	3	36	Par	72
Handicap	6	18	4	2	12	10	14	16	8			
RED	473	130	301	272	413	302	130	304	305	2630	RED	5232
Par	5	3	4	4	5	4	3	4	3	36	Par	72
Handicap	2	18	6	8	4	12	16	14	10			

Pro: Leo De Gisi, PGA　　　　　　**Supt:** Bruce Rickert
Architect: William Gordon 1963

MERCHANTVILLE CC

501 Chapel Ave. West, Cherry Hill, NJ 08002   **(856) 662-7835**

Merchantville is a 9 hole private course open 6 days a week all year. Guests may play accompanied by a member. Reserved tee times are not necessary.

Driving Range	•**Lockers**
•**Practice Green**	•**Showers**
•**Power Carts**	•**Food**
•**Pull Carts**	•**Clubhouse**
•**Club Rental**	•**Outings**
Caddies	•**Soft Spikes**

Course Description: Built around an array of natural creeks, every hole has water at Merchantville CC, the fifth oldest club in the US. It is relatively flat and there is an interplay of crossovers to make the course interesting from a different perspective. The contoured fairways have plenty of rough increasing the difficulty. The club pro here in the early nineteen hundreds, John McDermott, became the first American born golf professional to win the US Open, accomplishing this feat in 1910 and again in 1912. The new clubhouse, opened in 2004, has a panoramic view from the back of Philadelphia in the distance. The rating and slope from the forward tees will be changed in 2005.

Directions: Camden County, #19 on Southwest Map
NJTPKE to Exit #4. Then take Rte. 73 North to Rte. 38 West. At Chapel Ave. make a right; club is on left.

Hole	1	2	3	4	5	6	7	8	9	Out	BLUE	Rating 71.6
BLUE	505	589	145	323	335	202	289	375	400	3163		Slope 138
WHITE	485	568	130	298	325	190	270	345	393	3004		
Par	5	5	3	4	4	3	4	4	4	36	WHITE	Rating 70.7
Handicap	7	4	9	6	1	2	8	5	3			Slope 135
RED	342	458	112	304	433	348	137	366	334	2834		
Par	4	5	3	4	5	4	3	4	4	36	RED	Rating 71.5
Handicap	7	1	9	6	2	5	8	4	3			Slope 129
Hole	10	11	12	13	14	15	16	17	18	In		Totals
BLUE											BLUE	6231
WHITE											WHITE	6050
Par											Par	72
Handicap												
RED											RED	5342
Par											Par	72
Handicap												

Dir. of Golf/Pro: Blaise S. Straka, PGA   **Supt:** Kent Rickenback
Built: 1892   **Architects:** Members

MOORESTOWN FIELD CLUB

629 Chester Ave., Moorestown, NJ 08057   **(856) 235-2326**

Moorestown is a 9 hole course open all year, 7 days a week; (closes Mondays in Dec., Jan., and Feb.) Guests play accompanied by a member. Tee time reservations are not necessary. There is a long waiting list for membership.

•**Driving Range**	•**Lockers**
•**Practice Green**	•**Showers**
•**Power Carts**	•**Food**
•**Pull Carts**	•**Clubhouse**
•**Club Rental**	Outings
Caddies	•**Soft Spikes**

Course Description: The Field Club is an old style course; short, flat, straight and narrow with small well bunkered greens. The signature hole is the par 3 eighth; its green is virtually in the woods and is reached by hitting over a ditch. Different tees are used for the front and back nines to give variety. The engineers from Flexible Flyers (the well known sled company) built the original nine holes in 1910.

Directions: Burlington County, #20 on Southwest Map
NJTPKE to Exit 4. Then take Rte. 73 North to Kings Highway (Rte. 41) towards Moorestown where it becomes Main St. Make a left on Chester Ave. Club is 6 blocks up on the right.

Hole	1	2	3	4	5	6	7	8	9	Out	BLUE	Rating
BLUE												Slope
WHITE	313	311	323	148	457	412	510	143	360	2977		
Par	4	4	4	3	5	4	5	3	4	36	WHITE	Rating 68.9
Handicap	13	11	9	15	7	1	3	17	5			Slope 126
RED	313	311	323	148	457	412	510	143	360	2977		
Par	4	4	4	3	5	5	5	3	4	37	RED	Rating 74.1
Handicap	13	11	7	15	5	9	1	17	3			Slope 125
Hole	10	11	12	13	14	15	16	17	18	In		Totals
BLUE											BLUE	
WHITE											WHITE	6013
Par											Par	72
Handicap												
RED											RED	5851
Par											Par	73
Handicap												

Manager/Supt: John Carpinelli   **Pro:** Butch Schmehl, PGA
Established: 1892

OLDE YORK COUNTRY CLUB

228 Old York Rd., Columbus, NJ 08022   **(609) 298-0212**
www.oldeyork.com

Olde York is an 18 hole course open 6 days a week and closed in January. Guests may play accompanied by a member. Reserved tee times are recommended.

•Driving Range	•Lockers
•Practice Green	•Showers
•Power Carts	•Food
•Pull Carts	•Clubhouse
•Club Rental	•Outings
•Caddies	•Soft Spikes

Course Description: There are no less than 5 tees to a maximum of 9 tees at Olde York CC, which plays to a total of 6903 yards from the Blues. This accomodates golfers of varying proficiency and minimizes traffic. The course is heavily wooded with spectacular tee chutes; 5 of the holes are completely enclosed by woods. The fairways, tees & greens are bent grass; Kentucky Blue grass surrounds the 146 bunkers. Colorful fescue and native ornamental grass flank the out of play area. Stacked sod bunkers add to the traditional Scottish look. Designed by Gary Player, who considers this his signature course, it is world championship caliber. Golfers will notice the influence of Olde York's prior life as a stud farm by the attractive reminders of early history retained in the decorative setting.

Directions: Burlington County, #21 on Southwest Map
NJTPKE to Exit #7. Take Rte 206 S; after NJTPKE overpass, make 2nd U turn to Rte. 206 North. Take Old York Rd. on right. Go 3/4 mile to course on left.

Hole	1	2	3	4	5	6	7	8	9	Out	BLUE	Rating 71.2
BLUE	442	232	522	470	206	361	527	192	354	3306		Slope 132
WHITE	390	186	487	423	153	314	476	145	315	2889		
Par	4	3	5	4	3	4	5	3	4	35	WHITE	Rating 68.9
Handicap	3	13	9	1	5	15	7	17	11			Slope 125
RED	378	159	463	414	111	285	453	121	286	2670		
Par	4	3	5	5	3	4	5	3	4	36	RED	Rating 68.5
Handicap	3	13	9	1	5	15	7	17	11			Slope 122

Hole	10	11	12	13	14	15	16	17	18	In		Totals
BLUE	378	198	380	555	462	200	581	454	389	3597	BLUE	6903
WHITE	335	168	310	516	404	146	515	392	342	3128	WHITE	6017
Par	4	3	4	5	4	3	5	4	4	36	Par	71
Handicap	14	16	12	10	4	18	2	6	8			
RED	294	139	280	500	375	130	486	344	299	2847	RED	5517
Par	4	3	4	5	4	3	5	4	4	36	Par	72
Handicap	14	16	12	6	10	18	2	4	8			

Owners/Managers: Corinne & Ed Eget **Pro:** Tony Perla, PGA **Supt:** Mark Stallone
Architect: Gary Player 1994 (Orig. Estab. 1950)

PENNSAUKEN COUNTRY CLUB `SEMI-PRIVATE`

3800 Haddonfield Rd., Pennsauken, NJ 08109   **(856) 662-4961**
www.twp.pennsauken.nj.us

Pennsauken is an 18 hole semi-private township owned course open 7 days a week, all year. Memberships available for residents. Tee times: 1 week in advance. Carts are mandatory Fri - Sun.

Driving Range	• Lockers
• Practice Green	• Showers
• Power Carts	• Food
• Pull Carts	• Clubhouse
• Club Rental	• Outings
• Soft Spikes	

Fees	Weekday	Weekend
Resident	$31	$31
Non-res	$36	$36
Sr/Twi	$26/24	$26/24
Power carts	$16pp	

Course Description: Excellently maintained and highly rated in Southern NJ, Pennsauken has benefitted from its renovations, including rebuilt tees and improved fairway contouring. A tunnel was constructed to avoid crossing over a road on the course. It is well bunkered with small bent grass greens; water is in play on nine holes. The front is open while the back is somewhat more difficult. The course has been lengthened recently. The signature par 3 seventh is long measuring 216 yards from the white tees.

Directions: Camden County, #22 on Southwest Map
NJTPKE to Exit #4. Take Rte.73 North about 2 miles. Club is 1/4 mile past 3rd light. From Phila. Take Betsy Ross Bridge onto Rte. 90 East for 1 mile to Rte. 644S. Proceed 1 & 1/2 mi. to club on left.

Hole	1	2	3	4	5	6	7	8	9	Out	BLUE	Rating 68.1
BLUE	325	353	156	397	319	341	240	526	388	3045		Slope 119
WHITE	309	344	142	387	301	323	216	510	386	2918		
Par	4	4	3	4	4	4	3	5	4	35	WHITE	Rating 66.6
Handicap	15	10	13	2	14	12	4	8	6			Slope 117
RED	304	306	111	317	290	302	189	433	278	2530		
Par	4	4	3	4	4	4	3	5	4	35	RED	Rating 67.9
Handicap	13	8	14	1	15	10	3	9	5			Slope 111

Hole	10	11	12	13	14	15	16	17	18	In		Totals
BLUE	471	127	336	339	485	113	392	283	415	2961	BLUE	6005
WHITE	461	117	326	313	469	98	379	271	397	2831	WHITE	5663
Par	4	3	4	4	5	3	4	4	4	35	Par	70
Handicap	1	16	11	9	7	18	5	17	3			
RED	320	88	300	294	401	85	288	254	300	2330	RED	4966
Par	4	3	4	4	5	3	4	4	4	35	Par	70
Handicap	6	16	11	4	2	18	12	17	7			

Mgr: Robert Prickett   **Pro:** Quentin Griffith, PGA   **Supt:** David Hershey
Architect: Bob Prickett 1932

PINE HILL GOLF CLUB

500 W. Branch Ave., Pine Hill, NJ 08021   **(856) 435-3100**
www.golfpinehill.com

Pine Hill is a new 18 hole semi-private course open 7 days a week all year. Memberships are available. Tee times for members 14 days, 7 days for the public. GPS on the power carts. Pine Hill may be going private in the near future.

•**Driving Range**	•**Lockers**
•**Practice Green**	•**Showers**
•**Power Carts**	•**Food**
Pull Carts	•**Clubhouse**
•**Club Rental**	•**Outings**
•**Soft Spikes**	

Fees	Weekday	Weekend
Daily	$100	$100
Some discounts available		
Power carts included		

Course Description: Destined to be a lengendary course, Pine Hill inspires comments like awesome, spectacular and fabulous. Built mostly on the property of the former Ski Mtn, the unusual elevations are the highest in South Jersey. Views of Phila. can be seen from #s 3, 13 & 18. Tom Fazio, the architect, utilized exquisite environmental sensitivity in preserving wetlands, natural trees and contours as well as a federally protected trout stream in creating 80 acres of fairways and greens. Offering 5 sets of tees and thus playable by all levels of golfers, the intimidating carries over barranca, the elevated greens, the sedge bordered bunkers and its beauty all combine to make this close to 7,000 yard course a truly exciting challenge.

Directions: Camden County, #23 on Southwest Map
NJTPKE to Exit 3. Follow signs to Rte. 168 South & go for 4.1 m. to Church St., turn left (road becomes Blackwood-Clementon Rd.) for 3.2 miles and then turn right on Branch Ave. Pass Mountain View Village & turn right to club.

Hole	1	2	3	4	5	6	7	8	9	Out	BLUE	Rating 74.2
BLUE	520	174	467	437	210	410	577	205	448	3448		Slope 144
WHITE	480	150	416	395	171	370	546	170	397	3095		
Par	5	3	4	4	3	4	5	3	4	35	WHITE	Rating 71.0
Handicap	7	11	9	17	1	13	5	3	15			Slope 136
RED	389	107	331	326	105	315	387	95	292	2347		
Par	5	3	4	4	3	4	5	3	4	35	RED	Rating 68.3
Handicap	7	11	9	17	1	13	5	3	15			Slope 121
Hole	10	11	12	13	14	15	16	17	18	In		Totals
BLUE	477	408	399	170	534	471	203	453	406	3521	BLUE	6969
WHITE	430	369	375	145	477	409	155	422	371	3153	WHITE	6248
Par	4	4	4	3	5	4	3	4	4	35	Par	70
Handicap	10	12	16	18	4	14	8	2	6			
RED	360	332	289	93	390	341	122	338	310	2575	RED	4922
Par	4	4	4	3	5	4	3	4	4	35	Par	70
Handicap	10	12	16	18	4	14	8	2	6			

Manager: Eric J. Quinn   **Pro:** Matt Wentzel   **Supt:** Kevin Reis
Architect: Tom Fazio 2000

PINELANDS GOLF CLUB

PUBLIC

887 S. Mays Landing Rd., Winslow, NJ 08037   **(609) 561-8900**
www.allforeclub.com

Pinelands is an 18 hole public course located halfway between Atlantic City and Philadelphia. It is open 7 days a week all year. Memberships are available. Tee times may be made 7 days in advance. Carts mandatory on weekends in season.

•Driving Range	•Lockers
•Practice Green	•Showers
•Power Carts	•Food
•Pull Carts	•Clubhouse
•Club Rental	•Outings
Soft Spikes	

Fees	Weekday	Weekend
Daily	$25-$29	$39
Fri	$35	
Power carts included		

Course Description: Pinelands is a pretty course with tight tree lined fairways and small well maintained greens. The signature par 5 sixth hole, 581 yards from the blues, requires an approach shot over water to a two tiered green. The par 3 sixteenth is fashioned after a hole at Augusta and features landscaping of beautiful dogwoods and azaleas. The par 3s require great accuracy as the greens offer limited targets. The first hole has been lengthened to a par 5 and is a double dogleg right 525 from the tips.

Directions: Camden County, #24 on Southwest Map
GSP or NJTPKE to Atlantic City Xpressway to Exit #28 (Hammonton.) Take Rte. 54 South. Make a right at 1st light onto Mays Landing Rd. (Rte. 561 spur.) Course is 4 miles on left.

Hole	1	2	3	4	5	6	7	8	9	Out	BLUE	Rating 70.6
BLUE	525	180	351	485	187	581	157	353	472	3152		Slope 123
WHITE	490	163	338	475	178	573	142	344	465	3056		
Par	5	3	4	5	3	5	3	4	5	36	WHITE	Rating 69.5
Handicap	3	13	9	17	11	1	15	5	7			Slope 120
RED	420	155	320	450	158	473	133	340	457	2837		
Par	5	3	4	5	3	5	3	4	5	36	RED	Rating 69.9
Handicap	3	17	11	7	13	1	15	5	9			Slope 119
Hole	10	11	12	13	14	15	16	17	18	In		Totals
BLUE	323	183	360	368	507	347	170	456	403	3117	BLUE	6360
WHITE	313	178	349	358	493	336	163	448	394	3032	WHITE	6140
Par	4	3	4	4	5	4	3	5	4	36	Par	72
Handicap	14	12	4	2	10	8	16	18	6			
RED	275	142	311	296	423	309	131	410	311	2608	RED	5445
Par	4	3	4	4	5	4	3	5	4	36	Par	72
Handicap	14	16	6	4	2	12	18	10	8			

Mgr/Pro: Bob Cimino, PGA   **Supt:** Pete Pino
Architects: Brimfield Bros., Ralph Lespardi 1962

PINE VALLEY GOLF CLUB

Atlantic Ave., Pine Valley, NJ 08021   (856) 783-3000

Pine Valley is an 18 hole course open 6 days a week all year. Guests may play accompanied by a member. Tee time reservations are required.

•**Driving Range**	•**Lockers**
•**Practice Green**	•**Showers**
•**Power Carts**	•**Food**
Pull Carts	•**Clubhouse**
Club Rental	Outings
•**Caddies**	•**Soft Spikes**

Course Description: Chosen #1 in the world by Golf Digest year after year, Pine Valley deserves all its accolades. George Crump conceived the idea of this unique and tremendously difficult golf course. It is considered the ultimate in target golf as all the fairways and greens are surrounded by the sand & scrub characteristic of the NJ Pine Barrens. This irregular rough severely penalizes a wayward shot and makes intelligent, strategic club selection critical. The par 3 fifth, 226 yards over water, known as the hole "where only God can make a 3" has a heavily contoured plateau green with many bunkers. The par 3 tenth is rated the easiest on the scorecard, (more like the hardest at other courses) with a gaping right bunker luring the tee shot into trouble.

Directions: Camden County, #25 on Southwest Map
NJTPKE to Exit #4. Take Rte. 73 S past marker 19. At Franklin Ave. make a right; go to 3rd light. Go right onto Blackwood-Clementon Rd. & follow to amusement park. Make 1st left after park to E. Atlantic Ave. to front gate of club.

Hole	1	2	3	4	5	6	7	8	9	Out	BLUE	Rating 74.2
BLUE	427	367	181	444	232	388	578	319	427	3363		Slope 154
WHITE	416	357	169	433	221	369	544	309	411	3229		
Par	4	4	3	4	3	4	5	4	4	35	WHITE	Rating 72,4
Handicap	3	9	17	5	11	13	1	15	7			Slope 151
RED												
Par											RED	Rating
Handicap												Slope
Hole	10	11	12	13	14	15	16	17	18	In		Totals
BLUE	146	392	344	448	184	591	433	338	428	3304	BLUE	6667
WHITE	137	379	340	445	168	570	423	335	410	3207	WHITE	6436
Par	3	4	5	4	3	5	4	4	4	35	Par	70
Handicap	18	10	14	4	16	2	8	12	6			
RED											RED	
Par											Par	
Handicap												

Manager/Pro: Charles Raudenbush, PGA   **Supt:** Rick Christian
Architects: George Crump & H.S. Colt 1914

PITMAN GOLF CLUB

501 Pitman Rd., Sewell, NJ 08080   **(856) 589-6688**
www.co.gloucester.nj.us/golf

Pitman is an 18 hole course owned by Gloucester County and is open 7 days a week, all year. Tee time reservations may be made 1 week in advance for Fri to Sun and holidays. During the week no tee times are necessary.

•**Driving Range**	•**Lockers**
•**Practice Green**	•**Showers**
•**Power Carts**	•**Food**
•**Pull Carts**	•**Clubhouse**
Club Rental	Outings
•**Soft Spikes**	

Fees	Weekday	Weekend
Res w/ID	$19	$24
Sr w/ID	$13	$21
Non-res	$28	$34
Power carts	$15pp	Sr $10pp

Course Description: Appealing to all levels of golfers and very well maintained, Pitman is a scenic course that is convenient to Phila. and Camden. Relatively short, it has wide fairways and deep rough. The layout is constantly being upgraded with new bunkers and contour changes giving it more character. The signature par 4 429 yard eleventh, requires a well placed tee shot up a dogleg left fairway, then a shot over a ravine to an elevated green. Many consider this hole the most difficult although it is rated #2 handicap. Pitman now has a new clubhouse.

Directions: Gloucester County, #26 on Southwest Map
NJTPKE to Exit #3. Take Rte. 168 East (toward Atl. City) to Rte. 573 South and then a left onto Rte. 55 South to Exit 50B. Go to 1st light, turn right onto Lamb's Rd. for 1 mile to blinker & turn left. Course is 1/4 mile on right.

Hole	1	2	3	4	5	6	7	8	9	Out	BLUE	Rating 69.4
BLUE	329	346	528	204	296	382	422	138	383	3028		Slope 118
WHITE	302	328	497	186	268	356	398	122	373	2830		
Par	4	4	5	3	4	4	4	3	4	35	WHITE	Rating 67.4
Handicap	11	9	1	15	13	7	3	17	5			Slope 115
RED	263	268	425	143	222	317	335	103	349	2425		
Par	4	4	5	3	4	4	5	3	5	37	RED	Rating 68.7
Handicap	9	7	1	15	13	3	11	17	5			Slope 112
Hole	10	11	12	13	14	15	16	17	18	In		Totals
BLUE	386	429	338	421	129	432	415	158	389	3097	BLUE	6125
WHITE	328	408	321	404	110	409	388	128	368	2864	WHITE	5694
Par	4	4	4	4	3	5	4	3	4	35	Par	70
Handicap	12	2	14	4	18	10	6	16	8			
RED	310	336	300	359	95	377	348	98	294	2517	RED	4942
Par	4	4	4	5	3	5	4	3	4	36	Par	73
Handicap	12	2	6	10	16	4	8	18	14			

Manager/Pro: Orist Wells, PGA   **Supt:** Scott Hellerman
Architects: Alexander Findlay, James Chicwit 1926   **Renovation:** Brian Ault

RAMBLEWOOD COUNTRY CLUB

200 Country Club Pkwy., Mt. Laurel, NJ 08054   **(856) 235-2119**
www.ramblewoodcc.com

Ramblewood is a 27 hole semi-private course open 7 days a week all year. Memberships are available. Tee time reservations may be made up to 1 week in advance.

Driving Range	•**Lockers**
•**Practice Green**	•**Showers**
•**Power Carts**	•**Food**
•**Pull Carts**	•**Clubhouse**
•**Club Rental**	•**Outings**
•**Soft Spikes**	

Fees	Weekday	Weekend
Daily	$40	$48
Power carts	$15pp	$17pp

Description: Built on 220 lush acres with three distinct nines, Ramblewood is a public facility with a private style. The Blue course, where trees abound, is considered the most challenging although the shortest. The 418 yard par 4 eighth on the Red nine is a difficult hole requiring a shot over a creek to a green on a hill with hazards on right and left. It has been known to cause more than a few broken clubs over the years. The fairly large sized greens, flanked by well positioned bunkers, have been rated as the best in South Jersey. The scorecard below is for Red/White.

Directions: Burlington County, #27 on Southwest Map
NJTPKE to Exit #4 to Rte. 73 South or Rte. 295 to Mt. Laurel Exit (36A) to Rte. 73 S. Immediately after the intersection (Ramblewood Pkwy.) turn left onto Church Rd. for 1/2 mile to Country Club Pkwy. Turn left to club on left.

Hole	1	2	3	4	5	6	7	8	9	Out	BLUE	Rating 72.9
BLUE	380	367	549	485	250	490	391	418	161	3491		Slope 130
WHITE	375	354	526	457	176	464	382	409	144	3287		
Par	4	4	5	4	3	5	4	4	3	36	WHITE	Rating 71.3
Handicap	4	8	3	1	5	7	6	2	9			Slope 127
RED	352	345	439	439	122	415	369	354	131	2966		
Par	4	4	5	5	3	5	4	4	3	37	RED	Rating 72.7
Handicap	6	7	1	3	9	2	4	5	8			Slope 128
Hole	10	11	12	13	14	15	16	17	18	In		Totals
BLUE	390	384	200	513	400	210	537	386	372	3392	BLUE	6883
WHITE	384	353	168	503	385	196	502	365	355	3211	WHITE	6498
Par	4	4	3	5	4	3	5	4	4	36	Par	72
Handicap	3	9	7	2	1	8	6	5	4			
RED	279	323	132	457	374	152	423	292	343	2775	RED	5741
Par	4	4	3	5	5	3	5	4	4	37	Par	74
Handicap	3	6	8	1	4	9	2	7	5			

Mgr: John Goodwin   **Supt:** Trip Jones
Architect: Edmund Ault 1960

RANCOCAS GOLF CLUB

Clubhouse Drive, Willingboro, NJ 08046   **(609) 877-5344**
www.americangolf.com

Rancocas is an 18 hole semi-private course open to the public 7 days a week all year.
Memberships are available. Tee times: mbrs 8 days in advance, non-mbrs. 7 days.

- **Driving Range**
- **Practice Green**
- **Power Carts**
- **Pull Carts**
- **Club Rental**
- **Soft Spikes**

Lockers
Showers
- **Food**
- **Clubhouse**
- **Outings**

Fees	Weekday	Weekend
Daily	$46	$59
Power carts included		

Course Description: Formerly a private club and still maintained in that style,
Rancocas is considered one of the best public courses in NJ. With more than 100
bunkers throughout, the front is links style open to the wind while the back is more
wooded and tight. The par 4 320 yard 3rd hole is a dogleg left; the out of bounds on
the right requires a well placed tee shot to avoid going through the fairway. The fourth
is a long par 4 with an elevated green. On the back nine, water affects play on 4 holes.
The par 5 #13 is appropriately the #1 handicap needing accuracy off the tee; the
approach shot is to an undulating severely sloped green. Recently the bunkers and tee
boxes have been upgraded.

Directions: Burlington County, #28 on Southwest Map
Rte. 295 to Beverly Rancocas Rd. (Exit 45B). Go west through Willingboro, make left
onto Country Club Rd., then make the 2nd left onto Clubhouse Dr.

Hole	1	2	3	4	5	6	7	8	9	Out	BLUE	Rating 72.7
BLUE	585	192	355	420	380	390	202	348	523	3395		Slope 130
WHITE	549	156	320	396	346	350	167	316	485	3085		
Par	5	3	4	4	4	4	3	4	5	36	WHITE	Rating 70.0
Handicap	2	18	14	4	8	10	16	12	6			Slope 124
RED	251	113	306	260	489	147	447	221	339	2573		
Par	5	3	4	5	4	4	3	4	5	37	RED	Rating 66.6
Handicap	2	18	14	4	8	10	16	12	6			Slope 116

Hole	10	11	12	13	14	15	16	17	18	In		Totals
BLUE	406	165	330	568	402	396	400	165	402	3234	BLUE	6629
WHITE	365	126	301	522	368	381	374	145	373	2955	WHITE	6040
Par	4	3	4	5	4	4	4	3	4	35	Par	72
Handicap	11	17	13	1	5	9	3	15	7			
RED	334	57	254	409	284	368	344	120	345	2515	RED	5284
Par	4	3	4	5	4	4	4	3	4	35	Par	72
Handicap	11	17	13	1	9	7	3	15	5			

Manager: Andrew Derbyshire   **Supt:** Shawn Ross
Architect: Robert Trent Jones 1964

RIVERTON COUNTRY CLUB

Highland Ave., Riverton, NJ 08077   **(856) 829-5500**

Riverton is an 18 hole private course open 6 days a week all year. Guests may play accompanied by a member. Reserved tee times are not required.

•Driving Range	•Lockers
•Practice Green	•Showers
•Power Carts	•Food
• Pull Carts	•Clubhouse
•Club Rental	•Outings
•Caddies	•Soft Spikes

Course Description: Members of Riverton come predominantly from Moorestown and Cherry Hill although some are from other areas in New Jersey and Pa. as well. It is relatively busy with 375 memberships. Built by Donald Ross, the course offers a traditional layout with its multi-tiered well bunkered subtley breaking greens. Renovations were done a few years ago which improved the facility. Water affects play on four holes on the back nine. The 418 par 4 twelfth is the signature hole featuring a tee shot over water and a severely sloped green. The club has hosted Amateur tournaments recently.

Directions: Burlington County, #29 on Southwest Map
NJTPKE to Exit #4. Take Rte. 73 North (toward Phila.) to Rte. 130 and turn right. After Cinnaminson Mall make a left onto Highland Ave. to club on right.

Hole	1	2	3	4	5	6	7	8	9	Out	BLUE	Rating 71.5
BLUE	364	386	418	364	356	208	525	331	491	3444		Slope 129
WHITE	354	379	384	353	342	197	510	319	480	3318		
Par	4	4	4	4	4	3	5	4	5	37	WHITE	Rating 70.4
Handicap	13	7	1	17	5	11	3	15	9			Slope 126
RED	274	373	341	323	332	156	458	311	423	2991		
Par	4	4	4	4	4	3	5	4	5	37	RED	Rating 73.6
Handicap	15	9	5	13	3	17	1	11	7			Slope 130
Hole	10	11	12	13	14	15	16	17	18	In		Totals
BLUE	428	173	432	398	207	417	162	475	355	3047	BLUE	6491
WHITE	409	142	418	389	186	405	156	466	346	2917	WHITE	6235
Par	4	3	4	4	3	4	3	5	4	34	Par	71
Handicap	6	18	4	8	12	2	16	10	14			
RED	391	118	368	379	136	394	124	448	337	2695	RED	5686
Par	5	3	4	4	3	5	3	5	4	36	Par	73
Handicap	8	18	4	2	16	12	14	6	10			

Manager: Brad Scott   **Pro:** Fred Philipps, PGA   **Supt:** Doug Davis
Architect: Donald Ross 1900

RIVER WINDS GOLF CLUB

PUBLIC

River Winds Drive, W. Deptford Twp, NJ 08086

www.riverwindsgolf.com

(856) 848-1033

River Winds is an 18 hole course open to the public 7 days a week all year. Memberships are available. Tee times may be made up to 7 days in advance.

Driving Range
- **Practice Green**
- **Power Carts**
Pull Carts
- **Club Rental**
- **Soft Spikes**

- **Lockers**
- **Showers**
- **Food**
- **Clubhouse**
- **Outings**

NEW

Fees	M-Thurs	Weekend
Daily	$55	$69
Fri	$59	
Twi 3PM	$37	$37
Power carts included		

Course Description: The newest course in this region, River Winds, over 7,000 yards from the tips, sports a links style layout. Built with 5 holes along the Delaware River, the course offers spectacular views of Philadelphia in the distance. Players encounter sod faced fescue lined bunkers, large undulating greens and a variety of mounding. No 2 holes are alike. Wind can affect play as well. The signature par 3 17th features an island green; on #13, there is a double green. Golfers will not be frustrated with long waits as timely pace of play is encouraged here. This scenic course is part of the riverside redevelopment project that includes tennis courts, athletic fields and an impressive community center.

Directions: Salem County, #46 on Southwest Map
Take Route 295 South to Exit 21. Make a right at the end of the Exit ramp onto Crown Point Rd. At light, turn left onto Delaware Ave. Take that road to its end and the entrance to the complex.

Hole	1	2	3	4	5	6	7	8	9	Out	BLUE	Rating 72.3
BLUE	532	165	416	477	446	381	208	422	425	3472		Slope 132
WHITE	520	153	401	456	428	373	189	369	401	3290		
Par	5	3	4	5	4	4	3	4	4	36	WHITE	Rating 70.3
Handicap	8	14	12	18	2	16	10	6	4			Slope 128
RED	379	133	357	393	328	302	161	329	307	2689		
Par	5	3	4	5	4	4	3	4	4	36	RED	Rating 71.2
Handicap	8	14	12	18	2	16	10	6	4			Slope 123
Hole	10	11	12	13	14	15	16	17	18	In		Totals
BLUE	505	403	367	592	381	162	354	140	391	3295	BLUE	6767
WHITE	455	376	355	504	373	154	340	129	357	3043	WHITE	6333
Par	5	4	4	5	4	3	4	3	4	36	Par	72
Handicap	5	7	9	3	15	17	11	13	1			
RED	389	338	301	492	288	129	265	101	309	2612	RED	5301
Par	5	4	4	5	4	3	4	3	4	36	Par	72
Handicap	5	7	9	3	15	17	11	13	1			

Mgr: Nick Pileggi   **Dir. of Golf:** Dick Smith, PGA   **Pro:** Sean Driscoll, PGA
Architects: Pete Fazio, Ed Shearon 2002

RUNNING DEER CLUB

1111 Parvins Mill Rd., Pittsgrove, NJ 08318   **(856) 358-2000**
www.runningdeergolfclub.com

Running Deer is a private 18 hole course open 7 days a week all year, weather permitting. Guests may play accompanied by a member. Members call in for tee times. Power caddies may be rented.

•**Driving Range**	•**Lockers**
•**Practice Green**	•**Showers**
•**Power Carts**	•**Food**
•**Pull Carts(elec)**	•**Clubhouse**
Club Rental	•**Outings**
Caddies	•**Soft Spikes**

Course Description: 'Striving for The No Waiting Game,' is emphasized at rustic Running Deer, a secluded club with a lengthy tree lined entrance road. The pace of play here is strictly enforced. Each hole is unique; enormous canyons as waste bunkers, interesting mounding and native grasses interspersed on the fairways make this creation so intriguing. Just as you think you have played a hole that could not be surpassed, you come to another breathtaking challenge. Carved out of 350 acres of deep woods, the course has 3 par 4s over 480 yards. The six sets of tees make it playable for golfers of every skill level. Offering privacy and traditional etiquette, South Jersey is fortunate to have this outstanding course in the vicinity.

Directions: Salem County, #30 on Southwest Map
From North: Take Rte. 55 South to Garden Rd, Exit 35B. Turn right off exit for 2 miles and left onto Parvins Mill Rd. (Rte. 645). Go 1.4 m. to entrance on right (gravel road).

Hole	1	2	3	4	5	6	7	8	9	Out	BLUE	Rating 74.3
BLUE	405	495	390	530	175	425	185	420	495	3520		Slope 136
WHITE	380	450	350	500	150	400	160	400	470	3260		
Par	4	4	4	5	3	4	3	4	5	36	WHITE	Rating 73.0
Handicap	12	2	8	14	17	4	16	6	15			Slope 133
RED	330	380	300	445	105	345	95	340	400	2740		
Par	4	4	4	5	3	4	3	4	5	36	RED	Rating 72.2
Handicap	12	2	8	14	17	4	16	6	15			Slope 128
Hole	10	11	12	13	14	15	16	17	18	In		Totals
BLUE	425	365	485	250	560	360	195	575	490	3705	BLUE	7225
WHITE	400	345	420	205	515	330	165	550	460	3390	WHITE	6808
Par	4	4	4	3	5	4	3	5	4	36	Par	72
Handicap	11	13	1	9	7	10	18	5	3			
RED	340	300	305	140	445	290	140	430	390	2780	RED	5821
Par	4	4	4	3	5	4	3	5	4	36	Par	72
Handicap	11	13	1	9	7	10	18	5	3			

Manager: Edward Carman   **Pro:** J. R Carman, PGA   **Supt:** Theodore Carman
Architect: Edward Carman 2000

SAKIMA COUNTRY CLUB

383 Shell Rd. Rte. 130 Carney's Pt., NJ 08069   **(856) 299-0201**

Sakima is a 9 hole course open all year 7 days a week. Guests may play accompanied by a member. Tee time reservations are not necessary.

•**Driving Range**	•**Lockers**
•**Practice Green**	•**Showers**
•**Power Carts**	•**Food**
•**Pull Carts**	•**Clubhouse**
Club Rental	•**Outings**
Caddies	•**Soft Spikes**

Course Description: Sakima is a deceptively difficult, tight, tree lined course with narrow fairways and small greens. A second nine may be played changing the tees for the "back". There is no water on the course in the form of ponds or creeks but on the ninth and eighteenth, it is necessary to hit over drainage ditches. The signature par 3 third hole is long from the white tees and in the dead center of the course. It has a large back to front sloping green and with strategic pin placement can be quite challenging.

Directions: Salem County, #31 on Southwest Map
Rte. 295 South to Exit #4 (Penn's Grove.) Take Rte. 130 South and go 1 and 1/2 miles. Course is on left.

Hole	1	2	3	4	5	6	7	8	9	Out	BLUE	Rating
BLUE												Slope
WHITE	475	388	209	348	367	379	285	165	461	3077		
Par	5	4	3	4	4	4	4	3	5	36	WHITE	Rating 68.6
Handicap	9	1	7	13	3	5	17	15	11			Slope 115
RED	418	285	139	348	317	341	268	152	440	2708		
Par	5	4	3	4	4	4	4	3	5	36	RED	Rating 70.8
Handicap	1	13	17	7	9	5	11	15	3			Slope 116

Hole	10	11	12	13	14	15	16	17	18	In		Totals
BLUE											BLUE	
WHITE											WHITE	6150
Par											Par	72
Handicap												
RED											RED	5498
Par											Par	72
Handicap												

Manager/Pres: Jack Peak   **Pro:** Chris Lefperance   **Supt:** Garland Swanson
                              Built: 1898

COUNTRY CLUB OF SALEM

91 Country Club Lane, Salem, NJ 08079   **(856) 935-1603**

Salem is a 9 hole course open 7 days a week, all year. Guests play accompanied by a member. Although there is no actual driving range, there is a chipping area for practice.

Driving Range	Lockers
•**Practice Green**	Showers
•**Power Carts**	•**Food**
•**Pull Carts**	•**Clubhouse**
Club Rental	•**Outings**
Caddies	•**Soft Spikes**

Course Description: This small, friendly club is member-owned and professionally managed. The scenic views of the Delaware River are spectacular in all seasons; being near the water the golfers benefit from the exhilarating breezes. Salem has fast bent grass greens and is challenging for the scratch golfer as well as for the weekend duffer. The signature first hole, a 617 yard par 5 dogleg left, has a pond that comes into play. Water affects play on the second and seventh holes as well. Although it is 9 holes, alternate tees change the yardages adding interest to the second nine.

Directions: Salem County, #32 on Southwest Map
NJTPKE to Exit #1 (Pennsville). Take Rte. 49 East to Salem, over bridge to Chestnut St. Then turn right to club 3 miles ahead on right on Country Club Lane.

Hole	1	2	3	4	5	6	7	8	9	Out	BLUE	Rating
BLUE												Slope
WHITE	617	373	126	490	354	164	291	398	360	3173		
Par	5	4	3	5	4	3	4	4	4	36	WHITE	Rating 70.1
Handicap	1	8	18	12	3	16	14	4	7			Slope 118
RED	439	351	115	369	341	140	283	381	343	2762		
Par	5	4	3	4	4	3	4	5	4	36	RED	Rating 70.8
Handicap	8	6	18	1	4	16	13	12	3			Slope 120
Hole	10	11	12	13	14	15	16	17	18	In		Totals
BLUE											BLUE	
WHITE	451	363	187	480	369	150	299	386	370	3055	WHITE	6228
Par	5	4	3	5	4	3	4	4	4	36	Par	72
Handicap	10	9	11	13	2	17	15	5	6			
RED	400	360	126	408	292	153	240	307	353	2639	RED	5401
Par	5	4	3	5	4	3	4	4	4	36	Par	72
Handicap	9	5	17	11	10	15	14	7	2			

Manager: Ian Bambirck   **Supt:** John List
Built: 1898

SCOTLAND RUN NATIONAL GC `PUBLIC`

2626 Fries Mill Rd., Williamstown, NJ 08094 **(856) 863-3737**
www.scotlandrun.com

Opened in 1999, Scotland Run is an 18 hole semi-private course open 7 days a week all year. Memberships are available. Tee times: 30 days for mbrs. and 14 days for non-mbrs. Walking is permitted.

- •**Driving Range**
- •**Practice Green**
- •**Power Carts**
- Pull Carts
- •**Club Rental**
- •**Soft Spikes**
- •**Lockers**
- •**Showers**
- •**Food**
- •**Clubhouse**
- •**Outings**

Fees	M-Thurs	Fri-Sun
Daily	$95	$105
Twi 3	$70	$70

Power carts included
Reduced rates off season

Course Description: Built on a former sand quarry and carved out of the landscape with a backdrop of cliffs and an expansive waste area, Scotland Run offers breathtaking views. It has 5 sets of tees on a 6800 yard layout encompassing 200 acres of winding fairways, naturally blue ponds and elevation rises not characteristic of the flatlands of Southern NJ. Stephen Kay's design makes an unusual golfing experience giving players a host of different shots in a variety of settings. Outstanding among the holes is the 2d, a long par 4 with 2 greens; one is short to the right, the other long to the left. Either one provides excitement and challenge.

Directions: Gloucester County, #33 on Southwest Map
From Phila. take the W.Whitman Bridge to Rte. 42 South; continue & at 6th light go right to Fries Mill Rd. (Rte.655). Course is 3 miles on left. From Trenton & North, take 295 South to Rte.42 South & follow as above.

Hole	1	2	3	4	5	6	7	8	9	Out	BLACK	Rating 73.3
BLACK	520	454	370	165	457	315	372	406	223	3282		Slope 134
WHITE	493	418	332	143	431	303	340	353	191	3004		
Par	5	4	4	3	4	4	4	4	3	35	WHITE	Rating 70.4
Handicap	10	4	8	18	2	12	14	6	16			Slope 128
RED	420	371	241	90	367	230	285	281	135	2420		
Par	5	4	4	3	4	4	4	4	3	35	RED	Rating 69.5
Handicap	10	4	8	18	2	12	14	6	16			Slope 120

Hole	10	11	12	13	14	15	16	17	18	In		Totals
BLACK	545	404	465	217	315	164	402	486	530	352 8	BLACK	6810
WHITE	492	338	434	172	275	140	360	421	502	3120	WHITE	6138
Par	5	4	4	3	4	3	4	4	5	36	Par	71
Handicap	11	13	1	9	15	17	7	3	5			
RED	438	302	290	130	238	118	272	363	439	2590	RED	5010
Par	5	4	4	3	4	3	4	4	5	36	Par	71
Handicap	11	13	1	9	15	17	7	3	5			

Manager: John Igoe   **Pro:** Jeff Frederick, PGA   **Supt:** Andrew Franks
Architect: Stephen Kay 1999

SPRINGFIELD GOLF CENTER

PUBLIC

Jacksonville-Mt. Holly Rd., Mt. Holly, NJ 08060   **(609) 267-8440**

Springfield is an 18 hole semi-private par 68 course open to the public 7 days a week all year. Memberships are available. Tee time reservations are required on weekends in season. There is miniature golf and a chip & putt on the premises.

- **Driving Range**
- **Practice Green**
- **Power Carts**
- **Pull Carts**
- **Club Rental**
- Soft Spikes

Lockers
Showers
- **Food**
- **Clubhouse**
- **Outings**

Fees	Weekday	Weekend
Daily	$17	$20
Twi(3PM)	$14	$17
Power carts	$13pp	

Course Description: Fairly short, flat and open, Springfield has water in play on several holes. The back nine is more difficult than the front which has wider fairways and fewer hazards. A tee shot through a chute and over water on the par 5 signature 14th is followed by more water to the left and a drainage creek to the right. The nines have been reversed recently. The facility draws many players from local senior residence communities who appreciate the easily walkable terrain.

Directions: Burlington County, #34 on Southwest Map
NJTPKE to Exit #7. Take Rte. 206 South to Rte. 630 West and then turn right on Rte. 628 which is Jacksonville-Mt. Holly Rd. Course is on left.

Hole	1	2	3	4	5	6	7	8	9	Out	BLUE	Rating 63.4
BLUE	380	200	370	200	585	360	395	190	360	3040		Slope 110
WHITE	370	192	360	195	578	350	388	182	350	2965		
Par	4	3	4	3	5	4	4	3	4	34	WHITE	Rating 62.6
Handicap	10	16	6	14	2	12	4	18	8			Slope 109
RED	350	92	352	180	485	340	376	136	335	2646		
Par	4	3	4	3	5	4	4	3	4	34	RED	Rating 64.3
Handicap	10	16	6	14	2	12	4	18	8			Slope 111
Hole	10	11	12	13	14	15	16	17	18	In		Totals
BLUE	350	370	375	186	570	150	350	130	351	2832	BLUE	5872
WHITE	340	360	365	157	560	140	340	123	345	2730	WHITE	5695
Par	4	4	4	3	5	3	4	3	4	34	Par	68
Handicap	9	5	3	13	1	15	11	17	7			
RED	320	310	355	126	440	125	317	112	331	2436	RED	5082
Par	4	4	4	3	5	3	4	3	4	34	Par	68
Handicap	9	5	3	13	1	15	11	17	7			

Manager: Mike Santarian **Supt:** Jarry Smith
Architect: Garrett Renn 1965

TAVISTOCK COUNTRY CLUB   PRIVATE

Tavistock Lane, Haddonfield, NJ 08033   (856) 429-1827

Tavistock is an 18 hole course open all year 6 days a week. Guests play accompanied by a member. Tee time reservations are recommended on weekends.

- •Driving Range   •Lockers
- •Practice Green   •Showers
- •Power Carts   •Food
- Pull Carts   •Clubhouse
- •Club Rental   •Outings
- •Caddies   •Soft Spikes

Course Description: Alexander Findlay built 300 courses on the east coast and according to his grandsons, he believed Tavistock was the best work he had ever done. A variety of 28 different trees were planted on the property enhancing the beauty of the course. The twelfth hole is guarded by a buttonwood tree that golfers must avoid. The signature par 4 fourteenth hole has a lake parallel to the fairway beautified with azalea, rhododendrum and dogwood plantings. Tavistick's greens are undulating which makes positioning of the approach shot critical. Plans are in the works for a major renovation with new tee boxes and bunkers.

Directions: Camden County, #35 on Southwest Map
Rte. 295 South to Exit #30, Warwick Rd. Make a left at the STOP; go 800 yards to club. If traveling north, exit on Rte. 295 at Exit 29B and follow as above.

Hole	1	2	3	4	5	6	7	8	9	Out	BLUE	Rating 72.3
BLUE	354	535	403	146	523	392	341	189	362	3245		Slope 136
WHITE	323	518	378	166	444	532	194	486	408	3364		
Par	4	5	4	3	5	4	4	3	4	36	WHITE	Rating 70.9
Handicap	13	9	7	17	3	1	11	15	5			Slope 133
RED	287	455	352	122	424	326	278	152	315	2711		
Par	4	5	4	3	5	4	4	3	4	36	RED	Rating 72.8
Handicap	11	3	5	17	1	9	13	15	7			Slope 128

Hole	10	11	12	13	14	15	16	17	18	In		Totals
BLUE	345	391	398	166	444	532	194	486	408	3364	BLUE	6609
WHITE	334	388	389	148	414	518	168	479	389	3227	WHITE	6321
Par	4	4	4	3	4	5	3	5	4	36	Par	72
Handicap	16	10	6	18	2	4	14	12	8			
RED	312	371	368	123	328	460	127	411	341	2841	RED	5552
Par	4	4	4	3	4	5	3	5	4	36	Par	72
Handicap	14	12	6	18	10	2	16	4	8			

Manager: George Wolf   **Pro:** Rick Hughart, PGA   **Supt:** Thomas Grimac
Architect: Alexander Findlay 1921

TOWN & COUNTRY GOLF LINKS

197 East Ave., Woodstown, NJ 08098   **(856) 769-8333**
www.tcgolflinks.com

Town & Country Golf Links is open to the public 7 days a week all year. Memberships are available with tee times up to 14 days in advance, non-mbrs 7 days.

- •Driving Range
- •Practice Green
- •Power Carts
- •Pull Carts
- •Club Rental
- •Soft Spikes
- •Lockers
- •Showers
- •Food
- •Clubhouse
- •Outings

Fees	Weekday	Weekend
Daily	$45	$59
After1PM	$30	$45
Jr/Sr. & twi rates available		
Power carts included		

Course Description: Town & Country is a links style course in immaculate condition. Fescue grass abounds in the rough; decorative flowers and waterfalls draw the eye. The course, 6496 from the tips, is wide open in farm country. It is helpful to know the layout because of pin placements that are challenging on the subtly breaking greens. Thirteen holes are bordered by water. The outstanding signature par 3 13th features an island green. A state-of-the-art practice facility is illuminated at dusk. The course has been made more family friendly with extra forward tees set up for beginners.

Directions: Salem County, #36 on Southwest Map
NJTPKE to Exit 2 (Swedesboro) or Rte. 295S to exit 11A. Take Rte. 322 East to Mullica Hill, 5.5 miles. Turn right onto Rte. 45S & follow to Woodstown (6-7 Miles). Turn left onto Rte. 40 East (traffic light Mobil & Woodstown Bank). Follow 1/2 m. to club on left.

Hole	1	2	3	4	5	6	7	8	9	Out	BLUE	Rating 69.4
BLUE	420	393	492	203	353	355	360	160	533	3269		Slope 119
WHITE	393	387	398	173	327	332	343	145	518	3016		
Par	4	4	5	3	4	4	4	3	5	36	WHITE	Rating 67.1
Handicap	3	7	5	11	13	15	9	17	1			Slope 117
RED	303	303	353	117	293	257	310	110	438	2484		
Par	4	4	5	3	4	4	4	3	5	36	RED	Rating 66.1
Handicap	3	7	11	15	17	5	1	9	13			Slope 114
Hole	10	11	12	13	14	15	16	17	18	In		Totals
BLUE	490	317	320	144	465	295	160	298	375	2864	BLUE	6000
WHITE	462	307	307	127	448	278	140	277	357	2703	WHITE	5678
Par	5	4	4	3	5	4	3	4	4	36	Par	72
Handicap	6	18	16	14	4	8	12	10	2			
RED	405	280	273	104	383	213	103	256	310	2327	RED	4811
Par	5	4	4	3	5	4	3	4	4	36	Par	72
Handicap	4	18	10	8	2	6	16	12	14			

Mgr: Karen Pierson   Dir. of Golf: William Holmes   **Supt:** Paul Geer
Architect: Carl Gaskill 1999

VALLEYBROOK GOLF CLUB

200 Golfview Dr., Blackwood, NJ 08012   **(856) 227-3171**
www.valleybrookgolf.com

Valleybrook is an 18 hole semi-private course open to the public 7 days a week all year. Memberships are available. It is now owned by Ron Jaworski. Tee times: members 2 weeks, non-members 1 week.

- •Driving Range
- •Practice Green
- •Power Carts
- •Pull Carts
- •Club Rental
- •Soft Spikes
- •Lockers
- •Showers
- •Food
- •Clubhouse
- •Outings

Fees	Weekday	Weekend
Daily	$42	$54
11-2PM	$38	$49
After 2	$30	$40
Power carts included		

Course Description: The well maintained Valleybrook combines flat and open terrain with hills, valleys and some narrow tree lined fairways. The bent grass greens are undulating, fast and in very good condition. The par 4 7th requires a 150 yard carry over water to the dogleg left fairway with another pond to negotiate to reach a back to front sloping green. The 12th plays long; the narrow green is guarded by a bunker on the left and trees on the right.

Directions: Gloucester County, #37 on Southwest Map
NJTPKE to Exit #3. Then take Rte. 168 East to Rte. 42 South to Blackwood-Clementon exit (Rte. 534). Turn right off ramp 1/2 mile to Little Gloucester Rd. Turn left on Golfview Dr. for 1 mile; club on left. From Phila: Rte. 42 South & follow as above.

Hole	1	2	3	4	5	6	7	8	9	Out	BLUE	Rating 69.7
BLUE	488	322	177	342	186	296	347	479	411	3048		Slope 124
WHITE	482	318	167	337	182	293	342	475	406	3002		
Par	5	4	3	4	3	4	4	5	4	36	WHITE	Rating 68.5
Handicap	16	12	6	10	8	14	2	18	4			Slope 120
RED	452	277	132	312	140	257	301	428	328	2627		
Par	5	4	3	4	3	4	4	5	4	36	RED	Rating 67.4
Handicap	2	12	18	10	14	16	8	4	6			Slope 118
Hole	10	11	12	13	14	15	16	17	18	In		Totals
BLUE	385	487	217	324	176	326	328	341	501	3085	BLUE	6384
WHITE	380	482	197	319	170	316	321	336	487	3008	WHITE	6008
Par	4	5	3	4	3	4	4	4	5	36	Par	72
Handicap	3	9	1	15	13	11	7	17	5			
RED	336	441	173	291	128	271	301	319	432	2692	RED	5307
Par	4	5	3	4	3	4	4	4	5	36	Par	72
Handicap	5	3	15	11	17	13	9	7	1			

Manager: Robert Ewing   **Pro:** Ed Kramer, PGA   **Supt:** Dave Santana
Architects: David Beakley 1960   **Redesign:** Hal Purdy 1990

WASHINGTON TOWNSHIP GC

PUBLIC

Fries Mill Rd., Turnersville, NJ 08012   **(856) 227-1435**

Washington Township Municipal Golf Club is a 9 hole executive course run by the Department of Parks & Recreation. It is open 7 days a week all year. Tee time reservations are not necessary. Memberships are available.

Driving Range	Lockers
•Practice Green	Showers
Power Carts	Food
•Pull Carts	Clubhouse
•Club Rental	Outings
•Soft Spikes	

Fees	Weekday	Weekend
Daily Res	$10	$12
Sr	$7	
Non Res	$11	$13

Course Description: This municipal course is very well maintained with low rolling hills and no natural water. Accuracy is essential to make par on some of the more difficult holes. The 155 yard par 3 sixth is out of a chute and over a ditch to a small green. There are other ditches to traverse on holes 6, 7 and 9. Washington Township Golf Course provides excellent exercise as the golfers must walk. The word here is that this was one of the first courses designed by Tom Fazio.

Directions: Gloucester County, #38 on Southwest Map
From Phila: Walt Whitman Bridge & go South on Rte. 42 to split in road, then take Black Horse Pike bearing right. Before the 5th light, bear right onto Fries Mill Rd. Course is 3/4 mile on right. OR: NJTPKE to Exit #3 to Rte. 168 S to Rte. 42 & follow as above.

Hole	1	2	3	4	5	6	7	8	9	Out	BLUE	Rating
BLUE												Slope
WHITE	99	151	134	101	128	155	74	161	248	1251		
Par	3	3	3	3	3	3	3	3	4	28	WHITE	Rating
Handicap	8	5	6	7	4	1	9	2	3			Slope
RED	99	151	134	101	128	155	74	161	248	1251		
Par	3	4	3	3	3	4	3	4	5	32	RED	Rating
Handicap	6	9	2	8	5	4	1	7	3			Slope
Hole	10	11	12	13	14	15	16	17	18	In		Totals
BLUE											BLUE	
WHITE											WHITE	1251
Par											Par	28
Handicap												
RED											RED	1251
Par											Par	32
Handicap												

Manager/Supt: Wendell Beakley   **Architect:** Tom Fazio 1960s

WEDGEWOOD COUNTRY CLUB   PUBLIC

200 Hurffville Rd., Turnersville, NJ 08012   **(856) 227-5522**
www.wedgewoodcc.com

Wedgewood is an 18 hole course open to the public 7 days a week all year. Reserved tee times are suggested for weekends. Memberships are available. Power carts are mandatory Fri. through Sun. till 1PM.

Driving Range
- Practice Green
- Power Carts
- Pull Carts
- Club Rental
- Soft Spikes
- Lockers
- Showers
- Food
- Clubhouse
- Outings

Fees	Weekday	Weekend
Daily	$35	$45
Power carts $15pp		

Course Description: Completely renovated, Wedgewood is long, narrow and challenging. The improvements include new bent grass tees, fairways and greens. The signature and most difficult hole is the par 4 #13 where too long a tee shot can land in one of two ponds on the fairway. The drive should be about 210 yards and straight, followed by a second shot over water to a wide but short well bunkered green. When Wedgewood was used as a qualifying course for the PGA, the 18th hole was so difficult and tight that the pros didn't tee off from the blacks.. The bunkers have been upgraded recently.

Directions: Gloucester County, #39 on Southwest Map
NJTPKE to Exit #3. Take Rte. 168 East (Black Horse Pike) to Wilson Rd. (approx. 5 miles). Make a right and club is up ahead.

Hole	1	2	3	4	5	6	7	8	9	Out	BLUE	Rating 72.3
BLUE	424	522	371	150	539	378	392	188	383	3347		Slope 131
WHITE	380	500	349	138	531	365	379	178	359	3179		
Par	4	5	4	3	5	4	4	3	4	36	WHITE	Rating 70.6
Handicap	2	8	4	18	14	12	10	15	6			Slope 129
GOLD	328	430	332	126	396	330	318	122	320	2702		
Par	4	5	4	3	5	4	4	3	4	36	GOLD	Rating 72.1
Handicap	7	3	15	17	1	11	5	13	9			Slope 125
Hole	10	11	12	13	14	15	16	17	18	In		Totals
BLUE	381	551	188	421	367	408	181	486	388	3371	BLUE	6718
WHITE	365	524	178	411	355	375	163	464	342	3177	WHITE	6356
Par	4	5	3	4	4	4	3	5	4	36	Par	72
Handicap	3	9	13	1	17	11	18	7	5			
GOLD	346	457	171	404	257	341	150	400	326	2852	GOLD	5554
Par	4	5	3	4	4	4	3	5	4	36	Par	72
Handicap	6	8	10	2	14	4	18	12	16			

Manager: Tim Ahearn, PGA   **Supt:** Marty Musho
Architect: Gary Wren 1964

WESTWOOD GOLF CLUB

850 Kings Highway, Woodbury, NJ 08096   **(856) 845-2000**
www.westwoodgolfclub.com

Westwood is an 18 hole course open 7 days a week all year. Memberships are available. Tee time reservations req'd on weekends and holidays; Special discounts apply. Carts req'd until 12 on weekends. There is a driving range nearby.

Driving Range	•Lockers
•Practice Green	•Showers
•Power Carts	•Food
•Pull Carts	•Clubhouse
•Club Rental	•Outings
•Soft Spikes	

Fees	M-Thurs	Weekend
Daily	$24	$51/cart
Fri.	$25	
After 12		$30
Power carts	$15/pp	

Course Description: This pleasantly challenging course is in excellent shape and quite hilly for this part of Southern New Jersey. The fairways are narrow and the greens are large. The par 3 11th signature hole is extremely picturesque especially in Spring when 1,000 daffodils, crab apple and dogwood plantings blossom; its elevated green has been levelled to make it less difficult. A waste bunker has been added on the 7th with a grass island in the middle. The 6th hole has an uphill drive and then downhill to the redone green that is bunkered on the right and left giving the golfer a relatively narrow target.

Directions: Gloucester County, #40 on Southwest Map
NJTPKE to Exit #2 (Swedesboro/Rte. 322). Take 322 West. At light at Rte. 551 make a right turn onto 551 North. Club is 8 miles on the right (across from Wawa).

Hole	1	2	3	4	5	6	7	8	9	Out	BLUE	Rating
BLUE												Slope
WHITE	450	274	517	303	128	417	359	323	210	2981		
Par	5	4	5	4	3	4	4	4	3	36	WHITE	Rating 68.2
Handicap	7	15	3	11	17	1	5	9	13			Slope 120
RED	415	252	442	279	103	297	324	288	126	2526		
Par	5	4	5	4	3	4	4	4	3	36	RED	Rating 69.2
Handicap	1	15	3	9	17	11	5	7	13			Slope 116
Hole	10	11	12	13	14	15	16	17	18	In		Totals
BLUE											BLUE	
WHITE	360	190	383	180	390	325	442	374	343	2987	WHITE	5968
Par	4	3	4	3	4	4	5	4	4	35	Par	71
Handicap	12	14	4	18	2	16	10	8	6			
RED	315	172	305	148	352	280	419	352	313	2656	RED	5182
Par	4	3	4	3	5	4	5	4	4	36	Par	72
Handicap	16	12	14	18	6	8	2	4	10			

Owners/Managers: Janet, Ken Vogt & Jennifer Bell   **Supt:** Charles Hund
Architect: Horace Smith   **Built:** 1962

WHITE OAKS COUNTRY CLUB SEMI-PRIVATE

2951 Dutch Mill Rd., Newfield, NJ 08344   **(856) 697-8900**
www.whiteoaksgolf.com

White Oaks is an 18 hole course open to the public 7 days a week all year.
Memberships are available. Members may make tee time reservations 14 days in
advance, non-members 7 days.

Driving Range	
•Practice Green	•Lockers
•Power Carts	•Showers
Pull Carts	•Food
•Club Rental	•Clubhouse
•Soft Spikes	•Outings

Fees	Weekday	Weekend
Daily	$45	$59
Twi	$39	$45
Srs	$32	
Power carts included		

Course Description: White Oaks is situated on gently rolling terrain and cut out of the
pinelands. A large lake affects play on the first hole and must be carried on the
approach shot to the deceiving double 9th green. Tall oak trees encroach the narrow
fairways and most greens are large, undulating and well-bunkered. The course has
large sand waste areas dotted with shrubs. The par 5 7th hole, one of the longest in
South Jersey, is 621 yards from the tips. Asphalt cart paths are provided throughout;
a state of the art irrigation system helps maintain the course.

Directions: Gloucester County, #41 on Southwest Map
From Phila. area, take Rte. 322 East and turn right on Piney Hollow Rd. After 2 miles,
turn right onto Dutch Mill Rd. to club on right. OR Take GSP to Exit 36. Then take Rte.
322 West & turn left onto Piney Hollow Rd. Follow as above.

Hole	1	2	3	4	5	6	7	8	9	Out	BLUE	Rating 70.7
BLUE	368	342	487	197	343	410	621	190	375	3333		Slope 118
WHITE	349	312	455	176	328	382	562	179	350	3093		
Par	4	4	5	3	4	4	5	3	4	36	WHITE	Rating 68.8
Handicap	15	11	9	17	13	3	1	7	5			Slope 115
RED	320	270	400	124	302	363	446	143	310	2678		
Par	4	4	4	3	4	4	5	3	4	35	RED	Rating 68.9
Handicap	11	7	9	17	5	3	13	15				Slope 118

Hole	10	11	12	13	14	15	16	17	18	In		Totals
BLUE	570	438	168	401	338	344	312	240	366	3177	BLUE	6510
WHITE	510	438	168	401	338	344	312	240	366	3020	WHITE	6113
Par	5	4	3	4	4	4	4	3	4	35	Par	71
Handicap	6	2	18	4	14	16	12	8	10			
RED	518	308	114	360	274	254	235	170	284	2517	RED	5195
Par	5	4	3	4	4	4	4	3	4	35	Par	71
Handicap	2	8	16	4	14	6	12	18	10			

Mgr: Nick Pileggi   **Pro:** Todd Prohammerr, PGA   **Supt:** Pete Adams
Architect: Mike Gafney 1999

WILD OAKS GOLF CLUB

PUBLIC

75 Wild Oaks Drive, Salem, NJ 08079 **(856) 935-0705**
www.championshipgolfmanagement.com

Wild Oaks is a 27 hole privately owned course open to the public 7 days a week all year. Tee time reservations are necessary on weekends and holidays and may be made 1 week in advance. Memberships are available.

Driving Range
• **Practice Green**
• **Power Carts**
• **Pull Carts**
• **Club Rental**
• **Soft Spikes**

Lockers
Showers
• **Food**
• **Clubhouse**
• **Outings**

Fees	Weekday	Weekend
Daily	$25	$30
Twi(3PM)	$20	$25
Power carts included		

Course Description: At Wild Oaks there are 3 separate nines which may be played in a variety of combinations. On the longest, Willow Oaks, the first hole, a 431 yard par 4, is a wooded sharp dogleg left with a tree in the middle of the fairway and water in play. White Cedar is generally straight, wide open and is the easiest of the three nines. Pin Oaks is narrow with small greens that necessitate accurate approach shots. Wild Oaks attracts players from Phila. and parts of NJ and Del. The scorecard below is for Willow Oaks and White Cedar.

Directions: Salem County, #42 on Southwest Map
Rte. 295S to Exit 1C. Then take Rte. 551 2.5 mi. & turn left onto Rte. 49 through Salem to Quinton to light (only light in town). Make the 2nd right after light to club. OR: NJTPKE to Exit #1 to Hook Rd. (Rte. 551) to Rte. 49 through Salem & follow as above.

Hole	1	2	3	4	5	6	7	8	9	Out	BLUE	Rating 72.1
BLUE	431	461	429	169	397	412	566	190	372	3427		Slope 126
WHITE	416	448	417	155	377	394	550	175	360	3292		
Par	4	5	4	3	4	4	5	3	4	36	WHITE	Rating 71.0
Handicap	1	9	3	8	6	4	2	7	5			Slope 124
RED	352	383	336	141	304	324	398	159	276	2673		
Par	4	5	4	3	4	4	5	3	4	36	RED	Rating 71.4
Handicap	1	2	7	9	4	5	6	3	8			Slope 118
Hole	10	11	12	13	14	15	16	17	18	In		Totals
BLUE	543	417	381	183	375	151	396	393	460	3299	BLUE	6726
WHITE	523	400	365	168	361	144	377	380	445	3163	WHITE	6455
Par	5	4	4	3	4	3	4	4	5	36	Par	72
Handicap	2	1	6	7	5	9	3	4	8			
RED	452	334	297	155	253	125	328	325	380	2649	RED	5322
Par	5	4	4	3	4	3	4	4	5	36	Par	72
Handicap	3	6	7	4	9	8	2	1	5			

Mgr: Championship Golf Management   **Supt:** John Hogate
Architect: Joe Hassler 1979

WILLOW BROOK COUNTRY CLUB SEMI-PRIVATE

4310 Bridgeboro Rd., Moorestown, NJ 08057   **(856) 461-0131**
www.willowbrookcountryclub.com

Willow Brook is an 18 hole course open to the public 7 days a week all year. There are full, weekday and social memberships available. Members have preferred tee times, (Monday for the following week.) Non-mbrs 5 days. A variety of specials are available.

•Driving Range	•Lockers
•Practice Green	•Showers
•Power Carts	•Food
•Pull Carts	•Clubhouse
•Club Rental	•Outings
•Soft Spikes	

Fees	Weekday	Weekend
Daily	$32	$58/cart
Twi(3PM)	$21	$23
Power carts $16pp		
Cart req'd til 11AM weekends		

Course Description: At Willow Brook the new mounding has made the course more interesting. New greens, cart paths and bunkers are part of the recent upgrades. It is relatively flat, rather wide open and the excellent bent grass greens are contoured. Water affects play on five holes. The 418 yard par 4 18th is a challenging dogleg with a stream in front and a large lake near the green presenting a daunting approach shot. Greens have been redone recently and they are in excellent shape.

Directions: Burlington County, #43 on Southwest Map
NJTPKE to Exit # 4. Then take Rte. 73 North to Rte. 130 North to Rte. 613 East. Proceed 2 miles and club is on left. OR: Rte. 130 South to 613 East and follow as above.

Hole	1	2	3	4	5	6	7	8	9	Out	BLUE	Rating 71.2
BLUE	324	377	546	350	199	400	169	490	378	3233		Slope 125
WHITE	313	365	530	340	184	374	157	469	363	3095		
Par	4	4	5	4	3	4	3	5	4	36	WHITE	Rating 69.9
Handicap	17	7	1	11	5	3	13	15	9			Slope 118
RED	253	253	434	239	155	319	153	409	281	2496		
Par	4	4	5	4	3	4	3	5	4	36	RED	Rating 68.3
Handicap	17	7	1	11	5	3	13	15	9			Slope 110

Hole	10	11	12	13	14	15	16	17	18	In		Totals
BLUE	378	399	160	503	156	530	362	349	418	3255	BLUE	6488
WHITE	368	391	149	493	127	500	352	341	388	3109	WHITE	6204
Par	4	4	3	5	3	5	4	4	4	36	Par	72
Handicap	10	6	18	8	14	4	12	16	2			
RED	269	335	320	154	290	404	163	422	257	2614	RED	5518
Par	4	4	3	5	3	5	4	4	4	36	Par	72
Handicap	10	6	18	8	14	4	12	16	2			

Manager/Pro: Brian Feldschneider, PGA   **Supt:** Ed Klumpp, Jr.
Architect: William Gordon, 1967

WOODBURY COUNTRY CLUB

467 Cooper St., Woodbury, NJ 08096   **(856) 848-5000**

Woodbury is a 9 hole private course open 7 days a week all year. Guests may play accompanied by a member. Tee time reservations are not necessary.

Driving Range	•Lockers
•Practice Green	•Showers
•Power Carts	•Food
•Pull Carts	•Clubhouse
Club Rental	•Outings
Caddies	•Soft Spikes

Course Description: Chartered in 1897, Woodbury is one of the oldest clubs in New Jersey. It is very well maintained and was redesigned several years ago with new tees, greens and bunkers. The generally flat course has narrow fairways with mature trees lining them. To give variety, there are double greens and differing tee placements, as indicated on the scorecard below. The par 3 fourteenth signature hole is 189 yards requiring the shot from the tee to go over a picturesque lake. The 9th/18th green have been redone and the drainage improved recently.

Directions: Gloucester County, #44 on Southwest Map
NJTPKE to Exit #3. Then take Rte.168 (Black Horse Pike.) Make a left onto Rte. 573 and then right onto Rte. 544 which ends at Cooper St. Make a right onto Cooper to club. OR: Rte. 295 to Exit 25A to Rte. 45 South. At Cooper St. turn right to club.

Hole	1	2	3	4	5	6	7	8	9	Out	BLUE	Rating
BLUE												Slope
WHITE	366	310	200	481	160	367	365	445	372	3066		
Par	4	4	3	3	3	4	4	4	4	35	WHITE	Rating 69.2
Handicap	5	15	3	7	17	11	9	1	13			Slope 126
RED	332	251	196	466	135	358	357	420	366	2881		
Par	4	4	3	3	3	4	4	5	4	36	RED	Rating 73.4
Handicap	11	15	13	1	17	7	5	3	9			Slope 127
Hole	10	11	12	13	14	15	16	17	18	In		Totals
BLUE											BLUE	
WHITE	361	277	157	467	189	363	357	420	369	2960	WHITE	6026
Par	4	4	3	5	3	4	4	4	4	35	Par	70
Handicap	10	18	16	12	14	8	4	2	6			
RED	332	280	153	466	137	358	357	358	365	2806	RED	5687
Par	4	4	3	5	3	4	4	4	4	35	Par	71
Handicap	10	14	16	2	18	6	4	12	8			

Manager: Ellen Reese   **Pro:** Brian Madden, PGA   **Supt:** Charles Clarke
Architects: Geoffrey Cornish   (Orig. design H. Clark 1897)

WOODCREST COUNTRY CLUB   **PRIVATE**

Evesham-Berlin Rd., Cherry Hill, NJ 08003   **(856) 428-1243**

Woodcrest is an 18 hole course open 6 days a week all year and closed in Jan. Guests play accompanied by a member. Tee time reservations are necessary on weekends.

- •Driving Range •Lockers
- •Practice Green •Showers
- •Power Carts •Food
- Pull Carts •Clubhouse
- •Club Rental •Outings
- •Caddies •Soft Spikes

Course Description: Well maintained, Woodcrest Country Club can be justifiably proud of both the condition of its greens and fairways, and of the difficulty of the course (132 slope from the white tees). The course has a very narrow layout and small greens. On the par 4 third signature hole "The Oaks", the golfer is confronted by water and a large tree on the right. The ninth called "Long John" is a 538 yard par 5 from the white tees with water in play off the tee, very thick rough and a lake to carry on the approach shot. The recent redesign has the nines reversed.

Directions: Camden County, #45 on Southwest Map
From Phila: take Rte. 295 to Exit #32 (Haddonfield-Gibbsboro). Turn right to Rte. 561 & at 5th light make left to Evesham Rd. Club is 500 ft. ahead on left.

Hole	1	2	3	4	5	6	7	8	9	Out	BLUE	Rating 72.9
BLUE	361	511	443	187	430	348	409	177	547	3413		Slope 140
WHITE	347	489	425	178	425	338	363	154	538	3257		
Par	4	5	4	3	4	4	4	3	5	36	WHITE	Rating 71.4
Handicap	13	9	1	7	5	17	11	15	3			Slope 137
RED	334	434	378	124	416	299	347	140	427	2899		
Par	4	5	5	3	5	4	4	3	5	38	RED	Rating 71.8
Handicap	9	5	1	11	13	15	7	17	3			Slope 126
Hole	10	11	12	13	14	15	16	17	18	In		Totals
BLUE	405	521	175	505	154	320	211	429	362	3082	BLUE	6528
WHITE	385	511	163	494	146	312	203	408	360	2982	WHITE	6224
Par	4	5	3	5	3	4	3	4	4	35	Par	71
Handicap	4	8	12	2	16	18	10	6	14			
RED	317	474	144	415	133	255	176	379	355	2648	RED	5395
Par	4	5	3	5	3	4	3	5	4	36	Par	74
Handicap	4	8	12	2	16	18	10	14	6			

Manager: Greg Columbo   **Pro:** Dick Smith, Jr., PGA   **Supt:** Patrick Lucas
Architects: Howard Toomey & William Flynn 1929

LOWER SHORE REGION

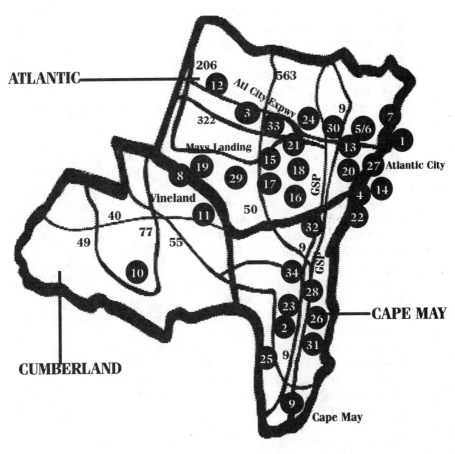

ATLANTIC

206

12

563

Atl City Expwy

3

24

9

7

322

33

30

5/6

1

Mays Landing

21

13

15

18

Atlantic City

19

20

27

8

29

17

16

4

14

Vineland

50

40

11

22

77

32

49

55

9

10

34

GSP

28

23

26

CAPE MAY

2

31

CUMBERLAND

25

9

9

Cape May

LOWER SHORE REGION

Public Courses appear in *bold italics*

	Map (#)	Page #
Atlantic City Country Club (1)		293
Avalon Golf Club (2)		294
Ballamor GC (3)		295
BL England Recreation Center (4)		296
Blue Heron Pines East GC (5)		297
Blue Heron Pines West GC (6)		298
Brigantine, The Links (7)		299
Buena Vista Country Club (8)		300
Cape May National Golf Club (9)		301
Cohanzick Country Club (10)		302
Eastlyn Golf Course (11)		303
Frog Rock CC (12)		304
Galloway National Golf Club (13)		305
Greate Bay Resort (14)		306
Green Tree Golf Course (15)		307
Hamilton Trails Country Club (16)		308
Harbor Pines Country Club(17)		309
Heritage Links (32)		310
Hidden Creek GC (18)		311
Latona Golf & Country Club (19)		312
Linwood Country Club (20)		313
Mays Landing Country Club (21)		314
McCullough's Emerald Golf Links (33)		315
Ocean City Golf Course (22)		316
Pines at Clermont (23)		317
Pomona Golf & Country Club (24)		318
Ponderlodge Golf Course (25)		319
Sand Barrens Golf Club (26)		320
Seaview Golf Resort (27)		321
Shore Gate GC (34)		322
Stone Harbor Golf Club (28)		323
Twisted Dune GC (29)		324
Vineyards at Renault (30)		325
Wildwood Golf & Country Club (31)		326

ATLANTIC CITY COUNTRY CLUB

Jackson & Leo Fraser Rd., Northfield, NJ 08225   **(609) 641-7575**

Atlantic City CC is an 18 hole course owned by Caesars Entertainment and is only available to hotel guests of the AC Hilton, Caesars or Bally's. It is open 7 days a week and closes in Jan. & Feb. Reservations are only made in conjunction with the hotels.

- •**Driving Range**   •**Lockers**
- •**Practice Green**   •**Showers**
- •**Power Carts**   •**Food**
- Pull Carts   •**Clubhouse**
- •**Club Rental**   •**Outings**
- •**Caddies**   •**Soft Spikes**

Course Description: This well-maintained seaside course in the temperate climate of the Jersey Shore is convenient for Atlantic City hotel guests. The back nine was cut out of a marsh and 6 holes have water in some way affecting play. Wind is always a factor here. Atlantic City CC is famous among golf aficionados because the word "birdie" was first used here to indicate a hole played in one under par. According to A. W. Tillinghast, this coinage occurred in 1903 when a player exclaimed as a second shot on the par 5 12th came to rest on the green, "that's a bird of a shot". Thus this popular golf term was born at the Jersey shore. Great views of the AC Skyline are apparent from many holes.

Directions: Atlantic County, #1 on Lower Shore Map
GSP to Exit 36, Tilton Rd. Take Tilton (Rte. 563) for 7 lights and then make left onto Shore Rd. Club is 1 mile ahead on the right. From Phila. take AC Xpressway to GSP and exit at #36. Follow as above.

Hole	1	2	3	4	5	6	7	8	9	Out	BLUE	Rating 72.0
BLUE	464	443	375	133	403	575	467	187	442	3489		Slope 128
WHITE	442	421	360	121	364	510	425	168	420	3231		
Par	4	4	4	3	4	5	4	3	4	35	WHITE	Rating 70.1
Handicap	1	5	13	17	11	9	7	15	3			Slope 124
RED	417	369	308	102	332	462	408	132	405	2935		
Par	5	5	4	3	4	5	5	3	5	39	RED	Rating 71.4
Handicap	5	9	13	17	11	1	7	15	3			Slope 125
Hole	10	11	12	13	14	15	16	17	18	In		Totals
BLUE	423	217	407	135	493	393	407	174	515	3164	BLUE	6539
WHITE	412	170	377	126	483	363	352	150	488	2921	WHITE	6172
Par	4	3	4	3	5	4	4	3	5	35	Par	70
Handicap	2	14	6	18	4	10	12	16	8			
RED	374	160	358	116	422	340	330	139	446	2685	RED	5324
Par	4	3	4	3	5	4	4	3	5	35	Par	70
Handicap	4	14	8	18	2	10	12	16	6			

VP of Golf: Billy Ziobro   **Pro:** Steven Sullivan, PGA   **Supt:** Jeff Kent
Architect: John Reed 1897   **Renovation:** Tom Doak 2000

AVALON GOLF CLUB

1510 Route 9N, Cape May Courthouse, NJ 08210   **(609) 465-4653**
www.avalongolfclub.net

Avalon is a semi-private 18 hole course open to the public 7 days a week all year. Tee times may be reserved up to 2 weeks in advance. Memberships are encouraged. Off season, discounted fees available. Call 1-800-MIDIRON for tee times.

•**Driving Range**	•**Lockers**
•**Practice Green**	•**Showers**
•**Power Carts**	•**Food**
•**Pull Carts**	•**Clubhouse**
•**Club Rental**	•**Outings**
•**Soft Spikes**	

Fees	Weekday	Weekend
Daily	$84	$84
Twilight specials		
Prices include cart		
Walking permitted off season		

Course Description: The public loves to play at this scenic bayside course. Warmer here than in northern New Jersey, it is not as hard frozen in the winter. Amidst the pines, oaks and dogwoods views of the bay can be seen. The course is basically level; the variable wind is a factor. With six natural lakes, water comes into play on many holes. The medium sized greens are in good condition.

Directions: Cape May County, #2 on Lower Shore Map
GSP to Exit 13. Go right at exit to Rte. 9 South and make a left at light. Golf course is about 1 mile ahead on the left.

Hole	1	2	3	4	5	6	7	8	9	Out	BLUE	Rating 70.7
BLUE	392	338	177	540	207	408	521	368	355	3306		Slope 122
WHITE	372	302	161	529	160	393	497	348	305	3067		
Par	4	4	3	5	3	4	5	4	4	36	WHITE	Rating 68.4
Handicap	7	15	9	1	11	3	5	13	17			Slope 117
RED	265	279	146	404	129	318	380	328	287	2536		
Par	4	4	3	5	3	4	5	4	4	36	RED	Rating 67.0
Handicap	7	15	9	1	11	3	5	13	17			Slope 111
Hole	10	11	12	13	14	15	16	17	18	In		Totals
BLUE	351	163	478	350	528	145	418	166	420	3019	BLUE	6325
WHITE	319	140	465	339	473	133	404	151	405	2829	WHITE	5896
Par	4	3	5	4	5	3	4	3	4	35	Par	71
Handicap	14	18	12	4	8	16	2	10	6			
RED	301	128	381	328	369	111	390	86	294	2388	RED	4694
Par	4	3	5	4	5	3	4	3	4	35	Par	71
Handicap	14	18	12	4	8	16	2	10	6			

Owners: Russell Buckingham, Stanley Casper   **Mgr./Pro:** Ted Wenner, PGA
Supt: Mike Robinson   **Architect:** Bob Hendricks 1971

BALLAMOR GOLF CLUB

6071 English Creek Ave., Egg Harbor Twp. NJ 08234 **(609) 926-9022**
www.ballamor.com

Ballamor is an 18 hole course open 7 days (in season) a week all year. Guests play accompanied by a member. Tee time reservations are not necessary.

•Driving Range	•Lockers
•Practice Green	•Showers
•Power Carts	•Food
Pull Carts	•Clubhouse
•Club Rental	•Outings
Caddies	•Soft Spikes

Course Description: Designed with tradition, variety and risk reward situations, Ballamor is carved out of gently rolling terrain and dense woods. With its 5 sets of tees, it is one of the finest private golf clubs in NJ. It is known as a "go out and stay out" routing; a halfway house for refreshments is available; play is continuous and fast paced. Wide fairways and large undulating well bunkered greens are typical of the course. The 3rd hole has a pond (one of 7) that needs to be negotiated. The scenic 6th is a short par 3 with a peninsula green and could be considered a signature hole. The 9th requires accuracy; it plays over a pond then along the existing wetland buffer. Golfers of all levels will find this course exceptional.

Directions: Atlantic County, #3 on Lower Shore Map
ACXE to Exit 9, go right off ramp 7/10 mile & go left on English Creek Rd. Go 2 lights, cross Ocean Hgts. Ave., club on right. OR (fr. South) GSP to Exit 30 & go left on Rte. 9/New Rd. Pass 5 lights, left onto Ocean Hgts. Ave. then left at Eng. Cr. Ave. to club.

Hole	1	2	3	4	5	6	7	8	9	Out	BLUE	Rating 72.5
BLUE	522	401	299	429	586	148	373	202	438	3398		Slope 130
WHITE	498	375	286	396	551	137	344	178	411	3167		
Par	5	4	4	4	5	3	4	3	4	36	WHITE	Rating 70.3
Handicap												Slope 125
RED	437	338	235	341	469	102	285	140	315	2662		
Par	5	4	4	4	5	3	4	3	4	36	RED	Rating 70.1
Handicap												Slope 122
Hole	10	11	12	13	14	15	16	17	18	In		Totals
BLUE	557	399	150	417	167	347	433	312	501	3283	BLUE	6681
WHITE	530	380	135	396	155	336	400	288	480	3100	WHITE	6267
Par	5	4	3	4	3	4	4	4	5	36	Par	72
Handicap												
RED	422	311	93	363	128	258	363	248	390	2576	RED	5238
Par	5	4	3	4	3	4	4	4	5	36	Par	72
Handicap												

President: Prudence K. Vipiani   **Pro:** Bucky Kenneff, PGA   **Supt:** Michael Miller
Architects: Ault, Clark, & Assoc., 2001

B L ENGLAND GOLF COURSE

PUBLIC

Route 9 P.O. Box 844, Beesley's Point, NJ 08215   **(609) 390-0472**

B L England is a regulation 9 hole course open to the public 7 days a week all year. Golfers may call 7 days ahead for tee times.

Driving Range
- **Practice Green**
- **Power Carts**
- **Pull Carts**
- **Club Rental**
- **Soft Spikes**

Lockers

Showers
- **Food**
- **Clubhouse**
- **Outings**

Fees	Weekday	Weekend
Daily (9)	$15	$20
Daily(18)	$25	$30
Power Carts	$6 (9)	$12(18)
(carts are per person)		

Course Description: B L England is a flat well maintained course with tree-lined fairways and lightning fast greens. Great Egg Harbor Bay can be seen from the clubhouse. Water is in play on 4 holes. The par 4 4th is a dogleg right with a tee shot out of a chute; trees and water make the hole difficult. The signature 6th hole is a par 3 with an elevated, small, well-bunkered green. Breezes from the bay keep the course cool and comfortable in summer.

Directions: Cape May County, #4 on Lower Shore Map
GSP to Exit 25. Make a right onto Rte. 9 North. Access to the course is on a road just before the Tuckahoe Inn. Go left at signs for Atlantic Electric (power plant). Do not go over bridge on Rte. 9 North.

Hole	1	2	3	4	5	6	7	8	9	Out	BLUE	Rating
BLUE												Slope
WHITE	271	143	320	331	457	99	341	205	311	2478		
Par	4	3	4	4	5	3	4	3	4	34	WHITE	Rating 63.7
Handicap	13	15	7	3	1	17	11	5	9			Slope 100
RED	252	126	296	313	385	81	322	135	235	2145		
Par	4	3	4	4	5	3	4	3	4	34	RED	Rating 63.3
Handicap	9	13	7	3	1	17	5	15	11			Slope 97

Hole	10	11	12	13	14	15	16	17	18	In		Totals
BLUE											BLUE	
WHITE											WHITE	4956
Par											Par	68
Handicap												
RED											RED	4290
Par											Par	68
Handicap												

Manager/Pro: Ron Threatt, PGA   **Supt:** Shawn Reynolds
Built: Atlantic Electric Co. 1961

BLUE HERON PINES EAST

600 Odessa Dr., Cologne, NJ 08213   **(609) 965-1800**
www.blueheronpines.com

Blue Heron Pines East is an 18 hole course open 7 days a week between Mar. & Nov 14. Memberships are available. Tee times may be made up to 10 days by phone and 14 days online.   Call 1-888-4STARGOLF for more info.

- •Driving Range
- •Practice Green
- •Power Carts .
- •Power Caddies
- •Club Rental
- •Soft Spikes
- •Lockers
- •Showers
- •Food
- •Clubhouse
- •Outings

Fees	Weekday	Weekend
Mar-Apr	$66	$81
Apr-May	$71	$91
May-June-	$81	$101
June-Sept	$101	$126
Carts included		

Course Description: Not far from Atlantic City, the new East course is distinctly different from the existing Blue Heron Pines West.   Measuring 7221 from the championship tees, it is built in a links style. Featuring wide fairways, generous tees and well bunkered challenging greens, golfers experience sweeping stretches of grasses and indigenous trees and shrubs. The play is "fast and firm" according to Smyers, to enhance the bounce and roll of the ball. The 510 yard 4th has a split fairway and places a premium on strategy. The course can measure up to some of the top private tracks in the state. Blue Heron East & West may be under one membership.

Directions: Atlantic County, #5 on Lower Shore Map
GSP to Exit 44. Take Rte. 575 S (Pomona Rd.), for 5 mi., then right onto Rte. 563N (Tilton Rd.) Course is 1/4 mi. on right.

Hole	1	2	3	4	5	6	7	8	9	Out	BLUE	Rating 72.9
BLUE	396	416	433	545	197	442	159	353	427	3368		Slope 133
WHITE	315	400	393	510	178	402	153	330	396	3077		
Par	4	4	4	5	3	4	3	4	4	35	WHITE	Rating 70.2
Handicap	12	10	8	2	14	6	18	16	4			Slope 128
RED	266	318	326	446	149	322	103	280	319	2529		
Par	4	4	4	5	3	4	3	4	4	35	RED	Rating 69.0
Handicap	12	10	8	2	14	6	18	16	4			Slope 120

Hole	10	11	12	13	14	15	16	17	18	In		Totals
BLUE	409	435	519	173	420	499	333	213	438	3439	BLUE	6807
WHITE	379	387	494	149	395	470	310	184	410	3178	WHITE	6255
Par	4	4	5	3	4	5	4	3	4	36	Par	71
Handicap	11	1	9	17	3	7	15	13	5			
RED	315	360	393	130	310	415	268	145	300	2636	RED	5165
Par	4	4	5	3	4	5	4	3	4	36	Par	71
Handicap	11	1	9	17	3	7	15	13	5			

Gen. Mgr.: Chris Arabio   **Dir. of Golf:** David Lee, PGA   **Supt:** Clark Weld
Architect: Steve Smyers 2000

BLUE HERON PINES WEST

PUBLIC

550 W. Country Club Dr., Cologne, NJ 08213   **(609) 965-1800**
www.blueheronpines.com

Blue Heron Pines is an 18 hole course open 7 days a week all year. Memberships are available. Tee times: 10 day advance by phone, 14 day online. Call 1-888-4STARGOLF for more information.

- •Driving Range
- •Practice Green
- •Power Carts
- •Pull Carts
- •Club Rental
- •Soft Spikes
- •Lockers
- •Showers
- •Food
- •Clubhouse
- •Outings

Fees	Weekday	Weekend
Mar-Apr	$66	$81
Apr-May	$71	$91
May-June-	$81	$101
June-Sept	$101	$126
Carts included		

Course Description: With a contemporary clubhouse that looks like a fine private club, Blue Heron Pines is worth a visit. The well maintained course has lush rye grass fairways and lots of woods that narrow the landing area. The greens are large with the back nine more of a challenge than the front; the bunkering throughout can be deceptive. The 11th and 14th holes are designed to be like Pine Valley, the 12th like Pinehurst. Other holes bring to mind Beth Page Black and Oyster Harbor on Cape Cod. It is the only public golf course in NJ that received both a Four Star rating and a Quality Service Rating from *Golf Digest* in their 2004 edition of *Places to Play*.

Directions: Atlantic County, #6 on Lower Shore Map
GSP to Exit 44. Take Rte. 575 S (Pomona Rd.), 5 mi., then right onto Rte. 563N (Tilton Rd.) Course is 1/2 mi. on left (across from Lenox China).

Hole	1	2	3	4	5	6	7	8	9	Out	BLUE	Rating 71.9
BLUE	307	165	517	173	405	400	305	555	370	3197		Slope 133
WHITE	290	150	485	160	390	366	283	520	347	2991		
Par	4	3	5	3	4	4	4	5	4	36	WHITE	Rating 70.1
Handicap	14	10	2	18	4	12	6	8	16			Slope 128
RED	221	119	369	138	348	284	225	443	308	2455		
Par	4	3	5	3	4	4	4	5	4	36	RED	Rating 68.4
Handicap	15	11	13	17	1	7	9	5	3			Slope 116
Hole	10	11	12	13	14	15	16	17	18	In		Totals
BLUE	382	124	405	365	498	408	196	438	511	3327	BLUE	6524
WHITE	367	114	386	342	483	383	176	401	471	3123	WHITE	6114
Par	4	3	4	4	5	4	3	4	5	36	Par	72
Handicap	5	17	15	9	1	3	11	7	13			
RED	315	90	330	305	358	321	132	342	405	2598	RED	5053
Par	4	3	4	4	5	4	3	4	5	36	Par	72
Handicap	2	14	6	12	10	4	18	8	16			

Gen. Mgr: Chris Arabio   **Dir. of Golf:** David Lee, PGA   **Supt:** Clark Weld
Architect: Stephen Kay 1993

THE LINKS at BRIGANTINE BEACH

1075 North Shore Drive, Brigantine Beach, NJ 08203 **(609) 266-1388**
www.brigantinegolf.com

Brigantine is an 18 hole course open to the public 7 days a week all year. Memberships are available. Tee times: 14 days in advance.

Driving Range	Lockers
•**Practice Green**	
•**Power Carts**	Showers
Pull Carts	•**Food**
•**Club Rental**	•**Clubhouse**
•**Soft Spikes**	•**Outings**

Fees	Weekday	Weekend
Daily(M-Th) $69	(Fr-Sun) $79	
Twilight (1PM) $40		$54
Reduced fees off season		
Power carts included		

Course Description: Built in 1927, The Links at Brigantine Beach is unique to the Northeast with its Authentic Scottish Links Design. True to its historic Scottish roots, this layout includes breathtaking bay views, native marshes and gently rolling, nearly treeless terrain. The challenge for the golfer here is playing the wind and steering around the berms, moundings and tidal water hazards including a peninsula green. With prevailing sea breezes, challenging par 3s, reachable par 5s, and newly renovated bunkers, this scenic par 72 course provides an exciting and ever changing experience for golfers of all skill levels. Recently awarded a "Top 100 Must Play Courses" by *Philadelphia Golf Monthly* and "3 & 1/2 Stars Places to Play" by *Golf Digest.*

Directions: Atlantic County, #7 on Lower Shore Map
GSP to ACXpressway East (Exit 38) ACX to Exit 1 Tunnel Connector. Take Exit 1 & follow tunnel connector thru Marina District to Brigantine Bridge (stay in middle lane). Go over Brig. Bridge onto Brig. Blvd.(3.5 mi)to Roosevelt Blvd. (Clipper Ship Motel on corner.) Take Roosevelt Blvd. to the bay.

Hole	1	2	3	4	5	6	7	8	9	Out	BLACK	Rating 70.2
BLACK	510	370	205	380	410	545	155	370	380	3325		Slope 123
SILVER	488	310	186	365	395	534	146	359	370	3097		
Par	5	4	3	4	4	5	3	4	4	36	SILVER	Rating 69.0
Handicap	14	16	4	12	2	6	18	10	8			Slope 122
GOLD	440	250	135	320	380	440	140	310	320	2735		
Par	5	4	3	4	5	5	3	4	4	37	GOLD	Rating 66.2
Handicap	4	16	8	12	6	2	18	14	10			Slope 115
Hole	10	11	12	13	14	15	16	17	18	In		Totals
BLACK	530	330	190	360	410	175	360	425	465	3245	BLACK	6524
SILVER	515	310	160	344	370	160	339	410	450	3059	SILVER	6214
Par	5	4	3	4	4	3	4	4	5	36	Par	72
Handicap	3	13	15	5	9	7	11	1	17			
GOLD	430	300	150	300	350	120	315	360	400	2725	GOLD	5230
Par	5	4	3	4	4	3	4	4	5	36	Par	73
Handicap	1	13	11	9	7	17	15	3	5			

Head Golf Pro: Chad Hoey, PGA   **Supt:** Tom Dale, CGCS
Architect: John Van Kleek, & Stiles 1927

BUENA VISTA COUNTRY CLUB   PUBLIC

Route 40, Box 307, Buena, NJ 08310   **(856) 697-3733**
www.allforeclub.com

Buena Vista is an 18 hole semi-private course open to the public 7 days a week all year.
Memberships are available. Mbrs. reserve tee times up to 7 days in advance, daily fee
5 days. Mbrs. pay cart fees only. Carts mandatory June -Sept. weekdays until 1PM.

•Driving Range	•Lockers
•Practice Green	•Showers
•Power Carts	•Food
•Pull Carts	•Clubhouse
•Club Rental	•Outings
•Soft Spikes	

Fees	Weekday	Weekend
(Mon-Th) $39	(Fri$45)	$49
After 1PM $39		
After 4PM $25		
Power carts included		

Course Description: Buena Vista is a Carolina style course, heavily wooded,
generously bunkered, and relatively narrow. Well maintained and golfer friendly, with
some water in play, the most interesting hole is the par 5 10th. A 200 yard bunker runs
along the left of this dogleg left; more sand protects the elevated and undulating green.
The eighth, a lengthy par 3, the slightly elevated green is well guarded, yet forgiving.
The 13th is a double dogleg par 5.

Directions: Atlantic County, #8 on Lower Shore Map
From Phil. area or GSP take Atlantic City Xpressway to Exit 28. Take Rte. 54S.
Proceed 8 miles and make a left onto Rte. 40 East. Go 1.5 miles to club on left.

Hole	1	2	3	4	5	6	7	8	9	Out	BLUE	Rating 71.8
BLUE	372	440	538	423	203	379	536	244	406	3540		Slope 127
WHITE	351	411	511	403	185	359	517	223	379	3339		
Par	4	4	5	4	3	4	5	3	4	36	WHITE	Rating 70.2
Handicap	17	1	5	3	13	11	7	15	9			Slope 124
RED	317	336	442	338	160	328	441	148	346	2856		
Par	4	4	5	4	3	4	5	3	4	36	RED	Rating 72.6
Handicap	13	3	5	1	15	11	9	17	7			Slope 124
Hole	10	11	12	13	14	15	16	17	18	In		Totals
BLUE	502	375	173	522	367	392	393	192	413	3329	BLUE	6869
WHITE	486	345	152	489	343	372	368	169	359	3083	WHITE	6422
Par	5	4	3	5	4	4	4	3	4	36	Par	72
Handicap	2	12	16	4	8	10	14	18	6			
RED	447	314	113	427	321	350	345	149	329	2795	RED	5651
Par	5	4	3	5	4	4	4	3	4	36	Par	72
Handicap	2	12	16	6	4	14	10	18	8			

Mgr: Eric Brandt   **Pro:** Bob Cimino   **Supt:** Ben Dunn
Architect: William Gordon 1957

CAPE MAY NATIONAL GOLF CLUB SEMI-PRIVATE

Route 9 & Florence Ave., Cape May, NJ 08204   **(609) 884-1563**
www.cmngc@dandy.net

Cape May National is an 18 hole course open to the public 7 days a week all year.
Memberships are available. Fees vary seasonally. Tee times may be made up to 7 days
in advance. For special hotel & golf packages call (1-888) CAPETRIP.

•Driving Range	•Lockers
•Practice Green	•Showers
•Power Carts	•Food
•Pull Carts	•Clubhouse
•Club Rental	•Outings
•Soft Spikes	

Fees* Weekday & Weekend
Daily $85 $85
Twi& mid-day reduced
Fees include cart
Golf packages available
*Considerably less off season

Course Description: At Cape May National the well maintained tees, fairways and
greens are of bent grass. In the heart of the course is a 50 acre nature preserve. Each
hole is distinctive with fast, undulating greens, some 2 or 3 tiered. After the golfer
chooses one of the multiple sets of tees, the well marked cart paths help him wend his
way through the wetlands. The beautiful and challenging 18th, rated one of the best
closing holes in NJ, offers water alongside on the left and a large sloped green half
surrounded by water. Cape May itself is a popular tourist attraction; after a round of
golf at this outstanding course, continue further south to see this town of Victorian
charm.

Directions: Cape May County, #9 on Lower Shore Map
GSP to Exit 4A. Follow road to 2nd light. Turn left onto Rte. 9. Club is 2 miles south
on the left.

Hole	1	2	3	4	5	6	7	8	9	Out	BLUE	Rating 72.1
BLUE	367	457	186	544	411	195	502	202	312	3176		Slope 135
WHITE	358	448	121	521	370	161	491	192	287	2949		
Par	4	4	3	5	4	3	5	3	4	35	WHITE	Rating 69.2
Handicap	11	3	13	1	7	17	5	15	9			Slope 125
RED	301	321	100	335	284	109	418	149	245	2262		
Par	4	4	3	5	4	3	5	3	4	35	RED	Rating 66.7
Handicap	7	5	17	3	9	13	1	15	11			Slope 116
Hole	10	11	12	13	14	15	16	17	18	In		Totals
BLUE	499	409	341	187	520	443	425	165	427	3416	BLUE	6592
WHITE	488	361	318	153	491	421	399	125	378	3134	WHITE	6083
Par	5	4	4	3	5	4	4	3	4	36	Par	71
Handicap	6	12	14	16	2	8	10	18	4			
RED	386	275	234	93	378	353	339	91	295	2449	RED	4711
Par	5	4	4	3	5	4	4	3	4	36	Par	71
Handicap	2	12	14	18	4	8	10	16	6			

Dir. Guest Services: Allison Maund **Pro:** John Petronis, PGA **Supt:** Keith Chapman
Architects: Carl Litten & Robert Mullock 1991

COHANZICK COUNTRY CLUB

PUBLIC

Box 149, Bridgeton-Fairton Rd., Fairton, NJ 08320   **(856) 455-2127**
www.allforeclub.com

Cohanzick is an 18 hole course open to the public 7 days a week all year. The golfer's weekday special includes green fee, cart and lunch for $25. Tee times may be made 14 days in advance.

- •Driving Range
- •Practice Green
- •Power Carts
- •Pull Carts
- •Club Rental
- Soft Spikes

- •Lockers
- •Showers
- •Food
- •Clubhouse
- •Outings

Fees	Weekday	Weekend
Daily	$15	$19
Twi	$9	$15
Power carts	$14/pp	

Course Description: This rustic golf course is hilly compared to others in south Jersey. Golfers encounter natural ponds and inlets as well as turtles, deer and herons as they make their way through this tight layout. The 15th hole overlooks the Cohansey River. The excellent drainage allows play shortly after rainfall. Trouble awaits an errant shot on the par 3 6th, a hole that straddles a craggy overgrown ravine. In the immediate vicinity, there is access to fishing, hunting, boating, water-skiing and tubing on the river.

Directions: Cumberland County, #10 on Lower Shore Map
NJTPKE to Exit #2. Follow signs to Rte. 322 to Rte. 77 South through Bridgeton to club. **OR** GSP to Exit 36. Go west.on Rte. 40 to Rte. 552 W to Rte. 553S. Make right onto Bridgeton-Fairton Rd. to club on left.

Hole	1	2	3	4	5	6	7	8	9	Out	BLUE	Rating 70.2
BLUE	415	345	173	394	533	175	474	384	390	3283		Slope 123
WHITE	405	335	163	384	508	150	464	334	375	3118		
Par	4	4	3	4	5	3	5	4	5	36	WHITE	Rating 69.1
Handicap	3	7	11	1	13	9	15	17	5			Slope 120
RED	395	325	127	374	463	137	454	266	330	2871		
Par	4	4	3	4	5	3	5	4	5	36	RED	Rating 70.5
Handicap	3	7	15	1	11	13	9	17	5			Slope 120

Hole	10	11	12	13	14	15	16	17	18	In		Totals
BLUE	143	549	313	293	391	190	167	416	540	3002	BLUE	6285
WHITE	135	539	303	283	381	164	150	406	530	2891	WHITE	6009
Par	3	5	4	4	4	3	3	4	5	35	Par	71
Handicap	12	14	8	18	4	10	16	2	6			
RED	118	516	246	260	366	150	145	382	416	2599	RED	5470
Par	3	5	4	4	4	3	3	4	5	35	Par	71
Handicap	14	4	10	18	2	8	16	12	6			

Manager: George Felice   **Supt:** Chris Hermenes
Architect: Alexander Findlay 1917

EASTLYN GOLF COURSE

4049 Italia Ave., Vineland, NJ 08361   **(856) 691-5558**

Eastlyn is an 18 hole executive course open to the public 7 days a week all year. Memberships are available. Tee time reservations are not necessary.

•**Driving Range**	Lockers
•**Practice Green**	Showers
•**Power Carts**	•**Food**
•**Pull Carts**	•**Clubhouse**
•**Club Rental**	•**Outings**
Soft Spikes	

Fees	Weekday	Weekend
Daily	$14	$16
Twilight rates available 4PM		
Power carts $14per cart $7pp		

Course Description: Meticulously maintained, Eastlyn is narrow with an abundance of diverse plants, trees and shrubs. Twelve holes offer natural water hazards. The par 3 10th has a slope away green protected by water on two sides and a bunker. The short dogleg par 4 7th also can prove difficult. The longest par 4, the 18th, is where the stronger hitters may use their drivers. Fairways are tight and greens are small providing a challenge for all levels of play. This property, formerly acres of swampland, is still a haven for wildlife.

Directions: Cumberland County, #11 on Lower Shore Map
NJTPKE to Exit #3. Take Rte.55 to Exit 26. Bear left & then 1st right onto Lincoln Ave. Follow to 2nd light & turn right onto Dante. At STOP, make left onto Panther Ave. for 1 block and then left onto Italia Ave.

Hole	1	2	3	4	5	6	7	8	9	Out	BLUE	Rating
BLUE												Slope
WHITE	135	149	136	217	160	249	285	265	165	1761		
Par	3	3	3	4	3	4	4	4	3	31	WHITE	Rating
Handicap												Slope
RED	130	139	126	210	155	240	275	255	155	1685		
Par	3	3	3	4	3	4	4	4	3	31	RED	Rating
Handicap												Slope
Hole	10	11	12	13	14	15	16	17	18	In		Totals
BLUE											BLUE	
WHITE	195	215	142	175	140	169	205	143	323	1707	WHITE	3468
Par	4	4	3	3	3	3	4	3	4		Par	62
Handicap												
RED	190	185	137	165	130	160	200	135	318	1620	RED	3305
Par	4	4	3	3	3	3	4	3	4		Par	62
Handicap												

Manager: Dana Smaniotto   **Supt/Owner:** Tom Galbiati
Architect: Francis Galbiati 1964

FROG ROCK COUNTRY CLUB

PUBLIC

420 Boyer Ave., Hammonton, NJ 08037   **(609) 561-5504**

Frog Rock is an 18 hole course open 7 days a week all year. Tee time reservations are not necessary.

Driving Range • **Practice Green** • **Power Carts** • **Pull Carts** • **Club Rental** • **Soft Spikes**	Lockers Showers • **Food** • **Clubhouse** • **Outings**

Fees	**Weekday**	**Weekend**
Daily	$20	$30
Power carts included		

Frog Rock has a rustic and park-like setting leading to an interesting golf experience. It is known for its rolling hills and tight fairways. The par 3 13th requires a well struck tee shot to carry over water. The greens are Penn Cross bent grass. From the clubhouse, the striking view is of the lake and beautiful flowers, making this an excellent site for catered affairs.

Directions: Atlantic County, #12 on Lower Shore Map
GSP to ACXpressway to Hammonton Exit. Take Rte. 54 North to Rte. 30. Watch for a sign saying "entering Hammonton." Pass a Chrysler dealership. As you make the curve, turn right onto Rte. 561. Keep straight & after STOP, club is on right.

Hole	1	2	3	4	5	6	7	8	9	Out	BLUE	Rating 67.6
BLUE	383	505	345	135	370	195	400	515	195	3043		Slope 113
WHITE	360	455	335	120	320	170	340	480	130	2710		
Par	4	5	4	3	4	3	4	5	3	35	WHITE	Rating 66.1
Handicap	1	7	11	17	9	13	5	3	15			Slope 108
RED	291	380	280	120	305	140	305	440	113	2374		
Par	4	5	4	3	4	3	4	5	3	35	RED	Rating 69.1
Handicap	1	7	11	17	9	13	5	3	15			Slope 111
Hole	10	11	12	13	14	15	16	17	18	In		Totals
BLUE	368	325	353	178	318	188	331	480	435	2976	BLUE	6101
WHITE	350	310	305	150	305	145	315	465	400	2745	WHITE	5500
Par	4	4	4	3	4	3	4	5	4	35	Par	70
Handicap	6	8	12	16	4	18	14	10	2			
RED	315	290	280	95	290	120	285	410	340	2425	RED	4799
Par	4	4	4	3	4	3	4	5	4	35	Par	70
Handicap	6	8	12	16	4	18	14	10	2			

Manager/Pro: Dennis Strigh, PGA
Built: 1970s

GALLOWAY NATIONAL GOLF CLUB ▌PRIVATE

270 S. New York Rd., Galloway, NJ 08205　　　**(609) 748-1000**
www.gallowaynationalgolf.com

Galloway National is an 18 hole championship course open 6 days a week all year.
Guests may play accompanied by a member. Reserved tee times are required.

- •**Driving Range**　•**Lockers**
- •**Practice Green**　•**Showers**
- •**Power Carts**　•**Food**
-   Pull Carts　•**Clubhouse**
- •**Club Rental**　•**Outings**
- •**Caddies**　•**Soft Spikes**

Course Description: Overlooking Reeds Bay, Galloway is considered a course for the
serious golfer. The layout is lined with bunkers and scrub pines and follows the
contours of the natural terrain. The beautiful par 3 5th faces the Bay and golf club
selection is critical due to prevailing winds and the salt marsh hugging the green. The
par 5 6th begins with a tee shot that crosses a quarry and climbs a hill to the left. The
second shot must be carefully placed to set up for the approach to the undulating and
slightly crowned green. Galloway is an outstanding example of fine golfing in New
Jersey.

Directions: Atlantic County, #13 on Lower Shore Map
GSP to Exit 48. Take Rte. 9 South toward Absecon. The club is on the left about 5
miles ahead on Rte. 9.

Hole	1	2	3	4	5	6	7	8	9	Out	GOLD	Rating 74.0
GOLD	400	146	375	446	189	548	390	196	539	3229		Slope 144
BLUE	366	138	336	415	175	520	357	170	504	2981		
Par	4	3	4	4	3	5	4	3	5	35	BLUE	Rating 71.4
Handicap	5	15	17	1	13	3	11	9	7			Slope 138
RED												
Par											RED	Rating
Handicap												Slope
Hole	10	11	12	13	14	15	16	17	18	In		Totals
GOLD	475	501	375	470	219	409	532	249	426	3656	GOLD	6901
BLUE	409	481	356	449	190	390	493	212	408	3388	BLUE	6374
Par	4	5	4	4	3	4	5	3	4	36	Par	71
Handicap	6	18	16	2	14	10	8	12	4			
RED											RED	
Par											Par	
Handicap												

Dir. of Golf/Pro: Mike Killian, PGA　　　　**Supt:** Scott McBane
Architect: Tom Fazio 1994

GREATE BAY GOLF CLUB

901 Mays Landing Rd., Somers Point, NJ 08244   **(609) 927-0066**
www.greatebay.com

Greate Bay is an 18 hole private course open 7 days a week all year. Guests may play accompanied by a member. Tee time reservations are suggested on weekends.

•**Driving Range**	•**Lockers**
•**Practice Green**	•**Showers**
•**Power Carts**	•**Food**
Pull Carts	•**Clubhouse**
Club Rental	•**Outings**
Caddies	•**Soft Spikes**

Course Description: The 169 acre classic Scottish links style Greate Bay Golf Club enjoys afternoon refreshing bay breezes in summer. In excellent condition, it is on the banks of Great Egg Harbor Bay between Somers Point and Ocean City. With elevation changes and small greens which are fast and well bunkered, this course is challenging and rewarding. The 12th is a long dogleg par 4 with a three tiered green. Golfers can experience the game as it was meant to be played. The clubhouse was completely renovated in 2003. This club is only minutes away from Atlantic City. Carts are mandatory.

Directions: Atlantic County, #14 on Lower Shore Map
GSP to Exit #30 (Somers Pt./Ocean City). At 1st light, go right onto Rte. 9 South to 1st light (Rte.559), Somers Point. Go left onto Mays Landing Rd. Club is on the left.

Hole	1	2	3	4	5	6	7	8	9	Out	BLUE	Rating 69.6
BLUE	381	439	126	386	408	548	426	421	216	3351		Slope 126
WHITE	364	414	120	358	389	537	409	406	183	3180		
Par	4	4	3	4	4	5	4	4	3	35	WHITE	Rating 67.6
Handicap	9	13	5	17	11	3	1	15	7			Slope 125
RED	309	346	97	320	326	466	368	325	133	2690		
Par	4	4	3	4	4	5	4	4	3	35	RED	Rating 71.9
Handicap	9	13	5	17	11	3	1	15	7			Slope 122
Hole	10	11	12	13	14	15	16	17	18	In		Totals
BLUE	424	423	410	185	387	549	151	423	402	3354	BLUE	6705
WHITE	396	402	364	164	374	535	129	386	385	3135	WHITE	6315
Par	4	4	4	3	4	5	3	4	4	35	Par	70
Handicap	4	8	18	2	16	14	6	10	12			
RED	326	331	316	135	299	441	111	355	345	2659	RED	5349
Par	4	4	4	3	4	5	3	4	4	35	Par	70
Handicap	4	8	18	2	16	14	6	10	12			

Director of Golf: Gary Massey   **Pro:** Tim DeBaufry, PGA   **Supt:** Chris Lynch
Architects: Willie Park, Jr. 1923 George Fazio 1972

GREEN TREE GOLF COURSE

PUBLIC

1030 Somers Pt.-Mays Landing Rd., Egg Harbor   **(609) 625-9131**
Twp., NJ 08234
www.atlanticcounty.inc

Green Tree is an 18 hole Atlantic County course open 7 days a week all year. Tee time
reservations may be made 7 days in advance. ID is available for county residents.

• Driving Range	• Lockers
• Practice Green	• Showers
• Power Carts	• Food
• Pull Carts	• Clubhouse
• Club Rental	• Outings
• Soft Spikes	

Fees	Weekday	Weekend
Daily(res/ID)	$12	$15
Non.res.	$24	$26
Twi(3PM)	$10	$16
Power carts	$14pp	

Course Description: Purchased from a private owner in the early nineties, Green Tree
is the only Atlantic County owned course. Short and relatively flat, it is well maintained
despite becoming quite crowded in season. The scorecard is very helpful with its
depictions of each hole and an overall layout scheme as well. Water comes into play
on nearly every hole on the back nine. The challenging par 4 8th needs the approach
shot to carry over a water hazard lurking in front of the contoured green.

Directions: Atlantic County, #15 on Lower Shore Map
From North: GSP to Exit #36. Then take Rte. 322/Rte.40 to Rte. 50 South. Make a left
onto Rte. 559S (*Somers Pt., Mays Landing Rd.) Course is 4 miles on left. OR From
South: GSP to Exit #29 onto Rte. 9N to Rte. 559N.* Course is about 10 mi. on right.

Hole	1	2	3	4	5	6	7	8	9	Out	BLUE	Rating
BLUE												Slope
WHITE	449	349	596	119	256	263	163	401	413	3009		
Par	4	4	5	3	4	4	3	4	4	35	WHITE	Rating 66.1
Handicap	3	7	1	17	13	11	15	2	5			Slope 109
RED	409	309	434	95	229	240	120	372	328	2536		
Par	5	4	5	3	4	4	3	5	4	37	RED	Rating 66.9
Handicap	3	7	1	17	13	11	15	2	5			Slope 106
Hole	10	11	12	13	14	15	16	17	18	In		Totals
BLUE											BLUE	
WHITE	165	319	275	240	397	181	312	326	485	2700	WHITE	5177
Par	3	4	4	4	4	3	4	4	5	35	Par	70
Handicap	18	8	12	14	4	16	10	6	9			
RED	118	257	251	219	375	119	254	251	424	2268	RED	4613
Par	3	4	4	4	5	3	4	4	5	36	Par	73
Handicap	18	8	12	14	4	16	10	6	9			

Manager: Edward McGettigan   **Supt:** Bob Miller
Architect: Horace Smith 1968

HAMILTON TRAILS CC

620 Harbor Ave., Mays Landing, NJ 08330   **(609) 641-6824**

Hamilton Trails is a regulation 9 hole course open 7 days a week all year. Tee time reservations are not necesssary.

• **Driving Range**	Lockers
• **Practice Green**	Showers
• **Power Carts**	• **Food**
• **Pull Carts**	• **Clubhouse**
• **Club Rental**	Outings
• **Soft Spikes**	

Fees	Weekday	Weekend
Daily	$14	$17
Power carts	$14/9	

Course Description: This easy to walk nine hole course is a good test of golf. The golfer encounters many interesting ditches and ponds throughout the layout. The tree lined open fairways are flat and the large bent grass medium sized greens are fast and well bunkered. Wind is a factor here. Hamilton Trails is close to Atlantic City making it a convenient place for a quick nine holes.

Directions: Atlantic County, #16 on Lower Shore Map
GSP to Exit #36. Take Rte. 563 (Tilton Rd.) West to Rte. 40. Go left on Rte. 40 (Black Horse Pike) to English Creek Rd. and turn left. Turn right onto Ocean Heights Ave. for 1.7 miles to Harbor Rd. Club is on right.

Hole	1	2	3	4	5	6	7	8	9	Out	BLUE	Rating 69.4
BLUE	405	390	520	410	170	345	370	465	190	3265		Slope 123
WHITE	395	370	495	395	160	325	350	445	160	3095		
Par	4	4	5	4	3	4	4	5	3	36	WHITE	Rating 67.3
Handicap	3	15	7	1	13	11	9	17	5			Slope 120
RED	380	310	470	380	115	320	335	340	145	2795		
Par	4	4	5	4	3	4	4	4	3	35	RED	Rating 66.0
Handicap	6	9	2	8	5	4	1	7	3			Slope 119
Hole	10	11	12	13	14	15	16	17	18	In		Totals
BLUE											BLUE	3265
WHITE											WHITE	3095
Par											Par	36
Handicap												
RED											RED	2795
Par											Par	35
Handicap												

Owners: Jack and Andrew Bucceri
Architect: Bill Sholtko 1983

HARBOR PINES COUNTRY CLUB **PUBLIC**

500 St. Andrews Dr., Egg Harbor Twp, NJ 08234   **(609) 927-0006**
www.harborpines.com

Harbor Pines is an 18 hole championship course open to the public 7 days a week all year. Memberships, both corporate and associate, are available. For tee times, calll extension 10, up to 30 days in advance for members, 14 days for daily fee golfers.

•Driving Range	•Lockers
•Practice Green	•Showers
•Power Carts	•Food
Pull Carts	•Clubhouse
•Club Rental	•Outings
•Soft Spikes	

Fees	Weekday	Weekend
Daily	$95	$130
Seasonal specials		
Twi rates available		
Fees include cart		

Course Description: Harbor Pines CC is a relatively level, well conditioned layout that takes advantage of the surrounding beauty and landscape to provide a challenging experience for all levels of golfers. With 5 sets of tees, breathtaking views and 17 acres of water, this parkland style course winds through 520 acres of dense pine forest. Strategically placed bunkers, wide fairway corridors, large, fast undulating greens and well mown rough are features of this highly rated course. The par 4 9th fairway, sloping on both sides, has water on the left and woods on the right. Within the contemporary clubhouse is the well stocked Pro Shop.

Directions: Atlantic County, #17 on Lower Shore Map
GSP to Exit 30. At first major intersection, turn left onto Rte. 9 North. At the 5th light, turn left onto Ocean Heights Ave. Go about 1 and 1/2 miles to club on left.

Hole	1	2	3	4	5	6	7	8	9	Out	BLUE	Rating 70.7
BLUE	480	360	153	395	422	364	502	190	435	3301		Slope 125
WHITE	465	340	143	370	402	345	474	170	419	3128		
Par	5	4	3	4	4	4	5	3	4	36	WHITE	Rating 69.1
Handicap	15	9	17	5	3	7	13	11	1			Slope 122
RED	412	271	123	296	360	263	418	137	367	2626		
Par	5	4	3	4	4	4	5	3	4	36	RED	Rating 68.8
Handicap	9	11	17	7	1	13	5	15	3			Slope 118
Hole	10	11	12	13	14	15	16	17	18	In		Totals
BLUE	530	172	333	383	325	158	385	437	479	3202	BLUE	6503
WHITE	511	162	291	351	315	150	367	409	458	3014	WHITE	6142
Par	5	3	4	4	4	3	4	4	5	36	Par	72
Handicap	8	10	14	6	16	18	4	2	12			
RED	419	130	233	296	252	108	298	335	402	2473	RED	5099
Par	5	3	4	4	4	3	4	4	5	36	Par	72
Handicap	4	16	14	8	12	18	6	2	10			

General Manager: Tim Krebs, PGA   **Supt:** Rick Broome
Architect: Stephen Kay 1996

HERITAGE LINKS GOLF CLUB

PUBLIC

1375 S. Shore Rd., Palermo, NJ 08230

heritagelinksgolf.com

(609) 390-4500

Heriitage Links is a 9 hole executive course open to the public 7 days a week all year. Memberships are available. Tee times may be made 7 days in advance.

Driving Range
- **Practice Green**
- **Power Carts**
- **Pull Carts**
- **Club Rental**
- **Soft Spikes**

Lockers
Showers
- **Food**
Clubhouse
- **Outings**

NEW

Fees	Weekday	Weekend
Daily	$25	$25
Twi (3PM)	$15	
Power carts $8pp		
Seasonal discounts		

Course Description: Heritage Links is an 1800 yard executive course which has 3 par 4's and 6 par 3's. It is in excellent condition. Water is in play on three holes. The signature par 3 third hole requires a tee shot over water to a well bunkered green. Wind may be a factor here. This facility is great for new golfers, Jrs. and Srs. to play. There is a family cemetary in the center of the course; a free drop is available if you land in it. A fast round of golf can be expected here.

Directions: Atlantic County, #32 on Lower Shore Map
GSP to Exit 25, Ocean City . Take the ramp and go right to Rte. 9 South for 2.& 1/2 miles; course is on the left.

Hole	1	2	3	4	5	6	7	8	9	Out	BLUE	Rating 29.5
BLUE	179	301	124	139	143	339	172	338	151	1886		Slope 105
WHITE	141	269	109	118	136	312	156	323	138	1702		
Par	3	4	3	3	3	4	3	4	3	30	WHITE	Rating 27.8
Handicap	9	5	17	11	15	3	7	1	13			Slope 92
RED	99	251	96	102	123	246	125	252	108	1402		
Par	3	4	3	3	3	4	3	4	3	30	RED	Rating 30.8
Handicap	9	5	17	11	15	3	7	1	13			Slope 109
Hole	10	11	12	13	14	15	16	17	18	In		Totals
BLUE											BLUE	1886
WHITE											WHITE	1702
Par											Par	30
Handicap												
RED											RED	1402
Par											Par	30
Handicap												

Manager: Jerry Donovan   **Supt:** Rob Prettyman
Architect: Mike Gaffney 2001

HIDDEN CREEK GOLF CLUB PRIVATE

75 Asbury Rd., Egg Harbor Township, NJ 08234 **(609) 909-2990**
www.hiddencreekclub.com

Hidden Creek is an 18 hole private course open 7 days a week between Mem. Day & Labor Day and closes on Tuesdays for the rest of the year Tee time reservations are not necessary. Guests play accompanied by a member.

- •Driving Range
- •Practice Green
- •Power Carts
- •Pull Carts
- •Club Rental
- •Caddies
- •Lockers
- •Showers
- •Food
- •Clubhouse
- Outings
- •Soft Spikes

Course Description: With a tumbling topography and nature as a backdrop, Hidden Creek is one of the top private championship courses in NJ and is a welcome addition to golf in South Jersey. Sculpted out of 750 acres of aged woodlands, the golfer encounters gently rolling hills, meandering streams and wildlife. The course features bent grass fairways, daring bunkers and dramatic elevation changes. There is no water in play but the difficulty lies in its construction. In pristine condition, it is actually quite challenging for the low handicapper and yet enjoyable for the neophyte.

Directions: Atlantic County, #18 on Lower Shore Map
GSP to Exit 36A(Northfield). At light at Fire Rd. go right and take Mill Rd. (Rte.662) to end where it meets Ocean Hgts. Ave. (alt. Rt. 559) & go right. Go straight thru light at English Creek Ave. for 1.3 mi. & go left on Pine Ave. Take Pine to end and turn right on Asbury Rd. to club.

Hole	1	2	3	4	5	6	7	8	9	Out	BLUE	Rating 72.2
BLUE	402	372	534	222	395	446	179	300	583	3433		Slope 131
WHITE	392	365	501	202	381	426	161	273	519	3220		
Par	4	4	5	3	4	4	3	4	5	36	WHITE	Rating 70.5
Handicap	12	10	4	8	14	2	16	18	6			Slope 127
RED	321	299	418	157	295	367	131	234	471	2693		
Par	4	4	5	3	4	4	3	4	5	36	RED	Rating 70.4
Handicap	8	14	2	10	12	4	18	16	6			Slope 120
Hole	**10**	**11**	**12**	**13**	**14**	**15**	**16**	**17**	**18**	**In**		Totals
BLUE	476	121	467	391	200	411	470	495	408	3439	BLUE	6872
WHITE	447	117	450	374	182	391	450	466	388	3265	WHITE	6485
Par	4	3	4/5	4	3	4	4	5	4	35/36		Par 71/72
Handicap	3	17	5	13	15	7	1	11	9			
RED	378	88	422	311	154	336	366	402	336	2793	RED	5486
Par	4	3	4/5	4	3	4	4	5	4	35/36		Par 71/72
Handicap	3	17	9	13	15	11	1	7	5			

Manager: Jennifer Hansen   **Pro**: Ian Dalzell, PGA   **Supt:** Jeff Riggs
Architects: Bill Coore & Ben Crenshaw 2002

LATONA GOLF & COUNTRY CLUB PUBLIC

Oak & Cumberland Rds., Buena, NJ 08310   **(856) 692-8149**

Latona is a 9 hole course open to the public 7 days a week all year. Tee time reservations are not necessary.

Driving Range
•**Practice Green**
•**Power Carts**
•**Pull Carts**
•**Club Rental**
Soft Spikes
Lockers
Showers
•**Food**
Clubhouse
•**Outings**

Fees	Weekday	Weekend
Daily	$15	$18
Twi(4PM)	$13	$16
Power carts $16 per cart		

Course Description: This well maintained 9 hole course is built on wide open terrain with very little water in play. The greens have subtle breaks and are hard to read; some say it has the "best greens in South Jersey." It is family operated and has a country-type friendly atmosphere.

Directions: Atlantic County, #19 on Lower Shore Map
Atlantic City Expressway West from the GSP or East from Phila.-Camden area (reached by NJTPKE) to Exit #28. Then take Rte. 54 South to Rte. 557 in Buena. Turn left and road becomes Cumberland Ave. Club is on right on Oak Rd.

Hole	1	2	3	4	5	6	7	8	9	Out	BLUE	Rating
BLUE												Slope
WHITE	360	480	390	185	330	155	440	495	225	3060		
Par	4	5	4	3	4	3	4	5	3	35	WHITE	Rating
Handicap	9	5	3	13	15	17	1	7	11			Slope
RED												
Par											RED	Rating
Handicap												Slope

Hole	10	11	12	13	14	15	16	17	18	In		Totals
BLUE											BLUE	
WHITE	370	490	400	195	340	165	450	505	235	3150	WHITE	6210
Par	4	5	4	3	4	3	4	5	3	35	Par	70
Handicap	10	6	4	14	16	18	2	8	12			
RED											RED	
Par											Par	
Handicap												

Manager: Joyce De Klerk   **Supt:** Nick Levari, Jr.
Architect: Garret Renn 1963

LINWOOD COUNTRY CLUB   **PRIVATE**

800 Shore Rd., Linwood, NJ 08221   **(609) 927-7374**

Linwood is an 18 hole course open 7 days a week all year. Guests play accompanied by a member. Tee time reservations are necessary on weekends.

- •**Driving Range**   •**Lockers**
- •**Practice Green**   •**Showers**
- •**Power Carts**   •**Food**
- Pull Carts   •**Clubhouse**
- •**Club Rental**   Outings
- •**Caddies**   •**Soft Spikes**

Course Description: Excellent views of the bay are prevalent at the well maintained Linwood CC. So near the water, the wind is a major factor. Golfers find the small greens difficult to putt and the breaks hard to read. The signature par 5 twelfth hole, 518 yards from the blues, has a lake running through the lay up area and is dominated by wind in your face. Stephen Kay has done some redesign to upgrade the course and produce a more links style feeling adding bunkers and waste areas.

Directions: Atlantic County, #20 on Lower Shore Map
GSP to Exit #36. Take Rte. 40 East (Black Horse Pike) to Rte. 585 (becomes Shore Rd.) Go right on Rte. 585 to club on left. From ACXpressway: exit at Rte. 585 and go South to club.

Hole	1	2	3	4	5	6	7	8	9	Out	BLUE	Rating 70.1
BLUE	348	363	167	421	357	171	377	205	531	2940		Slope 127
WHITE	333	323	127	387	328	164	360	198	505	2725		
Par	4	4	3	4	4	3	4	3	5	34	WHITE	Rating 68.7
Handicap	11	5	17	1	13	15	7	9	3			Slope 124
GREEN	319	314	114	280	312	157	289	121	409	2315		
Par	4	4	3	4	4	3	4	3	5	34	GREEN	Rating 68.2
Handicap	5	7	17	11	3	13	9	15	1			Slope 117

Hole	10	11	12	13	14	15	16	17	18	In		Totals
BLUE	366	365	518	345	389	404	173	532	376	3468	BLUE	6316
WHITE	355	325	433	333	370	346	164	463	362	3151	WHITE	5982
Par	4	4	5	4	4	4	3	5	4	37	Par	70
Handicap	10	18	6	8	2	14	12	4	16			
GREEN	345	264	407	319	351	333	151	414	348	2932	GREEN	5284
Par	4	4	5	4	4	4	3	5	4	37	Par	70
Handicap	8	16	4	14	6	12	18	2	10			

Manager: Bill Coulter   **Pro:** Jeff Lefevre, PGA   **Supt:** Alan Beck
Built: 1920s

MAYS LANDING COUNTRY CLUB `PUBLIC`

1855 Cates Rd., Mays Landing, NJ 08330 **(609) 641-4411**
www.mayslandinggolf.com

Mays Landing is an 18 hole course open to the public 7 days a week all year. Fees vary according to season; early-bird, twilight, lunch and midday specials are available. Tee time reservations may be made up to 7 days in advance.

- •Driving Range
- •Practice Green
- •Power Carts
- •Pull Carts
- •Club Rental
- •Soft Spikes

- •Lockers
- •Showers
- •Food
- •Clubhouse
- •Outings

Fees   Weekday   Weekend
Prices range from $35 to $70*
*(depending on season)
Power carts included

Course Description: Mays Landing is located on 175 acres in Atlantic County. It is a well designed and maintained course that wends its way through the pristine New Jersey Pinelands. The many trees encroach from the rough to produce narrow fairways. Water is in play on seven holes. The medium sized greens are rather fast. The huge waste bunkers edged with natural vegetation along with the recent upgrades make the course interesting. The par 4 13th is lengthy and features a somewhat elevated green. It was awarded 3&1/2 stars by *Golf Digest's Places to Play for 2002-2003*.

Directions: Atlantic County, #21 on Lower Shore Map
GSP South to ACXPressway to Exit #12. Go right at exit for 1/4 mile and turn left onto Rte.322/40. At Coastal Gas Sta., turn right onto McKee which turns into Cates. Course is on right.

Hole	1	2	3	4	5	6	7	8	9	Out	BLUE	Rating 71.8
BLUE	559	207	414	331	516	424	334	183	360	3328		Slope 123
WHITE	539	188	379	301	500	405	327	164	339	3142		
Par	5	3	4	4	5	4	4	3	4	36	WHITE	Rating 70.3
Handicap	3	11	7	17	5	1	9	15	13			Slope 120
RED	487	133	336	264	464	350	317	132	293	2776		
Par	5	3	4	4	5	4	4	3	4	36	RED	Rating 69.7
Handicap	1	15	5	11	7	3	9	17	13			Slope 114
Hole	10	11	12	13	14	15	16	17	18	In		Totals
BLUE	310	489	180	430	341	220	373	541	412	3305	BLUE	6624
WHITE	396	478	154	420	317	172	357	527	388	3109	WHITE	6251
Par	4	5	3	4	4	3	4	5	4	36	Par	72
Handicap	10	16	18	2	12	14	8	4	6			
RED	239	386	116	363	295	123	294	426	288	2530	RED	5306
Par	4	4	3	4	4	3	4	5	4	35	Par	71
Handicap	10	4	18	2	14	16	8	6	12			

Manager: Sean Donnelly   **Pro:** Bob Herman, PGA   **Supt:** Barry Anes
Architect: Leo Fraser 1962

McCULLOUGH'S EMERALD GOLF LINKS

3016 Ocean Heights Ave., Egg Harbor Twp., 08234   **(609) 926-3900**
www.mcculloughsgolf.com

Emerald Golf Links is a Billy Casper managed property. It is an 18 hole course open
to the public 7 days a week all year. Golfers may book tee time 10 days in advance.
(12 days on website). Various memberships are available with reduced fees.

- **Driving Range**
- **Practice Green**
- **Power Carts**
- **Pull Carts**
- **Club Rental**
- **Soft Spikes**

- **Lockers**
- **Showers**
- **Food**
- **Clubhouse**
- **Outings**

Fees	Mon-Thur	Fri-Sun
Daily	$60	$80
Atl Cty Res	$50	$65

Prices include cart

Seasonal, Jr & Sr Discounts

Course Description: McCullough's Emerald Links presents players with a distinctly
different Irish-Scottish golfing flavor characterized by wide open fairways, tricky
powerful winds, remarkable grass mounds and bunkers, vast natural waste areas and
true undulating greens. Minutes away from Atlantic City, this 18 hole, 6,600 yard
layout is a tribute to famed European courses. The 7th hole follows an Alistair McKenzie
design. With water on 5 holes and 100 foot elevation changes, players can enjoy a
scenic and challenging experience.

Directions: Atlantic County, # 33 on Lower Shore Map
GSP to Exit 36; go right on Fire Rd., right on Zion Rd., left on Ocean Hgts. Ave. to
club on left.

Hole	1	2	3	4	5	6	7	8	9	Out	BLUE	Rating 69.8
BLUE	390	173	481	345	212	490	422	400	166	3079		Slope 125
WHITE	363	140	461	323	196	457	380	385	160	2865		
Par	4	3	5	4	3	5	4	4	3	35	WHITE	Rating 67.8
Handicap	3	17	9	13	11	7	1	5	15			Slope 119
RED	302	105	413	298	158	401	333	370	123	2503		
Par	4	3	5	4	3	5	4	4	3	35	RED	Rating 67.2
Handicap	3	17	9	13	11	7	1	5	15			Slope 118
Hole	10	11	12	13	14	15	16	17	18	In		Totals
BLUE	437	314	434	180	491	272	126	451	348	3053	BLUE	6132
WHITE	380	289	419	154	458	259	113	431	332	2835	WHITE	5700
Par	4	4	4	3	5	4	3	5	4	36	Par	71
Handicap	2	6	8	10	14	18	16	4	12			
RED	354	143	342	126	422	221	92	400	253	2353	RED	4856
Par	4	3	4	3	5	4	3	5	4	35	Par	70
Handicap	6	8	2	10	14	18	16	4	12			

Manager: Tom Sullivan   **Pro:** Robert Bachman, PGA   **Supt:** Larry Motto
Architect: Stephen Kay 2002

OCEAN CITY GOLF COURSE

PUBLIC

Bay Ave. & 26th St., Ocean City, NJ 08226   **(609) 399-1315**

Ocean City is a 12 hole municipal course operated by the Ocean City Recreation Dep't. It is open 7 days a week all year. Tee time reservations are not necessary.

Driving Range
- **Practice Green**
Power Carts
- **Pull Carts**
- **Club Rental**
- **Soft Spikes**

Lockers
Showers
- **Food**
Clubhouse
Outings

Fees	Weekday	Weekend
Daily	$10	$10
Sr/Jr	$8	$8

Course Description: A considerable attraction at this golf facility is the warm and friendly atmosphere. Adjacent to an airport from which you can literally walk to the first tee, golfers who fly there in small planes can really enjoy this unique feature at this well maintained course. Ocean City is recommended for beginners, seniors and for those who want to practice their game at an inexpensive twelve hole layout. Due to environmental restrictions, no more holes may be built.

Directions: Cape May County, #22 on Lower Shore Map
GSP to Exit #25. Make a left onto Bay Ave and follow signs to airport and course.

Hole	1	2	3	4	5	6	7	8	9	Out	BLUE	Rating
BLUE												Slope
WHITE	70	145	135	115	140	105	135	180	165			
Par	3	3	3	3	3	3	3	3	3	27	WHITE	Rating
Handicap	12	7	9	10	8	11	6	1	3			Slope
RED												
Par											RED	Rating
Handicap												Slope

Hole	10	11	12	13	14	15	16	17	18	In		Totals
BLUE											BLUE	
WHITE	230	155	175								WHITE	1750
Par	4	3	3								Par	37
Handicap	5	4	2									
RED											RED	
Par											Par	
Handicap												

Club Manager: Mike Allegretto   **Supt:** Scott Gaskill
Built: 1962

THE PINES AT CLERMONT

PUBLIC

358 Kings Highway, Clermont, NJ 08210   **(609) 624-0100**

The Pines is a 9 hole regulation course open 7 days a week all year. Discounted green fee structures (Pac Pass) and memberships are available. Tee times are up to 10 days in advance for members and 7 days for daily players. A warm-up mat is available.

Driving Range	Lockers
•**Practice Green**	Showers
•**Power Carts**	•**Food**
•**Pull Carts**	•**Clubhouse**
•**Club Rental**	•**Outings**
•**Soft Spikes**	

Fees	Weekday	Weekend
Daily AM	$30	$30
12-4PM	$25	$25
4-8PM	$20	$20
Reduced rates off season		
Power carts $7pp/9holes		

Course Description: The Pines at Clermont is a wonderful 9 hole opportunity for New Jersey golfers. With lush bent grass tree-lined fairways, tees and greens, the waste bunkers and water in view make this an intelligently conceived and peacefully comfortable venue for a quiet golf getaway. There is beauty in the signature loop of holes 5, 6 and 7 around the lake; the layout is mature looking and well groomed. Relatively small greens and pot bunkers are featured here. The course is noted for hosting group outings, tournaments and leagues as well as for successful instruction programs catering to all skill levels.

Directions: Cape May County, #23 on Lower Shore Map
GSP to Exit 17. From ramp, turn left and then left onto Rte. 9 South. Go 1 mile to Academy Rd. and turn right. Go 1 mile to STOP. Course is 50 yards ahead on the left.

Hole	1	2	3	4	5	6	7	8	9	Out	BLUE	Rating 30.6
BLUE	359	127	403	340	188	183	161	273	168	2202		Slope 103
WHITE	339	117	379	320	165	166	134	256	135	2011		
Par	4	3	4	4	3	3	3	4	3	31	WHITE	Rating 29.7
Handicap	6	9	1	3	2	4	7	5	8			Slope 101
RED	326	113	344	304	154	152	114	247	119	1873		
Par	4	3	4	4	3	3	3	4	3	31	RED	Rating 31.0
Handicap	6	9	1	3	2	4	7	5	8			Slope 108

Hole	10	11	12	13	14	15	16	17	18	In		Totals
BLUE											BLUE	2202
WHITE											WHITE	2011
Par											Par	31
Handicap												
RED											RED	1873
Par											Par	31
Handicap												

Manager: Aaron McNair   **Supt:** Ken Sikora
Architects: Steve Malikowski & Vince Orlando 1999

POMONA GOLF CLUB

Moss Mill Rd. & Odessa Ave., Pomona, NJ 08240   **(609) 965-3232**

Pomona is a 9 hole executive course open to the public 7 days a week all year. Memberships are available. Tee time reservations are not necessary.

•Driving Range	Lockers
Practice Green	Showers
•Power Carts	**•Food**
•Pull Carts	**•Clubhouse**
•Club Rental	**•Outings**
Soft Spikes	

Fees	Weekday	Weekend
Daily	$14	$16
Power carts for members only		

Course Description: Formerly a vineyard, Pomona is a family owned and managed facility. It is a flat, wooded course not far from bustling Atlantic City. Water hazards come into play on three holes. The fairways are tree lined and many holes are doglegs. The bent grass greens are elevated. Accuracy with irons is a must to score well here. The friendly atmosphere and reasonable rates make it very appealing.

Directions: Atlantic County, #24 on Lower Shore Map
GSP to Exit#44. Make a right on Moss Mill Rd. and travel 3 miles to course.

Hole	1	2	3	4	5	6	7	8	9	Out	BLUE	Rating
BLUE												Slope
WHITE	295	150	295	290	290	275	126	365	340	2426		
Par	4	3	4	4	4	4	3	4	4	34	WHITE	Rating 62.5
Handicap												Slope
RED												
Par	4	3	5	4	5	4	3	5	5	38	RED	Rating
Handicap												Slope
Hole	10	11	12	13	14	15	16	17	18	In		Totals
BLUE											BLUE	
WHITE	295	150	295	290	290	275	126	365	340	2426	WHITE	4852
Par	4	3	4	4	4	4	3	4	4	34	Par	68
Handicap												
RED											RED	
Par	4	3	5	4	5	4	3	5	5	38	Par	76
Handicap												

Managers: Andrea Truitt & Pam Grenda   **Supt:** Bruce Ritchie
Built: 1940s

PONDERLODGE GOLF COURSE

PUBLIC

7 Shawmount Ave., Villas, NJ 08251   **(609) 886-8065**
www.ponderlodge.com

Ponderlodge is an 18 hole semi-private course open to the public 7 days a week all year. Memberships are available. Tee time reservations can be made up to 2 weeks in advance.

Driving Range	•Lockers
•Practice Green	•Showers
•Power Carts	•Food
•Pull Carts	•Clubhouse
•Club Rental	•Outings
•Soft Spikes	

Fees	Weekday	Weekend
Daily	$65	$65
After 1:00PM	$53	$53
Seasonal Discounts		
Power Carts included		

Course Description: At the end of a long, shaded, tree lined entrance road lies the golf course and the private Ponderlodge Conference Center. The wooded course is rather tight, scenic and interesting. Each hole has its own character with water in play on many of them. The long, narrow par 5 seventh is the signature hole and justifiably the #1 handicap. The par 4 ninth has water on the right and 2 tricky bunkers on the right side of the green. Formerly an estate owned by William Former of Schmidts's Brewery, horses are still stabled on the premises.

Directions: Cape May County, #25 on Lower Shore Map
GSP to Exit #4A (Rio Grande) to Rte. 47 North. Cross over Rte. 9 and turn left at Fulling Mill Rd. Turn left onto Bayshore Rd. Club entrance is 1 mile on the right side just past Bayshore Village.

Hole	1	2	3	4	5	6	7	8	9	Out	BLUE	Rating 69.6
BLUE	329	143	363	326	509	216	537	301	425	3149		Slope 120
WHITE	302	137	358	321	504	211	532	296	420	3081		
Par	4	3	4	4	5	3	5	4	4	36	WHITE	Rating 69.1
Handicap	11	17	7	9	3	15	1	13	5			Slope 119
RED	251	113	306	260	425	147	447	221	339	2509		
Par	4	3	4	4	5	3	5	4	4	36	RED	Rating 68.6
Handicap	11	17	7	9	3	15	1	13	5			Slope 117

Hole	10	11	12	13	14	15	16	17	18	In		Totals
BLUE	365	188	357	315	321	139	487	392	418	2982	BLUE	6200
WHITE	360	183	307	310	316	132	482	342	413	2845	WHITE	5928
Par	4	3	4	4	4	3	5	4	4	35	Par	71
Handicap	6	16	14	12	10	18	2	8	4			
RED	299	128	234	235	218	116	402	289	337	2258	RED	4767
Par	4	3	4	4	4	3	5	4	4	35	Par	71
Handicap	6	16	14	12	10	2	8	4	18			

Manager: Joe Sippa, PGA   **Supt:** Anthony Funari
Architect: Tony Funari 1977

SAND BARRENS GOLF CLUB

PUBLIC

1765 Route 9 North, Swainton, NJ 08210   **(609) 465-3555**
www.sandbarrensgolf.com

Sand Barrens is a 27 hole course open 7 days a week all year. Memberships are available with discounted rates and preferred reservation privileges. Tee times may be made 10 days in advance.

- **Driving Range**
- **Practice Green**
- **Power Carts**
- Pull Carts
- **Club Rental**
- **Soft Spikes**
- **Lockers**
- **Showers**
- **Food**
- **Clubhouse**
- **Outings**

Fees	Weekday	Weekend
Daily	$100	$115
Twi (4PM)*	$60/18	$35/9

Power carts included
Seasonal Discounts
*Twi: Same weekend & weekday

Course Description: Sand Barrens has wide gently rolling fairways and large relatively fast contoured greens, all of bent grass. The course has been created out of vast pine and oak forests; the environment has been treated with respect leaving wetlands, native grasses and bayberry vegetation in the rough. Unique are huge waste areas of sand in play on many holes where the golfer may ground his club. The new nine has been intermingled with the original back nine. These more heavily wooded holes are not as visually intimidating and have more formal bunkers and fewer waste bunkers. This beautifully maintained course has been rated in the top 100 by *Golf Magazine*. The scorecard below is for the South and West nines. The GPS tracking system is used here. Check web site for additional directions.

Directions: Cape May County, #26 on Lower Shore Map
GSP to Exit 13. Go right to Rte. 9 and turn right. Go north for 1 mile to course on left.

Hole	1	2	3	4	5	6	7	8	9	Out	BLUE	Rating 71.7
BLUE	365	188	399	439	439	546	204	295	511	3386		Slope 130
WHITE	329	163	354	391	415	491	157	276	485	3061		
Par	4	3	4	4	4	5	3	4	5	36	WHITE	Rating 69.0
Handicap	8	6	4	1	2	3	5	9	7			Slope 124
RED	254	105	308	339	328	443	109	210	387	2483		
Par	4	3	4	4	4	5	3	4	5	36	RED	Rating 68.3
Handicap	8	6	4	1	2	3	5	9	7			Slope 119

Hole	10	11	12	13	14	15	16	17	18	In		Totals
BLUE	386	561	175	398	514	203	384	448	440	3509	BLUE	6894
WHITE	362	530	141	356	478	177	343	413	409	3209	WHITE	6270
Par	4	5	3	4	5	3	4	4	4	36	Par	72
Handicap	6	3	9	8	2	7	5	1	4			
RED	250	448	113	279	400	97	242	351	308	2488	RED	4971
Par	4	5	3	4	5	3	4	4	4	36	Par	72
Handicap	6	3	9	8	2	7	5	1	4			

Head Pro: Fran Mulholland, PGA   **Supt:** Bruce Bailey
Architects: Dr. Michael Hurdzan, Dana Fry 1997

SEAVIEW GOLF RESORT

401 South New York Rd., Absecon, NJ 08201 **(609) 652-1800**
www.seaviewgolf.com

Seaview is a golf resort with two separate 18 hole courses that are open to the public and to hotel guests 7 days a week all year. Tee times may be made up to 30 days in advance for guests, one week for others. Call for other off-season rates.

•**Driving Range**	•**Lockers**
•**Practice Green**	•**Showers**
•**Power Carts**	•**Food**
Pull Carts	•**Clubhouse**
•**Club Rental**	•**Outings**
•**Soft Spikes**	

Fees	Weekday	Weekend
5/1-10/17	$99	$129
11/1-4/30	$79	$99
Twi (after 3PM) $59		$69
Power carts included		

Course Description: The legendary Bay Course on Reed's Bay was designed by Donald Ross in a "Scottish links" style and was completed in 1913. With 89 bunkers in a picturesque wind-swept setting, it features wide open mounded fairways and greens that are open in front to allow "bump & run" approach shots. The 1931 Pines course was updated in 1957 by William Gordon. Cut out of the NJ Pinelands, it features pine tree lined fairways, large, steep strategically placed bunkers and fast, undulating elevated greens. The Shop Rite LPGA Classic is held here. An Elizabeth Arden Red Door Salon and Spa is available on the premises. Scorecard below is for the Bay Course.

Directions: Atlantic County, #27 on Lower Shore Map
GSP to Exit #48. Go South on Rte. 9 for 7 & 1/2 miles. Seaview Resort is on right.

Hole	1	2	3	4	5	6	7	8	9	Out	BLUE	Rating 70.7
BLUE	357	434	484	360	301	393	190	319	425	3253		Slope 122
WHITE	345	421	464	347	292	380	180	302	401	3131		
Par	4	4	5	4	4	4	3	4	4	36	WHITE	Rating 69.5
Handicap	9	1	7	11	15	5	17	13	3			Slope 120
RED	293	341	394	290	255	319	110	288	325	2615		
Par	4	4	5	4	4	4	3	4	4	36	RED	Rating 68.4
Handicap	9	1	7	11	15	5	17	13	3			Slope 114
Hole	10	11	12	13	14	15	16	17	18	In		Totals
BLUE	419	204	377	115	230	320	476	352	501	2994	BLUE	6247
WHITE	403	193	366	104	221	311	463	337	482	2880	WHITE	6011
Par	4	3	4	3	3	4	5	4	5	35	Par	71
Handicap	2	16	8	18	14	12	6	10	4			
RED	322	150	294	92	179	275	411	272	408	2402	RED	5017
Par	4	3	4	3	3	4	5	4	5	35	Par	71
Handicap	2	16	8	18	14	12	6	10	4			

Director of Golf: Rob Bartley,PGA **Pro:** Robert Clark, PGA **Supt**: Mark Beaumont
Architects: Donald Ross 1913 *Bay*, William Flynn & Howard Toomey 1929 *Pines*

SHORE GATE GOLF CLUB

PUBLIC

35 School House Lane, Ocean View, NJ 08230   **(609) 624-8337**
www.shoregategolfclub.com

Shore Gate is an 18 hole course open to the public 7 days a week all year. Associate memberships are available with privileges and reduced rates. Off season rates lower; Twi & Sr. rates available. Non-members may book tee time 14 days in advance.

- •Driving Range
- •Practice Green
- •Power Carts
- •Pull Carts
- •Club Rental
- •Soft Spikes

- •Lockers
- •Showers
- •Food
- •Clubhouse
- •Outings

Fees	Weekday	Weekend
Mon-Th	$95	
Fri-Sun		$106

Prices include cart
Seasonal Discounts

Course Description: Great care was taken to preserve the wetlands and pristine environment of the picturesque Shore Gate Golf Club. Carved from over 245 acres of forest, and a few minutes from the Atlantic Ocean, this combination parkland and Scottish links style course is a wonderful new golf venue. Every hole is different and visually intimidating. The rough is made up of 14 inch fescue grass around the bunkers. With 5 sets of tees, 7 lakes, 88 bunkers and vertical dunes the course puts a premium on accuracy. The total yardage ranges from 5,200 to 7,200 yards. Shore Gate was named to *Golf Magazine's* list of "Top Ten US Public Courses".

Directions: Cape May County, #34 on Lower Shore Map
GSP to Exit 17/Sea Isle City. Turn left onto Sea Isle City Blvd., heading west to Ocean View. Go thru light at Rte. 9 and proceed to entrance to club on your left.

Hole	1	2	3	4	5	6	7	8	9	Out	BLUE	Rating 73.3
BLUE	365	401	386	345	149	565	388	204	616	3419		Slope 132
WHITE	333	398	374	324	136	537	371	188	577	3238		
Par	4	4	4	4	3	5	4	3	5	36	WHITE	Rating 70.8
Handicap	15	5	7	11	17	3	9	13	1			Slope 128
RED	256	332	310	270	91	459	284	145	457	2604		
Par	4	4	4	4	3	5	4	3	5	36	RED	Rating 68.8
Handicap	15	5	7	11	17	3	9	13	1			Slope 125

Hole	10	11	12	13	14	15	16	17	18	In		Totals
BLUE	435	376	387	536	130	378	526	185	422	3375	BLUE	6794
WHITE	400	345	355	512	112	350	509	179	391	3153	WHITE	6391
Par	4	4	4	5	3	4	5	3	4	36	Par	72
Handicap	6	16	12	2	18	4	10	14	8			
RED	301	128	381	328	369	111	390	86	294	2388	RED	5284
Par	4	4	4	5	3	4	5	3	4	36	Par	72
Handicap	6	16	12	2	18	4	10	14	8			

Manager: Douglas Turner   **Pro:** Greg Johnson, PGA   **Supt:** Kenneth Van Fleet
Architect: Ron Fream & David Dale 2002

STONE HARBOR GOLF CLUB PRIVATE

905 Rte. 9 North, Cape May Courthouse, NJ 08210   **(609) 465-9270**
www.stoneharborgolfclub.com

Stone Harbor is an 18 hole course open 7 days a week all year. Associate members pay cart & green fees in addition to their dues. Guests may play accompanied by a member. Members may request tee times up to 2 weeks in advance.

•Driving Range	•Lockers
•Practice Green	•Showers
•Power Carts	•Food
Pull Carts	•Clubhouse
•Club Rental	•Outings
•Caddies	•Soft Spikes

Course Description: The slope rating of 139 from the championship tees indicates how difficult the beautiful Stone Harbor course can be. Some consider it comparable to and as demanding as the famed Pine Valley. The well groomed fairways and fast greens are dotted with bunkers of unusual configurations. With water coming into play on well over half of the holes, the picturesque hilly course offers a multitude of photo opportunities. The par 4 6th hole features an island fairway with a green guarded by more water. Golfers encounter water on the par 3 7th hole everywhere but the tee and oval shaped putting surface which is surrounded by grass banks. Five sets of tees give variety to the course.

Directions: Cape May County, #28 on Lower Shore Map
GSP to Exit #13 and follow road to Rte. 9 South. Course is ahead on right.

Hole	1	2	3	4	5	6	7	8	9	Out	BLUE	Rating 73.9
BLUE	398	419	557	174	509	435	182	419	423	3516		Slope 139
WHITE	379	384	536	161	499	406	148	402	392	3307		
Par	4	4	5	3	5	4	3	4	4	36	WHITE	Rating 70.2
Handicap	17	3	7	15	13	1	11	9	5			Slope 129
RED	319	328	476	107	429	338	84	327	300	2708		
Par	4	4	5	3	5	4	3	4	4	36	RED	Rating 70.0
Handicap	17	3	1	15	13	5	11	9	7			Slope 119
Hole	10	11	12	13	14	15	16	17	18	In		Totals
BLUE	354	505	183	427	470	387	517	167	409	3419	BLUE	6525
WHITE	339	494	170	385	456	354	490	161	389	3238	WHITE	6075
Par	4	5	3	4	4	4	5	3	4	36	Par	72
Handicap	16	10	14	12	2	8	6	18	4			
RED	264	410	133	334	410	304	376	135	291	2657	RED	4423
Par	4	5	3	4	4	4	5	3	4	36	Par	72
Handicap	16	10	14	12	4	8	6	18	2			

Gen.Manager: Harry Bittner, PGA   **Pro/Dir.of Golf:** Marc Kimminau,
Supt: Dean Ferguson   **Architect:** Desmond Muirhead 1987

TWISTED DUNE GOLF CLUB

PUBLIC

2101 Ocean Heights Ave, Egg Harbor Twp. NJ 08234   **(609) 653-8019**
www.twisteddune.com

Twisted Dune is an 18 hole course open to the public 7 days a week all year. Memberships are available. Tee times may be made up to two weeks in advance.

• **Driving Range**   • **Lockers**
• **Practice Green**   • **Showers**
• **Power Carts**   • **Food**
• **Pull Carts**   • **Clubhouse**
• **Club Rental**   • **Outings**
• **Soft Spikes**

Fees	Weekday	Weekend
Daily	$95	$115
Sr (Tu-Th) $60 all day		
Power carts included		
Seasonal rates differ		

Course Description: Built on a former horse farm, the impressive, upscale Twisted Dune is like no other golf course in southern NJ. It offers a Scottish inland links look virtually devoid of trees, with up to 90 yard wide fairways, deep ravines, towering grass covered sand hills and over 100 bunkers. The terrain is basically scrub pineland with some dramatic elevations. The landing areas are firm giving substantial roll. The prominent dunes, covered in native grass, are sculpted out of gravel and clay whic produce a rugged appearance. The holes have descriptive names such as Dixie Dell named after the horse. The wind on this open course is unpredictable but you can be sure of a great golf experience .

Directions: Atlantic County, #29 on Lower Shore Map
GSP Exit #36; go right onto Tilton/CR563 then right onto Fire Rd/CR651. Right onto Mill Rd/CR662 then left onto Old Zion Rd, then right onto Ocean Hgts. Ave. to course.

Hole	1	2	3	4	5	6	7	8	9	Out	BLUE	Rating 74.8
BLUE	415	445	238	610	360	455	435	168	485	3611		Slope 132
WHITE	380	425	185	585	345	430	415	155	455	3355		
Par	4	4	3	5	4	4	4	3	4	35	WHITE	Rating 71.8
Handicap	13	7	11	1	15	5	9	17	3			Slope 126
RED	340	375	155	480	315	380	405	135	395	2935		
Par	4	4	3	5	4	4	4	3	4	35	RED	Rating 71.5
Handicap	7	11	9	17	1	13	5	3	15			Slope 124
Hole	10	11	12	13	14	15	16	17	18	In		Totals
BLUE	545	445	585	205	435	415	220	410	495	3725	BLUE	7284
WHITE	520	410	535	180	405	395	165	385	427	3422	WHITE	6786
Par	5	4	5	3	4	4	3	4	4	36	Par	72
Handicap	8	10	2	18	6	14	16	12	4			
RED	445	350	485	150	355	330	145	325	370	2935	RED	5831
Par	5	4	5	3	4	4	3	4	4	36	Par	72
Handicap	8	10	2	18	6	14	16	12	4			

Mgmt: Empire Golf   **General Manager:** Scott Dunn, PGA   **Supt:** Steve Lane
Architect: Archie Struthers 2001

VINEYARD GOLF COURSE

PUBLIC

2111 Bremen Ave, Egg Harbor City, NJ 08215   **(609) 965-2111**

www.renaultwinery.com

The Vineyards is an 18 hole course open all year, 7 days a week. Tee times may be made 8 days in advance. Memberships with privileges are available. Check web for alternate directions. Motorized pull carts available. Golf packages are available.

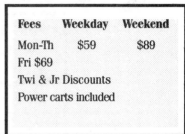

•Driving Range	•Lockers
•Practice Green	•Showers
•Power Carts	•Food
•Pull	•Clubhouse
•Carts	•Outings
•Club Rental	•Soft Spikes

Fees	Weekday	Weekend
Mon-Th	$59	$89
Fri $69		
Twi & Jr Discounts		
Power carts included		

Course Description: The 226 acre historic property at the Vineyards at Renault provide the perfect setting for a great day of golf at a one of a kind layout. Enjoy the majestic views of the vineyards and orchards as the course winds subtly through the pinelands of South Jersey. The grapevines and blueberries growing and blending in throughout different sections of the rough are unique indeed. Strategy is the key as each hole offers risk and reward opportunities to confront all levels of golfers on this 7,200 yard layout. There are 5 lakes in play and large waste bunkers adding to the challenge. The Tuscany Hotel and Restaurant are special attractions as is the original winery.

Directions: Atlantic County, #30 on Lower Shore Map

GSP to Exit 44. Take 2 immediate rt. turns onto Alt. 561 (Moss Mill Rd.) Follow signs 5 mi. to Bremen Ave. Turn right at the Wine Barrel onto Bremen Ave. Course on right.

Hole	1	2	3	4	5	6	7	8	9	Out	BLUE	Rating
BLUE												Slope
WHITE	349	321	391	155	446	507	437	193	413	3212		
Par	4	4	4	3	5	5	4	3	4	36	WHITE	Rating
Handicap	6	9	2	8	5	4	1	7	3			Slope
RED	327	300	353	92	440	410	422	180	380	2904		
Par	4	4	4	3	5	5	4	3	4	36	RED	Rating
Handicap	6	9	2	8	5	4	1	7	3			Slope
Hole	10	11	12	13	14	15	16	17	18	In		Totals
BLUE											BLUE	
WHITE	304	371	353	185	334	476	171	477	296	2967	WHITE	
Par	4	4	4	3	4	5	3	5	4	36	Par	72
Handicap	7	1	4	8	5	2	9	3	6			
RED	269	335	320	154	290	404	163	422	257	2614	RED	
Par	4	4	4	3	4	5	3	5	4	36	Par	72
Handicap	7	1	4	8	5	2	9	3	6			

Manager/Owner: Joe Milza   **Pro:** Paul Israel, PGA   **Supt:** Michael Renk
Architect: Arthur Hills 2002

WILDWOOD GOLF & CC

1170 Golf Club Rd, Cape May Courthouse, NJ 08210   **(609) 465-7823**

Wildwood is an 18 hole course open 7 days a week all year. Guests play accompanied by a member. Reserved tee times are advisable. Pull carts are permitted off season.

- **•Driving Range**
- **•Practice Green**
- **•Power Carts**
- **•Pull Carts**
- **•Club Rental**
- Caddies
- **•Lockers**
- **•Showers**
- **•Food**
- **•Clubhouse**
- **•Outings**
- **•Soft Spikes**

Course Description: The traditional links style Wildwood in Cape May County is a well groomed layout that surrenders to the breezes of the shore area affecting play much of the time. Within the course are several small lakes and mounds but it is relatively flat with a short, tight back nine. There are bent grass fairways and greens; the latter are small and well bunkered. The scenic par 3 seventh is considered the signature hole; it is short and interesting yet requires a carry over water. The course is kept up to date and is very well maintained. Ratings are as of 2004.

Directions: Cape May County, #31 on Lower Shore Map
GSP to Exit #9. At light, turn left and make 1st right onto Golf Club Rd. Club on left.

Hole	1	2	3	4	5	6	7	8	9	Out	BLUE	Rating
BLUE												Slope
WHITE	425	463	335	364	387	331	161	358	355	3179		
Par	4	5	4	4	4	4	3	4	4	36	WHITE	Rating 70.3
Handicap	6	2	10	14	4	16	18	8	12			Slope 123
RED	366	362	335	329	387	301	122	315	320	2837		
Par	4	5	4	4	5	4	3	4	4	37	RED	Rating 69.3
Handicap	3	1	9	11	7	15	17	5	13			Slope 115
Hole	10	11	12	13	14	15	16	17	18	In		Totals
BLUE											BLUE	
WHITE	384	390	213	410	345	508	140	397	378	3165	WHITE	6288
Par	4	4	3	4	4	5	3	4	4	35	Par	71
Handicap	5	9	15	1	13	3	17	7	11			
RED	369	355	152	330	311	353	113	354	343	2680	RED	5797
Par	5	4	3	4	4	5	3	4	4	36	Par	73
Handicap	6	2	16	10	14	12	18	4	8			

Manager: Robert Keating   **Pro:** Fred Riedel, PGA   **Supt:** Jeffrey Staeger
Architects: Stiles and Van Kleek 1916

INDEX

Key: Names of golf clubs or golf courses are in **bold**

Names of architects are in *italics*.

Towns indexed are locations of the courses.

Head golf pros are listed.

Counties are in CAPITALS

Abel, Vaughan 140
Absecon 321
Adams, Bill 108
Alaimo, Dick 248
Allison, Charles 98
Alloway 254
Alpine 25
Alpine CC 13
Anderson, Bill 144
Annandale 128
Apple Mountain G& CC 43
Apple Ridge CC 14
Architect's Club 44
Arcola CC 14
Ashbrook GC 95
ATLANTIC COUNTY 293-326
Atlantic City CC 293
Atlantic Highlands 189
Attara, Mike 202
Ault, Brian 111, 143,153, 270
Ault, Clark & Assoc 146, 202, 295
Ault, Edmond 135, 164, 173, 271
Avalon GC 294
Bachman, Robert 315
Baker, Gregory 82
Ballamor GC 295

Ballyowen GC 45
Baltusrol GC 96
Bamm Hollow GC 187
Banks, Charles 21, 67,103,106,110
115, 118, 139
Barker, Herbert 15,166, 231
Basking Ridge 127, 158
Basking Ridge CC 127
Battleground CC 188
Bayonne 97
Bayonne CC 97
Bayville 193
Beacon Hill CC 189
Beakley, David 282
Beal, Mike 155
Bear Brook GC 46
Beaver Brook GC 128
Bechsel, Mike 160
Beckett GC 245
Bedens Brook Club 129
Bedminster 138, 181
Beesley's Point 296
Bel-Aire GC 190
Bella Vista CC 191
Belle Mead 151
Belleville 110
Belvidere 43

Bendelow, Tom 101, 134, 162,182
BERGEN COUNTY 13-40
Bergen Hills CC 16
Bergen, Jim 252
Bergstol, Eric 97. 226
Berkshire Valley GC 47
Bernardsville 172
Bey Lea GC 192
Bishop, William 251
Black Bear G & CC 48
Black Oak CC 49
Blackwood 282
Blair Academy GC 50
Blairstown 50
Blaukovitch, Jim 248
B.L.England GC 296
Bloomfield 105
Bloomingdale 20
Blue Heron Pines East 297
Blue Heron Pines West 298
Bonicky, Jeff 232
Boswell, Bill 38
Bowers, Steve 156, 163
Bowling Green GC 51
Bowman, Allan 131
Boyle, Brendan 178
Branchville 54
Brick 2004. 218
Bridgewater 144, 166
Bridy, Raymond 135
Brielle 219
Brigantine 299
Brigantine Golf Links 299
Brigham, Don 231
Brock, Andy 154
Brooklake CC 52
Brown, Stephen 141
Bruno, Tony 239
Buena 300, 312
Buena Vista CC 300
Bunker Hill GC 130
Burgess, Bill 15
Burke, Mike Jr. 25
BURLINGTON COUNTY 245-290
Burlington CC 246
Burris, Michael 29
Busch, Peter 121
Calvaresi, Vic 132
CAMDEN COUNTY 245-290
Canoe Brook CC 98
CAPE MAY COUNTY 293-326
Cape May 301
Cape May Courthouse 294, 323
326
Cape May National 301
Carey, Brian 238
Carman, Ed 247, 275
Carman, J. R. 275

Carney's Point 276
Case, Roy 158
Cassano, Madeline 31
Cedar Creek GC 193
Cedar Hill CC 99
Centerton CC 247
Chamberlain, Bruce 20
Charleston Springs GC 194
Chatham 56
Cherry Hill 263, 290
Cherry Valley CC 131
Chick, Elliot 46
Chicwit, James 270
Chmura, Ron 142
Cimino, Bob 268, 300
Clark 11, 117
Clark, Robert 321
Clearbrook GC 132
Clermont 317
Clifton 37
Coakley-Russo GC 133
Coetzee, Oscar 84
Cohanzick CC 302
Cologne 297, 298
Colonia 134
Colonia CC 134
Colonial Terrace GC 195
Colt's Neck CC 196
Colt's Neck 196, 200, 211, 225, 233
Colt, H.S. 269
Columbus 265
Commins, J. Christopher 230
Concordia GC 135
Conticchio, Victor 66
Convent Station 75
Coore, Bill 311
Copper Hill CC 136
Cornish, Geoffrey 30, 51, 289
Cowell, Charles 105
Craig, George 224
Cranbury 132
Cranbury CC 137
Cream Ridge 197, 206
Cream Ridge GC 197
Crenshaw, Ben 311
Crestmont CC 100
Crump, George 269
Cruz Farm CC 198
Cruz, Evaristo 198
Crystal Springs GC 53
Culver Lake GC 54
CUMBERLAND COUNTY 293-326
Cupp, Bob 112
Curry, John 14
Dachisen, Chris 26
Dachisen, Peter 62
Dale, David 322

Dalzell, Ian 311
Darlington GC 17
Davis, Jay 220
DeBaufry, Tim 306
De Gisi, Leo 262
De Rosa, Davis 69
Deal 199, 210
Deal GC 199
Deer Run GC 55
Deerwood CC 248
Demarest 13
Denville 79, 82
DeVito, Steve 245
Dezic, Michael 21
Diehl, Jeff 145
Dietz, George 87
Dix, Wendell 201
Dow, Mahlon 151
Driscoll, Sean 274
Duane, Frank 25, 71, 134, 212
Due Process Stables 200
Dunn, Seymour 189
Dunn, William 174, 215
Durham, Rich 242
Dzergoski, Chris 191
Eagle Oak GC 201
Eagle Ridge GC 202
East Brunswick 177
East Orange GC 101
Eastlyn GC 303
Eaton, Hal 50
Eatontown 224
Echo Lake CC 102
Edgewood CC 18
Edison 154, 162
Edwards, Chuck 189
Egg Harbor Township 295, 307, 309,311, 315, 324
Emerson 19
Emerson CC 19
Emmet, Devereaux 82, 142
Englishtown 209, 227
Esposito, Frank 52
ESSEX COUNTY 95-124
Essex County CC 103
Essex Fells 104
Essex Fells CC 104
Fagan, John 166
Fairton 302
Fairmount CC 56
Fairway Mews GC 203
Fairway Valley GC 57
Falcon Creek GC 249
Famiano, Peter 100
Farmingdale 198, 201, 212, 237
Farmstead G & CC 58
Farrow, Greg 248
Fazio, George 60, 142, 148, 223, 306

Fazio, Pete 274
Fazio, Tom 168,181, 205, 267, 283
305
Feldschneider, Brian 288
Fiddlers's Elbow CC 138
Findlay, Alexander 127, 246, 270, 280, 302
Findlow, Paul 241
Findlay, William 261
Finelli, Hank 71
Finger, Joe 152
Fisher, Mike181
Flanders 59
Flanders Valley GC 59
Flemington 136
Flood, Val 39
Florham Park 52, 81
Flynn, William 174, 290, 321
Forest Hill Field Club 105
Forge Pond GC 204
Forsch, Ron 255
Forsgate CC 139
Fort Dix 250
Fort Monmouth 238
Foster, Robert 33
Fountain Green GC 250
Four Seasons CC 205
Fox Hollow GC 140
Frake, George, 2nd 259
Francis Byrne GC 106
Franklin 48, 90
Franklin Lakes 23
Franklin Township 173
Fraser, Leo 314
Fream, Ron 322
Frederick, Jeff 278
Fredon Twp 46
Freeway GC 251
Froes, Acacio 198
Frog Rock GC 304
Funari, Tony 319
Gaffney, Brian 39
Gaffney, Mike 286, 310
Galbiati, Francis 303
Gallagher, Mickie, 3rd 113
Galloping Hill GC 107
Galloway GC 305
Galloway Twp. 305, 325
Gambler Ridge GC 206
Gartner, Bob 196
Gaskill, Carl 281
Giuliano, Mark 56
Gladstone 145
Glass, Fred 157, 164, 173
Glen Ridge 108
Glen Ridge CC 108

Glenwild Greens 20
Glenwood CC 141
Glenz, Dave 45, 48, 53, 74, 91
Glenz, Dave 48, 49
GLOUCESTER COUNTY 245-290
Golden Pheasant GC 252
Gordon & Gordon 77
Gordon, William 144, 159, 163, 260, 262, 288, 300
Graygor, Ted 229
Great Gorge CC 60
Greate Bay GC 306
Green Brook CC 109
Green Knoll GC 144
Green, John 249
Green Pond GC 61
Green Tree GC 307
Green, Harold 64
Greenacres CC 142
Greenbriar Oceanaire GC 207
Greenbriar Woodlands 208
Greenbriar @ Whittingham 143
Griffith, Quentin 266
Hackensack GC 21
Hackettstown 73, 78
Haddonfield 280
Hainesville 64
Hamburg 45, 53, 91
Hamilton Farm GC 145
Hamilton Trails CC 308
Hammonton 304
Handwerg, John Jr. 38
Hanover CC 252
Hansen, Mort 190
Harbor Pines CC 309
Harkers Hollow G & CC 62
Harmon, Vincent 119
Harris, Mike 208
Harsin, Harry 208, 240
Haskell, Dan 261
Hassler, Joe 287
Hawk Pointe GC 63
Haworth 22, 39
Haworth CC 22
Hawtree, Frederick 258
Hearn, Raymond 232
Helwig, Russell 104
Hendricks Field GC 110
Henefer, Ron 205
Hendricks, Bob 294
Heritage Links GC 310
Herman, Bob 314
Heron Glen GC 146
Hidden Acres GC 64
Hidden Creek GC 311
Hicklin, Keith 44

High Bridge Hills 147
Highbridge 147
High Mountain GC 23
Highpoint CC 65
Hightstown 160
Hilliard, Tom 215
Hills, Arthur 207, 241, 325
Hillsborough CC 148
Hirt, Rob 43
Hoey, Chad 299
Hojnacki, Todd 85
Holmes, William 281
Hole-in One GC 209
Holland, Harvey 191
Hollterman, Glenn *76v*
Hollis, Daniel 111
Holly Hills GC 254
Hollywood GC 210
Hominy Hill GC 211
Hopewell 149, 176
Hopewell Valley GC 149
Howell Park GC 212
Hucknell, Robert 87
HUDSON COUNTY 95-124
Hughart, Rick 280
HUNTERDON COUNTY 127-183
Hurdzan/Fry 145, 157, 320
Hurdzan, Michael 136
Hyatt Hills GC 111
Indian Spring GC 255
Israel, Paul 325
Jackson 220, 226, 241
Jaeger, Tom 229
Jaggard, Burt 255
Jamesburg 139, 143, 169
Jefferson Township 47
Jersey City 172
Jerauld, Jill 171
Johnson, Greg 322
Jones, Rees 15, 21, 59, 78, 81, 131, 138, 210
Jones, Robert Trent 22, 36, 37, 74, 78, 107, 108, 133, 211, 220, 272
Jordan, Pat 240
Jumping Brook G & CC 213
Kallan, Mike 138
Kane, Ron 150
Karalis, Ben 30
Kauth, Bobby 153
Kay, Stephen 31, 44, 95, 165, 175, 191, 278, 298, 309, 315
Kelly, Joe 86
Kenneff, Bucky 295
Kenny, Kevin 203
Kidder, Dick & Loretta 245
Kidder, Richard 252

Killian, Mike 305
Kimball, Duke 149
Kimminau, Marc 323
King, Bill 236
King, Steele 67
Kite, Tom 112
Klocksin, John 51
Klose, Renee 59, 88
Knickerbocker CC 24
Knight, Michael 159
Knob Hill GC 214
Knoll East GC 66
Knoll West GC 67
Koch, Ed 81
Kohberger, Robin 77
Kompo, Scott 254
Korn, Ron 99
Kraeger, Robert 176
Kramer, Ed 282
Kresson GC 256
Kriews, Kevin 253
Kurlander, Jack 48
Lafayette 58
Laing, Charles 154
Lake Lackawanna GC 68
Lake Mohawk GC 69
Lakehurst 228, 230
Lakewood 202, 205, 215, 216, 242
Lakewood CC 215
Lambert, Fred 155
Lamp, Jason 199
Larsen, Keith 18
Latona G & CC 312
Laudien, David 194, 212
Laurel Creek CC 257
Lawlor, Joe & Pat 23
Lawrenceville 142, 150
Lawrenceville School GC 150
Lechardus, Babe 162
Lecker, Greg 98
Lee, David 297, 298
Lee, Sid 79
Lefevre, Jeff 313
Lefperance, Chris 276
Leisure Village East 216
Leisure Village West 217
Lenhart, Jason 147
Lespardi, Ralph 268
Liberty National GC 112
Lincoln Park 55, 71, 89
Lincroft 187
Lindsay, Craig 70
Links GC 258

Linwood 313
Linwood CC 313
Lions Head CC 218
Litten, Carl 301
Little Egg Harbor Twp 232
Little Mill CC 259
Livingston 99
Loomis, Steve 146
Long Valley 49
Luberecki, Randy 152, 177
Lyons 133
Lyons, Bill 250
MacDougal, Ron 210
Machala, Adam 172
Mack, Mike 246
Madden, Brian 289
Maddera, Baker 118
Madison 70
Madison GC 70
Mahon, Mark 158
Mahwah 14, 17
Malario, Matt 37
Malikowski, Steve 317
Manahawkin 222
Manalapan 214
Manasquan River GC 219
Manchester 217
Manziano, Terry 60
Maple Ridge GC 260
Maplewood 113
Maplewood CC 113
Marcella 61
Marine, Bill 197
Markt, Tim 47
Marlboro 191
Marlton 255, 258, 259
Martino, Kevin 260
Mattawang GC 151
Mays Landing CC 314
Mays Landing 308, 314
McAfee 74
McCarthy, Dan 174
McCarthy, Tom 213
McCluney, Bill 117
McCormick, Mark 122
McCullough's Emerald Links 315
McCumber, Mark 214
McDole, John 143
McGuiness, Tom 16
McNeil, Robert 55, 86
Meadows GC 71
Meadows at Middlesex 152
Medford 252, 261, 262
Medford Lakes 261

Medford Village CC 262
Meeks, Doug 27
Melody, David 225
Mendham 72, 85
Mendham GC 72
MERCER COUNTY 127-183
Mercer Oaks GC 153
Merchantville CC 263
Metuchen GC 154
Metedeconk National 220
Micelli, Dominick 107
MIDDLESEX COUNTY 127-183
Middletown 221
Millburn GC 114
Milford 159
Miller, Johnny 201
Miller, Thomas 200
Millstone Twp 194
Milne, Dennis 180
Milton 51
Mine Brook GC 73
Minerals GC 74
Miry Run CC 155
Miscoski, Frank 197
Mitchell, Mark 34
MONMOUTH COUNTY 187-242
Monrow, Lloyd 194
Monroe Twp. 135, 167
Montague 65, 83
Montammy GC 25
Montclair GC 115
Moore, Ben 179
Moorestown 264, 288
Moorestown Field Club 264
Moran, Kelly Blake 63
MORRIS COUNTY 43-91
Morris County GC 75
Morristown 87
Mountain Ridge CC 116
Mountain View GC 156
Mt. Holly 246, 279
Mt. Laurel 257, 271
Mt. Tabor 76
Mt. Tabor CC 76
Mugavero, Matt 80
Muirhead, Desmond 169, 323
Mulholland, Fran 320
Mullock, Robert 301
Mungeam, Mark 147, 194, 196
Myles, Mike 151
Navesink CC 221

Neptune 213, 235
Neshanic Station 148, 157
Neshanic Valley GC 157
New Jersey National GC 158
Newark 124
Newfield 286
Newton 77, 84
Newton CC 77
Nickelson, Jason 206
Nicolson, Robert 136
North Caldwell 109
North Hanover 253
North Jersey CC 26
Northfield 293
O'Laughlin, Martin 32, 154
O'Rourke, Ted 75
Oak Hill GC 159
Oak Ridge GC 117
Ocean Acres CC 222
Ocean City 316
Ocean City GC 316
OCEAN COUNTY 187-242
Ocean County-Atlantis 223
Ocean View 322
Old Bridge 141
Old Orchard CC 224
Old Tappan 27
Old Tappan GC 27
Olde York CC 265
Olear, Bill 167
Oradell 21
Orchard Hills GC 28
Orlando, Vince 317
Overpeck GC 29
Packanack GC 30
Packard, Edward 242
Palermo 310
Palmer, Arnold 139, 167, 257
Panther Valley GC 78
Paramus CC 31
Paramus 15, 28, 31, 35
Paris, Scott 161
Park, Willie Jr. 108, 306
Parsippany 66, 67
PASSAIC COUNTY 13-40
Passaic County GC 32
Pasternak, Dan 78
Pate, Jerry 233
Peace Pipe CC 79
Pebble Creek GC 225
Peddie School GC 160

Pedrazzi, Bob 187
Pennsauken CC 266
Perla, Tony 265
Petronis, John 301
Philipps, Fred 273
Phillipsburg 44, 62
Phillips, Shawn 137
Phoebus, Byron 58
Picatinny 80
Picatinny GC 80
Pinch Brook GC 81
Pine Barrens GC 226
Pine Brook GC 227
Pine Hill GC 267
Pine Hill 267
Pine Ridge GC 228
Pine Valley GC 269
Pine Valley 269
Pinelands GC 268
Pines at Clermont 317
Piscataway 165, 171
Pitman GC 270
Pittsgrove 247, 275
Plainfield CC 161
Plainfield 161
Plainfield West CC 162
Plainsboro 152
Player, Gary 179, 265
Podmayersky, Charles 22
Pomona 318
Pomona GC 318
Pompton Plains 88
Ponderlodge GC 319
Preakness Hills CC 33
Preston, Mike 102, 174
Princeton 130, 163, 179
Princeton CC 163
Prickett, Bob 266
Prohamerr, Todd 286
Pruden, Scott 58
Psiahas, Nicholas 17, 84, 99, 193
Purdy, Hal 14, 27, 34, 56, 59, 66, 85, 88, 109, 114, 132, 134, 138, 139, 140, 141, 171, 177, 183, 187, 188, 192, 204, 218, 221, 225, 235, 261, 282
Quail Brook GC 164
Quail Ridge GC 229
Quinn, David 258
Ramblewood CC 271
Ramsey 34
Ramsey CC 34
Rancocas GC 272
Raritan Landing GC 165
Raritan Valley CC 166
Rassett, Joey 168

Raudenbush, Charles 269
Raynor, Seth 75, 103, 119
Reasoner, Harry 35
Red Bank 234
Reed, John 293
Regency @ Monroe 167
Regner, Ron 95
Renaissance GC 250
Renn, Garrett 137, 279, 312
Rickenbach, Jeffrey 175
Ridge at Back Brook 168
Ridgewood CC 35
Riedel, Fred 326
Ringoes146, 168
Riverton 273
River Winds 274
Riverton CC 273
Rivervale 16, 18, 38
Robbinsville 155
Roberts, Alan 190, 194, 211
Robidoux, Art 230
Rocco, James 73
Rock Spring Club 118
Rock View GC 83
Rockaway River CC 82
Rockhill, Brian 206
Rockleigh 36
Rockleigh GC 36
Rolling Greens GC 84
Romano, Ralph 182
Roselle 119
Roselle GC 119
Ross, Donald 16, 24, 100, 102, 104, 115, 116, 161, 199, 273, 321
Rossmoor GC 169
Roxiticus GC 85
Royce Brook GC 170
Rulewich, Roger 15, 45, 46, 47, 91, 220
Rumson 231
Rumson CC 231
Running Deer GC 275
Rutgers GC 171
Sakima CC 276
SALEM COUNTY 245-290
Salem 277, 287
Salem CC 277
Sand Barrens GC 320
Sauer, George 109
Schaare, Mark 214
Schamback, Doug 129
Schlegel, Daniel 146
Schmehl, Butch 264
Scotch Hills CC 120
Scotch Plains 95, 120, 121

Scotland Run National 278
Sea Oaks GC 232
Seaview Golf Resort 321
Servis, Ted 169
Sewell 260, 270
Sewell, David 69
Shackamaxon G & CC 121
Shadow Isle GC 233
Shadow Lake Village 234
Shark River GC 235
Shearon, Ed 274
Sholtko, Bill 308
Shore Gate GC 326
Short Hillls 101, 114
Shukdinas, James 258
Sicklerville 251
Sieg, Steve 22
Silva, Brian 138
Silverstone, Sal 188
Siter, Len 116, 131
Skillman 129, 131
Sky View GC 86
Smith, Dick 274
Smith, Dick, Jr. 290
Smith, Horace 254, 285, 307
Smith, Kent 38
Smith, Orrin 16, 18
Smyers, Steve 170, 297
Somers Point 306
SOMERSET COUNTY 127-181
Somerset 164, 178
Somerset Hills CC 172
Somerville 140, 170
Sparks, Mike 170
Sparta 69, 86
Spicer, Bill 127
Spooky Brook GC 173
Spring Brook CC 87
Spring Lake 236
Spring Lake GC 236
Spring Lake Heights 203
Spring Meadow GC 237
Springdale GC 174
Springfield 96
Springfield GC 279
Stanhope 68
Stanton 175
Stanton Ridge GC 175
Staples, Tom 72
Steffan, Doug 96
Stiles & Van Kleek 299, 326
Stone Harbor GC 323
Stonybrook GC 176

Straka, Blaise 263

Strlekar, Mike 115
Strigh, Dennis 304
Strong, Herbert 52
Struthers, Archie 324
Studer, Brent 219
Suburban GC 122
Sullivan, Steven 293
Summit 98, 123
Summit Muni GC 123
Sun Eagles-Ft.Monmouth 238
Sunset Valley GC 88
SUSSEX COUNTY 43-91
Suter, John 63
Swainton 320
Swedesboro 245
Sweetra, Pat 247
Syring, Kevin 13
Tamarack GC 177
Tara Greens GC 178
Tavistock CC 280
Taylor, Ian Scott 213, 222
Taylor, Richard 222
Teaneck 29
Tenafly 24
Tennent 188
Ternyei, Alec 19, 23, 128, 148
Thomas, George Jr. 236
Threatt, Ron 296
Tillinghast, A. W. 13, 35, 37, 96, 103, 105, 108,
121, 122, 172, 224, 236, 238
Tinton Falls 240
Tom's River 192, 208, 239
Tom's River CC 239
Toohey, Todd 228
Toomey, Howard 174, 290. 321
Torlucci, Bill 255
Town & Country Links 281
TPC at Jasna Polana 179
Travis, Walter 26, 39, 98, 210
Trenton 180
Trenton CC 180
Trump National GC 181
Tucker, Willie 33
Tuckerton 223
Tull, Alfred 36, 39, 72, 95, 98, 142
Turnersville 283, 284
Twin Brook GC 240
Twin Brooks CC 182
Twin Willows GC 89
Twisted Dune GC 324
Tyrell, John 257

UNION COUNTY 95-124
Union 107, 122
Upper Montclair CC 37
Valleybrook GC 282
Valley Brook GC 38
Van Etten, Lawrence 199
Villas 319
Vineland 303
Vineyards @ Renault 325
Virga, Rudy 226
Vnuk, Frank 90
Von Hagge Robert 53
Voorhees 256
Vybihal, Marty 55
Wallkill CC 90
Wall 190
Wall Township 229
Wanamassa 195
Ward, Jeffrey 89
Waretown 207
Warms, Wayne 200
WARREN COUNTY 43-91
Warren Township 183
Warrenbrook GC 183
White, Robert 62, 109, 219
Whitman, Ed 24
Washington 57, 63
Washington Township GC 283
Watchung 182
Waters, Maura 178
Wayne 26, 30, 32, 33
Wedgewood CC 284
Weequahic Park GC 124
Wells, Orist 270
Wenner, Ted 294
Wentzel, Matt 267
West Caldwell 116
West Deptford 274
West Orange 100, 103, 106, 115, 118
West Trenton 156
West Windsor 137, 153
Westampton 248
Westfield 102
Westlake G & CC 241
Westwood CC 285
White Beeches G & CC 39
White Oaks CC 286
Wilcenski, Tony 169
Wild Oaks GC 287
Wild Turkey GC 91

Wildwood CC 326
Wilkinson Willard 107, 117, 213
Williamstown 278
Willingboro 272
Willowbrook CC 288
Wilson, Dick 129, 210
Wilson, Steve 103
Winslow 268
Winton, Thomas 149
Woodbury 285, 289
Woodbury CC 289
Woodcrest CC 290
Woodlake CC 242
Woodstown 281
Wren, Garrett 259, 284
Wrightstown 249
Yarbough, Holliss 130
Yevchek, Michael 226
Zakorus, Albert 22
Zauner, Don 73

335

ORDERING INFORMATION

Telephone: (201) 461-7960
              (201) 569-6605
     Fax# (201) 461-3383

By Mail: Weathervane Press
          2200 North Central Rd.
          Ft. Lee , NJ 07024

THE GARDEN STATE GOLF GUIDE
Send check or money order for $15.95 plus tax, shipping and handling.

THE GREATER NEW YORK GOLF GUIDE
Send check or money order for $18.95 plus tax, shipping and handling.

NJ Sales tax; Add 6% per book
NY Sales tax: Add 8.25% per book
Shipping and handling: $3.00 per book.

For quantity orders, please call Weathervane Press at telephone numbers above.